Green Suns and Faërie

Essays on Tolkien

Verlyn Flieg

The Kent State University Press

Kent, Ohio

For Vaughn with love

© 2012 by The Kent State University Press, Kent, Ohio 44242
ALL RIGHTS RESERVED
Library of Congress Catalog Card Number 2011047793
ISBN 978-1-60635-094-2
Manufactured in the United States of America

LIBRARY OF CONGRESS CATALOGING-IN-PUBLICATION DATA
Flieger, Verlyn, 1933–
    Green suns and faerie : essays on Tolkien / Verlyn Flieger.
        p.   cm.
    Includes bibliographical references and index.
    ISBN 978-1-60635-094-2 (hardcover : alk. paper) ∞
    1. Tolkien, J. R. R. (John Ronald Reuel), 1892–1973—Criticism and interpretation.
    I. Title.
    PR6039.O32Z6447 2012
    823'.912—dc23   2011047793

British Library Cataloging-in-Publication data are available.

16 15 14 13 12   5 4 3 2 1

Contents

Preface and Acknowledgments

The two terms that together form the title of this collection are taken from Tolkien's discussion of Fantasy in his great essay "On Fairy-stories." The first term, *green sun,* he intended to express the element of "arresting strangeness" that characterizes an imaginary world, that out-of-the-ordinary component that signals a departure from what he called the Primary World. A frog prince can be a green sun, as can a time machine or a unicorn or a space alien. Or a hobbit. Whatever it may be, the green sun sets the tone for the world it inhabits, and for the story that brings that world to life. The second term, *Faërie,* although it is less amenable to a single, concrete definition, may well be the most important word in Tolkien's creative lexicon. In his usage it has interconnecting meanings ranging from "the realm or state in which fairies have their being," to "Enchantment" as both a process and a condition, to "sub-creation," the making of a Secondary World

The essays in this collection rely on one or the other and often on both terms. They are grouped in three sections (though predictably there is some overlapping of topic and theme among the sections), each section examining Tolkien's work within a specific context: first sub-creation, next literary tradition, and lastly contemporary relevance. The essays include consideration, either straightforward or oblique, of a variety of green suns, from the silly Rivendell elves of *The Hobbit* to the dark but understandable malevolence of Old Man Willow to the ongoing process of bodily and spiritual dissolution effected in Frodo by the Ring. The larger term, *Faërie,* while equally applicable, has of necessity a wider scope, for I mean it to encompass not just the making of a fantastic Secondary World but also the varying treatments of that world from medieval reference to modern and postmodern literary techniques.

In assembling these essays my intent has been to present a body of work with a wide scope in both chronology and content, one that includes early and late opinions, lighter articles as well as more serious ones, and that conveys the extent and diversity of my efforts in Tolkien scholarship over many years. A few essays have been omitted on the grounds that they were the "germ" (as Tolkien might put it) of later books and became incorporated into the larger format. Inclusion here would simply rehash what is in the books. I suggest you read those instead. Some essays are here published for the first time. "Bilbo's Neck Riddle," "The Mind, the Tongue, and the Tale," and "Tolkien, *Kalevala*, and 'The Story of Kullervo'" belong in this category. Several of the essays go back twenty years or beyond and say more about where I entered a then-current conversation than they do about the state of Tolkien scholarship at the present time. Like their author, they show their age. Rather than revising them to reflect the present state of any question (which state itself must, to keep current, undergo continuous revision), I have chosen to let each stand as a milestone in my lifelong conversation with Tolkien's work. You can see where I've been as well as how far I've come.

I first encountered *The Lord of the Rings* in the winter of 1956–57. A colleague at the Folger Shakespeare Library, where I was then working, had been sent by her brother in England a remarkable three-volume fantasy novel that everyone over there was reading and talking about. At the Folger the books were passed around from department to department. We read it and we talked about it, in the halls, over lunch, and during tea breaks. My first reaction to the book was that I had never read anything like it. My second reaction was that I had. Being a lifelong lover of Arthurian literature, and having recently taken a course in translating *Beowulf,* I was struck by the many Arthurian and Beowulfian elements I recognized in the books. I gave myself a smug little pat on the back for understanding more about Tolkien than the ordinary reader.

Ten years later, reading *The Fellowship of the Ring* aloud to my three children one evening in 1967, I got my comeuppance. We were at the Council of Elrond and I was blundering through the unpronounceable gutturals of Gandalf's declamation in Black Speech of the first lines of the Ring verse: *Ash nazg durbatulûk, ash nazg gimbatul, ash nazg thrakatulûk agh burzum-ishi krimpatul.* Hardly fluent in Black Speech, I was trying to sound suitably ominous when my six-year-old daughter piped up from under the piano, where she was playing with her dolls. "*Ash nazg* means 'one ring,'" she remarked and went back to playing with her dolls. It was then I realized I had more to learn about Tolkien.

I have been learning ever since, as I hope the essays in this volume will bear witness, learning about invented languages and Elf-friends, about hobbits and sub-creation and the Red Book and the inner consistency of reality. Since this collection stretches over a period of some twenty-five years, it emphasizes certain motifs that come up repeatedly in my work and also illustrates the ways in which my understanding of Tolkien has widened and deepened over the years. Most of these essays began either as papers delivered at conferences or as essays submitted to journals—and not infrequently as both. In subject matter they range from the large and conceptual (Faërie, fate and free will, Tolkien the medievalist and the modernist, the Middle-earth manuscript tradition) to the small and specific (Bilbo's riddles, Frodo's wounds, consonant lenition in Sindarin).

Much has changed in Tolkien scholarship since *The Lord of the Rings* was first published in the middle of the twentieth century. His work has been called both an epic and a fairy tale; it has been classified as pseudo-medieval and discovered as surprisingly postmodern; it has been cataloged as fantasy and hailed as super-realistic; it has been characterized as both conventional and groundbreaking, as allegorical and mythological. It is all of these and more than these, for it stubbornly refuses to be confined within any genre. It is a book that has caught the imagination and held the loyalty of three generations of readers for over fifty years and shows no signs of stopping. It is what it is. And what it is has grown exponentially with Christopher Tolkien's monumental editing of his father's hitherto-unpublished mythology, including *The Silmarillion, Unfinished Tales*, and the twelve-volume *History of Middle-earth.* Our understanding of Tolkien's vision and our appreciation of the scope of his imagination are immeasurably greater than they could have been in the mid-twentieth century.

A number of the pieces, therefore, inevitably show their age, sometimes in light of new information contained in Tolkien's posthumously published work, often as a result of my later thoughts on a topic, not infrequently by comparison with the work of a growing number of newer scholars who are more and more enriching the world of Tolkien studies. I am grateful for their work and hope that mine can find a place in the continuum.

Many people have helped with the genesis of this book. First and foremost, thanks must go to the Tolkien Estate and to the J.R.R. Tolkien Copyright Trust for permission to quote from MS Tolkien MS A 13/1, *c* (folio 168), now in the Bodleian Library in Oxford, and from "Aotrou and Itroun," published in 1945 in the now-defunct *Welsh Review.* Special thanks go to Colin Harris, Catherine Barker, and the staff at the Bodleian Library Department of Western Manuscripts for all their cooperation in making manuscripts available. And to Cathleen Blackburn for all her help.

Thanks are due the members of the Tolkien Symposium as well as those of the Mythopoeic Society for their patience over many years in listening to papers and for their encouraging as well as constructive criticism. And thanks beyond measure to Vaughn Howland for his stringent and astringent editing of papers-in-progress.

A few essays are here published for the first time. "Tolkien on Tolkien: 'On Fairy-stories,' *The Hobbit,* and *The Lord of the Rings*" was presented at the Tolkien 2005 conference at Aston University in Birmingham, England, but was not published in the Conference *Proceedings.* A slightly different version of "The Mind, the Tongue, and the Tale" was presented at the 2010 Modena Conference on Tolkien and Philosophy. "The Body in Question: The Unhealed Wounds of Frodo Baggins" and "Bilbo's Neck Riddle," neither previously presented nor published, make their first appearance in this volume. The newest essay, "Tolkien, *Kalevala,* and 'The Story of Kullervo,'" grew out of my work with Tolkien's manuscript of the story and makes its debut here.

Abbreviations and Conventions

Since there are a number of different editions of *The Lord of the Rings* in hardcover and trade and mass-market paperback, some three-volume, some one-volume, all with different pagination, references to that work will be parenthetically cited from the second edition hardcover by abbreviated volume title (*FR, TT, RK*), book number in uppercase roman, chapter number in lowercase roman, and page number in arabic. Thus *FR* I, iii, 85.

FR = *The Fellowship of the Ring*
H = *The Hobbit*
HME = *The History of Middle-earth*
LM = *Language and Mythology*
LB = *Lays of Beleriand*
LotR = *The Lord of the Rings*
LR = *The Lost Road*
LT = *The Book of Lost Tales*
MC = *The Monsters and the Critics and Other Essays*
MR = *Morgoth's Ring*
OED = *The Oxford English Dictionary*
PD = *Poetic Diction*
PE = *Parma Eldalamberon*
RK = *The Return of the King*
RS = *The Return of the Shadow*
SD = *Sauron Defeated*
Silm = *The Silmarillion*
SME = *The Shaping of Middle-earth*
SWM = *Smith of Wootton Major*
TE = *Tolkien Encyclopedia*
TL = *Tree and Leaf*
TOFS = *Tolkien on Fairy-stories*
TT = *The Two Towers*
UT = *Unfinished Tales*

Part One

Tolkien Sub-creator

This section has as its common thread a principle central to Tolkien's fiction, the idea of a believable Secondary World faithful to its own norms and sustaining its own inner consistency. Such a Secondary World, commanding Secondary Belief, can be fantastic but must preserve a recognizable relationship to the Primary World out of which it grows. It must have "a recognition of fact, but not a slavery to it" (*MC* 144). Following Tolkien's dictum, this group of essays explores ways in which Tolkien both recognizes fact and frees himself from it.

"Fantasy and Reality: J.R.R. Tolkien's World and the Fairy-story Essay" introduces "On Fairy-stories," Tolkien's most important essay in terms of its creative principles and their application to his own fiction. "On Fairy-stories" is his definitive statement on the making of successful fantasy, and serves as an introduction to the whole subject of his sub-creation. "The Music and the Task" looks more specifically at a single sub-creative—and problematic—principle of his Secondary World, its inclusion of both free will and fate as separate operating systems in Middle-earth. "Tolkien and the Idea of the Book" proposes the Winchester manuscript of Sir Thomas Malory's *Le Morte D'Arthur* as a model and prototype for the extended conceit of the Red Book of Westmarch and its ancillary volumes as that body of stories was fictively imagined as being transmitted from oral tale to imaginary written version to actual printed book. His fictional tale-tellers, redactors, transcribers and translators, his pseudo-compilers and pseudo-editors, are parts of a chain of transmitters whose combined efforts both within and without the fiction have resulted in the actual appearance of his Secondary World's stories as texts in the Primary World.

"Tolkien on Tolkien: 'On Fairy-stories' *The Hobbit,* and *The Lord of the Rings*" takes the principles for successful sub-creation laid out in "On Fairy-stories," and assesses the extent to which Tolkien in his two best-known works, *The Hobbit* and *The Lord of the Rings,* succeeds in following his own rules. The question of "When is a Fairy-story a *Faërie* Story?" is answered by looking at his understanding and implementation of a word essential to his fiction, *Faërie,* in terms of its etymology, its historical usage, and his own depiction of it as a "perilous realm" in his last short story, *Smith of Wootton Major*. "The Footsteps of Ælfwine" traces the path throughout his fiction of a single archetypal figure, the Elf-friend, in all its guises.

"The Curious Incident of the Dream at the Barrow" examines the sub-created metaphysics and occult history of a brief but disturbing incident on the Barrow-downs, the hobbit Merry's living experience of a dead man's memory transmitted across time and space from one consciousness to another. "Whose Myth Is It?" considers Tolkien's awareness of point of view as an essential component of any mythology, and his willingness to allow conflicting, indeed, contradictory interpretations of the same phenomenon, that of the death-fate of Men, in his sub-created world.

Fantasy and Reality

J.R.R. Tolkien's World and the Fairy-Story Essay

In introducing students to the fiction of J.R.R. Tolkien, I often used to begin by quoting what I always felt was an especially relevant statement from his essay "On Fairy-Stories," that "fantasy depends upon reality as nonsense depends upon sense." Not long ago, I looked through the essay to verify the quote, largely so I could cite the page for inquiring students. To my surprise, although I turned page after page, I couldn't find it, and for a very good reason. It wasn't there. What I did find, to the considerable embarrassment of my memory, was that my oft-quoted dictum wasn't what Tolkien wrote at all. What he actually said was much richer and more complex than my snappy little one-liner gave him credit for.

> For creative Fantasy is founded upon the hard recognition that things are
> so in the world as it appears under the sun; on a recognition of fact but not
> a slavery to it. So upon logic was founded the nonsense that displays itself
> in the tales and rhymes of Lewis Carroll. (*MC* 144)

What this goes to show, which I should have known all along, is that you should not rely on memory, for the disparity between what I thought Tolkien said and what he really said is considerable. The difference is obvious. While the key terms—*fantasy* and *nonsense*—are the same, as is the semantic structure—seemingly opposed concepts which are actually interdependent—the resemblance stops there, for Tolkien's thought is more profound and his language more exact than my inadequate shorthand version.

Where in describing Carroll I used the word *sense*, a quality of thought, Tolkien more correctly and far more precisely cited *logic*, not an elusive quality but a system of rules governing words and their relationships. He saw how firmly grounded in the logic of language are the puns and literalities that create Carroll's fantasy, how reliant for their effect on the very system they seem to flout. He was equally percipient about fantasy. The phrase he opposes to it, "the hard recognition that things are so in the world," is more accurately descriptive as well as being more psychologically observant than is my word *reality,* a rather vague and general term. And although he does go on to talk about "reality" in his essay (it's easier to repeat one word than a whole phrase) his word *recognition* is the key to the whole idea, for it places the emphasis where it belongs: on the beholder rather than on something called "reality," about which there could be and often is disagreement. Recognition brings the idea home to the reader. We can neither understand nor appreciate a thing we cannot recognize. However apparently alien, however jarring to the imagination, fantasy, to be successful, must be recognizable by the perceiving human consciousness.

I'm not going to try to define fantasy. Excellent critics such as Tzvetan Todorov, Kathryn Hume, Harold Bloom, Darko Suvin, and Erik Rabkin have tried until the cows come home, and are no nearer a definition that does more than define their own theories. Tolkien, wiser than most, didn't try to define it, but he did in the fairy-story essay lay out the principles of *his* fantasy. We are all familiar with his working terms—*sub-creation, secondary world, inner consistency of reality,* but it is easy to lose track of their references—primary creation, the real world, and the outer reality of which consistency is the hallmark. In the section of the essay subtitled "Fantasy" Tolkien gets down to the nuts and bolts of the creative process, and his discussion stands as the best description anyone has made yet of his own art. It is his creative manifesto.

> Anyone . . . can say *the green sun.* . . . But. . . . To make a Secondary World inside which the green sun will be credible, commanding Secondary Belief, will . . . certainly demand a special skill, a kind of elvish craft. (*MC* 140).

It is in describing that elvish craft that he makes an implicit comparison with Carroll, for he declares unequivocally that, "Fantasy is a rational not an irrational activity" (*MC* 139). This statement could easily describe Lewis Carroll, who was a supremely rational individual. If he hadn't been, he could never have conceived the rational fantasy of the *Alice* books, whose apparent irrationality is so firmly grounded in syntactic and semantic logic. But Tolkien went on to say that, "Fantasy is made out of the Primary World" (*MC* 147), and here he was describing his own work. He declared about his own creation that, "Middle-earth is not an imaginary world" (*Letters* 239) and stated more directly that "Middle-earth is *our* world" (Carpenter 91). He also said (although *confessed* might be a better word, for while his statement is general, it is also clearly personal),

> Probably . . . every sub-creator wishes in some measure to be a real maker, or hopes that he is drawing on reality: hopes that the peculiar quality of this secondary world (if not all the details) are derived from Reality. . . . The peculiar quality of the "joy" in successful Fantasy can thus be explained as a sudden glimpse of the underlying reality or truth. (*MC* 155).

Here is the recognition to which he refers in the first quote, recognition not just that "things are so in the world," but also that there is a reality or truth that underlies that fact. And if the writer, the sub-creator, is an honest craftsman— and Tolkien certainly was—it will sometimes be "hard" recognition, for there are some underlying realities or truths that do not always bring joy. And if the secondary world is to reflect the primary one, it must acknowledge that.

Not only is fantasy made out of the Primary World, it must point back to its source if it is to be effective. But this requires the very elvish skill and craft that Tolkien cites, for he also argues that the attraction of fantasy as a genre is its "arresting strangeness" (*MC* 139). Fantasy allows us to escape into a world other than our own. Otherwise we could not call it fantasy. We desire escape, which of course implies strangeness. That is why we read fantasy. The particular skill of the writer of fantasy, especially in devising a sub-created Secondary World, lies in effecting the escape and still keeping the recognition; the craft resides in achieving and maintaining that delicate balance between fantasy and reality that will lead us to the underlying truth. Nobody does it better than Tolkien.

Indeed, I propose that nobody since Tolkien has managed to do it half as well. With the possible exception of Frank Herbert's Arrakis, and Ursula Le-Guin's Earthsea and Gethen and Anarres, Tolkien's Middle-earth outshines every sub-created world that has followed it, and most that came before. Not only do you have to be able to recognize reality before you can depart from it into fantasy, you have to have a pretty good sense of how far you can go before recognition disappears and there is no point of reference. In point of fact, Tolkien didn't go very far, much less far when you come to think of it than the worlds his work has inspired, the proliferation of Secondary World fantasies, the role-playing games, and their spin-off books.

It is no exaggeration to say that *The Lord of the Rings* is the most important and most influential fantasy of the twentieth century. But if you examine the book closely, you will find that for a major fantasy it has surprisingly few ac-tual fantastic elements in it—far fewer, indeed, than in the multitude of later fantasies his fiction has spawned. There is very little in his work that is not ei-ther derived from reality or rearranged from primary material. Tolkien's "fan-tasy" is both attractive and powerful not because of its fantasy but because of its reality, because his world shows us that things are "so" in our own world.

I propose to examine the way in which Tolkien follows his own principles, to look at his fantasy in the context of his reality and examine the relative pro-portions of each. I will show how un-fantastic is the quality of his world, and how grounded in reality are the elements of arresting strangeness in his work. There is some straight fantasy, of course. There are talking eagles. There is a Balrog. There are Elves, Orcs, Ents—creatures we certainly don't meet in the Primary World—and we see more of them than either eagles or Balrogs. But with the exception of the Ents (and even they destroy Isengard by acting like trees) the fantastic aspect of these characters is at the periphery of the action. It is largely decoration, and has very little to do with advancing the story.

In this respect, *The Lord of the Rings* is notably lacking in what any good science-fiction work displays—the integration of the science (or in this case the fantasy) with the plot. There is some integration or we couldn't call it a fantasy at all. Eagles can talk and carry people, and they do, twice, effect an important rescue. The Balrog is directly responsible for the death and therefore the resurrection of Gandalf. But out of eleven hundred or so pages that's not a great deal of fantasy. And for the rest, how much does the fan-tasy serve the plot? Gandalf has his staff, and he can command fire, but on the two occasions when he uses it, it doesn't help much. Saruman's flame-throwers mirror those of our own world, and aside from this technology he manifests remarkably little wizardly power. Galadriel's Mirror can range over time, but its function is to reflect action, not to affect it. Again, in so large a story, that does not seem very much.

To be sure, simply to call an individual an Elf is to invoke a quality of "ar-resting strangeness." It thus satisfies one of Tolkien's criteria. But what about the other? What about recognition? How elf-like is the behavior of Tolkien's Elves? Not very. They are recognizably human, in fact super human in looks and behavior. What is really strange about the Elves of Middle-earth (and Valinor, for that matter) is that we have trouble recognizing them as elves, for they depart radically from the folk and fairy tale conventions that tradition-ally govern the elven-kind. They are not diminutive in size. They are not pix-ies or corrigans or leprechauns or boggarts. They don't befriend poor wood-cutters' third sons. They don't mend shoes, or tidy up the house while you are asleep, or come out at night and dance in fairy rings, or steal human babies and substitute their own. They have neither wings nor wands. We can see in them reflections of ourselves. Legolas vies with Gimli over the number of orcs each has killed, and debates with him the relative beauties of forests and caves. Lórien makes use of Elven technology, not Elven magic, as the Elves themselves are careful to point out when Pippin asks them. Elven cloaks are effective camouflage, but they are not magic cloaks of invisibility, and when Aragorn, Legolas, and Gimli (wearing their cloaks) stand up, the Riders of Rohan have no trouble seeing them. Elven rope is tough and strong, but as far as we are told it is simply rope. Gollum's reaction to it, "Elves twisted it, curse them!" (*TT* IV, i, 224), and his pain when it binds him, are more psychological responses than they are the effects of magic.

The connection with Elves associates the rope with light, and its silvery gleam brings Frodo light in the darkness of the storm, but it is worthy of note that Tolkien leaves this phenomenon deliberately inexplicit. When Sam lets the rope down the cliff-face to Frodo, "The darkness seemed to lift from Frodo's eyes, or else his sight was returning. He could see the grey line as it came dangling down, and he thought it had a faint silver sheen." (*TT* IV, i, 214–15). Note the careful listing of possibilities. Either the darkness "seemed" to lift, "or else" his sight was coming back, as sight does when eyes become dark-adapted. The rope offers him a point to focus on, and his dizziness abates. These are all naturally occurring operations of the body, but readers can translate light into Light, focus into faith, as and if they choose. The rope itself acts like rope, and the final question of whether it unties itself after Frodo and Sam use it to descend the cliff is deliberately left unanswered.

Similarly, Elven bread, waybread, acts like bread. One cake will keep a traveler "on his feet for a day of long labour," as the Elves assure Gimli (*FR* II, vii, 386). This is what bread is supposed to do. It is nourishing and sustaining. It is the staff of life. Nevertheless, Sam and Frodo find it pretty dull as a steady diet, and it doesn't hit the spot like rabbit stew. Gollum's reaction to Elven bread, as to Elven rope, is more psychological than magical. He has met it before, when he was a prisoner of the Elves, and the memory still haunts him. He can't eat it, coughs and chokes, and spits it out. But we know the kind of food Gollum likes. "Worms or beetles or something slimy out of holes," as Sam conjectures (*TT* IV, ii, 232), and the thought of Gollum's food makes Sam choke and sputter. Again, we are free to make of this what we wish. The author has supplied a perfectly reasonable, natural rationale for Gollum's dislike. Those who wish can see in waybread a reference to the Way, but the author uses lower case and leaves interpretation to individual inclination. As the narrative progresses, both rope and bread undoubtedly acquire metaphoric value, but the metaphor is in the mind of the reader.

To call someone an Orc certainly invokes "arresting strangeness," since few readers are (or were before Tolkien) familiar with this word. Tolkien's first name for them was "goblins," and they are far closer to the goblins of literature than are his Elves to their fairy tale namesakes. But a closer look shows Orcs also to be recognizably human, and very little they do to be outside the realm of human behavior. Like soldiers everywhere, they march, they grouse, they bicker, they are insubordinate, they fight among themselves. They also snarl and murder and betray, and while this is not typical military behavior, it is certainly recognizable as human behavior. Orc food is simple meat and drink (although the meat is quite possibly human and the drink—described as "burning liquid—is probably alcoholic), but except for the cannibal implications these properties are even less fantastic than Elven bread. Indeed, the cannibal implications reinforce (albeit negatively) the Orcs' kinship with humanity, not their alienness from it. Orcs are certainly ugly, but while their looks can be seen as an external metaphor for an internal condition, these are no more a fantasy characteristic than is Elven beauty. We see our idealized selves reflected in the Elves. We see our shadow, the unadmitted, the worst side of human character in the unadmirable but depressingly human behavior of the Orcs. And we are forced to recognize it.

But what about hobbits? They are entirely Tolkien's invention, deriving from no established literary tradition, and they stand as his most striking, most enduring creation. They have added a word to the *Oxford English Dictionary* and a new folklore to children's literature. But how fantastic are they? How removed in nature and character and even appearance are they from the Primary World? They are half-sized humans. The Primary World is filled with little people. They have big appetites and hairy feet. So do lots of people we all know. They live in holes in the ground, but those holes are as spacious, as comfortably furnished, as "real" as any real-world household. The second line of *The Hobbit* takes the fantasy out of hobbit-holes, and the second paragraph relates them firmly to the recognizable, real world by means of doorknobs, panelled walls, tiles, carpets, bedrooms, bathrooms, cellars, pantries, wardrobes, kitchens, and dining-rooms. Hobbiton is modeled on a pre-industrial rural English village like the one where Tolkien spent his happiest years of childhood. Hobbits like to get presents, and have a tendency to accumulate objects. When they accumulate more than they have room for, they put the resultant clutter in a museum.

All the hobbit attributes I have cited and more besides are recognizable as aspects of humanity. The reason we dislike Ted Sandyman and love Sam Gamgee and develop a grudging respect for Lobelia Sackville-Baggins, the reason we admire Merry and develop an exasperated affection for Pippin,

and break our hearts at the tragedy of Frodo is not because they are hobbits, but because we recognize them as human beings. Ted Sandyman is
any unimaginative, scoffing skeptic who makes fun of weird tales. I've spent
most of my life arguing with Ted Sandyman. Sam's romanticism, his common sense, his devotion to his cooking-gear, his loyalty and self-sacrifice
are among the best and most appealing of human characteristics. Lobelia is
every nosey, busybody old lady who has ever triumphed over adversity by
sheer bad temper. The mature dependability of Merry and the adolescent
impulsiveness, curiosity, and big mouth of Pippin, are not just recognizable
human traits, they are typical.

Of fairy tale talismans the story has remarkably few—only two, in fact.
But neither, I suggest, will qualify as truly fantastic. The most mystical artifact in the story is the Phial of Galadriel, but no reader, I venture to guess,
would ascribe its light to magic, for the Phial transcends fantasy to become
myth in the best sense of that word. It is an object whose meaning is greater
than the sum of its parts. It is not founded on reality but on what for Tolkien
was Truth, and as such it offers precisely that "glimpse of underlying reality
or truth" which he said successful fantasy should bring. Within the story the
Phial is both a link to past history, the light of Eärendil's Silmaril, and a link
to the future when the three jewels will be recovered. Beyond the story it
is a metaphor for hope, and in this respect its light must be seen as at once
literal and symbolic. It is both *a* light and *the* Light, and as such is the most
symbolic reference to be found in the whole story. But for that very reason,
it will not stand as fantasy.

I will close with an examination of the most indubitably magical, most
prominent object in the whole story, the fantasy element that gives its name
to the whole work—the Ring. Just how magical, how fantastic an artifact is
the Ring? I suggest that it is more fantastic in *The Hobbit* than in *The Lord of
the Rings*, and that as the latter work developed, its magical properties came
more and more to recede behind its metaphorical and psychological significance. I grant its most obvious magical function, the ability to make people
disappear. This is un-recognizably so in this world and unarguably contrary
to the reality we know. But as the story progresses, this faculty becomes
less and less the nifty invisibility device of *The Hobbit* and more and more
a metaphor for a psychological state, and finally for a disastrous erosion of
moral and spiritual being and a perversion of the will, about which I will say
more in a moment.

But perversion of the will is actually a secondary function of the Ring. Its
primary function, the one on which the whole story turns, is to command
obedience. Here again, overt evidence of fantasy seems strangely lacking. The

one truly fantastic thing that the Ring is said to do—to confer absolute power, to be a super-weapon, to command armies and influence wars—is just what we do not see the Ring doing except in the very moment when it cannot do it any longer. That is, when it is destroyed and the Nazgûl are pulled in and down in the undertow of its descent. It is a measure of Tolkien's genius that he can convince us of the Ring's power without ever showing it. The hinge on which the whole story turns is at once the most and the least fantastic element in it. Look at it. It is a plain gold ring whose power is never conclusively demonstrated. Tolkien himself said,

> You cannot press the One Ring too hard, for it is of course a mythical feature. . . . The Ring of Sauron is only one of the various mythical treatments of the placing of one's life, or power, in some external object, which is thus exposed to capture or destruction with disastrous results to oneself. . . . (*Letters* 279)

What is shown instead of the actual power of the Ring is the reaction of characters to it. Bilbo lies to maintain his right to it, and cannot freely give it up. Gandalf is afraid of it, Galadriel is tempted by it, Boromir is corrupted by it (as is Denethor who has never even seen it), Grishnákh covets it, and Saruman loses his wisdom and his position as head of the White Council for it. We see all these manifestations, and we refer them back to the Ring. It is we, not Tolkien, who confer power on the Ring, and he was wise enough to know that we would, and to let us do it.

The most extreme operation of the Ring is the terrifying effect it has on Frodo—the eroding of his will as he is driven more and more to use it, until at the last he loses his very self. Nowhere more obviously than here does Tolkien's adjective "hard" in his phrase "hard recognition" become the operative word. Frodo's transformation is not just hard to watch, it is unbearable. It is even more unbearable to recognize, and yet it is impossible to deny, that things like this occur in the world, that what happens to him not only could happen to anyone, indeed it does happen—all the time. It happens when people fall victim to their appetites and surrender their humanity to their desires. It happens when soldiers come back from war, or when children are abused, or when anyone is damaged by catastrophe. Post-traumatic stress syndrome is not confined to hobbits.

So how fantastic is the Ring? Hardly at all; it is the very embodiment of reality as reality acts on people all the time—as they are affected by power, by greed, by envy, by violence, by shock, by serious injury to mind or body. It is Tolkien forcing us into "the hard recognition that things are so in the world." The Ring, then, is not so much a fantastic artifact of Tolkien's Secondary World as it is a direct reference to the Primary World, a sign pointing to and standing for an inescapable, underlying reality or truth, a hard recognition of the human condition. In this respect, the Ring is synecdoche, the part that stands for the whole. As the Ring is to humanity, so Tolkien's fantasy world is to our Primary one—founded on it, grounded in it, and standing for it.

The Music and the Task

Fate and Free Will in Middle-earth

[The Silmarillion] is nothing less than an attempt to justify God's creation
of an imperfect world filled with suffering, loss, and grief.
—John Garth, *Tolkien and the Great War*

During December and January of 1916–17, in the very center and depths
of World War I, the young J.R.R. Tolkien, newly returned to England from
the carnage of the Somme, began work on the stories which later became
the nucleus of his great legendarium the Silmarillion, correctly described by
John Garth in the epigraph to this essay. The Silmarillion was intended to
supply what Tolkien felt was missing from his country's literary pre-history,
an indigenous English (*not* British) mythology on the order of the Finnish
Kalevala and the Icelandic *Eddas*. He envisioned this ambitious project as
"a more or less connected body of legend" ranging from the "large and cosmogonic" to the level of "romantic fairy-story" (*Letters* 144). In the process
of creating his mythology, however, Tolkien did more than color in a blank
space; he invented a cosmology whose operation depends on a paradox, a
challenging teleological contradiction.

The contradiction resides in the simultaneous presence in his invented
world of two opposing principles, fate and free will, imagined as operating
side by side, sometimes in conflict, sometimes interdependent. The teleology
provides that this paradox, established at the beginning in his mythological
Creation narrative, will accomplish its end in both senses of that word: both
its purpose as described in the epigraph at the head of this article, and its
fulfillment. The challenge arises when fate and free will intersect, for this col-
lision of mutually contradictive forces engenders a cognitive disjunction that
works against readers' acceptance of its operation in the Secondary World.

The difficulty lies not with free will, but with fate. Readers who assume
(and most do) that characters in Tolkien's invented world are free to choose,
find the opposing notion that they are predestined hard to accept. And the

idea that both principles are concurrently at work (and apparently at odds) is a concept even harder to encompass. It is, nevertheless, a concept integral to a mythology whose overarching scheme is that fate, conceived as divinely inspired and celestially orchestrated music, governs the created world— with a single exception. Of all Middle-earth's sentient species, the race of Men (including Hobbits) is the one group given the "virtue" to "shape their lives" beyond the scope of this music. In contradistinction, the otherwise generally similar race of Elves (both races being the Children of [the god-head] Ilúvatar) is, together with the rest of Creation, ruled by fate.

A GREEN SUN

In its apparent impossibility of reconciliation, this fate/free will dichotomy is what in his essay "On Fairy-stories" Tolkien termed a "green sun." That is to say, it is an element, a feature, or aspect intentionally contrary to the Primary World but essential and formative in the Secondary one. The concept goes to the heart of what he called "sub-creation," the making of a believable imaginary world. "Anyone," he wrote, "can say *the green sun.* Many can then imagine or picture it." But neither the phrase nor the striking image it evokes is by itself enough to make his point, and Tolkien went on to explain what more would be necessary: "a Secondary World in which the green sun will be credible." This, he wrote, would not only "require labour and thought," it would " demand a special skill, a kind of elvish craft" (*MC* 140).

Labour and thought he most certainly gave it, as well as applying his own elvish craft, which was considerable. Yet for many even of his most devoted admirers, this departure of Tolkien's Secondary World from the laws or principles of the Primary World is not just a green sun, it is one green sun too many, putting a breaking strain on Secondary Belief already stretched by accepting Elves, Hobbits, talking eagles, and walking trees. Perhaps for that reason it has been largely ignored in the search for the keys to his cosmology. The assumption that either of the principles in question by definition obviates the other has tended to conceal this particular green sun, so that most readers seem disposed to look past it rather than at it. Like Poe's purloined letter, it is hidden in plain sight, openly displayed but easily overlooked.[1]

Readerly inattention notwithstanding, this green sun is not only a necessary and formative feature of Tolkien's Secondary World, it is the very mechanism by which it operates. In the Primary World the relative governance of fate or free will has been for millennia a topic for debate among philosophers and theologians, who argue the extent to which either factor may be in force. Tolkien had the daring and freedom of imagination to envision a world wherein both are co-existent, simultaneously in operation and co-operation.[2] So far as I am aware, this vision is unique in modern fantasy.[3]

Its uniqueness, however, is just what fosters its invisibility and permits scholars rather to view his cosmology through the lens of this or that more familiar and thus more readily perceived real-world philosophical system.[4] The impulse to associate the unconventional with the familiar is not unlike that of early genre-critics who wanted *The Lord of the Rings* to be a fairy tale or an epic or a romance, all the while conceding that it was a novel, though it certainly didn't read like one. Of course it is sui generis, and of course it contains elements from many genres, just as it also invites comparison with real-world philosophical systems. Comparison and similarity, however, are not necessarily the same thing. Most of these real-world systems specify fate *or* free will, and even when, like Boethius, they include some version of both, they do not, as does Tolkien, assign each to a different group existing in the same world at the same time.

A good question to start with, then, is *why?* Why would Tolkien deliberately contrive a system so at odds with itself, so cross-grained and contrary that nobody wants to see it, much less accept it? I suggest that he had three reasons, one strategic, the second personal, the last sub-creative. The strategic reason was to forestall or at least defuse the inevitable comparisons with real-world systems. The personal reason related to a major and then quite recent external event in Tolkien's life, the loss in 1916 of two of his closest friends, killed in World War I. The sub-creative reason was to give to an ordered universe a plausible mechanism for change. I'll tackle the strategic reason first, then the personal one, and save the sub-creative reason for more extended discussion

ELEMENTS IN SOLUTION

As to the strategy, I suggest that it was designed to assure that his mythology be taken on its own terms for the imaginative creation that it was, without being boxed in by any mythological, philosophical, or literary look-alike. In a literary culture where comparison is a standard practice and source-hunting a favorite pastime, such independence is hard to maintain, but Tolkien did his best. While scholars such as Tom Shippey and Marjorie Burns have offered good and clear evidence in Tolkien's work of influences from Old and Middle English and Old Icelandic, and Tolkien himself acknowledged the influence of the Finnish *Kalevala* on both his Quenya language and his epic story of Túrin Turambar, in all these cases he re-configured the borrowed material to fit his new context. Where mythology intersected religion he did no less. He specifically objected to "the Arthurian world" as a candidate for England's myth since it "explicitly contain[ed] the Christian religion," which seemed to him "fatal" (*Letters* 144). "Myth and fairy-story," he wrote, "must, as all art, reflect and contain in solution elements of moral and religious truth (or error), but not explicit, not in the known form of the primary 'real' world" (*Letters* 144). The operative word in this statement is *art*. Tolkien was writing fiction, not theology. His dismissal of the Arthurian world, a probable allusion to Sir Thomas Malory's allegorical Grail section of *Le Morte D'Arthur* (even in its toned down translation-adaptation of the French *Queste del Sainte Graal*) was a repudiation of its preachy didacticism.

The problem in a work of mythopoeic fiction is how to include "elements of moral and religious truth (or error)" without inviting association with this or that familiar system of belief, an inevitable pitfall of which Tolkien was well aware. Here is an example. His statement to Milton Waldman that, "there cannot be any 'story' without a fall—all stories are ultimately about the fall" (*Letters* 147) not only implies a shared language of belief, but goes beyond such sharing to accept the premise that a story, by virtue of having a plot, involves some kind of situational imperfection, a conflict whose resolution provides the story. Yet he was also aware that in Western Judeo-Christian tradition, *a* fall inevitably implies *the* Fall—the Eden story, the disobedience in the Garden, God's punishment, and humanity's expulsion from Paradise into a world of pain and suffering. For a story hoping to claim any originality, this is too much baggage to carry without collapsing under the weight, or inevitably turning into another and more familiar story. Writing as a Christian but trying not to write about Christianity, Tolkien avoided the pitfall by shifting his fall from creat*ed* humanity to the creat*ing* beings. He described it to Waldman as "a fall of Angels," hastening to add "Though quite different in form, of course, to that of Christian myth" (*Letters* 147).

Different in form it certainly is, and we may suppose deliberately so. First of all, it is creation by committee, not by a single Creator. As Tolkien's creation story the "Ainulindalë" recounts, the "One," his fictive godhead, first called Eru and then (by the Elves whose myth this is) Ilúvatar, declares a musical theme to "the offspring of his thought" the Ainur. These "offspring," separate aspects of "the One," make of his theme a "great music" which will be the blueprint for creation, but which is interrupted when one of their number, the rebellious Melkor, counters with his own theme. The performance is halted by Ilúvatar and started again with a new theme. This, too, is interrupted with a counter-theme by Melkor and halted by Ilúvatar. On the third attempt, Melkor's theme is taken up by Ilúvatar and woven in to his own theme so that there are "two musics progressing at one time." One is "deep and wide and beautiful, but slow and blended with an immeasurable sorrow," while the other is "loud, and vain, and endlessly repeated" (*Silm* 15–17). Tolkien has neatly captured the beauty and poignancy, as well as the pain and suffering of the world we live in. His fall is made to occur in the very act of creation so that the world thus set in motion is not, as in the familiar Judeo-Christian story of Genesis "good" until marred by human error but faulty and imperfect from the beginning. The obvious parallel has been avoided but the essential truth has been retained.

Both the truth and the human experience from which it derives—that the world is flawed, full of surprises, and seldom works the way we want it to—are dependent on and generative of the words used to express them. The names for things, as Tolkien well knew, operate to create the very world they describe. In the present context, such catchwords as *luck, accident, chance, happenstance, coincidence, fate, destiny,* all seek to name and thus to capture an aspect of human experience, the ways in which we categorize the ways things happen. They help us to relate to, if not always to understand, the incomprehensible, uncontrollable forces at work in our experiences with one another and with the world around us. Words are important, and an author's selection and use of words says much about the worldview he represents.

It is therefore worthy of note that such conceptually significant proper nouns as *God, Heaven, Grace, Paradise, Providence, Salvation, Damnation,* do not figure in Tolkien's major fiction. Equally worthy of note are the words which do figure, and which in fact play an important role in the structuring of his world. These include, as already noted, the noun *fate* as either a general concept (uncapitalized) or a proper noun/personification (capitalized), the opposing phrase *free will,* as well as related nouns such as *doom* and *choice,* and verbs such as *choose, will, shall,* and *must.* These had for Tolkien more specific and special meanings than those accepted (rather loosely) in the twenty-first century. Therefore, honoring Tolkien's position as a lover of words and the history of words, we need to look at where the words come from and what they once signified before we can understand fully what he meant them to mean.

Happened, Spoken, Settled

Among the literatures which he studied and taught, the Old English epic *Beowulf* was surely Tolkien's chief, though certainly not his only lexical model, important both for its heroic and tragic ethos and for the vocabulary through which that ethos is expressed. A familiar Old English word, *wyrd,* usually translated "fate," appears in that poem nine times (Branston 65).[5] It is there spelled in lower case, but can also be spelled with a capital W and personified, as it is in other Old English poems such as *The Dream of the Rood.* The word also appears (capitalized) as *Werdys* in the Middle English of Chaucer's *Legend of Good Women* (Branston 67), and culminates in the Shakespearean English of *Macbeth's* Weird Sisters. In the second half of line 455, Beowulf declares *Gǣð ā wyrd swā hīo scel,* "Fate will go as it must"(l. 455), but later says, *Wyrd oft nereð / unfǣgne eorl, þonne his ellen dēah,* "fate often saves/ an undoomed man [i.e., one not appointed to die] when his courage holds" (ll. 572–73). Compare the more current aphorism, "God helps those who help themselves." If the *Beowulf* poet could give fate some wiggle-room, Tolkien could (and did) do no less. Just how such wiggle-room might work both in *Beowulf* and Tolkien's own mythology, requires a brief dip into etymology.

Bosworth-Toller's Anglo-Saxon Dictionary glosses *wyrd,* related to the Old English verb *weorðan,* "to happen or become," as "What happens, fate, fortune, chance." Linguistically related is Old Icelandic *Urð,* described in Snorri's *Edda* as one of the three Norns or Fates, the others named as *Verðandi* and *Skuld. Urð* and *Verðandi* are respectively the past and present participles of the Old Icelandic verb *verða.* Cleasby-Vigfusson's Icelandic-English Dictionary gives the primary meaning of *verða* as "To become, happen, come to pass," with more specific meaning in sense IV as denoting necessity: *"one must, needs, is forced, obliged to do."* It further defines *Verðandi* (capitalized) as *"the 'Being,' the Weird,* the name of one of the Norns." Both Snorri's *Edda* and the earlier *Poetic Edda* personify *Urð* as the guardian of Urð's Well (Snorri 17; *Poetic Edda* 9, "Voluspø" verses 19, 20), which lies beneath the root of the World Tree Yggdrasil. Such personification makes it philologically reasonable to see *Urð* and *Wyrd* as similarly perceived forces, while *Skuld,* the present tense-preterite form of Old Icelandic *skulu,* implies "that which will have happened." Related to modern English "shall" or "should," it is closer in meaning to "must," Anglo-Saxon *motan,* with the force of necessity, and to sense IV (see above) of Old Icelandic *verða.*

Fate, the word most frequently used to translate both *Wyrd* and *Urð,* is defined by *The American Heritage Dictionary* as, "the supposed force, principle, or power that predetermines events." It comes from Latin *fāta* plural of *fātum,* the neuter past participle of *fārī,* "to speak." Fate, then, is what is *spoken,* that which has been declared to be. And finally, *doom,* which in modern English has negative connotations, is derived from Anglo-Saxon *dóm,* and means simply "judgment, judicial sentence, decree." In both "sentence" and "decree," then, it is not unlike *fate* as "that spoken." Dictionary definitions can only go so far, however, and it should be emphasized that they are not absolutes but meanings embedded in the history of the uses of certain words, meanings themselves subject to subtleties of usage and context. It must be emphasized as well that the words themselves are not things but only the words for things, the sometimes ill-fitted handles by which we try to grasp the import of what we cannot control and do not fully understand.

No one was more aware of this than Tolkien, who declared repeatedly that his legendarium was generated to provide a home for his languages. Thus he built linguistic concepts similar to these real-world examples into the vocabulary of his invented languages Quenya and Sindarin. An entry in the very early "Gnomish Lexicon" lists *gwalt, gwalod* as "good luck—any providential occurrence or thought" (*PE* 11, p. 44). In the "Quenya Lexicon" the later Quenya *Amarto, Ambar(rt)* is capitalized (therefore probably personified) as "Fate" (*PE* 12, 34). ENGET(OR) is translated "fate, hap" (35) with *engetor* listed under the stem NETE as "fate, luck" (66). ENGETOR also occurs in the Valar name-list (*PE* 14, pp. 13–14, note 12). Gnomish *Bridwen* is listed as "fate personified" (*PE* 11, 24), with lower case *pridwen* with the phrase *i-bridwen a-vridwen* glossed as "poetic justice, judgment of fate" (p. 64). The Primitive Eldarin stem √MBAR (see *Amarto* above), "to make a decision" (i.e., to choose) occurs in primitive Quenya *umbar*, "fate," as in *Túrambar* "Master of Fate," with the verbal base √TUR, "dominate, master, conquer" as a prefix. Quenya *ambar*, "world," is also derived from √MBAR, with the meaning "settlement or abode," as in a "decision" about dwelling or occupying land. Primitive Eldarin *ambar*(a), Quenya *ambar*, Sindarin *amar*, therefore carried the sense of "settlement, appointed place," as in the Earth/Arda as the appointed dwelling or home of the children of Ilúvatar (*PE* 17, 104–105). The other derivative of √MBAR, *umbar*, meant an ordinance or decree and thus the circumstances proceeding from such a decree, and is not unlike the notion of *fate* as what is spoken. Used of the dispositions and will of Eru,

> *Umbar* could thus correspond to *History*, the known or at least the already unfolded part, together with the *Future*, progressively realized. To the latter it most often referred, and is rendered *Fate* or *Doom*. But this is inaccurate, so far as genuine Elvish, especially high-elvish, is concerned, since it was not in that use applied only to evil events" (Tolkien quoted in *PE* 17, 105).

It is not difficult to see in *Umbar*, "fate," the notion of already-unfolded *History* and "the *Future*, progressively realized" a concept akin to Anglo-Saxon *Wyrd* and Norse *Urð* as "what happens" or "has "happened" or "will have happened." Though they are different words, the phonological connection between *umbar*, "decree or decision," and *ambar*, "appointed place" recalls Latin *fāta* in their concept of Arda as the appointed (i.e., fated) home or dwelling for Elves. They are confined to the circles of the world while it lasts, whereas Men, who "seek beyond the world and find no rest therein" (*Silm.* 41) are correspondingly unconfined.

Some of Tolkien's unpublished notes on Elven languages, many written after the publication of *The Lord of the Rings*, enlarge on such concepts, and although they remain in his possession have been made available by Christopher Tolkien. These are worth particular attention for their specifically Elven perspective on the actions and lives of Men (a category which includes Hobbits). Only a portion is quoted here, for the whole is lengthy and detailed, concluding with a move beyond the scope of the present essentially linguistic discussion into what might better be called theology, consideration of what may be unforeseen or unintended by characters in the drama, but is still present in the foreknowledge of Eru.

> [O]ne of the Eldar would have said that for all Elves and Men the shape, condition, and therefore the past and future physical development and destiny of this 'earth' was determined and beyond their power to change, indeed beyond the power even of the Valar, to alter in any large & permanent way. [*Marginal note:*] They distinguished between "change" and redirection. Thus any 'rational [?will-user] could in a small way move, redirect, stop, or destroy objects in the world; but he could not "change" [it] into *something else*. . . . The Downfall of Númenor was "a miracle" as we might say, or as they *a direct action* of Eru within time that altered the previous scheme for all remaining time. They would probably also have said that Bilbo was "fated" to find the Ring, but not necessarily to surrender it; and thus if Bilbo surrendered it Frodo was fated to go on his mission, but not necessarily to destroy the Ring—which in fact he did not do. They would have added that *if* the downfall of Sauron and the destruction of the Ring was part of Fate (or Eru's plan) then if Bilbo had retained the Ring and refused to surrender it, some other means would have arisen by which Sauron was frustrated. Just as when Frodo's will proved in the end inadequate, a means for the Ring's destruction immediately appeared—being kept in reserve by Eru as it were.

Tolkien goes on to say that,

> They [i.e., Elves] would not have denied that (say) a man was (may have been) "fated" to meet an enemy of his at a certain time and place, but they would have denied that he was "fated" then to speak to him in terms of

hatred, or to slay him. "Will" of a certain grade must enter into many of the complex motions leading to a meeting of persons; but the Eldar held that only those effects of "will" were "free" which were directed to a fully *aware purpose.*

To point out the obvious, all of this is from the Elven point of view and thus reflects what Tolkien intended to be a specifically Elven understanding of the world. Important here are the subjunctive constructions: "would have said," "would probably also have said," "would have added," "would not have denied," all suggest a projection of Elven perception not just on language but the worldview it expresses. Given that this discussion is linguistically based, given further that the languages and worldview concerned express perspectives generated and spoken by Elves (albeit invented by Tolkien), it is noteworthy that the entire discussion looks at how Elves "would see" the actions of Men within an Elven concept of fate. Indeed, Tolkien was at pains on several occasions to reiterate that the mythology was Elf-generated and thus not anthropocentric. The "high legends of the beginnings are supposed to look at things through Elvish minds" (*Letters* 145), and "the point of view of the whole cycle is the Elvish" (*Letters* 147).

GREATNESS MEANT

Now to the personal reason. I noted in my opening paragraph that Tolkien began serious work on his mythology in late 1916. The time is noteworthy for its proximity to his war experience and thus to the war-engendered deaths of two of his three closest friends. Rob Gilson, G.B. Smith, Christopher Wiseman, and Tolkien had formed, when all four were at King Edward's School in Birmingham, an informal fellowship they called the TCBS. [6] This was more than an ordinary gathering of friends; it was a brotherhood. Continued in their university years, maintained in the face of separation by war postings, the TCBS was a deeply bonded friendship of like-minded young men who shared a somewhat inchoate but deeply felt sense of artistic mission. Rob Gilson was killed on the first day of the Battle of the Somme, 1 July 1916. Geoffrey Bache Smith died behind the lines on 3 December 1916 of wounds from a stray shell.

By virtue of being the first, Gilson's death had the most dramatic effect. Tolkien's reaction was an almost physical one. "I don't feel a member of a little complete body now," he wrote to Smith (*Letters* 10). "I went out into the wood . . . last night and also the night before and sat and thought" (*Letters*

9). The scene is poignant, and the letter that came out of it shows Tolkien struggling with the third great loss in his life (his father when he was not yet four, his mother when he was twelve). Now he was in more than grief, he was in crisis over what Rob Gilson's death might portend for the three surviving members of their fellowship, and for his own sense of his place in the scheme of things.

The death of one man in a battle where in a single day 20,000 Allied lives were lost and nothing was won moved Tolkien to interrogate God's purpose not just for the dead but for the living. "I now believe," he wrote to Smith, "that if the greatness which we three certainly meant (and meant as more than holiness or nobility alone) is really the lot of the TCBS, then the death of any of its members is but a bitter winnowing of those who were not meant to be great—at least not directly" (*Letters* 9).[7] The repetition with changing connotation of the word *meant*—"greatness which we *meant*," "*meant* as more than holiness," "those not *meant* to be great"; the shifts from *meant* as "understood" to *meant* as "signified," to *meant* as "intended"—suggests a quest for certainty as well as for meaning. Was Gilson not "meant" to be "great" because he was killed? Was he killed *because* he was not meant to be great?

Unexpressed but implied is the inevitable personal corollary: was Tolkien alive because he was "meant" to be alive? "Meant" to be great? While Tolkien was still in England, Smith, already in combat in France, had urged him to publish his poems, declaring that Tolkien was " chosen like Saul among the Children of Israel," and if he [Smith] were to be "scuppered" [killed], there would still be "a member of the great TCBS to voice what I dreamed and what we all agreed upon" (Garth 118). Now Gilson, not Smith, had died, and Tolkien's sense "that the TCBS was destined to testify for God and Truth" (*Letters* 10) was called into question. What did *destined* mean? What did *chosen* mean?[8] Were their lives and their ambitions in their own hands to direct? Or were they, as events now overwhelmingly suggested, controlled by forces greater than any individual? And if that was so, how did their hopes and dreams fit into whatever larger scheme held sway?

Not long afterward, Tolkien fell sick with trench fever and was sent back to England. Here he got the news that G.B. Smith was also gone, like Gilson, killed in France; unlike Gilson, not in battle but by fragments from a stray artillery shell behind the lines. Although Smith's wounds were not in themselves life-threatening, they turned gangrenous, and he died four days after he was injured, doomed because of a random explosion not aimed at him. He and Tolkien had shared a particularly strong bond of like talents and ambitions. Both were poets, both critiqued one another's work, both had ambitions for publication. After the war, Tolkien saw to it that Smith's poems were

posthumously published as *A Spring Harvest*, the title a consciously ironic
choice for the work of a young poet cut down before he could ripen.

In the context of the hoped-for "destiny" of their fellowship, Tolkien's
own aspirations were then and afterward tangled with his feelings of grief
and loss and his struggle to see meaning in what had happened, a struggle
which would find an outlet in his own writing. In the years leading up to the
war he had been at work, albeit sporadically, on a body of poetry loosely focused on what he called "the Lonely Isle"—later to become Tol Eressea and
later still Valinor—but not yet coalesced into a structured mythology. Christopher Wiseman had written to him "You ought to start the epic" (Carpenter 90). Reprieved from war by illness, he now began seriously to consider
the direction of his own writing.

I do not propose that Tolkien came home from war and consciously sat
down to recreate his experience in words.[9] Unlike the war writers of his
generation such as Edmund Blunden, Wilfrid Owen, Robert Graves, and
Siegfried Sassoon (all of whom did exactly that), Tolkien turned instead to
mythology, then fairy tale, lastly fantasy, and filtered his experience through
the gauze of his imagination. Moreover, his most powerful depiction of
the horror of war and its effect on those who fight it—the long ordeal of
Frodo Baggins in *The Lord of the Rings*—emerged only years later and then
in a conspicuously different frame. Filtering and delay notwithstanding, it is
surely no accident that it was in 1916–17 and in the aftermath of two specific
losses that Tolkien began the story of an unending war and its never-ending
consequences, a legendarium that would as it developed come to explore
the interweaving of human desires and impulses with a fixed and overarching design.

The earliest stories—"The Fall of Gondolin," an unabashed war-story written in 1916–17, "The Tale of Tinuviel," a love-story in a war setting written in
1917, "The Music of the Ainur," a creation story written some time between
1918 and 1920, and "Turambar and the Foalókë," an epic tragedy centered on
warfare, and in existence by 1919—all came in the four years directly following his own war experience. While they would develop and change in the
ensuing years, they did not alter their essential nature, and formed the vital
heart of his "mythology for England," the Silmarillion.

I am aware that the terrain of biographical criticism is perilous territory,
with pitfalls for the unwary and dungeons for the overbold. The presence of
biographical elements in a work of art is easy to overemphasize, and too much
attention to such elements has the deleterious effect of privileging the creator
over the work created. Such concerns notwithstanding, it would be naive and
unrealistic to assume that the formative events of an author's life played a mi-

nor part in his creative process. To acknowledge the influence on his writing of an author's reading and at the same time to discount the influence of his immediate experience seems arbitrary and unnecessarily exclusive.

The Music and the Task

The sub-creative reason behind Tolkien's paradox will take us to the Silmarillion for a look at the earliest and subsequent versions of his creation story, the "Ainulindalë." This story, among the first he wrote, sets up the parameters for his Secondary World, parameters which remained, in one particular stipulation, unchanged throughout the course of many revisions. The first version, "The Music of the Ainur," was begun according to Christopher Tolkien between November 1918 and spring 1920 and set the tone for what was to follow. The theme of creation proposed by the godhead Ilúvatar and orchestrated by the Ainur is broken by the discord of the rebellious Melko, who introduces an independent theme of his own. The disharmony thus introduced creates the world, for after absorbing Melko's theme into his own, Ilúvatar proclaims "*Eä!* Let these things be!" The world thus brought into being is "a new thing: Eä, the World that Is." The final verb is important. Eä is not the World that *Should Be,* or the World that *Ought to Have Been,* but the world that *Is.* It is a portrait in music of the real world as it really appears—unfinished, conflicted, containing harmony and discord, love and hate, war and peace. To this picture, Ilúvatar adds a surprise component—his Children, the two races of Elves and Men which come direct from him, with but not in the third theme. The earliest, "hastily-pencilled" draft says:

> "but to Men I [Ilúvatar] will appoint a task and give a great gift." And he devised that they should have free will and the power of fashioning and designing beyond the original music of the Ainu, that by reason of their operations all things shall in shape and deed be fulfilled, and the world that comes of the music of the Ainu be completed unto the last and smallest. (*LT* I, 61).

This singling out of Men for something extra is explicit and must be deliberate. Men can transcend the Music. Their gift is free will, and their task is through the exercise thereof to "complete" and "fulfill" the heretofore-unfinished Music. This is fine for Men, but what about Elves? Their omission from this proclamation is obvious, and its implication significant. A second text, fuller, written in ink, and dated to the same period, spells it out,

"But to Men I will give a new gift, and a greater." Therefore he [Ilúvatar] devised that Men should have a free virtue whereby within the limits of the powers and substances and chances of the world they might fashion and design their life beyond even the original Music of the Ainur that is as fate to all things else. (*LT* I, 59).

The conjunctions "but" and "therefore" convey consequentiality, the words "as fate" define the Music, and the sweeping "all things else" must by default include Elves. The change of "will" to "virtue," with the retention of "free" says the same thing more obliquely. Tolkien is here using the word *virtue* not in its usual sense of moral excellence but in the older, now obsolete sense of "particular power, efficacy," definition 11 in the *Oxford English Dictionary*. Nonetheless, this free virtue is still bestowed only on Men. I propose that the free virtue/will of Men is Ilúvatar's wild card, intentionally outside the rules. In thirty years of re-vision this plan never changed. Of the "Ainulindalë" Christopher Tolkien has cited a direct tradition in which,

> from the earliest draft to the final version: each text is directly based on the one preceding. Moreover, and most remarkably, the earliest version . . . was so evolved in its conception that it underwent little change of an essential kind. . . . the fall of the original sentences can continually be recognized in the last version of the *Ainulindalë*, written more than thirty years later, and even many phrases survived. (*LT* I, 61–62)

Another version, called by Christopher Ainulindalë B and dated to "between 1930 and the end of 1937" (*LR* 107), keeps the same plan.

In the following years Tolkien wrote a further series of revisions called by Christopher Ainulindalë C*, C, and D (*MR* 3–4, 36–43). In all these revisions the relevant passage remains essentially intact. Although he cautions there is "no proof" that Tolkien was working on a revision of the "Ainulindalë" as early as 1946, Christopher cites "a torn half-sheet" with a passage from "Ainulindalë" among the "notes and jottings on the Adûnaic language" adjunct to the 1946 *Notion Club Papers* (*MR* 4). More reliably, he says there is "certain evidence" that Ainulindalë C* "was in existence by 1948" (*MR* 4). The version in *The Silmarillion* of 1977, the one most familiar to most readers, is expanded from but in all essentials the same as the preceding versions, stating that,

> the hearts of Men should seek beyond the world and should find no rest therein; but they should have a virtue to shape their life, amid the powers and chances of the world, beyond the Music of the Ainur, which is as fate

to all things else; and of their operation everything should be, in form and deed, completed, and the world fulfilled unto the last and smallest. (*Silm* 41–42)

The specific and explicit "virtue" to shape their lives is reserved for Men, not Elves. The scope of that "virtue," however, is left undefined. Rather than prescribing free will as a constant factor, Ilúvatar simply allows for its operation. Nor will Men always choose rightly. While this is addressed most explicitly in the early "Ainulindalë," the notion carries over in all the versions with the provision that Men, "being set amid the turmoils of the powers of the world, would stray often, and would not use their gifts in harmony" (*Silm* 42). Tolkien's vision encompasses the obvious fact that not only are good intentions not always enough, they can sometimes—and, in the case of a character like Túrin Turambar, often—lead to apparently bad outcomes.

Nevertheless, it is important to recognize the remarkable consistency with which Tolkien has retained Ilúvatar's declaration. Men have free will. All things else, including Elves, are ruled by the Music which is "as fate." As noted above, this is hard for readers to accept, and perhaps accounts for the fact that this aspect of the "Ainulindalë" has been under-examined by scholars of Tolkien's work. Dan Timmons' article on "Free Will" in the *J.R.R. Tolkien Encyclopedia* notes that "Ilúvatar . . . grants beings the ability to contribute to the 'Music' according to their 'will'" (*Encyclopedia* 221), but does not identify those "beings" as Men, or note that Ilúvatar's grant excludes all things else. In *Tolkien and the Great War,* John Garth correctly observes, "Whereas the cosmogonic Music prescribed the fate of the Elves . . . humans were granted a 'free virtue' to act beyond it" (Garth 275) but adds that, "Tolkien seems not to have tried to illustrate the implication that the Elves, the Valar, and Melko lack free will, which would surely have blighted his narrative" (275).[10] Others have voiced much the same objection. Three essays in vol. 1 of the essay collection *Tolkien and Modernity* (Weinreich, Fisher, and Fornet-Ponse) argue that both Elves and Men have free will. Only one (Fornet-Ponse) addresses the crucial statement by Ilúvatar, and then only to declare that it "contradicts the whole structure of *The Silmarillion*" (*Tolkien and Modernity,* 183). Therefore, in this reading, Ilúvatar could not possibly have meant what he said. This is many people's reaction, and one of the reasons I am writing now.

However, it is one thing to parse the "Ainulindalë," quite another to show its consequences in action. Eru's statement, through all the story's versions, seems simple, declarative, unequivocal. Its playing-out in the actions and interactions of characters within the story, however, is murky and deliberately ill-defined. It is when we leave the concept and look at its practice that the notion becomes problematic, and Tolkien has—I think wisely—allowed it to be so. He was not designing an inter-office flow chart by which responsibility could clearly be traced from one department to another; he was creating characters and situations through which he hoped to show how confusing the complex interaction of competing but interactive forces can be to both actors and beholders. It would be taxing and tedious if the reader had continually to be deciding if this or that action was the result of fate or free will. Moreover, such assignment would, if carried to its extreme, reduce the Elves to automata in a clockwork universe, moved by some external though hidden force. It would rob their actions, and consequently their story, of all narrative uncertainty and all readerly suspense.

Furthermore, it is important to remember that Tolkien's characters and situations are his inventions. They are not real people in a real world, but fictive characters in an arbitrary and invented one. In that sense they are all fated, their actions determined by their author's plan.[11] They have no independent existence, no lives beyond what the text gives them, no autonomy separate from Tolkien's intent. We cannot inquire what this or that character "would do" in a hypothetical situation; we can only accept what he or she actually does in the actual situation created by the author. And those situations are designed to reflect humanity's confusing perceptions of the operations of the real world. For while the narrative voice sometimes alludes to a character's "fate" (most clearly in the tale of Beren and Lúthien, but also in the story of Túrin Turambar[12]), the characters themselves, with two exceptional instances to be discussed below, nowhere make it explicit that one or anyone of them is consciously invoking free will or fate.

The few statements which seem to indicate free will are spoken by the characters themselves (for example, Frodo's "I will take the Ring" at the Council of Elrond). Likewise, statements implying an external controlling force—for example Gandalf's comment to Frodo that "something else" was at work (though he does not say what) in Bilbo's finding of the Ring, or his further statement that Bilbo was "*meant* to find the Ring" in which case Frodo also was "*meant* to have it" (*FR* I, ii, 65)—seem deliberately vague and obscure. They recall Tolkien's comment, cited above, that Elves "would have said" that Bilbo was "fated" to find the Ring but not necessarily fated to surrender it. These are presumptive Elven interpretations of events made at second hand and after the fact. Within the narrative, Bilbo's finding of the Ring is made to seem accident or chance, while his surrender of it is portrayed as a reluctant act of will (Bilbo needs a little help from his friend). Tolkien was first of all trying to depict the complex, often impulsive, and unpremeditated ways in which we respond to circumstances, ways in which separate people's separate actions perforce impinge upon one another and upon the world around them. Second, he was offering a structure within which those actions could be both framed and accounted for—the paradox introduced at the beginning of this discussion.

In support of that paradox, and operating on the assumption that Tolkien intended Ilúvatar to mean what he said, I will move now to some illustrative examples. These, I hope, will demonstrate that Ilúvatar's original statement, far from "contradicting" or "blighting" *The Silmarillion,* instead enriches and complexifies it, and furthermore that it enriches and complexifies its continuation which is Tolkien's masterpiece, *The Lord of the Rings.* I have chosen to look at the curious case of Fëanor and the Silmarils, at the conflicted triad of Beren, Lúthien and Thingol,[13] and to examine in some detail Tolkien's handling of key moments of decision in the representations of Aragorn, Sam Gamgee, and the dyad of Frodo and Gollum.[14]

THE SILMARILLION

Fëanor Against the Valar

As an Elven example I offer the most exceptional of the instances cited above, the perplexing passage in *The Silmarillion* wherein, after the Darkening of Valinor, Yavanna asks Fëanor to give her the Silmarils to renew the Two Trees. His response is explicit and noteworthy. "This thing I will not do of free will" (*Silm* 79). If we are to believe Ilúvatar, Fëanor does not have free will, thus its deliberate introduction here is confusing—superfluous if Fëanor has free will, and even more superfluous if he doesn't. Or else Tolkien is making a point. I choose to think he's making a point, and that he intends the phrase to operate at two different levels. One level is Fëanor's, his response to his perceived coercion by the Valar to give up the jewels. The other, larger level is Tolkien's, for when the tidings come that Melkor has stolen the Silmarils, he, in the voice of the narrator, adds the otherwise unnecessary comment that, "The Silmarils had passed away, and all one it may seem whether Fëanor had said yea or nay to Yavanna; yet had he said yea at the first, before the tidings came from Formenos, it may be that his after deeds would have been other than they were. But now the Doom of the Noldor drew near" (*Silm* 79).

This, as I read the situation, is exactly Tolkien's point. Fëanor is fated to lose the Silmarils, and the Silmarils are fated to pass out of his keeping. He could not give them to Yavanna if he chose, for they are no longer his.

But the editorial addendum implies that his answer to Yavanna, regardless of whether he could act on it, would affect his subsequent actions. While Christopher Tolkien includes this comment in "The Later *Quenta Silmarillion*" as published in *Morgoth's Ring* (*MR* 295), the passage does not appear in the earlier "Quenta Silmarillion" as given in *The Lost Road.* Here Fëanor, "distraught with grief for the slaying of his father, and anguish for the rape of the Silmarils," vows to pursue Morgoth (*LR* 234). The Oath of Fëanor and the flight of the Noldor are essentially as in *The Silmarillion.*

Three verb forms are critical in *The Silmarillion*'s version: the subjunctive "*had* he said" and the conditional "it *may* be" and "*would* have been." All three convey a sense of contingency, the possibility that things might have turned out differently. But could they? Could Fëanor have said otherwise than he said, done otherwise than he did? How much is in the Music? It seems *wyrd* in all senses of the word. Tolkien has again muddied the waters by suggesting that if Fëanor's response had been different, that difference might have affected his subsequent deeds. *But now* (my emphasis) his choice brings on the Doom of the Nolder. Free will can apparently invite fate. As noted earlier, *doom* is derived from Anglo-Saxon *dòm.* While its primary meaning is: "I. judgment, decree, ordinance, law," it has also a rare usage listed as "IV. will, free will, choice, option" (Bosworth-Toller). Thus Fëanor's impracticable choice to deny Yavanna the Silmarils, and his consequent oath to pursue Morgoth bring on the choice of the Noldor to follow him, which leads to their Doom. Though that doom is spoken in the voice of Mandos, it is the Noldor who in effect doom themselves.

If, as Ilúvatar decrees and as I argue, Fëanor is bound by the Music, his "after deeds" must be in that Music, therefore not subject to change. How then, could those deeds have been "other" than they were? The parallel passage from the Later, post-*Lord of the Rings* version of the *Quenta Silmarillion* written in 1951–52 (*MR* 141) reads, "had he said yea at the first, *and so cleansed his heart* ere the dreadful tidings came, his after deeds *would have been other than they proved*" [my emphasis] (*MR* 295). Here the potential for change in Fëanor is explicit; to have said "yea" would have "cleansed" his heart, which because of his intransigent "nay" remained filled with anger and resentment. The unequivocal comment that his deeds "would have been other" is far stronger than the conditional "it may be." But the question remains: how might his deeds have "been other" if they were in the Music? The problem seems deliberately unsolvable, but Tolkien's word *other* may offer a solution. Traditionally an adjective modifying a noun, *other* is here employed in its rarer adverbial usage of "otherwise, differently, in another way" as modifying a verb, in this case the implied verb *done,* as in "after deeds have been [done]" otherwise.

Tolkien may be saying that while the deeds themselves would inevitably be done, Fëanor's "yea"—if he had said it—could have changed his motive and perhaps his way of doing them. In that case, their quality might have turned out to be "other" than they "proved." The distinction, like that between killing for revenge and killing in self-defense, is in the motive behind the act. In the case of Fëanor the distinction is between getting back the Silmarils to be "lords of the unsullied light" (*Silm* 83), and recovering them to re-illumine Valinor. That in the end he cannot do either does not invalidate or alter Tolkien's point. I offer this as the best rationale I can think of for that otherwise inexplicable and unnecessary coda in two separate versions. It seems clear that Tolkien felt the addition served a purpose. Fate—the Music—cannot be changed by an Elf. Thus, the Silmarils are gone, their fate already decided and out of Fëanor's control. But his interior psychology could be changed, and that change could affect the nature of his subsequent actions.

Aragorn at the Falls

My Mannish example is Aragorn, who at the Falls of Rauros is forced to make a choice with too little information to go on. Realizing that Frodo is gone and Merry and Pippin have been captured, Aragorn must choose what to do next. His options are: to follow Frodo, to keep his promise to Boromir to go to Minas Tirith, to rescue Merry and Pippin. There is no easy or obvious choice, and his emotionally charged dialogue with himself signals his confusion and ambivalence. Hearing Boromir's horn as he comes down from the high seat he laments his absence from this crisis. "Alas! An ill fate is on me this day and all that I do goes amiss" (*TT* III, i, 15). Faced subsequently with Boromir's dying injunction to go to Minas Tirith, Aragorn asks without expectation of answer "What shall I do now?" (16).

Shall is here more than a simple future tense; it has, especially in the personified form of Old Norse *Skuld*, the force of *skulu* with its connotation of something already decided. Aragorn is questioning fate, and again comments, "All that I have done today has gone amiss" (17). Torn between following the Ringbearer or going after Merry and Pippin, he declares, "An evil choice is now before us" (17), and finally, deciding to follow the young hobbits, says, "now may I make a right choice and *change the evil fate* [my emphasis] of this unhappy day" (21). Unhappy," here, does not mean "sad," but "unfortunate, unlucky," the older, medieval usage as given in definition 4 under *unhappy* in the *OED*, "Of conditions: marked by misfortune or mishap." Aragorn's words constitute the closest the narrative comes to making explicit the interaction between the two forces, and is the only direct reference I can think of in *The Lord of the Rings* to the power of Men to go beyond the Music. It is significant for its clear implication that Aragorn is aware of this power. A more oblique reference comes only a few pages later, when in answer to Éomer's question "What doom do you bring out of the North?" Aragorn replies, "The doom of Choice" (*TT* III, ii, 36).

Thingol, Beren, Lúthien

Let us move now to the more complex interactions of Elves with Men. When free-willed Man meets fated Elf, who does what to whom? Tolkien has left the answers deliberately opaque. The story of Beren, Lúthien, and Thingol is the most tangled, for here Tolkien has inverted the language, using "fate" and "doom" for Beren and "free" for Lúthien, which makes it difficult to figure out who is doing what to whom. I argue that this is deliberate, intended to reflect the confused and confusing perceptions that characterize Tolkien's internal story-tellers, in this case those of his fictive bard, Daeron the minstrel. (It is also worth noting that Beren was originally an Elf and was later changed to a Man.) Beren comes to Doriath because it is "put into his heart that he would go down into the Hidden Kingdom." He passes through the mazes Melian has woven as she foretold, for "a great doom lay upon him." As Lúthien looks on Beren "doom fell upon her, and she loved him" (*Silm* 164–65). Of Beren's meeting with Lúthien Tolkien writes that, "he [Beren] began the payment of anguish for the fate that was laid on him; and in his fate Lúthien was caught, and being immortal she shared his mortality; and being free received his chain" (165–66).

This is piling contradiction on paradox. Lúthien is described as "being free." But free from what? Beren has a fate that "was laid on him." By whom? Are we to understand that Beren is fated and Lúthien has free will? Beren tells Thingol that his "fate" led him to Doriath, where he found what he "sought not," that is, Lúthien. Melian's statement that, "not by you [i.e., Thingol] shall Beren be slain; and far and free does his fate lead him, yet it is wound with yours" (167) muddies the water even further, yet the word "free" in this context, juxtaposed against "fate," suggests that Beren's fate is to make a free choice. If that is the case, however, freedom to choose doesn't always work. When he cuts the Silmaril from Morgoth's crown "it came into Beren's mind" (cp. "it was *put into* his heart" above) that he would go beyond his vow and take all three. "But," the narrative is at pains to point out, "such was not the doom of the Silmarils." The knife snaps, Morgoth stirs, and Beren and Lúthien flee with one Silmaril.

Let us suppose, since that is "what happens," (i.e., *wyrd*) that Thingol's fate in the Music is to die by violence.[15] That fate is directed by the free action of Beren, a Man whose appearance in Doriath and love for Lúthien arouse Thingol's anger and spark his request for a Silmaril. This leads to his obsession with the jewel which in turn leads to his death. That this death does not come about as a direct result of Lúthien's marriage to Beren but takes place years later and under other circumstances, is evidence of Tolkien's method of "winding" Thingol's fate with Beren's free will. Beren's free acceptance of Thingol's demand brings Thingol a Silmaril and wins Beren Lúthien, while Thingol's fated possession of the jewel becomes his doom as his greed conjoins the Silmaril and the Dwarf-necklace, leads to his quarrel with the Dwarves, and results in his death at their hands. The point seems to be simply that the choices of Men can trigger the fates of Elves and the fates of Elves can tilt the lives of Men, while both can affect the world they both inhabit.

Turning now from Elves and (Big) Men to Hobbits, my examples will show Tolkien working even more precisely at the lexical level, and will illustrate his careful and exact use of language, especially three verbs—*will*, *shall*, and *must*, whose philological history I have already discussed—as well as *choice*, *choose*, and *fate*.

Samwise at the High Pass

My first Hobbit example is Sam Gamgee. It is not by accident that an important chapter in the plot's development is titled "The *Choices* [my emphasis] of Master Samwise." Finding Frodo's dead (as he thinks) body, Sam goes through an agony of indecision over how to respond. His first despairing question to himself is "What shall I do, what shall I do" (*TT* II, x, 340). His options are to go home, to stay with Frodo, to kill Gollum, to kill himself, or to take the Ring and go on. He has no information that will help him to make a right decision. Having considered and rejected the first four options, Sam then considers "the hard answer," which is to take Frodo's burden and go on to the Cracks of Doom. The key words *will* and *must* follow one another now in rapid succession as Sam tells himself "I must make up my own mind. I will make it up" (341).

Knowing the precision with which Tolkien uses words, and the weight of internal historical evidence that lies behind them, we can see that Sam is not merely lecturing himself; he is unknowingly invoking both his destiny and his free will. He *must* "make up his own mind." He has to think for himself. He has to choose what to do. Nonetheless, Tolkien shows him still indecisive. "I've made up my mind," he says to himself, but the narrative adds, that "he had not," moreover, that "what he was doing was altogether against the grain of his nature." This leads Sam to self-doubt. "Have I got it wrong?" he asks, and then, as if there were someone present to tell him: "what ought I to have done?" (342). Sam's dilemma is that of someone facing a job he does not want but knows he has to do.

That having decided, he then changes his mind and starts back to Frodo is not so much evidence of Sam's vacillation as of Tolkien's intent to underscore the perennial human problem of how to act in light of too little information. The missing information, that Frodo is alive, leads Sam to his last and most practical question. "Now what is to be done?" (350) The difference between his earlier, despairing, semi-rhetorical "what ought I to have done?" and the pragmatic, down-to-business, "what is to be done?" is more than grammatical. The later phrase implies acknowledgment that there is a task appointed, while the former indicates helplessness, indecision, and despair.

Frodo and Gollum in the Looking-Glass

My last example is the dyad of Gollum and Frodo, who within themselves and with each other best embody Tolkien's fate-free will conjunction. When the Council of Elrond learns that Gollum has escaped the Wood-elves and is again on the loose, Gandalf reacts dismissively. "Well, well. He is gone. We have no time to seek for him again." And then he adds what seems an unnecessary tag: "He must do what he will" (*FR* II, ii, 269). This says it all. Tolkien has placed Gollum at a nexus of fate and free will in which each acts on the other and both act on Gollum. His wish (*willan*) for the Ring becomes necessity (*motan*), controlling his subsequent actions, especially his last and most desperate action at the Cracks of Doom. He is fated to follow his own desire. Gandalf's statement foreshadows Frodo's similar but opposite declaration on Amon Hen. Released from the Eye of Sauron, and in the liberation of being "free to choose" to take off the Ring, Frodo declares, "I will do now what I must" (*FR* II, x, 417). In both their mirroring and reversal the two statements reflect one another, and both derive directly from Ilúvatar's pronouncement concerning fate and free will at the close of the "Ainulindalë."

Tolkien clearly shows Frodo, Gollum's opposite and alter ego, voluntarily (*willan*) committing himself to the fate (*motan*) appointed for him. His free will accepts his fate. Other examples are easily passed over in the flow of the narrative, but stand out clearly when words like *fate, choice, must,* and *will* are highlighted. At the Falls of Rauros, when the Company must decide which way to go from there, Aragorn tells Frodo that even if Gandalf were there to advise them, "the choice would still wait on you. Such is your fate" (*FR* II, x, 412). Finding the Black Gate of Mordor closed, Frodo accepts Gollum's suggestion that they take the secret path of Cirith Ungol. "I must trust you once more," he tells Gollum. "Indeed it seems that I must do so, and that it is my fate to receive help from you, where I least looked for it, and your fate to help me whom you long pursued with evil purpose" (*TT* IV, iii, 248). Responding to Sam's suspicions both of him and the secret path, Gollum states that "If master says *I must go* or *I will go,* then he must try some way" (*TT* IV, iii, 251)

That Frodo and Gollum both freely participate in the Ring's destiny to arrive at the Cracks of Doom shows *their* free will collaborating with *its* fate.[16] *Doom* and *choice*, must and *will* are interlocking systems, cogs turned "by small hands" which move the wheels of the world while "the eyes of the great are elsewhere" (*FR* II, ii, 283). The final confrontation at the Cracks of Doom brings the conflict down to a contest of "small hands"—Frodo's hand now wearing the Ring and Gollum's hands as they "draw upward to his mouth" and then "[hold] aloft the Ring" as he falls into the fire (*RK* VI, iii, 224). But the wheels of the world are turned as much by words as by hands large or small, and it is in his words that we must look for clues to Tolkien's design. The key lies in Frodo's "I will," at Rivendell where he reluctantly volunteers for a job he does not want, and does not think he can do. "I will take the Ring," he announces, and the narrative adds the significant comment, "as if some other will was using his small voice" (*FR* II, ii, 284).

Given what we know about the background mythology and the intent of Ilúvatar for Men it seems reasonable to interpret this "other will" as Ilúvatar's. But Ilúvatar's will was to give Men free will. His will in this instance, therefore, must be that Frodo, like Beren, make a free choice. To complicate the matter, Frodo' voluntary "I will" is modified by Elrond's, "this task is appointed for you, Frodo," echoing in what is surely no accident Ilúvatar's, "to Men I will appoint a task." Elrond's comment that, "if you take it freely, I will say that your choice is right" (284), suggests that the rightness lies not just in acceptance of the task of carrying the Ring but also (though Frodo is unaware of it) in acceptance of the "task" of Men that is to transcend the Music. The Ring, however, like the Silmarils and "all things else," is bound by the Music, making it difficult to interpret this situation except as the interjection of free will into the operation of fate. Frodo's journey, and its yet-to-be-decided outcome, will affect the fate of all Middle-earth.

At the other end of Frodo's journey, as he claims the Ring at the Cracks of Doom, he again makes a declarative statement, now reversing his words at Amon Hen. "I do not choose now to do what I came to do. I will not do this deed." It seems a backhanded exercise of free will—to not choose to do. Nevertheless, the fact that in the manuscript this sentence is written above the line, replacing an earlier "I *cannot do* what I have come to do" (Marquette Archive Series 3, Box 8, Roll 11, p. 39), makes it clear that Tolkien intended, as Christopher Tolkien points out, that Frodo "fully willed his act" (*SD* 38). And although Christopher also comments that he "does not think that the difference is very significant," it is notable that Frodo's "I will not do this deed" harks back not just to his statement on Amon Hen but also to his earlier declaration at the Council of Elrond. It is at Mount Doom, in a climactic intersection of *will* and *must,* that the task appointed for Frodo, who now *will not* "do what he must," is inadvertently accomplished by Gollum, who *must* follow his will, wrest the Ring from Frodo and carry it where it is fated to go—into the fire. Frodo's and Gollum's inadvertent yet combined actions at the Cracks of Doom, actions of will both inevitable and spontaneous, between them operate to save Middle-earth.

THE POINT OF THE PARADOX

This leads back to my opening *why*, and Tolkien's sub-creative rationale for his green sun paradox, which was to provide a plausible mechanism for change in an ordered universe. *The Lord of the Rings*'s dramatic resolution in the destruction of the Ring by the conflicting and freely willed actions of Frodo and Gollum points thematically toward the telos, the final end of Tolkien's paradox. Tolkien described this telos as, "a vision of the end of the world, its breaking and remaking, and the recovery of the Silmarilli and the 'light before the Sun'—after a final battle which owes, I suppose, more to the Norse vision of Ragnarök than to anything else, thought it is not much like it" (*Letters* 149). Although at the story level he never reached this point, the concept makes clear that he envisioned an apotheosis in which the discord of the original Music would be harmonized in the Second Music, which explicitly includes Men in its performance. This is made clear in his letter to Waldman, where he states explicitly that "[t]he making, and nature, of the Children of God," the "two chief secrets" of "the Creator" withheld from the Valar, are intended "partly to redress the evil of the rebel Melkor, partly for the completion of all" (*Letters* 147). All the evidence points to his clear intention for Men to join in the Second Music, in which the themes will be played aright because the task of Men has been to enable that playing.

　　The Silmarillion states, "of old the Valar declared to the Elves in Valinor that Men shall join in the Second Music of the Ainur; whereas Ilúvatar has not revealed what he purposes for the Elves after the world's end" (*Silm* 42). That this was Tolkien's plan from the beginning is clear from a similar passage in the second 1919–20 draft in *The Book of Lost Tales* I, which states,

> Never was there before, nor has there been since, such a music ... though it is said that a mightier far shall be woven before the seat of Ilúvatar by the choirs of both Ainur and the sons of Men after the Great End. Then shall Ilúvatar's mightiest themes be played aright; for then Ainur and Men will know his mind and heart as well as may be, and all his intent" (*LT* I, 53).

It seems clear that in this "mightier far" music the "mightiest themes" will be played aright because the actions and choices of Men will have enabled their playing. The role of Elves in this denouement is deliberately left obscure, for, "while the Sons of Men will after the passing of things of a certainty join in the Second Music of the Ainur, what Ilúvatar has devised for the Eldar beyond the world's end he has not revealed" (*LT* I, 59–60).

I mentioned earlier that the words *God, Heaven, Grace, Paradise, Providence, Salvation, Damnation,* make no appearance in the mythology. Nor does the word *Redemption.* Like the others, it is a name for a concept for which Tolkien chose his own term, *free will.* By free actions over many years, his free-willed Men will have changed the Music and the world from what it is to what it has the potential to be. They will have fulfilled and completed the world and brought it to its intended but unforeseen apotheosis. Acting individually, sometimes acting wrongly, and acting always in ignorance of the ultimate outcome of their choices, they will over the course of time have the totality of their actions exert a self-correcting function that will lead them—and the Elves whose lives they intersect—to the right purpose and fulfillment of the Music of creation. While the inevitable comparison is with Saint Augustine's notion of the Fortunate Fall that expels humankind from Paradise but brings it the hope of heaven, the differences between Tolkien's imaginative vision and Augustine's Judeo-Christian one are important. In Tolkien's work the Fall is Melkor's, not Adam's. Tolkien's sub-created cosmos has no Paradise from which humanity is driven out, only a world flawed in the making into which they are introduced in order to change it. Elves and Men will carry the responsibility for illustrating, both in their interactions with one another and across the gap that divides them, just how living in an imperfect world might serve a larger plan.

The post-*Lord of the Rings* "Athrabeth Finrod ah Andreth" (see "Whose Myth Is It?" in this volume), written, according to Christopher Tolkien some time in 1959 (*MR* 304), supports this view. In a dialogue about death, the human woman Andreth remarks, "among us some hold that our errand here was to heal the Marring of Arda" and "'Arda Healed' (or Remade) shall not be 'Arda Unmarred,' but a third thing and a greater" (*MR* 351). Ilúvatar's original theme corrupted by Melkor into the Music would be replaced by the Second Music when the themes of Ilúvatar would be played "aright." A late linguistic commentary by Tolkien published in Parma Eldalamberon XVII, *Words, phrases & passages in The Lord of the Rings,* gives additional corroboration. His discussion of "The Knowledge of the Valar, or Elvish ideas and theories concerned with them" contains the following highly relevant comments:

> There was, however, one element in the design of Eru [Ilúvatar] that remained a mystery: the Children of Eru, Elves and Men, the Incarnate. These were said to have been an *addition* made by Eru himself *after* the Revelation to the primal spirits of the Great Design.

The same passage notes further that,

> Another purpose they [Elves and Men] had, which remained a mystery to
> the Valar, was to complete the Design by "healing" the hurts which it suf-
> fered, and so ultimately not to recover "Arda Unmarred" (that is the world
> as it would have been if Evil had never appeared) but the far greater thing
> "Arda Healed." (*PE* 17, 177–78)

Together, these passages from the "Athrabeth" and *Parma* make it clear
that the "*addition*" of the Children and their purpose to "complete the Design" were Eru-Ilúvatar's extended, drawn-out work in progress intended to
correct the harm done to the world by Melkor. They support the initial and
unchanged statement in "Ainulindalë" already discussed, and help to clarify
the "task" appointed to Men by Ilúvatar in the aftermath of Creation. I suggest that the purpose of the Children—that is, both Elves and Men—to complete the design must be twofold in its action, for otherwise there would be
no necessity for two separate races. Unless the interaction of the two was formative, the power given to Men to "shape their lives" would affect them alone
without any wider consequences for the world. Nor would there be wider
consequences unless there was some pre-existing circumstance on which
that power could work, the pre-determination of events that is the Music.
The energy in the contact of Men with Elves is the engine for change. The
free will of Men acting on and against the fate of Elves will bring about the
desired re-vision of the Music. It is worth noting that nothing is said in these
passages about free will or free virtue, but a further comment in the same
section that "the minds of the Children were not open to the Valar except by
the free will of the Children" (*PE* 17, 178) must be considered. "Children" is
clearly here an inclusive noun encompassing both Elves and Men, and I take
the operation of free will in this instance to be along the lines of Fëanor's in
saying yea or nay to Yavanna—an internal process not affecting events but
deeply influencing the inner nature of individuals involved in those events.

Finally, and this will loop back to my opening discussion, several points
should be re-iterated.

(1) Tolkien was writing fiction, not theology. He was not arguing for the
    validity of either fate or free will.
(2) The entire concept should be seen as an imaginary sub-creation in which
    the contending forces of fate and free will conjoin to form a green sun,
    an element or aspect deliberately contrary to the Primary World but es-
    sential and formative in the Secondary one

(3) The mythology in its entirety is meant to be read in the context of Tolkien's narrative strategy of using a multiplicity of storytellers and points of view rather than a single omniscient narrative voice. Among these fictive storytellers are the Elven sage Rúmil, the mortal voyager Eriol/ Ælfwine, the Elven minstrel Daeron, the mortal woman Andreth, and the mortal hobbits Bilbo and Frodo Baggins and Sam Gamgee, all of whom are allowed to tell it as they see it. No one, it seems, was intended to have the final word. Except Ilúvatar, who tells Melkor, "no theme may be played that hath not its uttermost source in me, nor can any alter the music in my despite" (*Silm* 17), and leaves it at that.

By establishing and following his own rules Tolkien has succeeded in giving his invented world the "inner consistency of reality" he insisted was essential. The intersection of fate and free will replicates the real world, where these concepts are also inextricably intertwined and interdependent. Fate assumes the absence (therefore the conceptual presence) of choice, while the freedom of free will must rely on its opposite as that from which to be free. As there is no concept of up without its opposite down, or of inside without an outside, so with fate and free will each depends on the other for its meaning. It is well to remember, moreover, that fate and free will, for all humanity's engagement with them as ideas, are neither facts nor principles. They are not easily demonstrable, like gravity, nor clinically testable, like a controlled experiment. Rather, they are human interpretations imposed upon phenomena that may or may not have them in actuality.

Excluding the exceptional circumstances of prophecy or second sight, a pattern seen as fate is nearly always recognized in retrospect, organized with hindsight out of a selection of salient circumstances that appear to relate most directly to one another and thus to make a coherent design. Free will is fate's opposite but also its corollary and partner, dependent on the appearance of choice in major areas of life. Few would bother to invoke free will in the performance of the small tasks of daily life, bathing and dressing, eating and drinking. The concept of free will comes into play when the importance of choice is significant, when humanity's "virtue" to influence events for good or ill is seen as an essential part of human activity in the world.

What emerges in Tolkien's depiction of Eä, the "World that Is," is a picture of the confusing state of affairs in the world that really "is," a state of affairs as it appears to us humans, an uncertain, unreliable, untidy, constantly swinging balance between fate and human effort, between the Music and the Task. Unlike philosophers past and present, Tolkien was not attempting to solve the puzzle, nor was he intending to show that one or the other principle governed the world and those within it. He was trying to show the world the way he saw it—as a place of hope and despair, cruelty and compassion. He saw it as a place where accidents happen, where plans go awry, where young men die in war and children lose their parents, where the right side can lose, where love is not always enough. But he also saw it as a place where human beings of good will and good intentions grope often blindly toward a more hopeful future that remains out of sight but not out of mind. His invented world deliberately included provisions for both fate and free will in order to reflect the often inevitable, sometimes unexpected, frequently incomprehensible unfolding of events as they happen in and shape humanity's perceptions of the real world. The whole elaborate enterprise was, as described in the quote from John Garth which forms my epigraph, "nothing less than an attempt to justify God's creation of an imperfect world filled with suffering, loss, and grief" (Garth 255).

The struggles undergone by the characters who inhabit Tolkien's fictive world require both order and spontaneity to justify them, to give them meaning, and above all to create that uncertainty of outcome which is a hallmark of effective fiction. The story needs its readers' awareness of both the Music and the Task. Thus, we as readers must recognize that the original great theme, proposed by Ilúvatar and spoiled in the making by Melkor, is embedded first in the ensuing Music and then in the world created through that Music. We must see that this spoiled Music goes uncorrected by the godhead, who instead assigns that task to one race of his created beings. We must honor the decision (not really Eru's but Tolkien's) to introduce into this unhappy, unfinished world the two unanticipated races of Elves and Men; and the further decision to give one race, Men, the freedom to change their lives and through those lives to change the Music and thus the fate of Middle-earth and its inhabitants. Only then can we understand the paradox with which I introduced this discussion as Tolkien's ultimately hopeful vision for what he saw as a fallen world: that in a flawed and faulty Creation it is the task appointed for flawed and faulty human beings—struggling with the world around them, sometimes making false starts, often following twisting paths of which they themselves cannot always see the ends—to lead themselves and that world out of error and into light.

Tolkien and the Idea of the Book

Near the end of "The Council of Elrond," a chapter essential to *The Lord of the Rings* and one that presents a variety of oral narratives by different speakers, Bilbo Baggins unexpectedly (and, it might seem, irrelevantly) intrudes the divergent concept of a written record. Volunteering to take the Ring to Mount Doom, he remarks plaintively: "I was very comfortable here, and getting on with my book. If you want to know, I am just writing an ending for it. . . ." And he adds, "There will evidently have to be several more chapters." After finding that he is not to go on the quest, he once more brings up his book a few days before the Company sets out, assuring Frodo, "I'll do my best to finish my book before you return. I should like to write the second book [meaning the story of Frodo's adventures], if I am spared" (*FR* II, ii, 283).

When I first read *The Lord of the Rings* in 1957 and for many years thereafter, I took such passages to be nothing more than a gentle running joke at the old hobbit's expense. It seemed that besides finding ways to connect *The Lord of the Rings* to *The Hobbit,* Tolkien was also poking fun at his own book and its runaway length. I was aware, of course, of the Appendices at the end of volume 3, and took for granted that their Annals and Chronologies were there to convey to the reader that there was, however remotely, a story behind the story. Nevertheless, the possibility that there might also be a book behind the book—that Bilbo's "book" might have developed a life of its own—did not occur to me.

It did occur to Tolkien. He wanted to justify the fact that those oral narratives told at the Council of Elrond were now in print. One way to do that was to make somebody other than the "removed narrator" (Tolkien) responsible for writing them down—some character within the fiction. Since Bilbo was known to have literary inclinations (he recited poetry, and had already "written" *The Hobbit*), since he was one of the few characters with the leisure and freedom from care to spend his time in writing, he was the obvious choice. Indeed, in this context, and quite aside from their necessary contributions to plot and theme, Bilbo, his heir Frodo, and Frodo's heir Sam,[1] are the sequentially obvious choices. Moreover, they can be seen collectively as the next-to-last in the long line of transmitters, translators, redactors, scribes, and copyists who have produced the varied history of Middle-earth.

These three are next-to-last because the last in the line is the primary author himself. Carrying the conceit about as far as it will go, Tolkien inserted his own name into the header and footer on the title-page of *The Lord of the Rings* (and thus into the history of the "book"), not as the author of the book but as its final transmitter/redactor. What appears to the first-time or untutored reader to be simply Tolkienian embellishment is in fact is a running inscription in Tolkien's invented scripts of Cirth and Tengwar. It can be put into English as follows: "THE LORD OF THE RINGS TRANSLATED FROM THE RED BOOK [in Cirth] OF WESTMARCH BY JOHN RONALD REUEL TOLKIEN HEREIN IS SET FORTH THE HISTORY OF THE WAR OF THE RINGS AND THE RETURN OF THE KING AS SEEN BY THE HOBBITS [in Tengwar]." He is not inventing this story, the running script announces, he is merely translating and recording.

With no other context in which to read it, this could easily be seen as mere playfulness, an author's tongue-in-cheek send-up of his own authorial role. To be sure, Tolkien had done something similar, though with considerably less mythological rationale, in the runes on the dust-jacket of *The Hobbit*, where he was (and is) credited not as the author but as the "compiler" of Bilbo's memoirs. During the course of the development of *The Lord of the Rings*, however, this strategy became as much a part of Tolkien's overall scheme as Bilbo's repeated references to finishing his book. If we accept the fictionalized Tolkien identified by the scripts in the header, then we must see that his persona of translator, just as much as those of Bilbo or Frodo or Sam as authors, is in the service of the "book." This carries the "book" beyond an authorial conceit, or an imaginary artifact within the fictive world of Middle-earth, to make it an actual volume in the real world and in the reader's hand. The more widely I read in Tolkien's work, especially those parts of *The History of Middle-earth* that deal with oral story-telling and written transmission, the more clearly I began to see that this endeavor to account within the fiction for something intended to exist outside it was a conscious and deliberate strategy on Tolkien's part.

Now that I have at last caught up with him, I propose to examine what I see as his intentional, interconnected efforts to bridge the fictive world of the story and the outside, real world, to connect inside with outside and fantasy with actuality through the idea of the book. The place to start is with the inside world. Here, the "book" is a conceit, an entirely fictive construct whose reality exists solely within and depends entirely upon the sub-created world, where it is designed to be both the rationale for and integration of all Tolkien's major fiction. Within the Middle-earth of *The Lord of the Rings,* its precursor volume, *The Hobbit,* is presented as Bilbo's "memoirs," the beginning of the book he "will do [his] best to finish" at Rivendell so that he can go on to write "the second book."[2] This serial volume concept will eventually extend itself both forward and backward in time, and will culminate in a comprehensive, "real," imaginary construct—the Red Book of Westmarch.

Granted, the whole world of Middle-earth is an imaginary construct, a sub-creation. The Red Book takes the idea one step further to become a sub-sub-creation that is intended paradoxically to give rise to a real creation in the real world. In "The Interlace Structure of *The Lord of the Rings,*" one of the all-time best articles on Tolkien, Richard West suggests that Tolkien's "use of the imaginary 'Red Book of Westmarch' is a medieval tradition adapted for a modern audience (Lobdell 91). West was writing in 1975, before the publication of *The Silmarillion* and *The History of Middle-earth,* but he was certainly on the right track about *what* Tolkien was doing. I intend to explore *how* and *why* Tolkien was doing it.

As to *how,* it seems clear that Tolkien's Red Book was intended to echo the great medieval manuscript books whose names sound like an Andrew Lang color series for the Middle Ages—The White Book of Rhydderch, the Black Book of Carmarthen, the Yellow Book of Lecan, and most important as his immediate color model, the real Red Book of Hergest. These are unique, anonymously authored manuscripts, collections of stories from different periods by different narrators, and brought under one cover by a scribe or copyist. As artifacts, these books may well be centuries younger than the stories they preserve. They are almost certainly copies of copies of copies of much earlier manuscripts now lost.

The fictive Red Book of Westmarch is the same, but different. Like the real-world books, it is imagined as a manuscript collection of tales from many periods. Like them, it has been copied and re-copied. Christopher Tolkien has noted that "in the original edition of *The Lord of the Rings* Bilbo gave to Frodo at Rivendell as his parting gift 'some books of lore that he had made at various times, written in his spidery hand and labeled on their red backs: *Translations from the Elvish, by B.B.*" (*RK* 1955, VI, vi, 265) But he adds that "in the second edition (1966) 'some books' was changed to 'three books.'" It is important to note that with this change, these three books had grown from "lore" to become "a work of great skill and learning in which . . . [Bilbo] had used all the sources available to him in Rivendell, both living and written" (*LT* I, 5).

The Foreword to the first edition of *The Lord of the Rings* also mentions that a copy of the Red Book is kept with the Fairbairns of Westmarch who are "descended from . . . Master Samwise" (*FR* 1954, I, 7). Expanding the range, the Prologue to the second edition lists copies in the Shire housed at Undertowers (home of the Fairbairns), at Great Smials (home of the Tooks), and at Brandy Hall (home of the Brandybucks), as well as a copy kept at Minas Tirith in Gondor (*FR* Prologue, 23–24). In addition, and like the real Red Book, by the time of the second edition of *The Lord of the Rings,* Tolkien's Red Book is a compendium of different stories from sources both "living and written" (24) stretching over many different periods and finally brought together in one place.

Unlike its medieval prototypes, Tolkien's Red Book has a traceable genealogy from earlier manuscripts, as well as a more coherent body of narrative than do many of the real-world books. Clearly, as Tolkien's concept grew, so grew the genealogy of the Red Book, from the first edition's ill-defined "lore" to the second edition's combination of orally transmitted information (the "living" sources) with material copied from written records that clearly reached farther and farther back into Middle-earth's pre-history. At first, according to the Foreword in the first edition of *The Lord of the Rings,* that narrative was intended to be "drawn for the most part from the 'memoirs' of the renowned Hobbits, Bilbo and Frodo, as they are preserved in the Red Book of Westmarch . . . compiled, repeatedly copied, and enlarged and handed down in the family of the Fairbairns of Westmarch . . . supplemented . . . in places, with information derived from the surviving records of Gondor, notably the Book of the Kings. . . ." (*FR* 1954, Prologue, 7). A few sentences later, *The Hobbit* is referred to as a "selection" from the Red Book (*FR* 1954, Prologue, 7).

However, by the time of the second edition of *The Lord of the Rings,* the Red Book had reached back into the First and Second Ages for its sources, and was extended both backwards and forwards in terms of transmitters. It acquired a line of identifiable author-redactors, among them Eriol/Ælfwine, Rúmil, Pengoloð, Gilfanon, and Findagil, as well as Bilbo and Frodo. From the "Note on the Shire Records" appended to the Prologue of the second edition we learn that the Red Book is now "*in origin* [compare with the first edition's *drawn for the most part*] Bilbo's private diary [*The Hobbit*]" (emphasis mine), added to by Frodo and then by Sam (*The Lord of the Rings*); but also that "annexed to it and preserved with it . . . were the three large volumes, bound in red leather that Bilbo gave to [Frodo] as a parting gift" (*FR* Prologue, 23). The key word is *annexed,* making clear what before was implicit, that the volumes, whether lore or work of great skill and learning, were to be attached to the more recently written private diary added to by Frodo and Sam.

Now as to *why* Tolkien was furthering this conceit. From the "Note on the Shire Records" I draw the fairly obvious conclusion that Tolkien's final scheme envisioned the combined set of these three volumes (Bilbo's "Translations") plus *The Hobbit* and *The Lord of the Rings* as comprising the "ideal" or archetypal Red Book of Westmarch. Moreover, I propose that this archetypal "book" was intended to encompass the entirety of his major fiction. The "Note" makes the point that only the copy at Minas Tirith in Gondor "contains the whole of Bilbo's 'Translations from the Elvish'" and thus includes all three author/translators—Bilbo, Frodo, and Sam. Thus the Red Book is written in what we might (with some license) call a Middle-earth equivalent of the "AB" language, since it shows traces of having originally been written by a scribe or scribes from a specific linguistic area and sharing a specific orthography.[3]

But what exactly are these "translations" of Bilbo's? We assume they are the Silmarillion, but what does that really mean in practical terms? What particular, specific texts might Bilbo have been imagined as using, and how was he supposed to have found them? As to where he might have found them, both the passage from *The Book of Lost Tales* I quoted above and the 1966 "Note on the Shire Records" added in the second edition of *The Lord of the Rings* show that over time Tolkien settled on Rivendell as the final repository. This is supported by his 1966 statement in an interview with Richard Plotz that the Silmarillion might be published as Bilbo's "research in Rivendell." Thus we have both written and oral confirmation of the content of those three annexed and preserved volumes.

That the actual texts of the stories were revised even more than the location of their eventual resting-place is less important in the present context than the scheme by which they were to be preserved. In answer to the question of what text Bilbo was using, the earliest candidate is likely to have been the Golden Book of Tavrobel, the record made by Eriol the Mariner of the tales he heard in what was to become Valinor.[4] The Golden Book as repository for the tales appears in Outline C of Tolkien's 1917 school notebook:

Eriol. . . . Goes to Tavrobel to see Gilfanon and sojourns in the house of a Hundred Chimneys. . . . Gilfanon bids him write down all he has heard. . . . The book lay [*sic*] untouched . . . during many ages of Men. The compiler of

the Golden Book takes up the Tale: one of the children of the fathers of the
fathers of Men. [*Against this is written:*] It may perhaps be much better to
let Eriol himself see the last things and finish the book" (*LT* II, 283). And in
the prefatory note to an "exceedingly difficult text titled *Epilogue*" is written: "Eriol flees with the fading Elves from the Battle of the High Heath. . . .
The last words of the book of Tales. Written by Eriol at Tavrobel before he
sealed the book" and left it in the House of the Hundred Chimneys, "where
it lieth still for such to read as may." (*LT* II, 287)

It had not "lain still" for very long before it picked up another author/
scribe, a shadowy compiler called Heorrenda[5] (the son of Eriol who later became Ælfwine), and became the Golden Book of Heorrenda. This need not
detain us, though it did lead Christopher Tolkien to caution future scholars
that "in the early notes and outlines there are different conceptions of the
Golden Book" (*SME* 274). The confusion between a book either "finished"
or "sealed" by Eriol and the notion of a later "compiler" who would add to it
is due to its creator's continual re-visioning of the concept, leading to those
"different conceptions" to which Christopher alludes, and culminating decades later in Tolkien's runic posture as the last compiler. If we could posit a
straight shot from the Golden Book to the Red Book, we might suppose Tolkien to have been launching his own color series to rival the actual ones.

Of course, it is not that simple. Later redactions and "translations" in-
tervened between the two books, as well as the not inconsiderable problem
of having the earlier book escape the Downfall of Númenor and manage to
survive the re-making of the world. Somehow, the "book" had to get from
the old world to the new one, and from the House of a Hundred Chimneys to Rivendell, the most likely place where it could be available to Bilbo.
Moreover, several languages were involved, for while the stories of the First
Age were presumed to have been written in the early Anglo-Saxon of Eriol/
Ælfwine, the later versions of the great tales of Beren and Lúthien and Túrin
Turambar were supposed to be in "Elvish" (most probably Sindarin).

In order to be read by any modern audience, both languages had to be
"translated" into modern English or "Common Speech." Moreover, this had
to be done by someone whom Tolkien could fictively authenticate as a translator. As his vision changed in the course of the re-visions of forty years,
so did his concept of the "book," the redactor, and the putative translator,
though not the strategy that lay behind the invention of all these. Over the
years, "Golden" was dropped from the title, Eriol/Ælfwine as redactor was
diminished, Heorrenda disappeared, and the book became just "the Book of
Stories" or "the Book of Tales," arriving in Númenor in time for the Downfall, and barely making it to Beleriand ahead of the tidal wave.

To untangle all these complexities would demand not just special skill but Elvish craft, and is beyond the capacity of the present discussion. I simply want to establish the centrality of the idea of a physical book, by whomever written and however titled, as the source and prototype for a publishable volume. And that is where the inside conceit connects to the external reality of the world outside Middle-earth, where Tolkien's concept of the "book" was to be not just an imaginary construct, but also a hoped-for actuality. For publication in the real world was his ultimate goal. Like any author, he wanted his work to be read, and for that to happen it had to be between covers and on bookstore shelves.

Within the fiction, he might imagine the Golden Book "lying untouched" in the House of a Hundred Chimneys, but outside the fiction, he wanted somebody to discover and publish it. Among the problems inherent in writing a fictive mythology was how to get it published as fiction but authenticate it as a mythology. At the time Tolkien was writing, collections of folk- and fairy-tales from Ireland to India had been and were being collected, published, and eagerly read by those whose interests lay in this area. The Folklore movement was in full swing. Not just the Grimms in Germany, but Jeremiah Curtin and Lady Gregory in Ireland, Lady Charlotte Guest in Wales, Joseph Jacobs in England, Moe and Asbjørnson in Norway, John Francis Campbell in the West Highlands of Scotland, and Elias Lönnrot in Finland had been and were providing a wealth of myth and folklore for their respective cultures. Tolkien's inside strategy had been to buttress his story by creating an imaginary artifact with the potential to be an actual outside volume publishable in the real world—the book behind the book, Bilbo's scholarly source.

In the curious way that life has of imitating art, just such a scholarly source was actually discovered at a crucial point in the arc of Tolkien's invention— when a version of the Silmarillion was near completion and before *The Lord of the Rings* was begun. This real-world analogue was the manuscript discovered in 1934 in the Fellows' Library of Winchester College, a major text in Arthurian mythology that pre-dated and was the obvious source for William Caxton's 1485 print edition of Sir Thomas Malory's *Morte D'Arthur.* In the context of Tolkien's vision, it was at once a serendipitous validation of the Golden Book, in that the Winchester too had been waiting undiscovered for "such to read as may," and a foreshadowing of his Red Book in that it brought a diversity of interrelated sources under one cover.

Like many fortunate discoveries, this one came about by accident. In June of 1934, while cataloguing and describing the early book-bindings of the Fellows' Library at Winchester College, the School Librarian, W.F. Oakeshott, obtained permission to open the safe in the bedroom of the College Warden. He needed to fill in gaps in his knowledge of the Library's holdings, and the safe contained the medieval manuscripts. Here is Oakeshott's account of what he found:

> I . . . was dashed to see at a glance that on the twenty or thirty manuscripts not a single medieval binding remained. . . . It was a disappointment. But . . . I pulled them out one by one and ran through one after another. . . . One was very fat, some 480 leaves, paper not vellum, the text prose not verse, clearly about King Arthur and his Knights, but lacking a beginning or an end. Be it admitted to my shame that I had never read Malory, and my knowledge of him was about as sketchy as my knowledge of most things has alas had to remain. But I made a vague mental note of this prose Arthurian manuscript, and passed on to the next item.

Oakeshott put the book back in the safe and went home to dinner. A few weeks later, preparing for an exhibit of early printed books including some by Caxton's successor Wynkyn de Worde, he consulted a reference work and came across a sentence which, he said, "made my heart miss a beat": "The compilation of the *Morte d'Arthur* was finished in 1469, but of the compiler little is known save the name . . . No manuscript of the work is known, and though Caxton certainly revised it, exactly to what extent has never been settled" (*Essays on Malory* 4).

The penny dropped. Oakeshott went straight to a bookshop, purchased the Everyman edition of the *Morte D'Arthur,* and asked permission to re-open the safe. Comparing the Everyman with the prose Arthurian manuscript, he realized straight away that the latter was not just a version of Malory; it was the manuscript of which Caxton's was the printed version. It was, as the colophon[6] makes clear, the "hoole book" of King Arthur.

The news immediately hit the papers, appearing in the *Daily Telegraph* on 24 June and with follow-up stories in the *Times* on 26 June and 25 August. Writing in his diary on Monday, 27 August 1934, C.S. Lewis's brother Warnie Lewis cited: "Saturday's *Times* which contains the very interesting news that the only known MS of Malory's *Morte d'Arthur* has just been discovered in the library of Winchester College" (W. Lewis 155). The dean of Arthurian studies, Eugène Vinaver, asked to see the manuscript, took on the job of editing it, and in 1947 published the three-volume *Works of Sir Thomas Malory* from Oxford University Press.

Vinaver had been a lecturer in French language and literature at Lincoln College, Oxford from 1924 to 1928, and university lecturer in French from 1928 to 1931. At the time of the discovery, he had moved to the University of Manchester, where he would later collaborate with Tolkien's friend E.V.

Gordon on a textual comparison of the Winchester and Caxton Malorys. In 1935, Vinaver gave a talk to the Arthurian Society at Oxford on "Malory's *Morte Darthur* in the Light of a Recent Discovery," the recent discovery being the Winchester manuscript. C.S. Lewis attended the lecture, as shown by a letter he subsequently wrote Vinaver inquiring about the meaning of a particular word and phrase (Lewis *Letters* vol. 2, 166).

It seems more than probable that Tolkien would also have attended Vinaver's talk. He would hardly have missed this opportunity to learn more at first hand about so important a discovery—a new text in what was then, and remains today (Tolkien notwithstanding), England's only native mythology. He would certainly have had a professional interest in the Winchester, first as a scholar (indeed, Lewis also consulted Tolkien on the textual problem[7]), second as the writer of a competitive work-in-progress, and third as an at-that-point unpublished author. Here was a discovery of a manuscript book of historical significance that, in circumstances uncannily like his fictive ones, had been lying untouched in plain sight for centuries. Furthermore it was going to be published.

The event affected Tolkien in at least two areas, one internal to the fiction, one external and related to his real-world problem as an author. First, the internal influence. I propose that the Winchester manuscript was the model for the book Sam Gamgee conjures in the conversation about stories on the Stairs of Cirith Ungol. In that passage so unnecessary to the plot but so appropriate in the context of Tolkien's myth-making strategy, Sam has been musing on the nature of stories, and on their serial transmission and continuance over many years. He tells Frodo he wants their story to be "read out of a great big book with red and black letters, years and years afterwards" (*TT* IV, viii, 321). Such specificity suggests reference to an actual book, a volume of stories from periods long years before.

Tolkien was familiar with medieval manuscripts, and knew that they come in all sizes. He knew the *Beowulf* codex, MS Cotton Vitellius A.xv, a modest, quarto-size book whose individual sections begin with large initial letters but which is otherwise devoid of calligraphic decoration. He knew the manuscript of *Sir Gawain and the Green Knight*, MS Cotton Nero A.x, for which he had edited the standard scholarly edition, and of which he made his own translation. Like the *Beowulf*, the *Gawain* codex is a modest quarto, though it does have ten full-page color illustrations, rare for a medieval manuscript. It also has ornamental colored capitals. However, neither book could properly be described as "great big," and neither makes a good match with Sam's description. Tolkien also knew (or knew of) the great medieval illuminated manuscripts such as the Book of Kells or the Book of Durrow, folio size and thus plausibly describable as "great big," with interlace borders and elaborate initial letters in many colors. These match somewhat better with Sam's imaginary book; nevertheless, they are a long way from a perfect fit.

There is one manuscript book that does fit Sam's description to a T, and that is the Winchester Malory. Like Sam's, it is a "great big book," a folio, not a quarto, of 480 leaves, copied out from an earlier, now lost manuscript by two different scribes. Like Sam's, it is a collection of stories. Most important for my argument is Sam's phrase "with red and black letters." This is the connecting link, for the Winchester manuscript is emphatically in red and black letters. While the narrative portions are in standard black ink, the proper names and all references to the Grail are carefully written in red ink. Thus, red and black letters appear on nearly every page. The introduction to the Early English Text Society facsimile edition of the Winchester manuscript cites this as a "remarkable feature" (Winchester xiv), one that, so far as I know, is unique to this manuscript. In light of this, Tolkien's desire to have the "fiery letters" of the Ring inscription printed in red (Carpenter 217) deserves fresh consideration. In addition, his own calligraphic manuscript page of *The Tale of the Years*, a color plate of which appears as the frontispiece of *Morgoth's Ring*, is carefully written out in red and black. Christopher Tolkien has called this "among the most beautiful [manuscripts] that he made" *MR* 49), and much of the effect comes from the use of the two colors. In both these instances, the specific red and black motif seems likely to have been inspired by the Winchester Malory.

Now for the external effect. It has to do with those three extra volumes annexed to the primary or nuclear Red Book. Quite unlike the medieval Red Book, the White Book, the Black Book, the Yellow Book, and all the other manuscript books of the Middle Ages, the Winchester manuscript could trace a clear line of descent from earlier texts. The author, Sir Thomas Malory, made no secret of the fact that he had drawn on previously existing sources, as his frequent references to the "Frenssh boke" make clear. Malory's "Frenssh boke" is in fact a number of texts in both French and English that were available to readers on both sides of the Channel in the years when he was writing his great work.

The stories of the Coming of Arthur, the romances of Tristan and Iseult and of Lancelot and Guinevere, the transcendent story of Galahad and the Grail Quest, and the final tragedy of the Death of Arthur, were to be found in various existing manuscripts. Among these were the cycle (from which only fragments survive) of Robert de Boron's *Joseph d'Arimathie*, *Merlin*, and *Perceval*; the *Queste del Saint Graal*; the prose *Tristan*; the French Vulgate Cycle, especially the *Morte Artu*; the *Suite du Merlin* that is the basis for the Post-Vulgate Cycle; and the Middle English Alliterative and Stanzaic *Morte* poems on the Death of Arthur. All were ready to hand. With due allowance for poetic license and his own genius, Malory "translated" them into his own Middle English.

Caxton's printed edition of Malory had fueled the speculation of scholars, but here was more immediate, primary manuscript evidence. Where Caxton had divided his printed edition into many chapters, the Winchester Malory is divided into a number of separate but interlaced "bokes,"[8] each given a separate title, and all but one, "The Tale of Sir Gareth of Orkney That Was Called Bewmaynes," having an identifiable outside source or sources. All the books are directly focused on the Matter of Britain, the interconnected sequence of myths and legends about Arthur and the Knights of the Round Table. This coherent content of myth and legend, stretching over a considerable span of time, fits remarkably with Tolkien's letter to Milton Waldman outlining his scheme for his own mythology. It was to be,

> a body of more or less connected legend. . . . redolent of the clime and soil of the North West, meaning Britain and the hither parts of Europe. . . . possessing . . . the fair elusive beauty that some call Celtic . . . it should be "high", purged of the gross. . . . The cycles should be linked to a majestic whole, and yet leave scope for other minds and hands, wielding paint and music and drama. (*Letters* 144–45)

If we did not know better, and could except the phrase "purged of the gross" (such as the adultery which is the plot pivot of the Arthurian story) we might easily imagine Tolkien to be describing the corpus of Arthurian myth and legend rather than his own mythology.

It is not unreasonable to conjecture that he was on a very private level comparing the two. It takes a special kind of confident imagination to make the leap from Malory's actual synthesis of earlier texts to the Red Book's fictive annexation of those three volumes with their separate but interconnected stories of the Singing of the Ainur, of Fëanor and the Silmarils, the romance of Beren and Lúthien, the tragedies of Thingol and Túrin, and the apotheosis of Eärendil. I argue that Tolkien had that kind of imagination and that he made that leap. To position Bilbo as not just the narrator of *The Hobbit* and part of *The Lord of the Rings*, but also, through his "researches in Rivendell," as the translator and redactor of the earlier "book" (by whatever title it had acquired by then), is to place that unassuming hobbit on a fictive editorial footing with Malory, and equally, to put Tolkien's Red Book on a Middle-earth par with the Winchester manuscript.

My external argument extends beyond the discovery of the Winchester in 1934 to its publication in 1947.[9] I suggest that this publication offered Tolkien not just a conceptual model, but a possible precedent as well. I propose this as a conjectural rationale for what otherwise seemed then, as it does now, his impractical and unrealistic insistence on twofold publication—having the Silmarillion and *The Lord of the Rings* brought out together. With the advantage of over fifty years' hindsight, we can see that there could not have been an audience for the Silmarillion until *The Lord of the Rings* created one, a circumstance that effectively precluded dual publication in the mid-twentieth century. No such hindsight was available to Tolkien. In its absence, the successful publication of the Winchester might have suggested to him that there could be an audience for so large a mythological work if it were presented in such a way as to attract that audience, as was the Winchester.

Vinaver described his goal in editing that manuscript as "the endeavour to produce the text in a form similar to that of a modern work of fiction" (Malory *Works* vol. 1, vi), and the motive was clearly to make it readable for a non-scholarly audience. If Vinaver could present a scholarly mythology in a form similar to that of modern fiction, why could not Tolkien publish his modern fiction in the form of a mythology? If despite post-war austerity, production costs, and paper shortages the Winchester manuscript could be brought out in a three-volume edition,[10] perhaps Tolkien's combined work could get similar treatment.

Although such twofold publication was impractical in terms not just of production expenses (letters between Tolkien and Sir Stanley Unwin during these years refer to paper shortages and mounting costs), but also of sales, he clung to that hope for three years, from 1949, when he first approached Milton Waldman at Collins publishers, to 1952, when he gave in and gave up. It was then that he wrote to Rayner Unwin, "I have rather modified my views. Better something than nothing!" (*Letters* 163) and settled for publishing *The Lord of the Rings* alone.

In addition to suggesting a possible rationale for an unrealistic hope, these circumstances may throw additional light on another and equally idiosyncratic aspect of Tolkien's stance as a British writer at that time. This was his dismissal of the story of King Arthur as the primary candidate for England's mythology. In his 1951 letter laying out the case for his own mythos to Milton Waldman, he had acknowledged the corpus of Arthurian material generally called the Matter of Britain, conceding that, "of course there was *and is* [my emphasis] all the Arthurian world." Nevertheless, he maintained that "powerful as it is," it did not meet his criteria. His grounds for its ineligibility were that its story was "imperfectly naturalized" (that is, native to the soil but not the language of England), that its Faery was "too lavish," and that it "explicitly contain[ed] the Christian religion" (*Letters* 139).

That it contained explicit Christianity is beyond question, for the Grail Quest had been an integral part of the story since the late twelfth century. That its Faery was too lavish is of course a matter of opinion. Imperfectly naturalized it might have been considered, though this is again a matter of opinion and open to question. However, this last judgment has a direct bearing on Tolkien's real reason for preferring his own myth, that in it he had created, as Christopher Tolkien has pointed out, "a specifically English [i.e. not British like Arthur] fairy lore" (*LT* II, 290).

Nevertheless, and even though the explicit "Englishness" of his own mythos diminished over the years, at the time when Tolkien wrote his letter, the story of Arthur was newly in print while his mythology was not. Had his negotiations with Waldman and Collins succeeded, the hoped-for tandem publication of the Silmarillion and *The Lord of the Rings* would have put Tolkien's mythological "book," which he described to Milton Waldman as "one long Saga of the Jewels and the Rings" (*Letters* 139), on a competitive level with its Arthurian counterpart.[11] It would have brought to fruition his ambition of dedicating a mythology to England, one that would rival the Arthurian one in actuality as well as in his private vision.

It was not to be. Not in its author's lifetime, at any rate. However, though this was for him a deep disappointment—indeed, Christopher Tolkien describes it as "grief to him" and cites his "despair of publication" (*MR* vii, viii)— the delay may not in other respects have been the drawback that it at first appeared. Ultimately, the dream deferred only increased the resemblance between Tolkien's fictive "book" and his most recent real-world model, for both were forced by circumstances to lie for years in one or another repository, uncatalogued and unread, before being rescued from obscurity, edited, and published for modern readers. As circumstances turned out, it was neither Eriol/Ælfwine nor Heorrenda, not even Bilbo Baggins, but Christopher Tolkien who finally produced in its entirety his father's "hoole book," the multivolume *History of Middle-earth.* Only the continuing popularity of *The Lord of the Rings* made possible the publication, three decades and more after that narrative's first appearance, of the vast and multi-voiced manuscript book that had lain unaccessed for so many years waiting for "such to read as may."

And that is we who come after, the generations following Tolkien who have found his "book" in all its aspects worthy not just of readerly enjoyment but also of scholarly study, of serious critical and textual examination through which we labor to enhance without dissecting his vision.

Tolkien on Tolkien

"On Fairy-stories," The Hobbit, *and* The Lord of the Rings

Writing to his American publisher Houghton Mifflin on 30 June 1955, Tolkien said of his essay "On Fairy-stories": "I think it is quite an important work, at least for anyone who thinks me worth considering at all" (*Letters* 220). I believe it is safe to assume that Tolkien is worth considering, so I intend to consider this important work in the context of two other important works, *The Lord of the Rings* and its immediate precursor, *The Hobbit.* The relationship between *The Hobbit* and *The Lord of the Rings* is clear enough, though I hope to point out some overlooked factors. But where does the essay fit in?

My argument is as follows: Tolkien's writing of *The Hobbit* was a learning process; indeed, the last half of the book is substantially better than the first half. He used the mistakes he perceived himself to have made in that book to develop and articulate in "On Fairy-stories" a theory of fantasy and sub-creation, which he then put into practice in *The Lord of the Rings.* The fairy-story essay covers many more aspects of fairy tales than there is room or time to discuss here, but its chief argument concerns the essential nature of fairy-stories, the character of their intended audience, and their uses as a literary genre. I will focus rather narrowly on two interconnected parts of his thesis. The first is audience, the relationship between fairy-stories and children. The second is the nature of fairy-stories, which includes the concept of Faërie as a Secondary World with the "inner consistency of reality" (*MC* 138).

I'll start with fairy-stories and children. On 7 June 1955, Tolkien wrote to W. H. Auden à propos *The Lord of the Rings:*

I had been thinking about "Fairy Stories" and their relation to children—
some of the results I put into a lecture at St. Andrews and eventually en-

larged and published in an Essay. . . . As I had [there] expressed the view
that the connexion in the modern mind between children and 'fairy stories' is false and accidental and spoils the stories in themselves and for
children, I wanted to try and write one that was not addressed to children
at all (as such). (*Letters* 216)

He was even more explicit when, on 22 November 1961, he wrote to his aunt
Jane Neave:

I am not interested in the "child" as such . . . and certainly have no intention of meeting him/her halfway, or a quarter of the way. . . . I have only
once made the mistake of trying to do it, to my lasting regret . . . in the
earlier part of *the Hobbit*. But I had not then given any serious thought to
the matter. . . . I had to think about it, however, before I gave an "Andrew
Lang" lecture at St. Andrews on Fairy-stories; and I must say I think the
result was entirely beneficial to *The Lord of The Rings*, which was a practical demonstration of the views that I expressed. (*Letters* 309–10)

The last sentence is my thesis in a nutshell and straight from the horse's mouth.

Here I must pause to note a minor snag—we don't have Tolkien's lecture
as he gave it. Delivered in 1939, it was extensively revised for publication in
the 1947 *Essays Presented to Charles Williams*, and revised again for inclusion in *Tree and Leaf*. Its final form is that edited by Christopher Tolkien
for the collection *The Monsters and the Critics and Other Essays*. That version is the one most people now are familiar with. Publication of *Tolkien on
Fairy-stories* (edited by myself and Douglas A. Anderson), which included
early drafts, has augmented but not materially changed Tolkien's original
position. However, even if we had the original lecture as delivered (and the
incomplete Manuscript A in *Tolkien on Fairy-stories* seems to have been the
earliest draft), we could not draw a straight line from *The Hobbit* through
"On Fairy-stories" to *The Lord of the Rings*, as Tolkien seems to be doing in
these letters. At best, he is in a holding pattern circling a rather large stretch
of time from late 1937 to early 1939.

Here is a brief chronology. *The Hobbit* was published on 21 September
1937. On 11 October 1937, Tolkien's publisher Stanley Unwin wrote to Tolkien
suggesting the possibility of a sequel. On 19 December 1937, Tolkien wrote
to Charles Furth of Allen & Unwin's editorial staff that "I have written the
first chapter of a new story about Hobbits—'A long expected party'" (*Letters*
27). By 4 June 1938, this promising momentum had ground to a halt. Tolkien
wrote to Stanley Unwin, "I have not had a chance to touch any story-writing

since the Christmas vacation. With three works in Middle English and Old English going to or through the press, and another in Old Norse . . . of which I am an editor . . . I cannot see any loophole left for months!" (*Letters* 36). However, a subsequent letter to Furth, this one dated 31 August 1938, announces, "I have begun again on the sequel to the 'Hobbit.' . . . It is now flowing along, and . . . has reached about Chapter VII [up to Bree]" (*Letters* 40). A little over six months later, on 8 March 1939, Tolkien gave his lecture at St. Andrews. It is possible (and, I would like to suggest, probable) that the lecture and the *Hobbit* sequel, at least the earliest drafts of that much-revised story, evolved together and mutually influenced one another.

One of Tolkien's targets in the essay is the writers of "literary" fairy-stories, which by way of *The Hobbit* certainly included Tolkien himself. He faulted such writers for (1) being "patronizing; or (deadliest of all) covertly sniggering, with an eye on the other grown-ups present" and (2) being affectedly dainty and over-refined, stressing the delicate and the diminutive in their depiction of fairies (*MC* 110–12). Though he tended to blame the French for such prettification, his prime example was the English Michael Drayton, whose mock-epic poem *Nymphidia* features a castle with walls of spider's legs,

> And windows of the eyes of cats,
> And for the roof, instead of slats,
> Is covered with the wings of bats (*MC* 111–12)

as well as a fairy knight named Pigwiggen who rides on a frisky earwig and carries a hornet sting for a lance. Tolkien called *Nymphidia* one of the worst fairy-stories ever written and dismissed its relentless cuteness as "Pigwiggenry." I will return to Pigwiggenry presently, but for now I want to look carefully at patronizing or sniggering with an eye on the grown-ups. Tolkien's example was that very Andrew Lang whom his lecture was to honor. He accused Lang of having had, in the *Chronicles of Pantouflia*, "an eye on the faces of other clever people over the heads of his child-audience" (*MC* 136).

Lang was no more guilty here than Tolkien himself, as Tolkien well knew and later acknowledged. In his 1951 letter to Milton Waldman written long after *The Lord of the Rings*, let alone *The Hobbit* and "On Fairy-stories," he conceded that "The . . . tone and style of *The Hobbit* is due, in point of genesis, to it being taken by me as a matter . . . susceptible of treatment as a 'fairy-story' for children. Some of the details of tone and treatment are, I now think, even on that basis, mistaken" (*Letters* 159). In *The Hobbit* he is as patronizing as Lang in *Pantouflia*, and if his eye is not on other grown-ups, it is certainly on his child audience in the complicit and sniggering narrative asides that mar the opening chapters. Here are some examples.

> "You will notice already that Mr. Baggins was not quite so prosy as he liked to believe" (*H* 14).
>
> "'[He is] as fierce as a dragon in a pinch.' If you have ever seen a dragon in a pinch you will realize that this was only poetical exaggeration" (*H* 24).
>
> "Yes, I am afraid trolls do behave like that, even those with only one head each" (*H* 37).
>
> "Bilbo suddenly discovered the weak point in his plan. Most likely you saw it some time ago and have been laughing at him; but I don't suppose you would have done half as well yourselves in his place" (*H* 157).

This is what Paul Thomas, in his essay on "Some of Tolkien's Narrators," terms the "self-conscious" narrator, hyper-aware of himself as a tale-teller (*Legendarium* 165). The real rhetoric of such asides is more than self-conscious; it is apologetic and dismissive as well. It says to the reader in effect, "You needn't take this story seriously. It's just for fun."

In all fairness to Tolkien, however, several things should be taken into account. First, those asides diminish noticeably as the story begins to gather momentum and disappear almost completely in the second half of the book. Second, the asides very probably arose directly out of the circumstances in which *The Hobbit* began, as a story originally *told*—not written—to Tolkien's own children. Third, this kind of direct address, the creation of a hypothetical "you" as listener/reader, was a convention of English children's stories in the early twentieth century. The master of the technique was E. Nesbit, whose children's books, among them *The Story of the Amulet, Five Children and It*, and *The Railway Children*, were popular in the 1920s and 1930s. Tolkien was no Nesbit. The authorial aside was not his natural mode, and his efforts in that direction seem both arch and awkward.

Direct address to a fictional "you" presumed to be smarter than the characters in the story, labored jokes about dragons in a pinch and trolls with only one head, asides that no serious author would address to an adult reader—Tolkien came to regret them all. Humphrey Carpenter notes that when Tolkien was sent the page proofs of *The Hobbit* by Allen & Unwin, he seized the opportunity to make numerous alterations to the text. "In particular," says Carpenter, "he did not like many of the patronising 'asides' to juvenile readers" (181). He took some but not all of these out and, as we see from his letters as well as from the essay, came to deplore those he left in.

How did this affect *The Lord of the Rings*? Christopher Tolkien's account in *The Return of the Shadow* of the many false starts and revisions to the first chapter is too complex to explore in detail here, but it does show Tolkien starting out to write in exactly this patronizing mode and working his way out of it as he laboriously wrote and rewrote. Here are some samples of the kind of thing he tried and rejected.

> *First version:* "There, I suppose it has become all too plain" (*RS* 16).
> *Second version:* "The fireworks of course (as you at any rate have guessed) were by Gandalf" (*RS* 21).
> "Now really we must hurry on" (*RS* 22).
> "What that meant only Bilbo and a few of his close friends knew (and you of course)" (*RS* 24).
> *Third version:* "It is no good telling hobbits about dragons: they either disbelieve you or feel uncomfortable" (*RS* 29).
> "I can tell you something more, in case you have not guessed" (*RS* 33).

This chatty and intrusive persona recedes further and further into the background in successive revisions, though traces remain in the published book, such as the party hobbits' reaction to Bilbo's speech: "This was the sort of stuff they liked: short and obvious" (*FR* I, i, 37). Nonetheless, it's clear that Tolkien has learned his lesson, and by the time he gets to the dark mood and the sober tone of "The Shadow of the Past," his narrator respects his audience—at that early stage still the child audience of *The Hobbit*—and his story enough to take both of them seriously.

Now to my second and related point, the requirements of Faërie and the inner consistency of reality: By the time he composed "On Fairy-stories," Tolkien had developed high standards for the integrity of both. He used *Faërie* to mean both "Magic . . . of a peculiar mood and power" (*MC* 114) and the Secondary World where such magic occurs. "If there is any satire present in the tale," he declared, "one thing must not be made fun of, the magic itself. That must in that story be taken seriously, neither laughed at nor explained away" (*MC* 114). "Anyone," he said, "can say *the green sun*," but a Secondary World in which a green sun would be credible would require "a special skill, a kind of elvish craft" (*MC* 140).

I'm going to assess several of Tolkien's green suns in terms of elvish craft, looking at magic and satire and belief. I'll start with the elves of Rivendell in *The Hobbit*. Remember their first appearance in the book, unseen but overheard sizing up the dwarves and Bilbo as they approach Rivendell.

O! What are you doing,
And where are you going?
Your ponies need shoeing!
The river is flowing!
    O! tra-la-la-lally
    here down in the valley!

O! What are you seeking,
And where are you making?
The faggots are reeking,
The bannocks are baking!
    O! tril-lil-lil-lolly
    the valley is jolly,
        ha! ha!

"So they laughed and sang in the trees," says the narrator, "and pretty fair nonsense I daresay you think it" (*H* 48–49). I daresay he's right. When a few paragraphs later the narrator tells us that "Elvish singing is not a thing to miss" (49), we may be pardoned for doubting his taste, if not his word. Sadly, the elves' conversational skills are no more magical than their song. "Just look!" they cry. "Bilbo the hobbit on a pony, my dear! Isn't it delicious!" (49). This is not Faërie; it is Pigwiggenry. These are not real elves as we (and Tolkien) know them from the Silmarillion. They are a joke built on popular misconceptions of the word "fairy" as gossamer and inconsequential. As green suns they are duds, impossible to take seriously. No one would confuse their nonsensical ditty with genuine Elven song. For comparison, here are some verses from the "Song of Nimrodel" that Legolas sings in Lórien.

When dawn came dim the land was lost,
    The mountains sinking grey
Beyond the heaving waves that tossed
    Their plumes of blinding spray.

Amroth beheld the fading shore
    Now low beyond the swell,
And cursed the faithless ship that bore
    Him far from Nimrodel. (*FR* II, vi, 354)

I think you can hear the difference.

I did note when I began that *The Hobbit* gets better in the second half, and Tolkien's marked alteration in his treatment of the Rivendell elves is one indication. He takes them much more seriously by the end of the book, as evidenced by their final song. He dismissed "O! What are you doing" as "pretty fair nonsense," but there is nothing nonsensical about "The dragon is withered." Although the narrator describes it as "of much the same kind as before" (*H* 249), he is mistaken. "The dragon is withered" is lyrical and elegiac and shares nothing with the elves' first song besides the meter and the refrain.

Just as bad as the elves are the trolls. Like elves, trolls are time-honored inhabitants of the magical world of fairy-stories and are standard characters in Scandinavian folktales and sagas. Unlike elves, they are large and lumbering creatures, but their size, like elven beauty, ought not be a subject for satire. Trolls are not terribly bright, but they are powerful and malevolent enough to be a menace to any human they encounter. The ones in *The Hobbit* are the first serious danger that Bilbo and the Dwarves encounter, and they are played for laughs—not mockery, as with the elves, but low comedy of the knockabout variety. Take their names, for instance. Not only are "Bert" and "Tom" and "William" markedly un-troll-like (trolls don't normally have proper names), but the names themselves clash culturally and chronologically and artistically with "Bilbo" and "Beorn" and "Bard" and the dwarf names from *Edda*. The mismatch is meant to be funny, but the joke rapidly wears thin.

The trolls are not just from a different world than Bilbo—they are from a different class, and that too is supposed to make them funny. They are stock comedy types, and in marked contrast to Bilbo's polite diction, their vocabulary comes not from ordinary speech but from the popular music hall and that quintessentially British theatrical form, the pantomime. Bilbo may say, "Good morning," to mean "Go away" and use words like "confusticate" and "bebother" to express annoyance, but these reveal his personality, not his station in life, whereas the trolls betray their origins with words like "blimey" and "blighter," "me" for possessive instead of "my," and slang expressions like "Look what I've copped." Not only do they drop their aitches, but so does William's magical talking purse. They are no more real trolls than the Rivendell elves are real elves. They sound more like Eliza Doolittle than traditional characters in a fairy tale.

Sensitive to sound and the nuances of language as he was, Tolkien has here failed spectacularly in maintaining the inner consistency of reality necessary for a Secondary World. The trolls and their dialogue bring the Primary World blundering into Faërie with the predictable result that enchantment and belief fly out the window. Like the Rivendell elves, the magic, the supernatural, is not taken seriously but used as the target for inappropriate satire and easy laughs. The difficulty is that the satire is too easy and the laughs are inappropriate. Neither comes naturally out of the subject matter but each relies on the built-in disjunction between the world of Faërie and the world of everyday. In this regard, Tolkien became in "On Fairy-stories" his own severest critic, and in *The Lord of the Rings* his own best pupil. His whole discussion of green suns and Secondary Belief in the essay can be applied to the troll chapter, and the lessons learned bore fruit in *The Lord of the Rings*.

Contrast the trolls of *The Hobbit* with the orcs of *The Lord of the Rings*. Contrast the speech as well as the names of Bert and Tom and William with both names and speech of Grishnákh and Uglúk, and Shagrat and Gorbag, and the nameless but immediately recognizable trackers who follow Gollum in Mordor. The language of these orcs, their guttural *Ar*'s and *Nar*'s and *Garn*'s, was almost certainly transposed directly from Tolkien's experience of the Allied trenches of World War I France to the war zones of his Middle-earth.

Here's Uglúk to Grishnákh: "I don't trust you little swine. You've no guts outside your own sties" (*TT* III, iii, 49).

Here's Grishnákh to Uglúk: "Who does [Saruman] think he is, setting up on his own with his filthy white badges?" (*TT* III, iii, 49).

And later, Grishnákh to Pippin and Merry: "Curse you, you filthy little vermin. . . . I'll untie every string in your bodies" (*TT* III, iii, 59).

Here's Shagrat to Snaga: "You little maggot. . . . Come here and I'll squeeze your eyes out. . . . I'll put red maggot-holes in your belly" (*RK* VI, i, 181–82).

Here's one of the orc trackers to the other in Mordor: "Not much use are you, you little snufflers? . . . I reckon eyes are better than your snotty noses" (*RK* VI, ii, 202).

No talking purses with London accents here, no "blimey" or dropped aitches, just the authentic gutter vulgate of real thugs whose inner consistency we have no difficulty accepting. It is the very realism of Tolkien's orcs that supports his Secondary World. If we accept them, we accept it. Grishnákh is not a stock character; he is a sharply delineated individual of a very particular kind: belligerent, defensive, cruel, ironic, clever enough to understand Pippin's game but not clever enough to see through it. Although not one of its more outstanding citizens, he nevertheless belongs in Middle-earth. Bert and Tom and William do not.

My final example examines Tolkien's disparate presentation of two sets of animals, contrasting the behavior of Beorn's animal servants with that of the eagles in *The Hobbit* and their counterparts in *The Lord of the Rings*. And since in *The Hobbit* the episode with the eagles comes before the Beorn episode, I must posit the latter as a surprising lapse in sub-creation, a detour in

Tolkien's progress from Pigwiggenry to true Faërie. Beorn's animals partake of Pigwiggenry. They are not magical; they are cute. They evoke not the true wonder and delight of Faërie but the patronizing incredulity of Dr. Johnson comparing the lady preacher to a performing dog—the wonder being not that the performance was well done, but that it was done at all. This is what Tolkien described as "a dreadful undergrowth . . . adapted to what was or is conceived to be the measure of children's minds and needs" (*MC* 136).

Beorn's animal servants—ponies, dogs, and sheep—respond to his instructions, uttered in "a queer language like animal noises turned into talk" (*H* 110), by lighting torches, rearranging furniture, and setting the table. The dogs, especially well trained, stand on their hind legs and use their forefeet like hands to carry dishes and utensils. This is not magic; it is circus tricks. It sorts ill with the truly supernatural shape-changing of Beorn himself, whose shift from man shape to bear shape, while it comes straight from the Icelandic sagas, finds a match in the fairy tale tradition. Similar man-beasts appear prominently in "Beauty and the Beast," "Snow White and Rose Red," and "East of the Sun and West of the Moon," the last two stories specifically featuring bears who are also human men. Although Beorn is a late and unforeshadowed entry into the story, his back-and-forth oscillation between bearlike human and actual bear brings a dark magic to the world of *The Hobbit,* while his shadowing in bear shape of the travelers' approach to Mirkwood injects a genuine note of mystery into the story. But the queer language "like animal noises" and the dog-and-pony show put the whole episode closer to the stories of Dr. Doolittle than to true fairy tale.

The eagles are a different matter. Indeed, though they are animals, they are actually closer to Beorn than to his dogs and ponies in that they act consistent with their animal nature, where his animals superimpose human behavior on theirs. True, the eagles act untypically as beasts of burden, carrying Bilbo and the dwarves on their backs. Nevertheless, their rescue of the party from incineration by the goblins places them firmly in the fairy tale convention of the animal helper who traditionally pulls the hero out of a tight spot. Moreover, they are able to effect this rescue precisely *because* they are eagles, flying high and far, and landing from the air on otherwise-inaccessible cliffs.

Rescue from the air by eagle becomes a motif in itself in *The Lord of the Rings,* where not just Gandalf, on three separate occasions, but also Pippin in the Battle at the Black Gate and Frodo and Sam at the Cracks of Doom are swooped out of danger by Tolkien's eucatastrophic eagles. Transportation of humans by large birds has a secure place in fantasy and myth. In the fantasy classic *The Wonderful Adventures of Nils,* the boy Nils flies across the North Sea on the back of the old goose Akka of Kebnekäse, while, even closer to *The Hobbit,* an eagle rescues the *Kalevala* hero Väinämöinen from the water and carries him to the magic region of Pohjola. Both stories may have had an influence on Tolkien, for he certainly knew and admired *Kalevala,* and it is not improbable that he knew of the adventures of Nils.

Far from being "animal noises turned into talk," the eagles' speech, like that of their counterparts in *Kalevala* and *Nils,* is the traditional seldom-explained fairy tale magic of communication between humans and beasts. This is what Tolkien described in "On Fairy-stories" as "one of the primal 'desires' that lie near the heart of Faërie: the desire of men to hold communion with other living things." He wrote further that "[t]he magical understanding by men of the proper languages of birds and beasts" is "near to the true purposes of Faërie" (*MC* 117). Here he was almost certainly going beyond Väinämöinen and Nils to the Norse hero Sigurd, whose accidental taste of the dragon Fáfnir's blood gave him the capacity to understand two birds chirping that his mentor Regin was planning to kill him. It is in this tradition that Gandalf in *The Hobbit* is able to understand "the dreadful language of the Wargs" (*H* 91), and Bilbo can understand the conversation between Gandalf and the Lord of the Eagles. The motif is refined in *The Lord of the Rings,* where Gandalf's three exchanges with Gwaihir the Windlord are presented without explanation as part of his capacities as a wizard.

This was for Tolkien so important an aspect of fairy-story that he returned to the topic near the end of the essay, where in the "Escape" portion of the section on "Recovery, Escape, and Consolation" he wrote again about "the desire to converse with other living things." We may be allowed to wonder if, when he wrote that "On this desire, as ancient as the Fall, is largely founded the talking of beasts and creatures in fairy-tales, and especially the magical understanding of their proper speech" (*MC* 152), he may have been describing himself as well as the properties of Faërie. We may speculate that in moving from *The Hobbit* through "On Fairy-stories" to *The Lord of the Rings,* he was moving closer to a primal desire that lay as near his own heart as that of Faërie.

I could add other examples to my list of green suns. But I think I've made my point. Admittedly, I have picked out the most awkward parts of *The Hobbit,* left out much that is good and transcends these weaknesses, and probably alienated legions of *Hobbit*-loving readers. Nevertheless, I stick to my guns and my argument. Tolkien learned from his mistakes in writing *The Hobbit* and translated them into a set of useful precepts in "On Fairy-stories," and the result, as he told his Aunt Jane, "was entirely beneficial to *The Lord of the Rings,* which was a practical demonstration of the views that [he] expressed" (*Letters* 310). By Tolkien's own criteria, *The Hobbit*, particularly in the early chapters, does not altogether succeed as fairy-story in some important areas. The narrator is intrusive, patronizing, and apologetic, and, even more important, the magic is too often made fun of, while the Faërie lacks the inner consistency of reality. In contrast, *The Lord of the Rings* gets full marks on both counts. The narrator keeps himself out of the picture and takes both his story and his audience seriously, treats magic with the respect it deserves, and makes a Secondary World of Faërie that is both sub-creatively consistent and fully believable.

When Is a Fairy Story a *Faërie* Story?

Smith of Wootton Major

It is a safe bet that when in 1939 J.R.R. Tolkien gave his Andrew Lang lecture "On Fairy-stories," with its extended discussion of what does (and does not) constitute a fairy story, he did not have *Smith of Wootton Major* in mind, since that story was not conceived until the mid-1960s. The reverse of that bet, however, seems equally safe, that when he wrote *Smith of Wootton Major* he very probably *did* have "On Fairy-stories" in his mind. For the two work together. Both *Smith of Wootton Major* and "On Fairy-stories," each in its own way, exemplify what Tolkien meant by the word *Faërie,* the essay by explaining it, the story by depicting it, with the result that the story becomes the practical application of the criteria set up in the essay. Among these criteria are the appropriate subject matter for fairy-stories, their proper quality, and the threefold attitude or "face" that fairy-stories show their readers. We will come back to these criteria in greater detail at a later point in the discussion.

But first, a word or two about the story. Of all Tolkien's works large and small, *Smith of Wootton Major* has perhaps received the least critical attention from both scholars and the public at large, though that has begun to change in recent years. In part, this is the story's—or Tolkien's—own fault. On its surface, the tale is misleadingly slight, causing many readers and reviewers either to dismiss it as trivial without examining it closely, or to take it at face value as a fairy tale—again, without examining it closely. Those who do look for deeper import have tended to allegorize its simplicities, to look for a message rather than a meaning in this story of a mortal man's visits to fairyland and what he finds there. While such visits and their opposite expression, the visits of fairies to the mortal world, are the standard stuff of fairy tales, *Smith* is more than just a fairy tale in the popular sense of that term. It is a *faërie* tale, that is, in Tolkien's own words, a tale about "*Faërie: the Perilous Realm itself, and the air that blows in that country*" (*MC* 114).

The poetic vagueness of a phrase like "the air that blows in that country" is the first clue to Tolkien's purpose in writing the story, for this was less to create a conventional narrative than to capture, like a butterfly in a net, the atmosphere, the essential nature of the Perilous Realm more traditionally known as Fairyland. Hence the story's lack of plot, and the absence of a "happy ending" in the accepted fairy-story sense. The hero Smith climbs no beanstalk, fights no giant, slays no dragon, brings home no golden goose or magic harp. He rescues no hapless maiden from the clutches of a witch or ogre, nor does he awaken any enchanted princess from her deathlike sleep with a kiss. He does not marry the princess. *Smith's* deliberate omission of the usual fairy tale motifs is one of the story's distinguishing characteristics.

Without such standard fairy tale machinery, the action is simple—its detractors might say simplistic. The background situation sets up the story. In search of trinkets to bake as party favors into the cake at a children's feast, the Master Cook of the village of Wootton Major finds a tarnished silver star in the bottom of the spice box. He is told by his apprentice Alf (in reality the King of Faery) that the star is "fay."[1] Though the unimaginative Cook has no notion what that means, he nevertheless puts the star into the cake batter along with all the other small prizes. A young boy at the party swallows the star without noticing, and it lies hidden, "tucked away in some place where it could not be felt" (*SWM* 19), until his tenth birthday, when it reappears to be put on his forehead. Few in the village can see the star, but all notice the sudden beauty of his voice and the unexpected grace and style of the utilitarian things he makes, for the boy becomes a blacksmith like his father before him.

With the fay-star as his entrée, Smith begins his journeys into Faery. This is the heart and purpose of the story, a highly compressed account (fifteen pages out of a total of fifty-five) of his wanderings in fairyland, the wonders he experiences there, the dangers he encounters, and the mysteries he witnesses but does not fully understand. His last visit is in response to a summons from the Queen of Faery, who gives him a message for the King, "*The time has come. Let him choose*" (*SWM* 38). The "time" is the time for Smith to relinquish the star, but with the special permission that he may choose to whom it should go next. He does so choose, and then, in bereavement and acceptance of his loss, returns to his family and ordinary life, "back to hammer and tongs" (*SWM* 52).

But where exactly has he been? The simple answer is Faery, of course, but what that word means, both to Smith and to Tolkien, takes some probing, for the narrative's gossamer surface at once conceals and reveals one of the most important words and concepts in Tolkien's lexicon—that is, Faërie,[2] the Otherworld of fairy tales and fantasy. The glancing and allusive description cited above, that Faërie is a "Perilous Realm," a country with a special "air" or atmosphere, shows only the tip of a particularly Tolkienian iceberg. Throughout his writing life (and that was a long one) *Faërie* was for Tolkien a word and an idea that embraced many meanings. It was at once a literary construct, an imaginal exercise, a make believe world, a place to go to, and an altered state of being—a series of ideas easier to picture than to explain, very like his spelling of the word.

His precedent was medieval. The word appears in Gower's *Confessio Amantis* (c. 1450), Chaucer's "Wyfe of Bath's Tale" (late fourteenth century) *Sir Orfeo*, (c. 1350), and *Sir Gawain and the Green Knight* (c. 1400), the latter two of which Tolkien edited and translated. In these, the word is used to refer variously to fairyland, and to an atmosphere of magic or enchantment: "the air that blows in that country." When the Wife of Bath asserts that in the days of King Arthur "Al was this land fulfild of fayerye" (ll. 857–60) she means the land was filled full of magic and enchantment, both as practice and as atmosphere. When Gower, in an example later cited by Tolkien, describes a young man "as he were of Faierie" (*MC* 112) he means as if he came from or belonged to Faierie, a specific place, if only an imaginary one.

A note in Tolkien's edition of *Sir Gawain and the Green Knight* calls the Green Chapel "nothing else than a fairy mound" (*SGGK* p. 86). It seems clear that Tolkien carried these interlinked meanings—the practice of magic, the place where magic is practiced, and the quality of magic that imbues that place—into his own discussion of the term in "On Fairy-stories." Some twenty-five years later, with the essay as his standard, he deployed all these meanings in *Smith of Wootton Major.*

The story began as Tolkien's effort to correct what he saw as a serious misapprehension of the word *fairy* on the part of George MacDonald, for whose story *The Golden Key* he had been asked to write an introduction. Finding MacDonald's notion of fairies not to his taste, Tolkien attempted to correct the sugary Victorian idea of fairies and fairyland as "little" and "pretty." Searching for a way to explain (once again) the difference between the popular or Disney concept of fairies as gossamer winged creatures living in daffodils, and his own much older, sterner notion of Faërie, he gave as negative example a cook who "thought of making a cake for a children's party. His chief notion was that it must be very sweet . . ." (*SWM* 75).[3]

And with the cake, now containing the fay-star, we are back to the conjunction of practice and theory, the intersection of *Smith of Wootton Major* with "On Fairy-stories." To show how patently the story is the essay's exemplar, let us look at the criteria Tolkien established in the essay. First there is sub-ject matter. Fairy-stories, Tolkien maintained, are not about fairies, but about Faërie, "the realm or state in which fairies have their being." This realm, he insisted, contains many things besides the supernatural creatures that are the usual trappings of fairy tales, the giants, dragons, fays, and dwarfs. It also holds the visible, "real" world as we know it: "the seas the sun, the moon, the sky; and the earth, and all things that are in it: tree and bird, water and stone, wine and bread, and ourselves, mortal men, when we are enchanted" (*MC* 113).

The significant terms here are *Faërie* and *enchanted,* characterizing both the quality of the magical otherworld and the change it effects in the hu-mans who interact with it. For it is the last-mentioned item in Tolkien's list, "ourselves, mortal men, when we are enchanted" who comprise the cen-ter of any good fairy tale, who supply the one essential human ingredient. "Most good 'fairy-stories'" declares Tolkien, "are about the *aventures* of men in the Perilous Realm" (*MC* 113). This is explicitly the case with *Smith of Wootton Major.* The story's central character, the Smith whose craft is also his name, is the enchanted mortal man, the reader's guide into the Perilous Realm. Smith himself, however, has no guide, nor indeed any stated reason for going. He has no goal, no quest, no pot of gold or giant's daughter to win. Unlike the hero of a typical *echtra,* a Celtic Otherworld journey, he follows no beckoning supernatural figure; nor like some does he stumble into Faery by accident. He goes there with intent but no purpose, content simply to wander and experience and marvel. He can and does go where he will, his passport the fay-star that came to him in his slice of cake.

The function of the star is limited, however. It will conduct, but not ex-plain. Smith can explore, but is never given any clue to the marvels and mys-teries he encounters. He is a tourist without a guidebook. True for the hero of the story, this is equally true for the reader, who wandering through Faery with Smith, experiences but has no way to understand the wonders there seen. The story depicts, but does not elucidate. In accord with its Faery set-ting, the tale enacts mysteries but declines to solve them. In this regard, *Smith of Wootton Major* stands as Tolkien's severest, most uncompromis-ing, least accessible piece of fiction, stubbornly refusing like his Faery it-self to give the reader any key with which to unlock its secrets. And that is precisely the point. The land of Faery is what it is, no more and no less. It is entire and other and self-sufficient, and has no need to explain itself to any outsider. In the essay (his second on the subject) that Tolkien wrote to ac-company his story, he noted that "Faery is a vast world in its own right, that does not depend for its existence upon Men, and which is not primarily nor indeed principally concerned with Men" (*SWM* 93).

How does this fit with the second criterion, the necessary quality of the story? Tolkien is explicit that fairy-stories must create a Secondary World inside of which all that occurs must have both "a quality of strangeness and wonder," and "the inner consistency of reality" such that however marvelous the sights or events, they can command "Secondary Belief," and the reader can accept them as credible (*MC* 139, 138). Yet in *Smith of Wootton Major* Tolkien has gone to some lengths to create a world whose chief quality seems to be its incomprehensibility to outsiders. His dictum in "On Fairy-stories" that to make a world where a green sun will be believable will take not just imagination but elvish craft (*MC* 140) seems in direct opposition to *Smith*, for without a credible explanation for that story's wonders, just what is their "inner consistency"? How can we as readers believe them? Why should we? Just how skilled was Tolkien at elvish craft? What is his green sun?

I suggest that the green sun in *Smith of Wootton Major* is the fay-star which conveys Smith, and with him the reader, on the journeys into the story's Faery. If readers accept the star, they will accept as well the rules governing the Perilous Realm to which it gives access. The mystery of the star is validated first by the word of the Apprentice, a mysterious figure who knows something about the star that the Master Cook does not know, and second by the patronizing skepticism of the Master Cook, who is clearly incapable of understanding anything beyond the ordinary and precious little even of that. Readerly sympathy is aroused for the one, and contemptuous dislike for the other. When the star reappears on Smith's forehead, it is perceived by only a few, chiefly Smith's own family, but also by the reader, who is thereby enlisted as one of the perceptive few and one of the chosen.

Having a star as the magic talisman was a wise choice. It was also Tolkien's second choice, as the various drafts of the story make clear. His first candidate for the magic trinket was a ring which the boy would then wear on his finger. It did not take long for Tolkien to realize that this particular image carried too much baggage. It would inevitably be associated with the Ruling Ring of his great work *The Lord of the Rings* and thereby carry all that token's negative associations of evil and power and dominance. The switch from ring to star was not, however, a mere substitution; it changed subtly the direction and quality of the magic, for the very word *star* carries connotations of *unearthly, inhuman, unattainable,* all of which carry over from the star itself to the Faery world it represents.

Last of all Tolkien's criteria, and most complex in execution, is the attitude of the story, first internally toward the events and characters within it, and second externally toward the reader for whom it must "command Secondary Belief." For just as the reader looks at, enters in to the story, so the story looks at, and both challenges and engages the reader. Fairy-stories, Tolkien wrote, have three faces: "the Mystical towards the Supernatural; the Magical towards Nature; and the Mirror of scorn and pity towards Man" (*MC* 125). Has *Smith of Wootton Major* these three faces? Where and how are they manifest?

Undoubtedly the story has a mystical face towards the supernatural, and the fay star conveys its expression. If we accept the dictionary definition of *mystical* as "suggesting the existence of realities beyond intellectual apprehension" (*American Heritage Dictionary*) it is certainly possible to see exactly this in Tolkien's depiction of the supernatural elements in his story. Although we have seen how Tolkien persuades his readers to accept the presence and power of the star, the reality that lies behind it, and the reason for its existence are nowhere explained.

Having swallowed it at the party, the boy Smith does not notice what has become of it, waiting patiently inside him until its day will come. On his tenth birthday the boy wakes early and hears the dawn-song of birds beginning far away, coming towards him, rushing over him and passing on "like a wave of music into the West. He begins to sing, "high and clear, in strange words that he seemed to know by heart" (*SWM* 20), and in that moment the star falls out of his mouth. Catching it, he claps his hand to his forehead, and there the star stays "for many years." The light of the star passes into his eyes, and his voice, "which had begun to grow beautiful as the star came to him, became ever more beautiful as he grew up" (20). Possession of the star admits Smith to Faery, but we are not told how; nor are we shown the passage from one reality to the other, contiguous though they seem. The star also protects him, though again we are not told how, and only obliquely from what. "The Lesser Evils avoided the star, and from the Greater Evils he was guarded" (*SWM* 24). The capital letters underscore but do not explain the dangers inherent in Tolkien's Perilous Realm, and suggest a complex and unfathomable range of powers against which the star is Smith's defense.

Of the Magical face toward nature, there are a number of examples, perhaps the most awe-inspiring being Tolkien's description of the Sea of Windless Storm with its silent waves rolling endlessly out of Unlight. Surely the most benign is the flower placed in Smith's hair by the elven maiden (actually the Queen of Faery), who dances with him. "The flower did not wither or grow dim," says the story, and Smith makes a casket in which to keep it and it is handed down in his family, a magical Living Flower, for many generations (*SWM* 35). Most impressive is the King's Tree, springing up out of a hill of shadow "tower upon tower" into the sky with a light in it like the sun at noon, with leaves and flowers and fruit growing simultaneously on its boughs (*SWM* 28). The Tree has at once a magical nature and a natural magic that derives from its very being as a tree, albeit a superlative one.

And finally and perhaps most importantly, there is the Mirror of scorn and pity toward Man. This face has a more complex expression than the other two, for scorn and pity, while at first glance they seem to be separate emotions, are not always that easy to distinguish from one another. Certainly the story displays scorn toward Nokes the Master Cook, whose own patronizing (not quite pitying) scorn for his Apprentice Alf ("elf") betokens his inability to see beyond the mundane. The original of Nokes is, of course, the cook in Tolkien's introduction to *The Golden Key,* whose notion of a very sweet cake as most suitable for children is the measure of his ignorance of the deeper implications of Faery. Nokes unwittingly disobeys one of the strictest rules in Tolkien's essay, thereby invoking it against himself. "There is one proviso: if there is any satire present in the tale, one thing must not be made fun of, the magic itself. That must in that story be taken seriously, neither laughed at nor explained away" (*MC* 114). Nokes is Tolkien's negative example. He makes fun of the star and belittles its magic, thus turning the satire against himself and inadvertently making him the butt of his own joke.

Moreover, on two separate occasions, in the village scenes that bracket Smith's journeys into Faery, Alf himself shows both scorn and pity for Nokes. There is scorn in his speakingly silent response to Nokes' smirks and heavy-handed jokes on the subject of *fairy* at the party, and at the end of the story he is first over-polite in listening patiently to Nokes' musings on what became of the star, and then scathing in his rebuke: "You are a vain old fraud, fat, idle and sly" (*SWM* 59). Alf's final revelation of himself as the King of Faery leaves Nokes cowed and cringing. There is pity in his final gift to the old man, who has joked that if one of Alf's "fairy friends. . . . waves his little wand and makes me thin again, I'll think better of him" (*SWM* 58). The gift is even then one that Nokes cannot understand and so talks himself out of accepting it with gratitude, reasoning that, "If you stop eating you grow thinner. That's natural. Stands to reason. There ain't no magic in it" (*SWM* 60)

But there is a darker, bleaker face shining the mirror of scorn and pity, this time on Smith himself. The most complex and perplexing episode in *Smith of Wootton Major*—Smith's venture onto the Lake of Tears,[4] its consequences, and the subsequent conversation between Smith and the birch tree—reveals as nothing else in the story Smith's ignorance of the deeper implications of the perilous realm of Faery, what Tolkien's essay calls its "pitfalls for the unwary and dungeons for the overbold." And both unwary and overbold Smith certainly is when he sets his foot on the lake and is unexpectedly and violently attacked for his trespass. He is "filled with wonder" at the shapes of flame and the fiery creatures he sees in the lake's "immeasurable depth," and tries the water with his foot, only to find that it is "harder than stone and sleeker than glass" (*SWM* 29).

Emboldened—we might say overboldened—Smith steps onto the surface and promptly falls, and with a sound like winter ice cracking with cold the lake itself gives a ringing boom that wakes the Wild Wind. Swept ashore and driven up the slopes by the Wind, Smith clings to a birch tree that, bent double by the force of the Wind, encloses him in its branches. When the Wind passes on, Smith sees that the birch is naked to the elements, its boughs having been stripped of their leaves by the blast. The birch weeps, its tears falling "like rain" from its branches. Both grateful for his rescue and contrite at the tree's sacrifice, Smith commends the birch. The scene and its attendant dialogue, among the least sentimental in the entire Tolkien corpus, reveal— as much to the reader as to Smith—ignorance of and unimportance to the larger operations of Faery that is the lot of "ourselves, mortal men, when we are enchanted."

> He set his hand upon its white bark, saying: "Blessed be the birch! What can I do to make amends or give thanks?" He felt the answer of the tree pass up from his hand: "Nothing," it said. "Go away! The Wind is hunting you. You do not belong here. Go away and never return!" (*SWM* 30)

Speaking, it seems clear, for Tolkien, the tree does not explain to Smith what he has done wrong, only tells him the bitter truth—that he does not belong in Faery. He has been a visitor and is now a trespasser. The scorn and pity directed at Smith in this episode are those of Faery itself, which needs no visitors and encourages no trespassers. Though Smith disobeys the birch tree's injunction against returning, and does in fact visit Faery again, it is with the knowledge that he is there on sufferance, and that his passport may be revoked. This, of course is exactly what happens, and makes the story's and Tolkien's final and major point.

Much critical speculation has been expended on the possible presence of autobiographical elements in the story, for the temptation, if one knows anything at all about Tolkien's life and work, is to see the author in the protagonist. If Tolkien's earlier short story "Leaf by Niggle" chronicles the struggles of the artistic temperament with the demands of daily life, *Smith of Wootton Major* can be read as dramatizing the relationship of the artist with the world of imagination, the ongoing engagement of the creator with the act of creation. In this regard, the story has been called Tolkien's farewell to his art, his Prospero speech. He himself called it "an old man's story, filled with the presage of bereavement," and it is not difficult to identify the bereavement that Smith feels on giving up the star with what may have been Tolkien's heartache toward the end of his life that his best years were spent, his best work was behind him. Humphrey Carpenter suggests that the "appalling depths of gloom" into which Tolkien sank from time to time toward the end of his life, coupled with his "growing grief at the approach of old age," led him to write *Smith of Wootton Major* (Carpenter, 242).

This is an easy and obvious connection to make, and without doubt a valid one. I do not challenge it. Nevertheless, an equally significant autobiographical element may reside in Tolkien's first-hand account of what it is like to wander in Faery (read "the realm of imagination") and his deliberate refusal to unlock for Smith or the reader the mysteries of the Perilous Realm. Describing himself in "On Fairy-stories" as "hardly more than a wandering explorer (or trespasser) in the land, full of wonder but not of information," he had gone on to say that although,

> In that realm a man may, perhaps, count himself fortunate to have wandered . . . its very richness and strangeness tie the tongue of a traveler who would report them. And while he is there it is dangerous for him to ask too many questions, lest the gates be shut and the keys be lost. (*MC* 109)

Wandering explorer. Trespasser. Shut gates. Lost keys. These words and phrases capture as much for Tolkien as for Smith the Faery of *Smith of Wootton Major.* The figure of the Smith as maker, as craftsman, wandering in the enchanted world of Faery, apprehending marvels but not comprehending them, most certainly embodies for himself as well as his author the tongue-tied traveler who would report them, as Tolkien had tried to do. Smith exemplifies for his creator the instinct without understanding that is the lot of the artist, who can use imagination and even to some degree direct it, but who cannot analyze it or explain its workings. For, as Tolkien said of *Beowulf,* "myth is alive at once and in all its parts, and dies before it can be dissected" (*MC* 15). Like Smith, Tolkien knew well enough that his art was a gift and not a purchase, that it could be polished by skill but never replaced by it. He knew that like the fay-star it came in its own time, unsought and unforced, and that it could not be bought or traded or commanded, but only accepted with gratitude for its presence and used with reverence for its power.

Smith of Wootton Major is thus a Faërie story in Tolkien's purest sense of that word. It is "a tale about *Faërie,* the Perilous Realm itself, and the air that blows in that country."

The Footsteps of Ælfwine

> '*Ælfwine* elf-friend? That at any rate is what their more or less literal translation comes to. Though as most of you will know . . . these two-part names are pretty conventional, and not too much can be built on their literal meaning.'
>
> 'But they must originally have been made to have a meaning,' said Ramer.
> —*The Notion Club Papers*

Although now unrecoverable except as elements of myth and folklore, the presence of elves in the world, attested to by numerous mentions in Norse and Anglo-Saxon poetry and by the very existence of the word—Norse *alf*, Anglo-Saxon *ælf*—was at one time a part of the pagan belief system of Northern Europe. It follows, then, that however conventional it may since have become, the name *Ælfwine*, a compound combining the Anglo-Saxon word for "elf" with the word for "friend," must, as Ramer suggests above, have originally had a literal meaning, describing or alluding to one who was in actuality an elf-friend. Although Ælfwine continued to be a proper name long after belief in elves had dwindled to folk-superstition, the word itself no longer conveys the old meaning or indeed any meaning at all except to a student of onomastics. It has no literal reference, nor even a metaphoric one. In its modern appearance it is now a mere fossil, one of the myriad words in English or any language whose bones are preserved as shape and sound, but whose living embodiment has decayed and fallen away. This is not the case, however, in the fictive world of Tolkien's mythology, wherein Elves are a viable species inhabiting Middle-earth, and in which the original meaning of the name is restored. Tolkien has re-imagined the concept of elf-friend, created a world in which such a figure could live and move, and bestowed the name or epithet on some of his most memorable characters.

Readers of *The Lord of the Rings* first meet the term in its English translation early in that story, in an exchange that at first reading seems of little significance. Responding to Frodo's Elvish greeting, *"Elen síla lúmenn' omen-tielvo,"* the Elf Gildor replies, "Hail, Elf-friend!" At this point in the story it seems to be simply polite elf-hobbit talk. (*FR* I, iii, 90). Even when, in a later, more serious moment, Gildor says to Frodo, "I name you Elf-friend," this still seems largely a formal rather than a substantive locution (94). With every repetition, however, the meaning deepens, and when, in the house of Tom Bombadil, Goldberry says to Frodo "I see you are an elf-friend; the light in your eyes and the ring in your voice tells it" (135), we begin to realize that more than politeness is involved; elf-friend is some kind of special identity. This is confirmed when, still later, the Elf Legolas introduces Aragorn to Haldir of Lórien as "an Elf-friend of the folk of Westernesse" (*FR* II, vi, 357).

However, it is not until the Council of Elrond that we discover that the phrase has a history beyond the present moment. Formally accepting his of-fer to carry the Ring to Mount Doom, Elrond Halfelven tells Frodo, "though all the mighty elf-friends of old, Hador, and Húrin, and Túrin, and Beren himself were assembled together, your seat should be among them" (*FR* II, ii, 284). What seemed at first a polite form of address, later a complimentary epithet, can now be seen as the sign of election to a special company. None-theless, for the first twenty years of the story's publication there was little evi-dence beyond what I have cited to indicate to readers that the phrase carried any extra meaning beyond the context of the immediate narrative. Not until *The Silmarillion* was published in 1977 did the figures of Beren and Túrin and Húrin truly come to life and take their proper places in the legendarium. And only since the appearance of Tolkien's full mythology in The History of Middle-earth has been possible to see all of the Elf-friends in a larger context, and to understand the name and some of the most memorable of those who bear it as emblems of a continuing and developing concept.

With the entire range of Tolkien's mythology now accessible, we can at last survey the full scope of Tolkien's treatment of the Elf-friend figure, and begin to appreciate its place and importance in the unfolding narrative. We know now that Frodo, Aragorn, even Húrin and Túrin and Beren, are only a few out of many Elf-friends. We know as well, that however formally or informally the epithet is bestowed, it is more than a polite term of address. It is at once the name, the description, and the function of one of that history's earliest and most multiform figures, a figure who is both inside and outside the story, who is at once a character in the drama and a frame for the narrative.

The list of Elf-friend figures who fill this role stretches over the whole of Tolkien's mythology. In addition to those cited in *The Lord of the Rings* either explicitly or implicitly (for we must surely include Bilbo among them), there are Ælfwine the Mariner and his alter ego, Eriol the Mariner, from Tolkien's earliest work *The Book of Lost Tales*. From his two unfinished time-travel stories *The Lost Road* and *The Notion Club Papers* there are the Númenorean Elendil (Quenya for Elf-friend) and his English avatars Alboin Errol and Alwin Lowdham, as well as Lowdham's father, old Edwin Lowdham (also and not coincidentally a mariner). And in Tolkien's last short story *Smith of Wootton Major*, the Elf-friends include not just Smith himself, but also his mysterious grandfather, the first Master Cook. These figures have widely different characteristics and fulfill a variety of different plot functions in the stories in which they appear, but the important position they all share is that of the link, the connector or mediator between the "real" or natural world and the world of Faërie—the super-natural world of myth and the imagination.

Why is such a link necessary? Why not just tell the story and allow it to stand on its own? First, because to Tolkien the value of a story is in its transmission as well as in its existence. Indeed, its transmission *is* its existence. The tale only exists in the telling. And for the telling there has to be a narrator, a link between the event and the hearer or reader. "I . . . Aneirin . . . sang *The Gododdin*" (*Gododdin*, 32). So proclaims the poetic voice in an early medieval battle-poem. Aneirin was a sixth-century bard, but the earliest existing text of his song is in the thirteenth-century *Book of Aneirin*. The poem survives today not just because Aneirin sang it but because others heard it and finally some hearer wrote it down. So it was transmitted and so it survived. The story which is *The Lord of the Rings* would not survive today (so runs the conceit) if Bilbo had not begun his Book nor Frodo continued it. Tolkien was too knowledgeable a story-teller not to recognize and affirm the importance of the Teller to the Tale.

Nevertheless, while the link is the crucial element in the transmission, we can still ask in Tolkien's case why the linking figure should be specifically an Elf-friend. Tolkien could easily have used some other kind of mediator as a way into his mythology—a pseudo-editor, or a fictive scholar-collector of old stories. In other circumstances, for example the Introduction to *The Adventures of Tom Bombadil* or the editorial frame for *The Notion Club Papers*, he did just that. What can an Elf-friend do for the story beyond establishing the validity of the material, a function that these other devices also fulfill? A possible answer is that, as the name implies, the Elf-friend can participate in both worlds, whereas by definition an editor or scholar can be in only one. An editor, a collector, a scholar, would be a complete outsider, and the result would be not stories but artifacts, suffering from the same kind of fossilization that overtook the name Ælfwine. Such a figure would be excavating for artifacts, not immediately experiencing myth. In contrast, the Elf-friend— not an Elf but a friend of Elves—is neither wholly outside nor completely inside but in between, and thus qualifies as a true mediator.

The earliest of Tolkien's Elf-friend figures functions as just such a mediator in *The Book of Lost Tales*. Originally he was neither called Elf-friend nor
named Ælfwine, but Eriol, a name of Tolkien's own invention. In keeping
with his early intention to link his mythology to English myth and history
Tolkien also gave him several Old English epithets. According to Christopher Tolkien he was "named by the Gnomes [later the Noldor] *Angol,* after
the regions of his home. *Angol* is also "given as the Gnomish equivalent of
Eriollo," and probably refers to "the ancient homeland of the 'English' before
their migration across the North Sea to Britain" (*LT* I, 24). So to begin with
(although in the text the name is translated as "one who dreams alone"),
Eriol in its earliest conception may have been simply the Elvish word for
English. As if these names were not sufficient, Tolkien gave the figure still
another name. Eriol, we are told, "called himself *Wæfre,*" an Old English
word meaning "restless, wandering" (23).

In the preliminary stages of the myth, before Tolkien had settled on
Ælfwine, the epithet *Wæfre* may have carried the greater significance, for
it recalls Eriol-Wæfre's real-myth counterpart Gangleri (Old Norse "wanderer") in a book that Tolkien knew well, Snorri Sturluson's 13th century
Prose *Edda,* one of the primary sources for Norse mythology. An Icelandic
scholar-politician and a committed Christian, Snorri knew but clearly did
not believe in the pagan myths which Christianity had superseded. Yet he
felt that the old gods and heroes, and the kennings, the poetic figures of
speech, which characterized them, were the proper material for poetry. He
wanted to educate the poets of his time, and in so doing he preserved for
them and for posterity one of the world's great mythologies.

Snorri's device for re-introducing these myths to his Christian audience
was to create a fictive interlocutor, a pagan king called Gylfi who, disguised
as Gangleri "the Wanderer," traveled to the world of the gods in search of
information. The *Edda*'s first and most comprehensive section, *Gylfaginning*
("The Deluding of Gylfi"), consists of Gangleri's interrogation of three mysterious figures—Hár (High One), Jafnhár (Just-as-High), and þrið (Third)—
who answer his questions by giving their account of creation, the nature of
the world, and the names, natures, and adventures of its gods and goddesses.
Gangleri thus becomes the primary recipient of the tales, and through him
Snorri gives his readers quite a lively account of Norse mythology while
safely maintaining his own distance from it.

Eriol-Wæfre performs the same service for Tolkien. Described as "a man
of great curiosity," and like Gangleri a wanderer, Eriol the mariner voyages
to the isle of Tol Eressëa, where he questions the Gnomes about their history. He thus functions as the quasi-insider, the man on the scene who is yet
a stranger and can be the primary recipient for the stories, allowing Tolkien

the author to be discreetly invisible. Moreover, the fact that both *Gangleri* and *Wæfre* mean "wanderer" or "wandering," the circumstance that both are epithets or assumed identities—these parallels suggest deliberate borrowing, as does the question-and-answer format, a conventional medieval literary technique used by Snorri and re-used by Tolkien.

As cues for the Norse stories, Gangleri asks such questions as: "Who is the foremost or oldest of all the gods?" "What was the origin of all things?" "How did they begin?" "What is the way from earth to heaven?" "What goddesses are there?" Snorri emphasize the importance of the gods' replies by having Gangleri exclaim, "Great tidings [literally translated from Icelandic *mikil tiðindi*] I'm hearing now." Eriol's questions follow a strikingly similar format: "Tell me of this island . . ." (*LT* I,18); "Who be these Valar; are they the Gods?" (45); "Who was Ilúvatar?" (49). And most important of all: "Tell me . . . what was the Music of the Ainur?" (49). Tolkien underscores the significance of the dialogue by putting in the mouth of Eriol a phrase so like the one Snorri gives to Gangleri that the similarity can hardly be accident: "Great are these tidings" (64).

The question about the Music of the Aiur deserves special notice, chiefly for the comment it elicits from Christopher Tolkien as editor: "Thus it was that the *Ainulindalë* was first to be heard by mortal ears, as Eriol sat in a sunlit garden in Tol Eressëa" (*LT* I, 49). The phrase "by mortal ears" is the key, for Eriol is to be the witness, the repositor and transmitter of these stories, the link between their Elven tellers and the humans who will hear (and read) the tales. Christopher Tolkien writes of Eriol that:

> his role was at first to be more important than (what it afterwards became) simply that of a man of later days who came to 'the land of the Fairies' and there acquired lost or hidden knowledge which he afterwards reported in his own tongue: at first, Eriol was to be an important element in the fairy-history itself—the witness of the ruin of Elvish Tol Eressëa. (*LT* I, 23)

As significant as "by mortal ears" is the word *witness,* for the act of witnessing leads the reader into the story. It is his role as witness which characterizes this Elf-friend figure.

That the witness should be somehow alien to the mythology described is important, for as an engaged outsider he can link the "outside" reader or hearer to the "inside" culture which generates the myths. Indeed, the word *mythology,* which means "a collection of myths" also means "the systematic collection and study of myths" (*American Heritage Dictionary*), and describes both the process and the product. In the second definition especially, the word is explicitly an outsider's term used by myth-scholars to de-

scribe the stories of other peoples' cultures—their origin-myths, hero-leg-
ends, early history, and religious beliefs. Emphasizing "the *study* of myth,"
as opposed to its experience or belief, this meaning of the word implies a
distance from the society described within the stories. As Snorri's author-
ship of the *Edda* gives evidence, myth frequently find their way into print
because somebody who may no longer believes them wants to retell them to
somebody else who may not believe them either.

The specific function of Gangleri is to have (like many in Snorri's reading
audience) no previous knowledge of the stories he hears. Thus he is constantly rebuked by High One, Just-as-High, and Third for not being "a well-
informed man," one who by definition ought to know the stories of his own
world. But if Gangleri was not well-informed, Snorri's audience must have
been even less so, for his desire to amend their ignorance led to his writing
of the book. Compendious mythologies, then, are not tales recounted by a
story-teller to a spellbound audience sitting at a fire on a winter's night. They
are instead collections of those tales; they have become texts transmitted by
"authorities"—by anthropologists, philologist, historians, folklorists—all of
them scholars of one kind or another who supply the texts with footnotes
and learned commentary, all of them hearing and recording someone else's
stories. In other words, outsiders.

By definition, then, Tolkien as author of a mythology must be such an
outsider. An entire primary mythology can not be written, it can only be
written *down* or written *about*. Here was the problem for Tolkien as myth-
fabricator. His authorial voice, directly transmitting the narrative, would
reveal his mythology as art, not living myth. He could be a Snorri but he
needed a Gangleri, a credible, non-scholarly observer who could be inside
the story but not of it, and who could both experience and explain it. And so
to give his Elven mythology what he called the "inner consistency of reality,"
he created as his Gangleri not an Elf but an Elf-friend, someone who could,
within the framework of the story, become the receiving consciousness for
a myth foreign to his own experience.

Tolkien's original question-and-answer device was eventually discarded,
as were Eriol's multiple by-names. But the figure itself was retained. In the
process of many revisions he became more clearly English (or proto-English)
and his name settled down as Ælfwine, Elf-friend. But whatever his name,
his function as a witness and connecting device remained an essential part
of the plan. Christopher Tolkien emphasizes the centrality of this character
to Tolkien's original design.

> From the beginning of this history, the story of the Englishman Ælfwine,
> also called Eriol, who links by his strange voyage the vanished world of the

Elves with the lives of later men, has constantly appeared. So in the last words of the *Quenta Noldorinwa* (IV. 165) it is said:

To Men of the race of Eärendel have they [*the tales of the Quenta*] at times been told, and most to Eriol, who alone of the mortals of later days, and yet now long ago, sailed to the Lonely Isle, and came back to the land of Leithien [*Britain*] where he lived, and remembered things that he heard in fair Cortirion, the city of the Elves in Tol Eresseä. (*SD* 279–80)

Over the course of time and in the labor of countless revisions, Tolkien refined his concept, and in the process this elaborate framework, like the rather cumbersome question-and-answer format, gradually diminished in importance. "All this," notes Christopher Tolkien, "was to fall away afterwards from the developing mythology; but Ælfwine left many marks on its pages before he too finally disappeared" (*LT* II, 327). Those marks on the pages are worth our scrutiny, for as Frodo Baggins' courtesy title makes clear, the figure of Ælfwine took on a life beyond its original context, and the concept of the Elf-friend walked the pages of Tolkien's fiction from then on. The many marks left by Ælfwine are the footprints of one who never completely vanished from Tolkien's mythology, a witness and participant who observes, often experiences, and in some fashion transmits to others the stories in which he appears.

It is in this capacity that the Elf-friend figure acts as a semi-transparent mask for the real Elf-friend, who is actually Tolkien himself. The paradox of Tolkien as author is that he was as it were his own Gangleri, his own link to Faërie. Recall that he stated on a number of occasions that he was not entirely inventing, but was indeed in some sense receiving the tales that made up his mythology. "They arose in my mind as 'given' things and as they came, separately, so too the links grew. . . . always I had the sense of recording what was already 'there', somewhere: not of 'inventing'" (*Letters* 145). To call someone "Elf-friend," as Gildor does Frodo, as Tolkien does other, later characters, was to confer on that character something of Tolkien's own position as hearer and recorder of a mythology which, he maintained, "arose" in his mind as an unfolding narrative somehow external to his imagination.

In whatever tale he appeared, then, and whatever his particular character in the story, the Elf-friend figure provided a fictive persona through whose agency the author Tolkien could convey the stories to the reader and at the same time gratify some of his own most deeply held desires—to participate in myth first-hand, to converse with other kinds of beings, to visit other dimensions of time and space, to experience—in human form and in human terms—something of the believer's sense of awe and wonder at the

supernatural. Ælfwine provided Tolkien a way to participate in his own mythology. And over time, both the name and the concept had a shifting and
variable relationship to his developing vision.

Let us look now at some representative Elf-friends, and explore how each
figure works in his particular story. The original Elf-friend and earliest Ælfwine figure, whom I will call Eriol-Ælfwine, was, as we have seen, primarily
a framing device, providing an occasion for Tolkien's elven-fairy narrator to
launch the mythology. Eriol-Ælfwine was to be the link between Elven myth
and English myth and history. However, the shifts and developments undergone by this figure over the course of the mythology are a story in themselves, a complex and at times perplexing history. Of his father's treatment
of this figure Christopher Tolkien says, "The 'Eriol-story' is in fact among the
knottiest and most obscure matters in the whole history of Middle-earth and
Aman" (*LT* I, 23).[1] While Eriol-Ælfwine was part of Tolkien's vision from the
very first, Tolkien never quite settled on what to do with him, never quite
let go of him, but continually worked and re-worked his story. "Ælfwine as
recorder and pupil was still present in my father's writings," Christopher Tolkien comments, "after the completion of *The Lord of the Rings*" (*LR* 21).

To round out what we already know of this most complicated character,
who appears and reappears over several volumes of *The History of Middle-
earth*, I can do no better than to quote in full Christopher Tolkien's summing
up, which condenses to a manageable minimum the essential elements:

[Ælfwine] is seen in Tavrobel of Tol Eressëa translating *The Annals of Valinor* and *The Annals of Beleriand* from the work of Pengolod the Wise
of Gondolin, and parts of his Anglo-Saxon text are preserved (IV. 263,
281 ff.); the *Ainulindalë* was spoken to him by Rúmil of Tún (V.156); the
Lhammas of Pengolod was seen by Ælfwine 'when he came into the West'
(V.167). To the *Quenta Silmarillion* his note is appended (V.203): 'The
work of Pengolod I learned much by heart, and turned into my tongue,
some during my sojourn in the West, but most after my return to Britain';.
. . . going back to one form of the old story *Ælfwine of England* (II. 322 and
note 42), was the story that Ælfwine never set foot on the Lonely Isle. So
in my father's sketches for those further reaches of *The Lost Road* that he
never wrote, Ælfwine on the one hand (V.78) awakes on the beach of the
Lonely Isle 'to find the ship being drawn by people walking on the water',
and there in Eressëa he 'is told the Lost Tales'; but in other notes of that
time (V. 80), after 'the vision of Eressëa'. the 'west wind blows them back',
and they come to shore in Ireland. In the note to the final version of the
poem *The Song of Ælfwine* (a version which I suggested was 'probably

from the years after *The Lord of the Rings,* though it might be associated with *The Notion Club Papers* of 1945, V.100) it is told (V.103):

Ælfwine (Elf-friend) was a seaman of England of old who, being driven out to sea from the coast of Erin, passed into the deep waters of the West, and according to legend by some strange chance or grace found the 'straight road' of the Elvenfolk and came at last to the Isle of Eressëa in Elvenhome. Or maybe, as some say, alone in the waters, hungry and athirst, he fell into a trance and was granted a vision of that isle as it once had been, ere a West-wind arose and drove him back to Middle-earth. (*SD* 280)

With this as background, we may for the moment leave Eriol-Ælfwine on the Straight Road, and turn to other Elf-friend figures. Alboin Errol of *The Lost Road,* the first of Tolkien's time-travel stories, written probably in 1936 or 37,[2] was to be, like Eriol-Ælfwine, the link between present-day England and Tolkien's own Númenor, where, like the original Eriol, he was to be the witness to its downfall. Alboin is both functionally and nominally an Elf-friend, for his name, as Tolkien is careful to make clear, is simply updated from the Anglo-Saxon Ælfwine to the medieval Lombardic form. More-over, his family surname Errol is, as Christopher Tolkien points out, too close to Eriol to be happenstance. When Alboin recites for his father, Oswin Errol, a scrap of Anglo-Saxon verse about Ælfwine Wídlást—"Ælfwine the far-travelled"—Oswin replies "good for Ælfwine-Alboin" (*LR* 44), leaving unclear (perhaps deliberately so) whether in linking the names he is refer-ring to the Anglo-Saxon figure or to his own son or to both at once. When later on in a dream Alboin hears a voice announcing itself as "Elendil, that is in Eressëan 'Elf-friend,'" and identifying the speaker as "the father of many fathers before you" (48), we are clearly meant to understand that, in a sense, this is Ælfwine speaking to Ælfwine, the Númenorean Elf-friend addressing his modern-day avatar and counterpart.

The next Elf-friend to be considered is Alwin Arundel (Arry) Lowdham of Tolkien's second time-travel story, *The Notion Club Papers,* written over the winter of 1945–46.[3] According to Lowdham, his father wanted to name him Ælfwine but was persuaded to update the name to modern English Alwin. The narrative goes into some detail over the meaning of the name, as the epigraph to the present study gives evidence. To make Lowdham's role perfectly clear, Tolkien has one of the members of the Notion Club refer to him (although he is actually quite a large man) as "your little Elf-friend" (*SD* 245). Lowdham was to perform much the same function in this later story as Alboin was to perform in his, that is, to link England and Númenor and be the witness to Númenor's downfall. A far more vivid character than the quiet and retiring Alboin, Lowdham is a dramatic, almost haunted link with Númenor, for his memory-flashbacks into Middle-earth mythology torture him as much as they tease the reader with portentous glimpses of half-remembered history.

Describing his dream-visions of the Eagles of the Lords of the West to his fellow Notion Club members, Lowdham tells them, not altogether happily, "They [the eagles] shake me badly when I see them. I could, I could—I feel I could tell some great tale of Númenor" (238). The "great tale" is Tolkien's narrative goal and climax, the Drowning of Anadûne or the Downfall of Númenor, and like Alboin Errol before him, Alwin Lowdham is to be both the means of arriving at the event and the witness to (and probable recorder of) the Downfall itself. Both time-travel stories make it clear that Alboin and Lowdham are explicitly meant to be descended from and retain the race-memory of Tolkien's Númenorean Ælfwine-figure, Elendil.

Lowdham's account to the Notion Club of his dream of Ælfwine is continued in several unfinished outlines and sketches. One note, offering insight into the care with which Tolkien considered his theoretical substructure, explains:

> The theory is that the sight and memory goes on with *descendants* of Elendil and Voronwë (= Tréowine) but *not* reincarnation; they are different people even if they still resemble one another in some ways even after a lapse of many generations. (*SD* 278)

Elendil and Voronwë are to be the Númenorean ancestors of Anglo-Saxon Ælfwine and Tréowine, who are in turn ancestors of the modern-day Lowdham and his friend Jeremy. All three pairs apparently share the same, serially inherited race-memory.

As Tolkien's notes show, the tantalizing, fragmentary accounts of Ælfwine of England are clear efforts to link not just England and Númenor, but stories of the past with present events. Christopher Tolkien writes:

> With . . . a 'time-travel' story in which the very significant figure of the Anglo-Saxon Ælfwine would be both 'extended' into the future, into the twentieth century, and 'extended' also into a many-layered past, my father was envisaging a massive and explicit linking of his own legends with those of many other places and times: all concerned with the stories and the dreams of peoples who dwelt by the coasts of the great Western Sea. (*LR* 98)

The briefest of jotted notes continue Tolkien's grand design, unfortunately never realized, part of which has Ælfwine and Tréowine sailing westward:

> Tréowine sees the straight road and the world plunging down. Ælfwine's vessel seems to be taking the straight road and falls [sic] in a swoon of fear and exhaustion.
>
> Ælfwine gets view of the Book of Stories; and writes down what he can remember.
>
> Later fleeting visions.
>
> Beleriand tale.
>
> Sojourn in Númenor before and during the fall ends with *Elendil* and *Voronwë* fleeing on a hill of water into the dark with Eagles and lightning pursuing them. Elendil has a book which he has written.
>
> His descendants get glimpses of it.
>
> Ælfwine has one. (*SD* 279)

Although his story was never fully realized in any of its versions, Ælfwine of England left his imprint on the shape of the mythology in the form of the "book," the fictive frame device, which gradually became absorbed into the narrative itself. Elendil's book, of which his descendants get glimpses, and which is probably the item referred to in Tolkien's note "Ælfwine has one," is undoubtedly the text which preserves the stories. The similarity in function between Elendil's book and the extended memoir of Bilbo Baggins, left for his nephew Frodo to finish and labeled *Translations from the Elvish* "by B. B.," is unmistakable. Bilbo's book becomes the Red Book of Westmarch and is the presumed source for both *The Hobbit* and *The Lord of the Rings*.

To anyone acquainted with medieval literature, Tolkien's choice of title will recall the actual Red Book of Hergest, an early source of Welsh myth and history which together with the Black Book of Carmarthen, the Book of Aneirin, and the Book of Taliesin make up the venerable Four Ancient Books of Wales, a series of manuscripts in various hands dating from the twelfth to the fifteenth centuries. The Red Book of Hergest, now housed in Jesus College, Oxford, is a compilation of prose and verse covering aspects of Welsh myth, legend, and history from the sixth century to the mid-fifteenth.

The fictive rationale for Tolkien's Red Book of Westmarch is that it is just such a compilation, started by Bilbo, continued by Frodo, and completed by various other hands. The actual frame device is confined to the Prologue, which is, in fact, not the book but a commentary *about* the book. By this time the "book" as such, and the Elf-friend character(s) are no longer a simple frame. Not only are they deeply woven into the fabric of the story, they have in fact become the story.

Begun shortly after Tolkien abandoned *The Lost Road* in 1937, and briefly interrupted in 1944–45 when he turned to *The Notion Club Papers*, *The Lord of the Rings*—to no great surprise—has several Elf-friend characters. The first we meet is Sam Gamgee, who on a less explicit, certainly less psychic level than Tolkien's serially incarnated time-travelers, is an instinctive Elf-friend even before he meets one. Sam's love of old tales, his romantic desire to see an Elf just once, make him a natural bridge between the skeptical Shire and the wonders beyond it—and thus a bridge for the reader between the real world and Tolkien's invented one. Sam's imagination takes over for Tolkien's, and though we know he is hopelessly romantic, we instinctively side with him against the sneering skepticism of Ted Sandyman, and even the advice of his father, the Gaffer. "Elves and dragons!" the Gaffer tells Sam, "Cabbages and potatoes are better for me and you. Don't go getting mixed up in the business of your betters" (*FR* I, i, 32). But Sam is not persuaded, and when Gandalf sentences him to go with Frodo he exclaims, "Me, Sir! . . . Me go and see Elves and all! Hooray!" (*FR* I, ii, 73).

When later, in Lórien, Frodo asks him "What do you think of Elves now, Sam?" the question is addressed as much to the reader as to Sam. And Sam tells us how we should respond:

> I reckon there's Elves and Elves. They're all elvish enough, but they're not all the same. Now these folk aren't wanderers or homeless, and seem a bit nearer to the likes of us; they seem to belong here, even more even than Hobbits do in the Shire. (*FR* II, vii, 376)

As Sam experiences the myth, as Sam understands the Elves, so too does the reader.

Frodo himself, the starting-point for this discussion and the first Elf-friend to whom readers are formally introduced, is not so explicit a link with an older myth as are Alboin Errol, Arry Lowdham, or even Sam Gamgee. Nevertheless, like Sam, Frodo has grown up listening to Bilbo's own re-countings of his adventure with the Elves, and his stories and poems of older times. Through Bilbo Frodo has met Elves, and can speak their language. Through Gandalf he becomes the agent for Sam's first ecstatic encounters with the Elves he has heard about but never seen. Moreover, Frodo is more at home with Elves than are the other hobbits, and far more sensitive than they to the special, otherworldly quality of Lórien, where he has the almost-psychic experience of being in an earlier, long-past, mythic time.

Of equal importance to the Elf-friend concept, Frodo's journey, without which the whole story would not take place, provides many occasions for re-tellings of the songs and legends of the history of Middle-earth—from Bilbo's

verses about Eärendel at Rivendell to the tale of Tinúviel which Strider tells
on Weathertop to Gimli's song of Dúrin to Legolas's song of Nimrodel—stories which deepen and enhance *The Lord of the Rings* by revealing something
of the mythology behind it. And though it is not explicit in the narrative
itself, part of the larger fiction is that Frodo himself becomes a story-teller
in that his is presumed to be the hand which continues what Bilbo began in
the story's own pre-history—the Red Book. Thus in *The Lord of the Rings* the
Ælfwine character moves inward from the frame to the body of the narrative,
and by implication out again to complete the circle—and the story.

The ultimate refinement of the function of Ælfwine as a mediator comes
in the last story published in Tolkien's lifetime, *Smith of Wootton Major*, written in 1965. Unlike Gangleri or Eriol-Ælfwine, unlike Sam or Frodo, Smith
is not even fully aware that he is an Elf-friend, nor is the reader. In fact, if
we define the term strictly, the real Elf-friend figure in *Smith of Wootton
Major* is not Smith, but his grandfather, the Master Cook, who disappears
on holiday and returns bringing Alf the Apprentice. Although most people
call him Prentice, we learn much later that Alf (Elf), is the King of Faery. He
it is who manages the disposition of the star which is Smith's passport into
the magic world. The story tells little of this Master Cook, only that when
he comes back with Alf he seems "rather changed." He is "merrier," he does
"most laughable things," and sings "gay songs" (*SWM* 9). And in three years
he disappears again, saying farewell only to his Apprentice in a speech that
strikingly recalls Bilbo's farewell to Gandalf at the end of the first chapter of
The Lord of the Rings.

> 'Goodbye for now, Alf', he said. "I leave you to manage things as best you
> can, which is always very well. I expect it will turn out all right. If we meet
> again, I hope to hear all about it. Tell them that I've gone on another holi-
> day, but this time I shan't be coming back again.' (*SWM* 10)

Like Frodo following Bilbo, or Lowdham, who longs to follow after his
father, Smith, although he does not know it, follows in the footsteps of his
grandfather. However—and here we meet Tolkien's theme at its sternest—
unlike the others, Smith brings nothing back from his journeys but the
flower the Queen of Faery puts in his hair. He neither hears nor recounts
any tales. He asks no questions and gets no answers. If he is a link between
the "real" world and Faery, his purpose is to show how mysterious, how
fragile, how contingent on the good-will of Faery is the connection. Nevertheless, we see the faery world through his eyes and experience its mystery
through his perceiving consciousness.

This brief, ephemeral story is perhaps Tolkien's most presentation of a mythology, for the narrative makes little or no concession to the reader's curiosity. In contrast to the question-and-answer technique of the earliest tales, where everything is explained in painstaking detail but there is very little immediacy of action, in *Smith* everything is shown and nothing is explained. Readers familiar with *The Silmarillion, Unfinished Tales,* and The History of Middle-earth can hazard some educated guesses as to what might be going on in some of the Faery episodes, but the narrative itself makes no concessions. We are obliged to take Smith's (that is, Tolkien's) Faery—his mythology—on its own terms or not at all.

Here is no interrogative device; there are no old tales; we are given no explanation of the meaning behind events. Structurally this story is Tolkien's most integrated work, for the frame and the action are seamlessly interwoven. Wandering in a myth he does not understand, Smith of Wootton Major witnesses a whole world to which he does not have the key, nor, in consequence, does the reader. He sees the Sea of Windless Storm, blue waves rolling silently out of Unlight, white ships returning from battles on the Dark Marches, but gathers no information about the history of these places, nor about their importance. He see elven mariners land from a great ship and march inland, but does not know their purpose, or anything about the battle to which they go. A sudden, inexplicable attack of violent wind drives him to the shelter of a birch tree, whereupon the birch tells him "Go away! The Wind is hunting you! You do not belong here!" (*SWM* 32). But it does not tell him why. The questions are not just unanswered, they are unasked, making Smith the least obtrusive of Tolkien's Elf-friends. The story itself is of all Tolkien's efforts the most uncompromising in its treatment of myth, the most demanding in its attitude toward the reader, and therefore perhaps, the most effective in its dramatic presentation.

The negative counterpart of all Tolkien's Elf-friends is the one mortal who witnesses nothing but absence in Faërie and brings back no knowledge, no insights or history, only frustration at the inaccessibility of Faërie to mortal consciousness. This is the lonely speaker in "The Sea-bell," who sails to Faërie but can make no contact with the elven world, the traveler whom the Elves avoid, leaving for all his beseeching only the sound of their singing echoing on the empty air. It is worth noting that when the poem was originally published as "Looney" in the *Oxford Magazine* for 18 January 1934, it had a kind of open-ended frame. It began with a nameless questioner inquiring "Where have you been, what have you seen / walking in rags down the street?" The rest of the poem provided the answer, detailing the adventures of a voyager who sailed to "another land" but could make no contact with the faërie inhabitants. When Tolkien re-wrote the poem as "The Sea-bell" he removed the frame questioner, leaving the story, like that of Smith, to stand on its own. When the voyager (in either version of the poem) returns at last to mortal lands, his inability to communicate his experience isolates him from the human community as well: "ragged I walk. To myself I talk; / for still they speak not, men that I meet" (*The Adventures of Tom Bombadil* 60). Sometimes not even the mystery is available to the perceiving consciousness. Where there is no access at all there is no myth, and the imagination and the spirit are impoverished.

Even more than the isolated speaker in "the Sea-bell," Smith of Wootton Major's reluctant farewell to Faery, and his renunciation of the magic star which is his passport, have been interpreted as Tolkien's own farewell to and renunciation of the mythic world he loved so much. If this is indeed what they are, we must be grateful that he walked there at all, grateful that we as readers have had such an Elf-friend. For of course the ultimate, the over-arching Elf-friend is Tolkien, no other. He is the bridge between the worlds. The footsteps of Ælfwine, sometimes faint, sometimes clear, are Tolkien's footsteps. We could not remove them if we tried, and we certainly would not want to try. His footsteps lead us as readers from character to character, from story to story, to a fuller understanding of the world of his imagination and to a deeper understanding of the man himself. And finally, as The History of Middle-earth has shown us, they lead Tolkien's audience to a more complete apprehension of his mythology and a more profound appreciation of the breadth and depth of his vision.

The Curious Incident of the Dream at the Barrow

Memory and Reincarnation in Middle-earth

Did J.R.R. Tolkien believe in reincarnation? Based on his avowed Catholic faith, the answer to that question would have to be "no," for such belief is not congruent with orthodox Catholic doctrine. Yet there are elements in his work which suggest the possibility of a different answer. These explicitly concern the inhabitation of a living individual by the perceptions, experiences, and memories of a past persona—a circumstance generally characterized as reincarnation. To be sure, such episodes are fiction not fact, and caution should be exercised in extrapolating from one to the other. Nevertheless, the products of a man's imagination can be clearer indicators of his natural inclination than his day to day observances, albeit with occasional unanticipated results for both his audience and himself. Some sharp theological questions from a concerned Catholic reader about reincarnation among Tolkien's Elves elicited a surprisingly unorthodox answer (see below), while the most anomalous example of re-inhabitation of the present by the past, Merry Brandybuck's dream at the barrow, goes un-remarked by most readers.

The principle of reincarnation can be linked to a larger theme running through Tolkien's major works, that the past is not just tributary to the present, but formative of it and immediate in it. His fiction itself is the largest example, making the recent past of *The Hobbit* a recurrent part of *The Lord of the Rings*, and interweaving both works as well as his two unfinished time-travel stories into the present, past and even the future of the Silmarillion. Tolkien repeatedly underscores the immediacy of time past in time present and time future by introducing prophecies, old songs, and legends into his narrative, as well personal recollections of events in history both near and distant. Since from a literary perspective these are standard narrative devices, it is worthy of notice that Tolkien also carried the concept to its extreme to introduce not just old songs in new situations, but old memories in new bodies, recollections of extra-personal past experiences that motivate and direct present actions.

In imagining these episodes, he borrowed from the psychological and metaphysical speculation of his own time, which explored the possibility of memory as a direct channel to extra-personal experience through the operations of the unconscious mind in dreams. Drawing on such concepts as Carl Jung's theory of archetypes and the collective unconscious, and J.W. Dunne's notion of serial memory, Tolkien in three separate examples used the concept of dream-memory as the psychic or psychological connector/channel between characters in the narrative present and a distant past beyond their waking memory.[1]

Two of these examples are his unfinished science fiction stories, "The Lost Road" and "The Notion Club Papers," written nearly ten years apart but making use of the same concept and method. These treat time-travel as a psychic or psychological mode whereby two modern-day Englishmen travel back to Númenor through the unconscious memories of a succession of ever more ancient forebears. The third example, and by all odds the most extreme and puzzling, involves the anomalous experience of Merry Brandybuck at the barrow in *The Lord of the Rings*. In the context of one another, these three examples show Tolkien's varying treatments of the matter, and his exploration into the problematic (for a devout Catholic) area of human reincarnation.

Two elements of Tolkien's own personal experience found their way into his treatment of time-travel, and have some bearing on his perspective. The first is what he called his "Atlantis haunting," his own recurrent dream of the "Great Wave" towering above him, from which he said he awoke "gasping out of deep water" (*Letters* 213, 347). In both "The Lost Road" and "The Notion Club Papers" he transferred that experience to his time-traveling Englishmen, characters who witness (in their dreams) the drowning of Númenor in a great wave that overwhelms that land. The second, also bestowed on his fictive time-travelers, is inherited memory of language. In both stories, the time-travel is triggered by words from un-familiar languages, words that are "remembered" in dreams. This unambiguously replicates Tolkien's statement, in a letter to W. H. Auden dated 7 June 1955, that he "took" to west midland Middle English as a "known tongue" as soon as he saw it (213). In the same letter, he made the notable suggestion that linguistic tastes might be as good a test of ancestry as blood groups (214), a sort of language DNA. (It is worth noting that Tolkien's letter to Auden postdates the discovery of DNA, first proposed by Watson and Crick in 1953 in the British Journal *Nature*.)

Indeed, in an explicitly autobiographical allusion, Tolkien had his character Alwyn Arundel Lowdham of "The Notion Club Papers" duplicate his own experience by reporting knowledge of a real-world language, Anglo-Saxon, before they learned it from books. He (Tolkien) amplified the concept by having another of his characters in the same story, Ramer, draw attention to the "native" (or inherited, first-learned) language (SD 201). Both Alboin Errol in the 1936 Lost Road and Arry Lowdham in the 1945–46 Notion Club Papers experience direct memory of hitherto unknown languages which Tolkien variously calls Elven-Latin, Avallonian, and Adunaic and which neither character could have encountered in waking life (LR 47; Sauron 241).[2] Such autobiographical references woven into the stories suggest a more-than-fictional interest in the notion of past lives or extra-personal memory.

The narrative structure of "The Notion Club Papers" must stand as one of Tolkien's most complex and sophisticated treatments of time. The story takes place within a nest of three interlocking time-frames. Writing in the nineteen-forties of the twentieth century, he set the narrative present of the story forward to the nineteen-eighties from which his time-travelers go back to the pre-history of Númenor. He then further advanced the time by placing it in a twenty-first century frame, the year 2012.[3] This is the year when a bundle of papers discovered in the basement of the Examination Schools at Oxford turns out to be the minutes of a twentieth-century Oxford club, the Notion Club. These minutes are "edited" and "published" by their fictional discoverer, "Mr. Howard Green" in Tolkien's fictive twenty-first century.

Tolkien links the separate times not just by concentric framing, but also by flashback, his most contemporary, psychological use of memory. In this context, flashback is not simply the ordinary literary technique by which the reader is switched from the narrative present to the narrative past to fill in a gap or to supply part of the back-story. Rather, it is his authentic treatment of a psychological phenomenon, the actual re-living of a past incident such as is frequently experienced by people who have undergone violent trauma. By its very nature as the re-living or re-experiencing of an event, flashback also functions as the bridge or channel between the present and the past.

In the climactic episode of the story, Night 67 of the Club minutes' chronology, Tolkien's protagonists Lowdham and Jeremy, in their everyday lives two modern Oxford scholars, are overtaken and possessed by memories of the destruction of Númenor as experienced by their remote ancestors, memories which violently erupt into, and materially and psychologically alter the two men's present experience. For a brief space of time, while they are physically and observably in a college room in Oxford, they also have the sensation of being in Númenor at the time of its destruction. In this time-doubling mode, they address one another by their Númenorean names Abrazān and Nimruzīr, and give the impression to others in the room of being aboard a ship in a violent storm—the storm that destroys Númenor.

So powerful is this flashback that it brings the reality of ancient Númenor irrupting not just into the individual experiences of the two protagonists, but those of their confreres and all of modern-day Oxford as well, for the same storm and tidal wave simultaneously sweep over both locations in both times. This is memory with a vengeance, for unlike modern trauma victims, Lowdham and Jeremy are not repossessed by memories of their personal experiences but by those of their remote Númenorean ancestors. It is here that a phrase much-used by Tolkien, "waking thought," becomes operative through its opposite, dreaming thought, the operation of the unconscious mind in the sleeping/dreaming state

Outline sketches for time-travel sequences appended to both "The Lost Road" and "The Notion Club Papers" make it clear that Tolkien intended travel backward in time to be travel backward in memory, accomplished though dreams that accessed or tapped into the recurring identities of two men carrying some form of names having the meanings "Elf-friend" and "Bliss-friend." As Ælfwine (Anglo-Saxon *Ælf,* "elf," Anglo-Saxon *wine,* "friend") and Tréowine (Anglo-Saxon *tréow,* "truth, troth")[4] Alwyn Lowdham and Trewin Jeremy of "The Notion Club Papers" were to dream their way back to Nú-menor, where they were to experience that island's destruction. More than witnesses of the cataclysm, they were to arrive on the scene in time to get a glimpse of (or actual possession of—the notes are not clear) the Book of Stories which is the mythology of Middle-earth, a body of lore which they were then to transmit in some fashion to present-day England.

It is in his treatment of identity recurring over serial lives that Tolkien modified the theologically difficult question of reincarnation to the less-problematic concept of inherited memory. At first glance, they would seem to be the same, or nearly so, but Tolkien went to some lengths to differentiate them. A note attached to "The Notion Club Papers" suggests that he found a way around the difficulty that enabled him to retain the mechanism without theological unorthodoxy by substituting genetics for metaphysics. Here he states unequivocally that,

> The theory is that the sight and memory goes [*sic*] on with *descendants* of Elendil and Voronwë (=Tréowine) but *not* reincarnation: they are different people even if they still resemble one another in some ways even after a lapse of many generations. (*SD* 278)

His terms for this process were "serial longevity" and "hoarding memory," (*Letters* 284), and he worked out the idea in some detail, at the same time carefully working around any mention of reincarnation.

Nevertheless, the distinction he draws is a fine one, and open to interrogation. Transmitted memory may be defensible as genetic inheritance, but sight, the actual alteration of physical experience would seem to call for some further process. It is not improbable that Tolkien was trying to have it both ways; to be theologically orthodox and yet retain his time-travel device using the idea of an ancestral unconscious that could irrupt into and alter present identity. Although this could conceivably be explained by the presence of some genetic trigger which released or called up neurologically encoded experience, the fact is that it takes over the bodies and identities as well as the minds of Lowdham and Jeremy, controlling present experience by past memory.

In his later writings, however, notably in the section "Of Death and the Severance of Fea [spirit] and Hrondo [bodily form]" in *Morgoth's Ring,* Tolkien dealt at some length with Elven reincarnation, going so far as to employ the terms *rebirth* and *re-born,* with the rationale that by this process, "the evil and grief that they [Elves] had suffered in the curtailment of their natural course might be redressed" (*MR* 219). It is hard to ignore the likeness of this concept to that of *karma,* the working out in one life of actions or relationships left unfinished in a previous life. Nevertheless, this is applied to Elves, not Men. The concept is safely confined to imaginary beings, avoiding the apparent heresy of proposing it, albeit in fiction, for actual human beings. Even so, Tolkien was on theological thin ice here, for Catholic doctrine, which upholds the immortality of the soul and its resurrection in the body at the Last Judgment, does not therefore admit of the soul's transference through time, or its residence in more than one body.

It may be for this reason that although he did address it, the concept of reincarnation as applied to humans was a subject about which Tolkien expressed such conflicting viewpoints, sometimes within the same work. Part One of "The Notion Club Papers" presents a viewpoint at odds with that contained in the Note. During a theoretical argument (as among writers) about how to believably accomplish space travel in science fiction, the Club's minutes-keeper, Guildford, in early drafts identified as Tolkien (*SD* 150), maintains that,

> 'For landing on a new planet, you've got your choice: miracle, magic; or sticking to normal probability, the only known or likely way in which any one has ever landed on a world.'

'Oh! So you've got a private recipe all the time, have you?' said Ramer sharply.

'No, it's not private, though I've used it once.'

'Well? Come on! What is it?'

'Incarnation. By being born,' said Guildford.

At that point Dolbear woke up. (*SD* 170)

Commenting on this exchange, Christopher Tolkien's Note 15 to Part One adds that "In the original text A (still followed in B) Dolbear, waking up, says with reference to these words of Guildford's ('Incarnation. By being born'): 'Then try reincarnation, or perhaps transcarnation without loss of memory'" (*SD* 213).

That neither *reincarnation* nor *transcarnation* made it into his "D" text, the final typescript published as Part One of the "Papers," suggests that Tolkien had second thoughts about using either word, and substituted the less controversial *incarnation* as Guildford's "private recipe for landing on a world," which he defines as "being born." This seems safely uncontroversial, although the fact that Guildford says he has used it "once" suggests (albeit obliquely) the possibility that it could be used more than once. It seems clear that Tolkien was of several minds about espousing, even in fiction, a concept so radically opposed to his Catholic belief.

The notion of hereditary memory offered an alternative. This concept was part of a climate of fictional thought in the 1920s, most probably fostered by Carl Jung's theory of the collective unconscious as a repository of universally shared memories. Such notions were widespread in the early twentieth century. Freud argued for the transmission of memories in several works (e.g., *Totem and Taboo* and *Civilization and Its Discontents*) and it can be found in the writings on fairy-tales by R.G. Collingwood, who like Tolkien was at Pembroke College. E.R. Eddison also made the concept central to his novels, most notably in his Zimiamvian trilogy. Tolkien had met Eddison, who came to an Inklings meeting in 1944, and was familiar with his works.

A prime American example from about the same time is Leonard Cline's 1927 novel, *The Dark Chamber*.[5] Moreover, Cline's novel was the impetus for a series of "hereditary memory" stories among writers of speculative fiction in the late 20s and 30s, most notably H.P. Lovecraft. It is not demonstrable that Tolkien knew any of these, though his reading in contemporary science fiction was wide. In a letter to Charlotte and Dennis Plimmer, who in 1967 had interviewed him for an article published in the *Daily Telegraph Magazine,* he mentioned reading "many books (notably so-called Science Fiction and Fantasy)" (*Letters* 377). The concept behind Cline's novel comes out of a recognized branch of literary thought and practice with which Tolkien was undoubtedly familiar, and may well have been behind the note about Elendil and Voronwë. Nevertheless, the distinction there made between reincarnation and hereditary memory seems a fine one. That the sight and memory of an ancestor can be transmitted to a descendent so that the descendent not only remembers them in another life but re-enacts them as well, appears to be little different in its effects from reincarnation.

Nonetheless, the preponderance of evidence so far for Tolkien's belief or non-belief in reincarnation seems to come down on the side of non-belief, or at least extreme caution. His "Notion Club" note was written sometime in 1945–46, and was addressed to himself alone. It is worth noting, however, that he spoke of reincarnation more boldly and in less equivocal terms at a later time and in an even more direct context. An unsent letter addressed to a fellow Catholic who protested the concept on specifically theological grounds shows Tolkien thinking more radically. In 1954, Peter Hastings, manager of the Newman Bookshop in Oxford, wrote expressing concern that Tolkien might have "overstepped the mark in metaphysical matters," particularly in the case of the concept of reincarnation of the Elves, which Tolkien had mentioned to him in a conversation. Hastings argued that,

> God has not used that device [reincarnation] in any of the creations of which we have knowledge, and it seems to me stepping beyond the position of a sub-creator to produce it as an actual working thing, because a sub-creator, when dealing with the relations between creator and created, should use those channels which he knows the creator to have used already. . . . (*Letters* 187–88).

The draft of Tolkien's letter of reply makes his opposing position clear. Here he wrote to Hastings that, "We differ entirely about the relation of sub-creation to creation. . . . I should have thought it a curious metaphysic . . . that declared the channels known (in such a finite corner as we have any inkling of) to have used, are the only possible ones, or efficacious, or possibly acceptable to and by Him!" He went on to declare that,

> 'Reincarnation' may be bad *theology* (that surely, rather than metaphysics) as applied to Humanity; and my *legendarium,* especially the 'Downfall of Númenor' which lies immediately behind *The Lord of the Rings,* is based on my view: that Men are essentially mortal and must not try to become 'immortal' in the flesh. But I do not see how even in the Primary World any theologian or philosopher, unless very much better informed about

the relation of spirit and body than I believe anyone to be, could deny the *possibility* of re-incarnation as a mode of existence prescribed for certain kinds of rational incarnate creatures. (*Letters* 188–89)

The draft is marked in Tolkien's hand "Not sent," with the addition, "It seemed to be taking myself too importantly" (196). The self-deprecating phrase, "too importantly" notwithstanding, he certainly took the metaphysics of *The Lord of the Rings* importantly. After reminding Hastings of the obvious, that his story is "a tale, a piece of literature, intended to have literary effect, and not real history," Tolkien went on to write a lengthy response to Hastings' criticisms that runs to seven single-spaced printed pages in the published *Letters*.

The fact that the letter was never sent leaves the question open. It is tempting to speculate that beyond his professed modesty, Tolkien might have had the same kind of second thoughts about opening so unorthodox an argument with the manager of a Catholic bookstore that made him eliminate the words *reincarnation* and *transcarnation* from the "D" typescript of "The Notion Club Papers." Certainly the views expressed in the unsent letter are explicit, and make it plain that by 1954 Tolkien himself would not and did not deny the possibility of reincarnation "for certain kinds of rational incarnate creatures."

Other, more oblique references in his work would seem to support this position. In his 1939 lecture-essay "On Fairy-stories" Tolkien had declared (without further elucidation) that "[i]n dreams strange powers of the mind may be unlocked" (*MC* 116). The reference to "dreams" and the "strange powers," I suggest, are powers of recall by the unconscious mind capable of taking memory beyond personal experience and history into a realm which Tolkien clearly saw as metaphysical, and just as clearly believed to be possible. Indeed, he had one of his characters in "The Notion Club Papers," Ramer, declare that "a pretty good case had been made out for the view that in dreams a mind can and sometimes does, move in time (*SD* 175).

Call it inherited memory or reincarnation or both, the process is the central mechanism of both the time-travel stories, without which their action cannot occur. However, the same idea hardly seems necessary to the structure or the plot of Tolkien's more serious endeavour, *The Lord of the Rings*. It is true that dream experiences are used as foreshadowing throughout that narrative, dreams in which Frodo's perceiving mind can move laterally in space, as in his vision of Gandalf at Orthanc, or forward in time, as in his vision in the house of Tom Bombadil of the green country he sees at the end of the book. One dream experience, however, assigned to a less plot-driven part of the story, foreshadows nothing but itself. In this singular instance, Tolkien went out of his way to introduce into his story a dream and memory episode entirely unconnected to plot or character. Not surprisingly the episode occurs in a landscape already haunted by history and oral tradition, the Barrow-downs.

In the preliminary to this episode, Frodo, waking to find himself captive in the barrow, realizes that he is "probably under the dreadful spells of the Barrow-wights about which whispered tales spoke" (*FR* I, viii, 151). Frodo's "waking thought" connects the barrow to oral tradition, folklore and "whispered tales," but a following incident will explicitly connect it to both history and dreaming memory as well. This incident is the extraordinary and to all appearances anomalous episode involving Merry Brandybuck, who, on awakening after his rescue by Tom Bombadil, undergoes much the same kind of flashback as that experienced by Tolkien's science fiction time-travellers, but without the rationale of their serial link to ancestral memory.

The chronology of composition is worth noting here, for the Barrow-wight chapter was first drafted near the end of 1938, not long after the abortive 1936 "Lost Road" but before the equally unfinished 1945–46 "Notion Club Papers," both of which deal explicitly with inherited memory and reincarnation (*RS* 112), and may well have influenced the barrow episode both in retrospect and anticipation. In the context of *The Lord of the Rings*, it would be hard to imagine any race less likely to experience a para-normal memory than the earthy, workaday hobbits, or any individual less metaphysically inclined than the steady, practical, responsible Merry Brandybuck. Yet precisely the same kind of para-psychological memory that possesses Tolkien's time-travelling Englishmen in his science fiction stories overtakes the hobbit Merry at the barrow when, awakening after his rescue to find himself dressed in rags and crowned with gold, he undergoes a sudden, unexpected experience of what can only be read as extra-personal memory.

> 'What in the name of wonder?' began Merry, feeling the golden circlet that had slipped over one eye. Then he stopped, and a shadow came over his face, and he closed his eyes. 'Of course, I remember!' he said. 'the men of Carn Dûm came on us at night, and we were worsted. Ah! The spear in my heart!' He clutched at his breast. 'No! No!' he said, opening his eyes. 'What am I saying? I have been dreaming.' (*FR* I, viii, 154)

An earlier draft of the incident is even more explicit. After "What in the name of wonder," this version continues, "Then he stopped, and a shadow came over his face. 'I begin to remember,' he said. 'I thought I was dead—but don't let us speak of it.'" (*Shadow* 128). The question of who it is who "begins to remember," is confused here, for whether the "I" is Merry or some past individual is not made clear, perhaps deliberately. Christopher Tolkien notes that in this draft there is "no mention of the Men of Carn Dûm" (128). The published version adds the specific details of the battle, the manner of death, the physical experience of pain, and Merry's conclusion that he has "been dreaming," a significant addition to the metaphysics of the episode.

This explicit, intentional reference to extra-personal knowledge is directly connected to, indeed is apparently caused by, first the landscape in which Merry finds himself—the barrow; and second by his tactile experience of the "golden circlet" on his head. Tolkien's (or Merry's) word-choice signals the change of identity, shifting from the colloquial "What in the name of wonder?" to the archaic, formal "we were worsted." It cannot be doubted that Tolkien's final version intended Merry to experience and express the actuality of some long-ago battle, to relive (or re-die) some unknown person's last moments down to the final detail of the spear going into his heart. Opening his eyes on his own present, Merry concludes that he has been dreaming. And that is precisely Tolkien's point. He has not made Merry's allusion to dream lightly, and he seems plainly to be drawing on the same dream mechanism used in "The Lost Road" and "The Notion Club Papers."

But where did the memory or the dream come from? Who is the fallen warrior? What is the link to the barrow? Neither "hoarding memory" nor "serial longevity" will answer here, for there are no descendants to hoard recollection, no series of ancestors through which to transmit it. Tom Shippey discusses the episode in *The Road to Middle-earth*, suggesting that Merry "seems to have taken on the personality of the body in the barrow." Nevertheless, he does not explore the metaphysics of this, which is not surprising, as his subject here is barrow-wights, not Merry (*Road* 99–100). Shippey does not speculate on who "the body in the barrow" might be except to observe that it "can hardly be the wight." Tom Bombadil bears this out in his account to the hobbits of the barrows as the biers of dead kings and queens covered by mounds. "[S]oon the hills were empty again. A shadow came out of dark places far away, and the bones were stirred in the mounds. Barrow-wights walked in the hollow places with a clink of rings on cold fingers and gold chains in the wind" (*FR* I, vii, 141). The wights are transient squatters, later inhabitants of the burial mounds of kings and queens.

A back story identifying the mound's original occupant can be pieced together from scattered references in Appendix A. Here we find that Carn Dûm was the chief city of Angmar, the kingdom ruled by the Witch-king, later known as the Lord of the Nazgûl. He and his host were defeated by the forces of Cirdan and Glorfindel at the Battle of Fornost, after which the

Witch-king "fled northwards, seeking his own land of Angmar. Before he could gain the shelter of Carn Dûm the cavalry of Gondor overtook him" (*RK* Appendix A, 331). The Appendices also tell us that the barrows, many of which were built in the First Age as grave mounds for the Dúnedain (cf. Tom Bombadil above), came to be haunted by "evil spirits out of Angmar" who "entered into the deserted mounds and dwelt there" (*RK* Appendix A, 321).

We now have a direct link from Angmar and "the men of Carn Dûm" to the barrow and the Wight. But this does not answer the questions nor solve the mystery. The memory that overtakes Merry is neither that of a Barrow-wight nor of a man of Carn Dûm, but rather someone who was "worsted," indeed, slain, by a man of Carn Dûm, stabbed through his heart with a spear. However, when the Appendices further inform us that hobbits from the Shire were actually at "the battle in which Angmar was overthrown" (*RK* Appendix A, 322–23), we can imagine a link from Merry to a possible ancestor who could have been at the battle and been killed by the men of Carn Dûm. But this turns out to be not a real clue but a red herring, for that battle was not at the site of the barrow, but a hundred or so miles farther north, at Fornost on the North Downs.

Something else, then, must account for the memory at the barrow. We turn back to the Appendices again, which tell us in good oral style that, "Some *say* [my emphasis] the mound in which the Ring-bearer was imprisoned had been the grave of the last prince of Cardolan, [a Dunedan] who fell in the war of 1409 [against Angmar]" (*RK* Appendix A, 321). To further refine the picture, Appendix A tells us that, "A remnant of the faithful among the Dúnedain of Cardolan also held out in Tyrn Gorthad[6] (the Barrow-downs)" (*RK* Appendix A, 321). We now have someone (though not a hobbit) who was killed by the men of Carn Dûm and buried in the barrow. Could it be his memory that invaded Merry's dream and the pain of his death that Merry experienced? There seems no other ready explanation. The possibility is strengthened by Tolkien's insistence that hobbits are a subspecies of men, which makes the transference more believable than if Merry had re-lived the experience of an elf.

Nevertheless, there can be no mistake about the nature of this episode. Merry is not reliving the genetically transmitted memory of some remote ancestor, for there is no demonstrable connection among hobbits, the barrow, and the battle with the men of Carn Dûm. Someone else's long past experience has, if only momentarily, overtaken and overpowered him, and he has identified with it. Finally, however, the question remains, why is the episode included in the story? What is its purpose? It is not followed up in any way, and has no apparent bearing on the further conduct or character

of Merry. It adds nothing to plot and seems to have no explicit relationship
to theme. The immediate influences, I suggest, were the two science fiction
stories that bracket this portion of the book, the first written in 1936, the
year before he began work on *The Lord of the Rings*, and the second composed in 1945–46, after Tolkien's writing of the Barrow-downs chapters.
Time-travel and dream-memory were still in his mind as he wrote. Beyond
that, the episode has much the same general function as the poems, oral
stories, wise sayings and old saws that are sprinkled throughout the book,
to insist on and underscore the immediacy of the past in the present, and (in
this case) to do so through one of the narrative's least metaphysical characters—the hobbit Merry Brandybuck.[7]

After his rescue of the hobbits from the barrow, Tom Bombadil had given
them blades from the barrow's treasure, "long, leaf-shaped, and keen, of
marvellous workmanship." They were forged, Tom told them, by the Men of
Westernesse, foes of the Dark Lord who were "overcome by the evil king of
Carn Dûm in the Land of Angmar. Few now remember them," Tom continued, "yet some still go wandering, sons of forgotten kings walking in loneliness" (*FR* I, viii, 157). The hobbits do not understand him, but they have a
vision of "a great expanse of years behind them, like a vast shadowy plain
over which there strode shapes of Men, tall and grim with bright swords.
. . . then the vision faded and they were back in the sunlit world" (157). Up
until this episode the hobbits have experienced chiefly that sunlit world, but
Tom's words now carry them back into the "great expanse of years" that is
the past. Part of that past is contained in the barrow. It is in direct relationship to the barrow that Merry enters in his dream of the older world, the
"shadowy plain," only to die there with a spear in his heart.

What most clearly distinguishes this episode from the two time-travel
sequences is the absence of any overt connection, either in the narrative itself or in any of the ancillary documents in the Appendices, between Merry
and that sequence of the past that touches him at the barrow. The story carries no thread of repeated Ælfwine-like names, there is no pattern of lineal
descent, no link through language, no indication whatsoever of any special
circumstance that would associate Merry Brandybuck with the prince of
Cardolan or with the barrow. Only the gold crown on Merry's head ties
his physical presence to the dream-memory of that earlier event and un-
ancestral person. In the re-experience of death, the prince of Cardolan actually if only momentarily inhabits Merry. This cannot be Merry's inherited
memory, for there is no genealogy through which he can inherit, no genetic
pathway along which such memory could be transmitted.

The episode of Merry's dream at the barrow remains, then, the most irregular, least explicable and least historically prepared for event in the entire book, singular in its mystery, and significant in its power to bridge past and present. It is surely no accident or random choice on Tolkien's part that this reinhabitation occurs where it does. Like so much of the landscape of Middle-earth, the Barrow-downs are more than mere scenery or topography, more than human-made relics become monuments of history. They are at once repositories of the past and gateways to it, portals through which old memory can touch the present, and the present can connect back to the past.

Memory is alive and active and always with us, Tolkien seems to be saying, not just in our eyes and in our ears, not just in our languages and the stories we tell and the books we read, but embedded in the deepest recesses of the world we live in and the deepest recesses of our minds which are at all times and in all circumstances that world's mirror. In light of this, and returning now to the opening question, I would say that while the evidence is not unequivocal, the final answer must be a qualified "yes probably." It seems safe to say that at some level and in his own particular fashion, Tolkien did at least not disbelieve in reincarnation.

Whose Myth Is It?

The "Athrabeth Finrod ah Andreth," (Debate of Finrod and Andreth) is a late, post-*Lord of the Rings* text, conjecturally dated to 1959 by Christopher Tolkien (*MR* 304). It is a problematic addendum to Tolkien's mythology, raising serious questions about a central tenet of his creation story, that death is the "gift" of the godhead Eru/Ilúvatar to Men, a gift withheld from Elves, who are condemned to immortality. The piece is couched as a dramatic dialogue between an elf, Finrod, and a mortal woman, Andreth. The subject of their argument is the death fate of Men in Middle-earth. Finrod sticks with the conventional (within the fiction) view of death as a gift; Andreth challenges this with the real-world idea that death is a punishment. The argument ends inconclusively, with neither debater winning the argument.

The conversation opens with Finrod expressing sorrow for the recent death of Andreth's grandfather, Boron. Finrod assumes, as do readers of *The Silmarillion,* that the death of Men is the "gift" of Ilúvatar. It is part of the plan and is therefore not only necessary but right. To Finrod's surprise, Andreth disagrees, contending that the death of Men has not always been in the plan, that it is neither necessary nor right, that it was not always so, and that it is not a gift but a punishment. What began as a friendly conversation slides rapidly into an argument in which the both characters reveal hidden emotions and entrenched ideas based on the preconceptions of each about their relative places in the scheme of things. The conversation becomes surprisingly heated. Andreth is angry and bitter. Finrod is superior and condescending. She is resentful of his condescension. He is taken aback by her anger.

The apparently philosophical tone of their argument masks an emotional sub-text, the real reason for Andreth's bitterness—a broken love-affair. The differing life-spans of Elves and Men has divided her fate from that of her only love, Finrod's brother Aegnor. She will grow old, and wither. He will remain youthful. She will die. He will not. This turns debate into tragedy, and would be enough for most authors. It was not enough for Tolkien. Beneath both the philosophical tone and the emotional subtext lies the real rationale behind the "Athrabeth," its author's exploration of the meaning of purpose and death through interrogation of his invented world. Christopher Tolkien characterizes the "Athrabeth" and other of his father's re-visions of about that same time as "the record of a prolonged interior debate" (*MR* 369), which debate is exteriorized and dramatized as the argument between Finrod and Andreth.

Since it is presented as a debate, the question of authority immediately arises. Whose myth is it? Who within the invented world is the authority or authorities for what Finrod and Andreth each say and assume? Tolkien's well-known dictum, that a sub-created Secondary World must have "the inner consistency of reality," that it must adhere to its own norms, requires that such authority be provided. In the earliest versions of the creation story in *The Book of Lost Tales* "The Music of the Ainur," that authority is Rúmil the Elven sage, who conveys the words of Eru to Eriol the Mariner. Moreover, Tolkien's 1951 letter to Milton Waldman giving an overview of the mythology declares unequivocally that, "the point of view of the whole cycle is the Elvish" (*Letters* 147). This sounds like the last word; but it isn't. At some time during his much earlier composition of the prose Túrin saga (for which there is no definite date) Tolkien had scribbled a note to the effect that, "The cosmogonic myths are Númenórean, blending Elven-lore with human myth and imagination" (*MR* 374). And in or about 1958 "or later" according to Christopher Tolkien, Tolkien wrote that, "the Mythology must actually be a Mannish affair. . . . What we have in the *Silmarillion* etc. are traditions . . . handed on by *Men* in Númenor and later in Middle-earth . . . blended and confused with their own Mannish myths and cosmic ideas" (*MR* 370).

Apparently he intended, or came to realize, that there could be no last word, that all stories reflect human and imperfect, un-omniscient narrators, that all truths (as Gandhi said) are partial. The "Athrabeth" embodies the quandary, for it is driven by two different, indeed contending points of view, "Elven-lore" against "Mannish myths." Far from "traditions blended and confused," these traditions not only refuse to blend, they actually compete. Finrod and Andreth each stake a claim to their own interpretation of the myth, and the trap for the reader is to read the debate with the same either-or assumption, the fallacy that if either side is right the other side must be wrong. A close look at Tolkien's seemingly confused and conflicting statements will show that he was aware of the trap. It seems clear that while on one level writing the stories of what he hoped would be a viable work of fiction, he was on another level aware that all stories and all the texts that record them are filtered through the sensibilities and perceptions of their narrators and must therefore reflect those narrators' individual and differing points of view. This is scrupulous, but confusing to the ordinary reader. Yet a closer look at the words Tolkien uses in the above-cited quotes may clarify the matter. *Lore. Imagination. Point of view. Traditions handed on. Ideas blended and confused.* In this context, one of the phrases cited above holds the key to the "Athrabeth." It is "point of view." The "Athrabeth" is not a final statement, by Finrod or Andreth or Tolkien. It is a dialogue between contending points of view, those of Elves and Men. As Tolkien himself said of it, it is "an example of the kind of thing that enquiring minds on either side, the Elvish or the Human, must have said to one another" (*MR* 329). The apparent contradictions are parts of a process, not a final pronouncement. Each of the debaters has his or her separate point of view shaped by background, history, and personal identity.

But we are readers, not umpires, and not accustomed to awarding credibility on points. Taken at face value, Andreth's argument would seem to set the whole mythology on its head, for if Andreth is right, not just Finrod, but Eru himself is wrong, and his statement that death is a gift to Men which as time goes on "even the Powers will envy" is called into question (*Silm* 42). So whose myth is it? Granting the obvious fact that the whole legendarium is Tolkien's invention, and that he can handle it however he pleases, it is well to remember that it has been presented all along as *tales told* by various tellers. As far back as the *Lost Tales*, and not forgetting the conceit of the multi-authored Red Book of Westmarch, we have had texts both Elven and Human coming from different times, different Middle-earth cultures, and speaking in various voices—Eriol/Ælfwine, Rumil, the sage, Pengoloð, Daeron the minstrel, Edwin Lowdham, Bilbo and Frodo Baggins. In this context, the contending voices of Finrod and Andreth are only the latest in a long line.

The narrative frame for the "Athrabeth" provides that it was "recorded in the ancient lore of the Eldar" as a conversation " in Beleriand long ago" between Finrod Felagund and Andreth the Wise-woman, and that it is "here given in one of the forms that have been preserved" (*MR* 304–5). Nevertheless, the argument raises the question of Secondary Belief, that acceptance of the Secondary World which is necessary for readers to enter into it. One of the principles of Tolkien's sub-creative process was that the imaginary world thus created had to have "the inner consistency of reality" (*MC* 138). This did not mean just the appearance and action of earth and sky, flora and fauna; it meant also the way the inhabitants saw themselves in relation to the world around them. The conflicting views of Finrod and Andreth seem to subvert that inner consistency, introducing doubt where we had all grown used to certainty.

Doubt is not what most of Tolkien's readers want. They want his invented world to stand still, to stay the way it always was (or seemed to be) when they first encountered it. In appearing to change the rules of his invented world, Tolkien was putting at risk the inner consistency of everything he had already written, gambling on his readers' intelligence and ability to accept change. This is a big chance for any author to take, especially an author whose invented world rivals the "real" one in the minds of many of his readers. The problem, then, lies not just in the debate itself, but first in its author's decision to question his own invented world-view, and second in its impact on readers grown used to a fixed picture but now confused by what seems like not just revised sub-creation but revisionist theology.

The presence of death in the world, and the rationale behind it, are issues that every mythology must deal with sooner or later. In a world, even an invented one, where some people die and others do not, it seems reasonable to suppose that those who die are going to wonder why. Calling death the "gift" of Ilúvatar sounds nice in theory, but is finally not much consolation, especially when that gift is conspicuously withheld from a large and highly visible part of the population. Tolkien came to see that he could not in good conscience avoid the question, and so he wrote the "Athrabeth." To fine-tune his world's inner consistency, his Men had to come to terms with death, had to question the circumstances of their own mortality. Let us give Tolkien the credit he deserves for having the authorial honesty to question a bedrock assumption of his invented world, and the courage and daring to make that interrogation an integral part of its myth.

He did not, however, try to publish it. That responsibility fell to his literary executor, Christopher Tolkien, who with equal honesty made the decision to publish on the basis that it was "a major and finished work" and was "referred to elsewhere as if it had for [his] father some 'authority'" (*MR* 303). This means that as readers, we must match honesty with honesty. We must accept the "Athrabeth" not as an answer, but as a question, the one that gives the title to this essay—whose myth is it?—and allow the competing voices to speak for themselves, each to make its own case. There are mythological precedents for this. Recall the two versions of creation in chapters one and two of the Book of Genesis, the conflicting portrayals of Norse gods by Snorri and Saxo, the marked differences among the Greek gods as portrayed by Æschylus, Euripides, and Homer. In such primary mythologies it is a given than any and all versions are particular interpretations coming from particular voices, times, and stages of development. The "Athrabeth" simply speeds up the process by putting the competing voices on stage at the same time and having them argue with one another.

Tolkien made sure that neither of these voices spoke with final authority. When Andreth remarks sarcastically, "All ye Elves deem that we die swiftly by our true kind," Finrod replies that the Elves "speak out of knowledge, not out of mere Elvish lore (*MR* 308). Andreth counters by citing "the Wise" among her people, who say that Men were not made for death, although she admits that they (the Wise) do not have the "sure knowledge" which Finrod boasts. They have only "'lore,' from which truth (if it can be found) must be winnowed" (*MR* 308–9). Most readers, relying on *The Silmarillion* as published and the earliest versions of myth as given in *The History of Middle-earth,* will probably prefer Finrod's "knowledge" to Andreth's "lore," which sounds folkloric and less than reliable.

Tolkien will not permit so easy an answer. Finrod's knowledge is not as secure as he would have it seem. In Tolkien's Commentary on the "Athrabeth" he cautioned, "it must be understood that [Finrod] starts with certain basic beliefs, which he would have said were derived from one or more of these sources: his created nature; angelic instruction; thought; and experience" (*MR* 330). What Finrod calls "knowledge" Tolkien calls "beliefs," a scarcely more verifiable source than Andreth's lore. It is worth noting, moreover, that Tolkien casts Finrod's position in the subjunctive mode; it is based on "beliefs which Finrod *would have said* [my emphasis] were derived" from the sources cited. This is probability rather than certainty, and shows Finrod as less authoritative than he seems. Both he and Andreth argue in terms of their own beliefs, hopes, and fears. Andreth declares that her people "say" that Men were not made for death, and that for Men to die is the work of Morgoth. Finrod's response raises what is clearly the central problem with the Debate. "[I]f your tale is true," he tells Andreth, "then all in Arda is in vain." A crucial premise of Tolkien's creation story is called into question. And he adds, "I do not believe your tale" (*MR* 313). Finrod may not believe it, but do we as readers? Should we? Does Tolkien?

For Tolkien, Christian and Catholic, human mortality, death, is a direct result of the Fall. In his letter to Milton Waldman, however, he had stated that in his invented world, "mortality is not explained mythically: it is a mystery," and so [t]he first fall of Man nowhere appears" (*Letters* 147). Yet only a few years later he deliberately introduced the subject. Granting his mortal Men permission to question their mortality, he had to let them devise an answer. The Fall of Men had to appear. Nevertheless, a note in a very early draft gives evidence that Tolkien was aware of a potential hazard:

Query: Is it not right to make Andreth refuse to discuss any traditions or legends of the "Fall"? Already it is (if inevitably) too like a parody of Christianity. Any legend of the Fall would make it completely so? (*MR* 354).

At this point the original question of whose myth it is takes a left turn out of the secondary world into the primary one. Even though in his Commentary, Tolkien stated unequivocally that the Debate was "not presented as an argument of any cogency for Men in their present situation (or the one in which they believe themselves to be)", but was "in fact simply part of the portrayal of the imaginary world of the *Silmarillion*" (*MR* 329), he is now no longer imagining a fictive contest between fictive voices, but asking a real question about the relationship of his mythology to a real-world belief system, Christianity.[1] It was a question he had seen coming (cf. the word "inevitably" in the note just cited). In his letter to Waldman he had disqualified the Arthurian world as England's mythology because it was "involved in and explicitly contained the Christian religion" (*Letters* 144), and now he saw his own "mythology for England" teetering on the brink of the same pitfall. Christopher Tolkien cites this as the primary reason for his father's original insistence that the Fall of Men must happen offstage (*MR* 355).

Nevertheless, although Tolkien was clearly aware of the threat to his story's autonomy, he did not surrender to his own warning doubts. Although the "Athrabeth" was already potentially "too like a parody of Christianity" which any "legend of the Fall" would make completely so, he went ahead and added to it a legend of a fall, the "Tale of Adanel," adding still another unreliable voice to the debate. Now the "Athrabeth" itself is not about the Fall per se, it is about death. There is no mention in the dialogue of any Fall, only veiled suggestions by Andreth that something (she does not specify what) must have happened to doom Men to death. But late in the argument, Tolkien has Finrod pin her down: "Therefore I say to you, Andreth, what did ye do, ye Men, long ago in the dark? How did ye anger Eru? For otherwise all your tales are but dark dreams devised in a Dark Mind. Will you say what you know or have heard?"

Andreth answers unequivocally, "I will not. . . . We do not speak of this to those of other race."

Finrod persists: "Are there no tales of our days before death, though ye will not tell them to strangers?" (*MR* 313). He has a point. If Men had in the past committed some misdeed whereby they had so angered Eru that he punished them with a death-doom, there would surely in this world of taletellers be tales told about it. If there was such a tale, and if Andreth knew it, or knew of it, surely the "inner consistency of reality" would demand that Finrod's question be the cue for its introduction into the conversation. That does not happen. Concerned, with good reason, that to introduce such a tale would turn his myth into a "parody of Christianity," Tolkien did not include the "Tale of Adanel" as part of the "Athrabeth" proper; he attached it as an appendix to his Commentary on the Debate.

Even there, he took care to present it as lore, not knowledge or even belief. The "Tale of Adanel" adds not just one more voice, but several, and these voices, like Finrod's and Andreth's, are not authority but unconfirmed report. The "Tale of Adanel" begins in traditional oral story-telling style with the indeterminate "Some say." We are given hearsay, and hearsay moreover, at several removes—from the unnamed "some" to Adanel to Andreth to Finrod to the Eldarin record of ancient lore in which the whole conversation is presumably set down. Tolkien explicitly said in a note that "Nothing is hereby asserted concerning [the story's] 'truth,' historical or otherwise" (*MR* 344). He seems almost bending over backward to make sure the reader does not take any of the voices as authoritative.

It is worth noting, moreover, that through the "Tale of Adanel" Tolkien replaced a Fall, which is by definition immediate and precipitous, with a Decline, which is by nature gradual both in time and steepness. A watershed moment in which by one action all is lost is replaced by a continuing process played out over an indeterminate period. Here is how it seems to work. At a time "before any had yet died," says Andreth quoting Adanel quoting the "some" who are her source, Men ceased to listen to the Voice (apparently the voice of Eru, who calls Adanel's people "my children"), and turned instead to worship of the Enemy (apparently Morgoth). At the end of this indeterminate period, the Voice is said to have spoken only once again, saying, "Ye have abjured Me, but ye remain Mine. I gave you life. Now it shall be shortened, and each of you in a little while shall come to Me" (*MR* 347). The choice of words is significant: not, as in Genesis, "ye shall surely die," but "ye shall come to Me." Death, with its inescapable biblical echoes, is avoided, implicit though it may be in the threat of shortened life. In addition, it would seem that even then death did not come to everyone, for Adanel says only and rather ominously that "some began to die in horror and anguish, fearing to go out into the Dark" (*MR* 347–48).

Through his device of multiple voices whereby one speaker answers another speaker by quoting a third speaker who in turn cites an indeterminate fourth speaker, Tolkien was able to introduce the question of the meaning of death without answering it, and keeping both options—death as gift or death as punishment—on the table. The Tale of Adanel is Andreth's third-hand answer to Finrod's questions: "what did you do to anger Eru?" and "are there no tales of your days before death?" But while that tale supplies answers to both his questions, neither Finrod speaking from within the mythos nor we as readers seeing it from the outside have any assurance that those answers are the right ones, or that her story is anything more than speculation. In these circumstances, it becomes difficult to take her argument as the definitive Middle-earth Fall of Men, nor her introduction of the hearsay of the Old Hope as a pre-vision of the Advent of Christ. Nonetheless, an ancillary question arises, one that Tolkien himself raised; does the Tale of Adanel, not to mention the add-on of the Old Hope, make his legendarium "too like a parody of Christianity?" Or are his mythos and that of Christianity simply trying each in its own way to do the same thing, to answer with whatever means are at hand the same cosmic questions, to find a way to derive meaning from the terrible and beautiful Middle-earth in which we live and have our being?

To these questions, as to the question that opens this discussion, "whose myth is it?" Tolkien leaves us to find our own answers. It is Tolkien's myth, of course, but within that context he is careful to present both sides, both Finrod's and Andreth's interpretations, as well as Adanel's addition of other voices to Andreth's argument. Christopher Tolkien's statement in his 1977 foreword to *The Silmarillion* that his father came to envision the legendarium as a "compilation," a narrative made "from sources of great diversity" including oral tales (*Silm* viii), shows the intentional similarity of Tolkien's invented mythology to those of the real world, to the competing and confused versions of events we find for example in Greek, Hindu, Welsh, and Finnish myths. That Andreth and Finrod do not and cannot agree about Eru's plan for humanity gives verisimilitude to Tolkien's texts; their conflicting interpretations add to rather than detract from the inner consistency of reality in his Secondary World. And if readers can accept the inconsistency of that inner consistency, the "Athrabeth Finrod ah Andreth" will in its own multi-voiced, mythological way foster Secondary Belief.

Part Two

Tolkien in Tradition

Part Two, Tolkien and Tradition, seats his work in the context of mythic literature from the Middle Ages to the nineteenth century. "Tolkien's Wild Men from Medieval to Modern" looks at Tolkien's many variations—ranging from Ghân-Buri-Ghân to Gollum to Frodo Baggins—on a traditional figure in medieval romance and history: that fugitive from society and the outlier on the edge of civilization known as the Wild Man. As its title implies, "Tolkien and the Matter of Britain" investigates the relationship between the Matter of Middle-earth and the longest-running and most famous cycle of stories in English literature, that of King Arthur and his court. "Frodo and Aragorn: The Concept of the Hero" pairs, compares, and contrasts the two hero-figures from *The Lord of the Rings,* showing how Tolkien has mixed and matched his characters with their epic and fairy tale archetypes. "Bilbo's Neck Riddle" puts the central question of *The Hobbit,* "What have I got in my pocket?" in the context of its medieval forebears in Icelandic prose and poetry.

"Allegory Versus Bounce" offers a variation on the format, being not one essay on a subject but two in collegial disagreement. It is a debate between myself and that dean of Tolkien scholarship, Tom Shippey, on the appropriate reading of Tolkien's short story, *Smith of Wootton Major.* Whomever you decide to agree with, I hope you will find the dispute informative and entertaining. Tom and I certainly did.

"'There would always be a fairy tale': Tolkien and the Folklorists" examines Tolkien's position, stated in "On Fairy-stories" in the debate between two schools of thought in Comparative Mythology/Philology, that of solar myth proposed by Max Müller and his followers, and that of anthropology offered by Andrew Lang, Edward Tyler, George Cox, and others. Not surprisingly, Tolkien didn't agree with either school. "A Mythology for Finland: Tolkien and Lönnrot as Mythmakers" looks at Tolkien's legendarium in the light of its real-world inspiration, Elias Lönnrot's compilation of oral Finnish *runos* or songs. Lönnrot's *Kalevala,* as Tolkien wrote to his publisher, "set the rocket off in story" as the spark that ignited his own stories of Middle-earth and Valinor.

"Brittany and Wales in Middle-earth" investigates ways in which Tolkien's mythos was influenced by, imitative of, or directly borrowed from the medieval Celtic cultures of Wales and Brittany, their stories, ballads, and languages. "The Green Knight, the Green Man, and Treebeard," is just that, placing everybody's favorite Ent in the context of his medieval literary and folkloric ancestors. "Missing Person" looks at what Tolkien left out of his mythology and how that omission adds to the poignance and tragedy of his story.

Tolkien's Wild Men from Medieval to Modern

The form and subject matter of J.R.R. Tolkien's major fiction clearly derive from the medieval genres of epic, romance, and fairy tale. This said, it should also be noted that Tolkien puts a modern spin on many of his characters, reconfiguring the contexts and situations in which they play a part while at the same time keeping faith with the medieval types from which they derive. Of the many elements that make his work both classic and unclassifiable and energize his stories with a life of their own, this must be counted not the least important. His medieval roots are plain to see—from the surface texture of costume, custom, battle-gear, and speech to the deeper borrowings of theme and pattern from *Beowulf,* Malory, and the *Gawain* poet. His modernity of treatment is less clearly obvious, largely because it is so seamlessly integrated into the medieval structure.

One of the areas in which his medievalism and his modernism join most fruitfully is in his handling of one of the less-imitated medieval character types—the Wild Man. A familiar figure in the literature and folklore of the Middle Ages, he was called *wudu-wása* in Anglo-Saxon, *wodwos* in Middle English, *sylvestre* in Old French. His proper title is Wild Man of the Woods. A refugee from civilization, he is a prowler lurking both actually and metaphorically on the borders of society. His home is the forest, the wilderness outside the boundaries set by civilization. The word *forest* apparently originates from the Latin *foris,* meaning "outside" (Saunders, 1). The Wild Man is the archetypal outsider, the prowler on the borderlands between the wild and tame, exiled either by his fellow men or by his own misanthropy. The prototype is Enkidu, the hairy buddy of the eponymous hero in the Babylonian epic of *Gilgamesh,* or perhaps Nebuchadnezzar of biblical fame, crawling on all fours, gnawing grass and letting his fingernails grow. But these are only the precursors of a whole crew of medieval manlike monsters from the Grendel of *Beowulf* fame to Glamr, the walking dead terror of *Grettissaga.*

In his book *Wild Men in the Middle Ages,* Richard Bernheimer gives a general description of the type. The Wild Man is,

> a hairy man curiously compounded of human and animal traits, without, however, sinking to the level of an ape. It exhibits upon its naked human anatomy a growth of fur, leaving bare only its face, feet, and hands. . . . Frequently the creature is shown wielding a heavy club or mace, or the trunk of a tree; and since its body is usually naked except for a shaggy covering, it may hide its nudity under a strand of twisted foliage worn around the loins. (Bernheimer, 1)

Bernheimer elaborates this picture with phrases culled from European folklore: "Huge, hairy, and mute," "so large that his legs alone have the size of trees," "a creature of woods and rocks" (23–24). He observes that, "[t]he creature itself may appear without its fur, its club, or its loin ornament. Any one of its characteristics may be said to designate the species" (2). The type, then, is a convention, and as Bernheimer notes, individual specimens vary.

A representative example might be the Wild Man in Chrétien de Troyes's *Yvain* who appears to Calogrenant, a knight of Arthur's court, near the opening of the poem. Riding through the wood of Broceliande in search of adventure, Calogrenant comes upon a prototypical specimen. First, he is huge.

> *si vi qu'il ot grosse la teste*
> *plus que roncins ne autre beste,*
> *chevox mechiez et front pelé*
> *s'ot pres de deus espanz de lé*
>
> [I saw his head's size was enormous,
> a huger head than any horse's
> or other beasts, with tufts of hair.
> His forehead was completely bare
> and measured more than two spans wide.]

He is also a sort of cross between flora,

> *oroilles mossues et granz*
> *autiex com a uns olifanz,*

[a huge ear filled with mossy plants,
just like the ears of elephants.]

and fauna:

les sorcix granz et le vis plat
ialz de çuete, et nes de chat,
boche fandue come lous,
dans de sengler aguz et rous

[His brows were full, his face was flat,
with owlish eyes, the nose of a cat.
His wolfish mouth was split apart
by wild boar's teeth, bloodred and sharp.]

He is hairy,

Barbe rosse, grenons tortiz

[His beard was red; his whiskers in
great knots;]

and misshapen.

Et le manton aers au piz,
longue eschine torte et boçu;

[his chest merged with his chin.
His long spine twisted in a hump.]

He carries a club,

Apoiez tu sor sa maçu

[The creature sat upon the stump
and leaned upon his club.]

and dresses in skins.

qu'il n'avoit ne lin ne lange,
einz ot a son col atachiez

deus cuirs de novel escorchiez,
ou de deus tors ou de deus bués.

[He wore
no wool or linen clothing, for
instead the fellow was arrayed
in two wild bulls' hides, newly flayed.]

Calogranant ends his quasi-comic description by reiterating the Wild Man's size:

Et fuz montez desor un tronc,
S'ot bien dis et set piez de lonc;

[He leaned against a fallen tree,
and then I realized that he
was seventeen feet tall, at least]
(Chrétien, ll. 291–320; Cline trans., ll. 271–99).

And yet when Calogrenant asked him what he is, the creature replied "qu'il ert uns hom" [that he was a man] (l. 328).

An equally conventional, but considerably briefer, appearance of the Wild Man occurs in *Sir Gawain and the Green Knight,* where the *wodwos* harry the bewildered Sir Gawain as he rides through the winter forest on the way to his meeting with the Green Knight.

Sumwhyle with wormeʒ he wereʒ, and with wolues als,
Sumwhyle wyth wodwos, þat woned in þe knarreʒ
(Tolkien & Gordon, 23)

At whiles with worms he wars, and with wolves also,
at whiles with wood-trolls that wandered in the crags
(Tolkien trans., *Sir Gawain,* 43)

The paradigm is roomy enough to hold a number of variations from the Grendels and Glamrs, bestial or uncanny but clearly related to humanity, to the outright shape-changers, the were-beasts who can assume either human or animal form and whose animal shape is most often that of wolf or bear. Best-known, perhaps, are the Norse hero Sigmund and his son Sinfjotli from *Völsungasaga,* who, when they find and put on wolf skins to hunt in, are trapped in the wolf shape, and come close to killing one another before they get free. Such werewolf stories abounded in the Middle Ages and seem to be equally popular today, if Stephen King is anything to go by.

Another example is the battle-mad berserkers, whose reputation is explicit in their name, derived from "bear-sark," or "bear-shirt." The exemplar here is Böðvar Bjarki of *Hrolfs Saga Kraka,* whose *fylgja,* or "fetch," appears and fights as a bear while Böðvar sleeps. But such man-beasts were not always seen as men transformed into beasts; they could be beasts elevated above ordinary humanity. The Celtic Horned God Cernnunnos is of this type, a supernatural figure, man-shaped but with the antlers of a stag. All these testify to the fearsomely close connection between human and animal that haunted the pagan mind and that the Christian church worked so hard to eradicate.

A more refined use of the Wild Man figure supplies us with a psychological variation on the type. Neither the medieval version of the missing link that Bernheimer describes nor the were-beast of myth and legend, this Wild Man is simply a man with what we would now call a severe personality disorder. The psychological Wild Man is not born wild but has wildness thrust upon him by some shock or trauma that produces bizarre but usually temporary aberrant behaviour. One example of this type is the Merlin of Geoffrey of Monmouth's *Life of Merlin.* When his brothers are killed in battle, Merlin goes mad, forsakes civilization, and runs wild in the woods with only the beasts for company. A better-known example is Sir Thomas Malory's Lancelot, who falls into a similar madness, but for a slightly different reason—he too has lost a loved one, Queen Guinevere, who in a jealous rage has banished him from her sight. He first swoons and then runs mad.

> And whan Sir Launcelot awooke oute of hys swoghe, he lepte oute at a baywyndow into a gardyne, and there wyth thornys he was all to-cracched of his vysage and hys body, and so he ranne furth he knew nat whothir, and was as wylde [woode] as ever was man. And so he ran two yere, and never had man grace to know hym. (Malory, 487)

Lancelot and his malady exemplified one of the most popular literary treatments of the Wild Man, a malady to which medieval lovers were particularly susceptible, and to which Malory's Tristram and Chrétien's Yvain also succumbed. Indeed Richard Bernheimer describes this madness as almost an "occupational disease of knight-errantry," explaining that,

> When they believe they have been slighted in love, these warriors have a way of breaking all bonds, sometimes stripping themselves naked, and invariably repairing to the woods, expressing their sadness and degradation by leading the life of the wild man. (Bernheimer, 14)

Yet another variation on the conventional Wild Man type is the medieval outlaw, the masterless man. As his name implies, the outlaw is on the run from society not because of his primitive nature or as the result of a psychotic break, but because of some legal transgression. He too is a prowler on the borderlands, a lurker in the woods. But his avoidance of society is no irrational aberration but a quite reasonable fear of the law. At its best this outlaw type is personified in Robin Hood, living merrily in the greenwood and occasionally drawing a bow against some stuffy bureaucrat.

But this is rare. In life, which tends to be scruffier than literature, the outlaw type shows up in England as the brushwood men, in France as the Jacquerie, escaped serfs with nothing to lose, desperate men living wild because they could not risk a return to civilization. By those more fortunate, wealthier, and on the right side of the law, they were seen as very low on the scale of humanity, hardly better than the standard Wild Man. A fourteenth-century tale, *Le Despit au Vilain,* says of them, "they are a sorry lot. . . . Should they eat meat? Rather should they chew grass on the heath and go naked on all fours"—phrases which make the comparison plain. (Joly, 461, quoted in Tuchman, 175). In all his guises, then, the Wild Man was to the Middle Ages just what he is to the twentieth century—an ever-present threat to our thin veneer of socialized behaviour, the image of what we fear, of what we all might become.

Like their medieval counterparts, Tolkien's Wild Men come in all varieties. He has forest trolls, wood-elves, outlaws, and shape-changers, all of whom fit more or less comfortably into the general category. His first attempt at taking the convention and updating it may be Beorn, the man-bear of *The Hobbit.* Beorn is described as "a huge man with a thick black beard and hair, and great bare arms and legs with knotted muscles. He was clothed in a tunic of wool down to his knees and was leaning on a large axe" (*Hobbit,* 104–5). He towers above Gandalf, and the hobbit Bilbo "could easily have trotted through his legs without ducking his head" (105). So far, though he is certainly better-dressed, he closely approximates the Wild Man of Bernheimer's description, including the massive legs and the weapon. But Beorn is a modern version, friendly, hospitable, fully capable of speech, and possessed of a house, farm animals, and a sense of humor. He is a twentieth-century children's Wild Man, hearty and jolly and not really frightening, just mysterious. True, he seems to be a shape-changer, and it is strongly implied that he has a habit of occasionally turning into a bear. Nevertheless, he is never actually seen as a bear, and the character and the episode in which he figures are treated with disarming jocularity.

A more typically medieval Wild Man is Ghân-Buri-Ghân, one of the aboriginal Drúadan, who makes a cameo appearance late in *The Lord of the*

Rings. In that civilized society he is seen by the other characters as a leftover, a prehistoric figure surviving in a modern world, a "remnant," as one of them says, "of an older time . . . wild and wary as the beasts" (RK V, v, 105). Viewing Ghân-Buri-Ghân from the darkness outside Theoden's tent, Merry Brandybuck is reminded of the Pukelmen, the primitive stone figures he saw on the road to Dunharrow. Borrowing straight from the Gawain poet, Tolkien calls him a "Wose," and glosses this in the text as "Wild [Man] of the Woods" (105).

Ghân-Buri-Ghân is "a strange squat shape of a man, gnarled as an old stone," with the "hairs of his scanty beard" straggling "on his lumpy chin like old moss." He is "short-legged and fat-armed, thick and stumpy, and clad only with grass about his waist" (105–6), all of which brings him pretty close to the standard type of Bernheimer's description. Still, though Tolkien clearly wanted to give the standard Wild Man a place in his pseudo-medieval world of Middle-earth, this one, too, is not wholly typical. Like Beorn, he also talks, though his dialogue sounds like Hollywood Tarzan: "Wild Men live here before Stone-houses," "fight not," "kill orc-folk," "we help" (106). For another thing, he is not a menace but a good guy, guiding the Men of Rohan to Gondor for the battle and asking no reward except to be let alone.

Tolkien's more complex versions of the figure exceed the convention by their lengthier treatment and fuller development as characters. I will offer three and a half examples. My first example is an unlikely one: Strider, the guide and rescuer of the hobbits who becomes Aragorn, the uncrowned king. As one of the two major heroes of *The Lord of the Rings*, Strider seems an odd candidate for Wild Man status. But a close look shows that he has the requisite characteristics to fit him into the outlaw type. He is first introduced to both Frodo and the reader as a figure both actually and metaphorically on the edge of society, sitting alone in the corner of the common-room at Bree among "vague figures difficult to make out in the shadows and corners" (*FR*, 167). Thus introduced, he is made to seem just one among many strangers, men on the move, squint-eyed, ill-favoured types. "One of the wandering folk—Rangers we call them," says Butterbur the innkeeper (168), and it is clear that the word *ranger* carries its own suspicion, suggesting someone too much at home in the wild, living rough and sleeping out, not like civilized folk who live in houses.

Others have the same opinion. "That's Stick-at-nought-Strider," Bill Ferny tells the hobbits, "[t]hough I've heard other names not so pretty" (193). Even after the hobbits meet and talk with him, Strider seems too tough-looking a character for their Shire-bound sensibilities to accept. Frodo suspects uneasily that he has "fallen in with a rascal" and reflects with considerable anxiety that he has very little money with him. "All of it would hardly satisfy a rogue," he thinks, and moreover "he could not spare any of it" (175). He clearly expects that such a suspicious-looking character must be a robber of the highway variety. Sam's opinion is no better. "He comes out of the Wild," says Sam, "and I never heard no good of such folk" (178). With grim humor Strider consciously plays up this side of himself. "I have a rather rascally look, have I not?" he asks the hobbits, with a "queer gleam in his eye" (176).

It seems clear that our first view of Strider is intended as a deliberately negative picture of the outlaw or brushwood Wild Man. Tolkien has purposely presented him in the worst light in order to make his transformation all the more effective when he is subsequently revealed, first, as a kind of Robin Hood figure—from the greenwood, not the brushwood—and then, as the noble Aragorn, the crownless who shall be king. Tolkien is playing variations on the medieval variation itself and playing mind-games with the reader as he does it. He takes Strider from rascal to forest ranger to king, progressively peeling away the layers that have concealed his identity until we see this Wild Man as in some ways the most civilized man in the book—certainly the one with the longest lineage, the most distinguished heritage, and the most brilliant future.

The next example is Túrin Turambar, the hapless protagonist of one of the most poignant episodes in Tolkien's mythology, "The Tale of the Children of Húrin." As a character, Túrin is based on Kullervo, an equally hapless character from the Finnish *Kalevala*, which Tolkien much admired. Kullervo is a mixture of outcast and misanthrope, and Túrin is another. Both are orphaned; both are social misfits. Their energies cannot be harnessed to civilized pursuits, and their affinities are with the wild rather than the human world. Both exist on the fringe of society, always solitary, always on the outside looking in. In the line of Tolkienian Wild Men, Túrin is a greater mix of types than Strider, combining outlaw and psychological Wild Man. Tolkien's modernity comes into play here, and Túrin is presented as a civilized man paving his own road to self-destruction and betrayed at last by his own wrongheadedness. Thus the character is more sympathetic, his story more tragic because he is the architect of his own defeat.

What gives Túrin a special poignance as a Wild Man is that his tragedy need not have happened. What he becomes makes us constantly aware of how different he might have been. Tolkien has made Túrin a paradigm of modern alienation, a self-exiled outsider driven by emotions he does not understand, wilful and conflicted, coming to painful self-awareness only at the end of his life. Moreover, Tolkien supplies a greater than medieval range of causes for his Wild Man behaviour. For example, Túrin, like Merlin or Lancelot or Tristram, suffers attacks of madness, but Túrin's come not, like theirs, from loss of relatives, or from disappointment in love, but from shock and horror at his betrayal of those who love him. When he discovers the death of Finduilas, the elf-maiden whose unrequited love for him has led her to her death, he swoons, and when he finds that he has unknowingly killed Beleg, his best friend, he becomes truly mad, catatonic. He suffers loss of speech and memory and must be led about by others while his madness lasts.

Also extra-medieval is Túrin's habitual appearance, although it too supports his Wild Man identity, for he is in a sense "hairy," that is, unshaven, untrimmed, and uncombed. But unlike his medieval counterpart, this is not from natural inclination but rather because he is a guerrilla warrior with little opportunity to attend to his appearance, to shave or get his hair cut. Though his fosterfather, Thingol, offers him a place among his knights, Túrin chooses "the north-marches" (*march* = "borderland") and walks "far and wide in the wild woods" (*UT*, 79). There he cares "no longer for his looks or his attire, but his hair [is] unkempt, and his mail covered with a grey cloak stained with the weather" (79). Coming into Thingol's hall one day from the wild, unkempt and with ragged garments, he is taunted by a jealous Elf, Saeros, who with ironic solicitude offers him a comb for the "thicket of brambles" which is his hair, describes him as "wild and fell," and explicitly calls him a "woodwose" (80). In revenge, Túrin ambushes Saeros, strips him naked, and chases him through the woods to his accidental death.

This incident provides yet another aspect that links Túrin with the Wild Man: nakedness. But again, the motif is re-worked, and the context changed. Instead of being himself naked, he imposes nakedness on someone else, in revenge for his insults turning Saeros into a kind of inadvertent Wild Man running naked in the wild wood. But the episode has other Wild Man repercussions, for it is this incident that sends Túrin into the woods for good, so to speak. He flees to the forest at first out of fear of apprehension, but stays out of stubbornness and wounded pride. Tolkien has made Túrin's affinity for the wild at once practical, psychological, and archetypal. He chooses the forest over Thingol's hall, first as refuge, and then because he cannot bring himself to be judged, or to sue for a pardon he feels he does not need. It is a conscious choice, a clearly rhetorical gesture, intended as a reproach to those he leaves behind. Both the act of choosing and the choice of venue recall the meaning for "forest" cited earlier, "outside." Feeling himself an outsider, alienated, Túrin has made metaphor into fact and put himself beyond the pale.

A telling clue to Túrin's psychological Wild Man status comes with his most exasperating and revealing quirk. He keeps changing his name as if he had no real sense of self, taking on a succession of abstract identities, each of which is a marker of his alienation from himself and the world around him. After the Saeros episode, convinced that his motives have been mis-construed, he calls himself Neithan, "the Wronged." Refusing to apologize or explain what is obviously a tragic accident, he exiles himself to the woods and joins a band of outlaws, themselves recognizable Wild Man types. But these outlaws are not Robin Hoods. They are true brushwood men, thieves and rascals, and Túrin finally leaves them in disgust.

Once more on the side of right, given a chance to re-form himself, he takes the battle-name Gorthol, "Dread Helm," thus dehumanizing his own and ev-eryone else's view of him. When by tragic accident he kills Beleg Strongbow, his best friend, he again takes a new name, calling himself Agarwaen son of Umarth, "Bloodstained, son of Ill-fate." Next he takes the name Mormegil, the "Black Sword," another dehumanization. Most telling of all, when asked his name he says only, "I am Wildman of the Woods" (*UT*, 110). If that does not make it clear, nothing will. It is Tolkien's gift, however, that he makes us see this Wild Man as all too human and therefore tragic, as a real Wild Man could never be. Treating a medieval character with twentieth-century psychological insight, Tolkien shows us in Túrin an existential man, creating meaning out of his own perception, searching for his identity, yet unwilling to accept it.

My next example is the most complex, and both the most and the least typical. It is, as may be guessed, Gollum, Tolkien's most brilliant creation, a medieval Wild Hobbit with distinctly modern overtones. Gollum is an amalgam of all the types. Readers of *The Lord of the Rings* first encounter him offstage, so to speak, described to Frodo by Gandalf as being "of Hob-bit-kind; akin to the fathers of the fathers of the Stoors" (*FR*, I, ii, 62). He is thus an aboriginal. He is the murderer of his friend Déagol, the original finder of the Ring, and is thus an outlaw, shunned by his relatives, expelled from his family, and driven into the wild. We are told that,

> He wandered in loneliness, weeping a little for the hardness of the world, and he journeyed up the River, till he came to a stream that flowed down from the mountains, and he went that way. He caught fish in deep pools with invisible fingers and ate them raw. . . . So he journeyed by night up into the highlands, and he found a little cave out of which the dark stream ran, and he wormed his way like a maggot into the heart of the hills, and vanished out of all knowledge. (63)

Like the conventional medieval Wild man, Gollum becomes a degenerate, feral figure, constantly associated with animal images. But Gollum's animals are from the bottom of the evolutionary scale. The passage quoted above compares him to a maggot. Other animal images include spider, squirrel, and frog. At his first appearance, crawling down the cliff-face of the Emyn Muil, he is repeatedly referred to as "it," as if he had no humanity. He is "a small black shape" whose "clinging hands and toes were finding crevices and holds that no hobbit could ever have seen or used, but it looked as if it was just creeping down on sticky pads, like some large prowling thing of insect-kind" (*TT,* 219). Like an animal, Gollum goes on all fours. Like an animal's, his eyes gleam green when caught in the light. Like an animal, he is naked. Nowhere in the narrative is there any mention of clothing, as if, like a real animal, he does not need to be provided with covering.

Gollum is also psychotic, driven mad by his obsession with the Ring. It is just here, however, that Tolkien's modernity takes over, for Gollum's madness is distinctly of the twentieth century rather than the Middle Ages. Gollum's split into the dual personas that Sam calls Slinker and Stinker is a psychological division into conflicting, even opposing selves, the kind of division that the Middle Ages regularly treated allegorically, often personifying the split as Soul and Body. In Tolkien's hands it becomes a paradigm of the twentieth century, the age of anxiety. More than just a psychological Wild Man in the Merlin-Lancelot tradition, Gollum is a case study, a textbook example of what the popular psychoanalytic terminology of the mid-twentieth century called a split or multiple personality, a schizophrenic.

Gollum hears voices, and is haunted by their demands. Not only does he talk to himself, but his two voices/selves are in deep conflict with one another. In addition, his madness has skidded him backwards down the developmental scale. Where the conventional Wild Man is evolutionarily regressive, slipping from a civilized town-dweller or court habitué to a hunter-gatherer, Gollum is psychologically regressive. He is infantile. Ghân-Buri-Ghân talks like a Hollywood Tarzan. Gollum talks baby-talk: "Nice little hobbitses . . . they jumps on us like cats on poor mices . . . cruel little hobbitses" (221). And like the brushwood men he is a refugee from civilization, indeed, it is his experience as a fugitive that qualifies him as a guide for Sam and Frodo on their way to Mordor.

But I promised three and a half examples. My half example, part of Gollum and yet separate from him, is Tolkien's most modern, most moving depiction of the Wild Man. It is, of course, the least likely Wild Man in the book—Frodo Baggins. When we see Gollum and Frodo side by side, day after day, we see also the potential Gollum in Frodo as well as his struggle against being wholly taken over by the madness that has wasted and destroyed that lost creature. As the narrative progresses, the two characters move nearer to one another. One by one, Gollum's Wild Man characteristics are transferred, albeit sometimes only momentarily, to Frodo.

First he is stripped of his clothes. In the Tower of Cirith Ungol Sam finds him lying naked on a heap of filthy rags. Then he is temporarily reclothed, which should make him more human but instead makes him more animal-like, for like Calogrenant's Wild Man he is clothed in orc garments made of animal skin, "long hairy breeches of some unclean beast-fell" (*RK*, 189). Finally, on Mt. Doom, too weak to stand erect, he is reduced to crawling up the mountain on his hands and knees like an animal. And at the last, as they go up Mt. Doom, Frodo's nakedness becomes symbolic, a metaphor for his loss of self: "I am naked in the dark," he tells Sam, "and there is no veil between me and the wheel of fire" (215).

The reference to the wheel of fire—the Ring—is the final evidence of another Wild Man characteristic, madness, the madness that has been growing on Frodo since the Ring came into his possession. Though its visits are fitful, it increasingly takes possession of him, altering his behavior and lessening his humanity. Approaching the tower of Minas Morgul, Frodo feels "his senses reeling and his mind darkening. Then suddenly, as if some force were at work other than his own will, he began to hurry, tottering forward, his groping hands held out, his head lolling from side to side" (*TT*, 313).

It is an ugly picture of a creature bereft of rational mind, and both Sam and Gollum have to run after him and turn him around to bring him to his senses. When Sam finds Frodo in the Tower of Cirith Ungol, his confession that he has the Ring and his offer to carry it cause Frodo to turn on him like a maddened beast. Later, on the slopes of Mt. Doom, when Sam again offers to carry the Ring, Frodo tells him with sad self-knowledge, "If you tried to take it I should go mad" (*RK*, 214). At that moment he is sane, for self-knowledge is sanity. In the ensuing moments he loses that self-knowledge, and then he does go truly mad. He is mad when, having come to Mt. Doom to destroy the Ring, he instead puts it on and claims it as his own. At that moment he becomes the most possible, the most persuasive, the most modern of all Tolkien's Wild Men—the madman who thinks he is sane, who has had self-knowledge and has lost it.

In medieval literature the Wild Man is a stock character, sometimes a figure of fear, sometimes a figure of fun—as with Calogrenant's Wild Man—sometimes a figure of sympathy, as is the case with Merlin and Lancelot. But he is not often a figure who shows us something of ourselves, something essential, pitiable, and typical of the human condition. In Gollum and Frodo, and in Túrin as well, Tolkien has made the medieval Wild Man into a figure at once medieval, modern, and timeless.

Tolkien and the Matter of Britain

Throughout the Middle Ages the three great "Matters" of European heroic romance comprised a library of myths and legends, poetry and prose, that would have been known to any educated reader. These were the Matter of Britain (the Arthurian stories), the Matter of Greece and Rome (the romances of antiquity, especially those of Alexander), and the Matter of France (the *chansons de geste* centering on the court of Charlemagne). While the Matter of Greece and Rome and the Matter of France are now largely the domain of scholars and literary critics, the Matter of Britain is still read and enjoyed by a wide audience. Not only it is readily available, it has spawned a number of modern re-tellings, and is rivaled in size and scope only by J.R.R. Tolkien's Matter of Middle-earth, whose appearance in the middle and late twentieth century has given Arthur a shot in the arm and a run for his money.

Nowhere that I know of did Tolkien refer to his legendarium as the Matter of Middle-earth. Nevertheless, the designation has come more and more to be used by Tolkien scholars as the phrase that aptly captures both the scope of his work and its long (over half a century) history of composition. Taken together, *The Lord of The Rings, The Silmarillion* and its companion volume of *Unfinished Tales,* and the multi-volume History of Middle-earth comprise a body of work worthy to be considered a fourth great Matter in the tradition of its three medieval predecessors. More important, the relationship between two of the four, the Matters of Britain and Middle-earth, is closer than at first appears.

In his oft-quoted letter to Milton Waldman of Collins Publishing, Tolkien referred to what he called the mythological "poverty" of England, in that it had "no stories of its own"[1] and went on to describe the mythology he

once hoped to dedicate to his country. Worth noting is his disqualification
of the obvious candidate for the position, the "Arthurian world," which he
dismissed as "imperfectly naturalized, associated with the soil of Britain but
not with English. . . . For one thing its 'faerie' is too lavish, and fantastical,
incoherent and repetitive. For another, and more important thing: it is involved in, and explicitly contains the Christian religion. . . . that seems to me
fatal" (*Letters* 144). In its place, Tolkien offered his own mythos as:

> a body of more or less connected legend. . . . somewhat cool and clear, be
> redolent of our 'air' (the clime and soil of the North West, meaning Britain
> and the hither parts of Europe) . . . and, while possessing . . . the fair elusive
> beauty that some call Celtic . . . it should be 'high', purged of the gross, and
> fit for the more adult mind of a land long now steeped in poetry. (*Letters*
> 144–45)

The two descriptions, when considered in the context of one another, as well
as the audience Tolkien was addressing, the time in which he wrote, and the
situation which gave rise to it, add up to something greater than the sum of
their parts. Let us consider first the audience. Unlike most letters, this was
aimed at a multiple audience. Its immediate addressee was Milton Waldman, but its ultimate target was the firm Waldman represented—Collins
Publishing. The letter's agenda was to make a case for joint publication of
The Silmarillion with *The Lord of the Rings*.

Equally relevant is the time at which the letter was written. This was (conjecturally, the letter is undated) some time in 1951, thirty-five years after his
first serious efforts at contriving an English myth in *The Book of Lost Tales*,
begun in 1916–17. The second passage thus reflects, albeit in terms of the
past, Tolkien's most recent thinking about his mythology, which by 1951 had
been re-written many times. The first passage, then, must perforce reflect
Tolkien's recent thinking about Arthurian myth, and it is not unreasonable
to suppose that with the passage of time this too may have undergone revision. While it seems plain that Tolkien wanted Waldman to think of him as
creating rather than imitating, his very dispossession of Arthurian myth is
negative evidence of its power, for it shows that Arthur was in his mind.

Finally, the situation which gave rise to the letter. George Allen & Unwin,
publishers of *The Hobbit*, who had urged Tolkien to begin a sequel—(the
new Hobbit which became *The Lord of the Rings*)—had reluctantly declined
Tolkien's proposal to include *The Silmarillion* as part of the package. Tolkien
then turned to Collins, writing Waldman a description intended to persuade
him that the two works were interdependent and indivisible, that they nei-

ther could nor should be separated (*Letters* Headnote, 143). Such a massive publication was a risk, made doubly so by the post-war shortage of paper, and Tolkien made every effort to promote the venture by giving Waldman what remains to this day the best single account of his own mythology. The combined rhetoric of the two descriptive passages was first to dispossess the one legend—the Arthurian world—as England's myth, and then to replace it with a fresh one—Tolkien's many-layered and potentially multi-volumed myth of Middle-earth. Yet the very fact that he raised the issue of the Arthurian world to Waldman suggests that Tolkien was well aware of its hallowed place in England's literary heritage.

He could also have been aware of its place in his own, for both before and after he wrote to Waldman, Tolkien had set his hand to his own treatment of the Arthurian legend. At some time in the mid-1930s, that is, more than a decade *before* he wrote to Waldman, he had begun a long poem which he called The Fall of Arthur. And in 1955, four years *after* the letter to Waldman, he still cherished the hope of finishing it. "I write alliterative verse with pleasure" he wrote to his American publisher Houghton Mifflin, and added, "I still hope to finish a long poem on *The Fall of Arthur* in the same measure" (*Letters* 219).

Tolkien's biographer Humphrey Carpenter describes The Fall of Arthur as a "major" work, although he also notes that this was Tolkien's "only incursion into the Arthurian cycle." A point worth noting in view of the decided objections quoted above to the overt Christianity in the Arthurian cycle is that his own poem did not touch on the Grail. Instead, according to Carpenter, Tolkien,

> began an individual rendering of the Morte D'Arthur, in which the king and Gawain go to war 'in Saxon lands' but are summoned home by news of Mordred's treachery. The poem was never finished, but it was read and approved by E.V. Gordon, and by R.W. Chambers, Professor of English at London University, who considered it to be 'great stuff—really heroic, quite apart from its value as showing how the *Beowulf* metre can be used in modern English'. (Carpenter 168)

The poem is in the possession of Christopher Tolkien. Its relevance to the present discussion lies not just its survival, but in Tolkien's comment to Houghton Mifflin that he "still" hoped to finish it. This suggests that his dismissal of Arthur in the Waldman letter may to some extent have reflected an immediate, specific, and possibly context-determined critical position, a re-vision (in every sense of the word) of the relationship of the Arthurian corpus to his own invented legendarium.

Returning now to the two quoted passages, let us examine their implications both singly and together. While the first passage seems to define what is *not* a proper mythology for England, the second passage (intended to describe what to Tolkien *was* such a mythology) rather begs the question, for his account of his own legendarium could easily pass for a description of the Arthurian world he so emphatically dismissed in the first passage. The likenesses are clear. Both myths comprise "bodies of more or less connected legend." Both are "redolent of the clime and soil of Britain and the hither part of North West Europe." Both possess "the fair elusive beauty that some call Celtic."

Although these might seem mere generic similarities, Tolkien's juxtaposing of the two myths invites their comparison. It also raises some specific questions about the relationship between "the Arthurian world" and his own invented world. How much are the likenesses between the two cycles a function of the generic resemblance that all mythologies share, rather than the conscious imitation of one by another? Beyond the general resemblance, are there any shared particulars that might be ascribed to conscious borrowing? How well do Tolkien's criteria for disqualifying the Arthurian world stand up against his own work? What are the major points of similarity and how much do they owe to conscious intent and how much to inadvertence or circumstance?

It could certainly be argued that other mythologies besides that of Arthur might fit Tolkien's general description. Tom Shippey has ably demonstrated similarities in shape and layering to the poems and stories constituting the Völsung material in the *Poetic Edda* and the prose *Völsungasaga*.[2] Norse is not the only example. It is the nature of mythologies to be made up of different kinds of narrative and to be the accumulated work of many voices. This is the case, for example, with the combined mythology of Greece and Rome, gathered as it was over many centuries from poets, dramatists, and historians. However, while this mythology is certainly a body of "more or less connected legend," I would eliminate it as an influence on the grounds that Tolkien had no particular affinity for what he called "Southern" myth, greatly preferring the *Eddas* and sagas of Iceland and the Scandinavian peninsula. Moreover, Greek and Roman myth can hardly be said to be "redolent" of the air of Britain and North West Europe.

But were there existing European models other than the Arthurian that might have influenced Tolkien's own? Yes, there were. He wrote to W.H. Auden that he had once made "an attempt to unify the lays about the Völsungs from the [Icelandic] Elder Edda, written in the old eight-line fornyrðislag stanza" (*Letters* 379), a reference to his then-unpublished "Volsungakviða" and "Guthrúnarkviða" poems, now edited and published by Christopher

Tolkien as *The Legend of Sigurd and Guthrun*. His story of Túrin Turambar draws on the exploits of the greatest hero of Northern myth, Sigurð the Völsung, most notably in the treatment of Túrin's killing of Glaurung, which is explicitly modeled on Sigurð's slaying of the dragon Fáfnir. The Völsung material certainly influenced Tolkien, but powerful though it is, it does not approach the chronological and compositional sweep of either the Arthurian material or Tolkien's own.

There is, of course, the *Beowulf*, which arguably had a greater influence on him than any other single work. Certainly it informed his imagination. The Beowulfian themes of the struggle against monstrous forces, the inevitability of failure, and the imminence of death, are the backbone of *The Lord of the Rings*. More specifically and concretely, Tolkien's appropriation for his invented kingdom of Rohan of Old English language, architecture, customs, poetic tradition, heroic code, and even the king-figure from *Beowulf* is so direct and so obvious that it comes close to endangering the integrity of his sub-created world. Nevertheless, the *Beowulf* cannot be said to have provided a conceptual model for his mythos. Although it is undoubtedly part of some greater, now largely lost, bardic tradition, the poem itself is singular, and can be associated with only a few scattered Old English poems—the epic fragment (barely a page in length) of *Waldere*, and the comparatively short verses of *The Seafarer*, *The Wanderer*, and *Deor's Lament*. It has literary parallels and references in other literatures, most notably Old Icelandic, but no family tree.

What about the Finnish *Kalevala*, which by Tolkien's own account was his direct inspiration for the character of Túrin, and was the genesis of *The Lay of the Children of Húrin?* While *Kalevala* unquestionably influenced that particular work, it had less impact on the narrative aspects of his mythology as a whole, although it was a significant influence on his Elven language, Quenya. Though the Finnish poems are wonderful in their own way, they are, unlike the Arthur material and (of course) Tolkien's own, entirely oral in genesis, preserved orally, and only committed to writing in the late nineteenth century by their compiler, Elias Lönnrot. Furthermore, they are primitive in origin, and do not approach the sophistication and complexity of the later medieval Arthurian narratives either in verse or prose. In addition, the poems were selected and arranged in a shape they did not originally possess by Lönnrot, who culled from a collection of over 85,000 songs the fifty which he chose to edit, organize, and publish as *Kalevala*. So, while certainly an inspiration, *Kalevala* also does not seem an apt conceptual model.

There remains the Arthurian legendarium. We have already noted that sometime in the 1930s and while immersed in his own mythology, Tolkien had begun his own Arthurian poem. He was re-visioning Arthur even while en-visioning his own myth, and it would hardly be surprising if the two my-thologies overlapped. There can be little doubt that Tolkien was not only aware of the overlap, he was consciously employing it in *The Lord of the Rings.* Examples of character and episode abound. For all his Odin-like trap-pings of staff and hat, and his predilection for wandering, Tolkien's Gandalf out-Merlins Merlin, and indeed has cast his own retroactive shadow over that most famous of wizards. Frodo's final wounding by his shadow-nemesis Gollum recalls Arthur's wounding by Mordred in the last battle. The maimed Frodo's departure oversea from Middle-earth to be healed in Valinor explic-itly echoes the wounded Arthur's departure by barge to be healed in Avalon. And Sam's bewildered protest at Frodo's decision to leave the Shire, answered by Frodo's rueful explanation of its necessity, are strongly reminiscent of the last exchange between the despairing Bedivere and his departing king.

I would add as well (though I am aware that not everyone will agree) a more subtle reverberation that occurs early in *The Lord of the Rings* in Fro-do's acceptance at Rivendell of the sword Sting, thrust "deep into a wooden beam" by Bilbo. The narrative records that "Frodo accepted it [the sword] gratefully" (*FR* II, iii, 290). He would most naturally have done this simply by pulling it out. Tolkien's immediate source was probably the Norse *Völ-sungasaga,* in which Sigmund the Völsung's withdrawal of the sword from the tree Barnstokk signals his emergence as a hero. Nonetheless, Frodo's "acceptance" of Sting at the beginning of his quest also re-enacts what is arguably the most significant gesture in all of English literature, Arthur's withdrawal of the sword from the stone in the London churchyard at the beginning of his reign.

One inescapable and obvious dissimilarity must be noted before we go fur-ther, and that is the absence in Tolkien's mythos of a central and uniting figure around which the stories gather. *The Silmarillion* has no Arthur. Indeed, the lack of any one heroic protagonist is one of the hallmarks of Tolkien's leg-endarium. There are heroic figures aplenty—Fëanor, Fingolfin, Beren, Túrin, Húrin, Tuor, Finrod, Aragorn, Frodo, to name only the most prominent. But there is no central character, no hub from which all the spokes radiate. That still point is embodied not by character but by artifact, a factor central to Tolkien's story. No court, no king-figure, but the Silmarils (and to a lesser extent the Ring) are the center of the mythic activity of Middle-earth. The Silmarils drive the action. The Silmarils light the way, and show the reader the gap as it were between earth and heaven. It might not be pressing things too far to propose the Silmarils as both the Arthur and the Grail of Tolkien's story.

These likenesses notwithstanding, the Waldman letter, wherein he listed his objections one by one, gives evidence that at that time Tolkien gave greater importance to his arguments against the Arthurian story. One: the Arthurian world was too lavish and fantastical. Two: it was imperfectly naturalized. Last and seemingly worst of all, it contained explicit Christianity. Let us see how well these criticisms stand up against his own story. I'll begin with Christianity and immediately concede the point. Unlike the Arthurian canon with its miracles, pious hermits, heavy-handed symbolism, and allegorical preachiness, Tolkien's fantasy has no explicit Christianity. It is not preachy, it has no miracles, no holy hermits, no Grail, no didactic allegory, all of which is greatly to its credit.

Further, I will agree with him that the inclusion of such material in his own mythology would have been "fatal" to its credibility and integrity, its inner consistency as a sub-creation. Indeed, Tolkien wrote to Father Robert Murray that he had "not put in, or [had] cut out, practically all references to anything like 'religion', to cults or practices, in the imaginary world," making it clear that he consciously made every effort to keep religion *out* of his legendarium (*Letters* 172). Absence of explicit Christianity is the strongest supporting evidence for Tolkien's distinction between his myth and Arthur's.

Next, Arthurian versus Tolkienian faerie. This is more complicated. Tolkien's description of the Arthurian brand as too lavish, fantastical, incoherent, and repetitive constitutes a sweeping condemnation of qualities on which he obviously had some strong views. But how lavish is "too" lavish? And who is to decide? Without illustrative examples, these are vague terms, and even with examples they are dependent to a large extent on the taste of the beholder. Tolkien's own fantasy has been subjected to the very same kinds of condemnation by critics not in tune with his particular brand of imagination. By his own definition (*vide* his "Fairy-story" essay) fantasy is related to faerie, and in this respect Tolkien's faerie is no less lavish or fantastical than is Arthur's. Both make use of wizards, little people, dragons, mysterious queens, enchanted fountains, shape-changers, time-warps, and magic talismans. The magic storm-inducing Fountain in Chrétien's *Yvain* is no more fantastical than the Mirror of Galadriel, while one has only to range Gandalf against Merlin, hobbits against the ubiquitous dwarfs of Arthurian romance, Galadriel against Morgan le Fay, or the Silmarils and the Ring against the Grail to see the similarities.

The Arthurian world undoubtedly reflected the medieval imagination from which it sprang and answered the needs of the medieval audience to which it spoke. That it might seem unsatisfactory to a modern reader, even one so steeped in medieval tradition as Tolkien, is as much a function of time and taste as of any flaw in the matter itself. Incoherence and repetitiveness are matters of opinion, and what is lavish and fantastical to one reader may be satisfyingly sub-creative to another. If Arthurian faerie appeared incoherent to Tolkien, as it did to Matthew Arnold and as it does to many modern students, that may well be because the key to unlock its inner meaning has been lost. For all its Christian overlay, Arthurian faerie derives primarily from the Celtic mythology native to the "soil of Britain" but imperfectly transmitted by its Christian redactors. Their late and certainly many times copied manuscripts are the only witnesses to what it might have been, but the manuscripts themselves are centuries removed from the origins of the tales. Tolkien's inability to perceive any formal vision underlying Arthurian faerie might be less a measure of its actual incoherence than of the faulty texts which are all he or anyone of his time had to go on. In this respect, his concern over its incoherence might derive from a Germanic impulse to tidy it up, rather than a Celtic inclination to let it rip.

As to repetitiveness, that also is in the eye (or ear) of the beholder, as the forceful, if possibly apocryphal comment on Elves by Hugo Dyson bears witness.[3] And whether Dyson liked them or not, Tolkien's immortal Elves—the Vanyar, the Noldor, the Teleri, the Sindar, the Wood-elves in all their hidden kingdoms and Elven fastnesses of Doriath and Gondolin and Nargothrond and Lórien and the Undying Lands—are as faërian, as otherworldly, as dangerously beautiful and typically Celtic a bunch as any who ever came out of a fairy mound, or peopled the haunted woodlands and enchanted keeps and castles of the Arthurian world.

Finally, naturalization to England. Tolkien's contrasting of a landmass with a language in his distinction between "the soil of Britain" and "English" seems somewhat arbitrary in light of the many-layered culture that English has become. The Celtic Arthur is no more or less "naturalized" than the Anglo-Saxon Alfred or the French Henry II. They are all folded into English history. Indeed, for all Tolkien's distinction between British soil and English history, the Arthurian legend is unquestionably one of the foundations of the island's literature, its culture, and—increasingly with new information—its history. If England has a culture hero in the mythic sense of that term it is Arthur the Celt, not Alfred the Saxon. In this respect, it is surely *The Silmarillion,* far more than the Arthurian cycle, which would have to be naturalized, awarded a citizenship that it was not born into. Tolkien tried to accomplish this through the Ælfwine character of the early versions, but apparently found Ælfwine and his link to English history less and less viable, and finally abandoned any explicit treatment of either.

Having balanced Tolkien's criticism of Arthur against his own mythos, I'd like now to go into more detail about some similarities of structure and external history which, while they are more circumstantial than deliberate,

are part of the close resemblance between the two Matters. Tolkien's references to tales "drawn in fullness" and tales merely "placed" or "sketched"
are apposite here. Some of the Arthurian stories, for example *Sir Gawain
and the Green Knight,* the alliterative and stanzaic *Morte Arthurs,* and several of the romances of Chrétien de Troyes, are finished works of art. Others, however—among them some of the most important, such as Chrétien's
Perceval—were either left unfinished by their author and later continued
by other hands, or—like Robert de Boron's *Roman del Graal*—were lost or
mangled and now exist only in a corrupt or fragmented state.

Comparatively few of Tolkien's stories were ever finished, but we can certainly count *The Lord of the Rings* as a major effort, comparable in its sweep
to Malory's *Le Morte D'Arthur.* Of the many he left unfinished we can cite
the account of Tuor's coming to Gondolin, one of the most provocatively
unfinished of all his *Unfinished Tales,* as well as the attempts to tell in prose
and verse the story of Túrin. Of tales merely sketched there is the outline of
tales appended to "The Lost Road" and "The Notion Club Papers," of which
"King Sheave" is the only actual narrative, while the rest are sketched or in
most cases only mentioned.

Both the verse and prose versions of the tale of Beren and Lúthien, perhaps
the single most important story in the whole corpus apart from *The Lord of
The Rings,* were never completed to Tolkien's satisfaction. Nevertheless, their
presence in his myth may provide an added clue to what I call the negative
aspect of Tolkien's involvement with the Arthurian world. One phrase in his
description of his own mythology, "purged of the gross," invites inquiry, for
Tolkien does not explain what he means by the word *gross.* Read in the context of his dismissal of the Arthurian world, it might be understood as a reference to the two adulterous love triangles of Tristan, Iseult, and Mark, and
Lancelot, Guinevere, and Arthur which occupy so large a place in the story.
Certainly there are no comparable situations in Tolkien's myth. There is, in
fact, only one love story worthy of the name, that of Beren and Lúthien. Their
love, while it is complicated by Thingol's reluctance to give up his daughter, is
neither forbidden nor illicit, and its successful outcome in Beren's quest for
the Silmaril is a formative component of the entire myth.

Both cycles of stories are "redolent" of the clime and soil of the North West
of Europe, Arthur's because that's where they started and where they found
their highest expression, Tolkien's because that's what he intended them to
be. Moreover, Tolkien's own statements show his awareness of the overlap
of language and thus of mythology between the Continent and the island of
Britain. In his O'Donnell Lecture, "English and Welsh," he states unequivocally that, "The north-west of Europe . . . is as it were a single philological

province, a region so interconnected in race, culture, history, and linguistic fusions that its departmental philologies cannot flourish in isolation" (*Angles and Britons* 33).

The interconnection of culture, history, and linguistic fusion cannot be ignored, either in Arthur's case or Tolkien's. Arthurian myth is the cumulative product of intense cross-fertilization, having been translated, retranslated, and re-retranslated by successive hands, and crossed and re-crossed the Narrow Sea so often it could have qualified for a free trip through the Chunnel. It was originally Celtic, shared among the related Celtic communities of Wales, Cornwall, and Brittainy. Geoffrey of Monmouth made it a major part of his *History of the Kings of Britain.* Wace translated Geoffrey into French; Layamon translated Wace into English. Chrétien and his followers brought the story back to France. Anonymous English poets re-cast it into Middle English; and at last the Sir Thomas Malory conflated all the material into one great whole to demonstrate that, in the words of William Caxton, "there can no man resonably gaynsaye but there was a kyng of thys lande named Arthur" (Malory xiv). As with Arthur, so with Tolkien's own mythos. Tolkien's co-option of Old English language for his men of Rohan is as bold a linguistic fusion of the real with the imaginary as anyone ever made. And although it was a late entry into Tolkien's world, the Shire, as typical a rural English village as anyone could want to see, is now and forever a part of Middle-earth.

Both legends certainly display "that fair elusive beauty that some call Celtic." The Elven strongholds of Gondolin and Doriath are as beautiful, as glittering, and as gracious as the magical courts of Arthur's realm, and both recall the under/otherworld of the Welsh Annwfn and the Irish Tír na nóg or Mag Mell, or Tír inna mBóo. Mirkwood may be Germanic in name but it is unmistakably Celtic in character, drawn straight out of the darkly haunted woods of Celtic legend and Arthurian romance. Like Fangorn and Lórien it could pass in a pinch for the magical Breton forest of Broceliande—which, let us not forget, was the original form of the name that later became Beleriand (*LB* 160).

Finally, the Arthurian stories are plainly "linked to a majestic whole," but scope has certainly been left for "other hands and minds." We can cite Edmund Spenser, Sir Thomas Malory, Alfred, Lord Tennyson, T. H. White, and indeed Tolkien himself, although these work with words rather than Tolkien's projected "paint and music and drama." Thanks to Christopher Tolkien the bulk of Tolkien's mythology is now available and we can see its shape, which is certainly "majestic." And for all its gaps and competing overlaps there can be no doubt that *The Silmarillion* is a "whole" vision, whole at least in conception if not in execution. Furthermore, much as we might dislike the idea, in the years to come there will undoubtedly be new stories of Middle-earth contributed by other hands and minds. It is in this area of comparison, that of compositional and textual history, where the greatest kinship between the two myths resides, and where the rest of my discussion will be focused.

The introduction to Jane Burns' translation of *Lancelot*, a thirteenth-century French prose narrative, notes that for the early Middle Ages prose was "a mode of composition that mimic[ed] the writing of chronicle,"—that is to say, history, whereas poetry was reserved for romances—that is to say, fiction (Burns xxix). Chronicles were about the real world while romances described a world of the imagination. Prose, moreover, was meant to be read for elucidation or education while poetry, even when committed to paper, was meant to be chanted or sung as entertainment. It followed, therefore, that a prose rewriting of an earlier poem, such as the prose *Lancelot*'s rewriting of an earlier poetic *Lancelot*, had the effect of lending its subject veracity. The result was that as part of a many-layered and ongoing process, the many Arthurian authors/redactors cast their material first as poetry and then recast it in prose to validate its authenticity. The ultimate consequence, according to Jane Burns, was that there arose a manuscript tradition deriving "ultimately from the cumulative efforts of successive author, scribes, and reader/reciters" that allowed texts to be constantly recast and rewritten in many variants (xix).

Anyone familiar with the composition history of Tolkien's mythology can see that both intentionally and through the vagaries of his own creative process, Tolkien's stories followed this kind of temporal layering. The result is that Tolkien's mythos, like that of Arthur, has its own extended history of transmission, its own complex manuscript tradition. *The Silmarillion* consists of multiple and often overlapping story variants in both poetry and prose, a circumstance that by design or accident mimics the Arthurian manuscript tradition and bestows a counterfeit textual authenticity on the whole corpus.

And as with the Arthurian tradition, although the progression is by no means straightforward we can, with caution, infer a commensurate movement from poetry to prose both in Tolkien's external chronology of composition and in the internal chronology of the myth itself. The Túrin story offers a good illustration. Although according to Christopher Tolkien, "[t]he development of the legend of Túrin Turambar is in some respects the most tangled and complex of all the narrative elements in the story of the First Age" (*UT* 6), we do have some chronology. We know that according to Tolkien's own statement, the earliest version of the poetic Túrin was "begun c. 1918" (*LB* 3), while Christopher Tolkien tells us that the prose *Tale of Turambar* was "in existence . . . by the middle of 1919" (*LT* II 69).

Circumstantial evidence (one page written on the back of a letter) suggests that at least part of the second version of the alliterative Túrin was in existence by 1923 (*LB* 94n). Tolkien carries the conceit even further to provide a fictive "translation" into prose of a (presumed) Elvish version of the story, the *Narn I Hin Húrin*, with the implication that the prose translation (in English) is a late redaction. Now *narn* is an Elvish verse form, so that strictly speaking any mention of "the" *Narn* must be supposed to refer to a specific poem in Elvish. There is no evidence that any poem about Túrin in Elvish exists. As nearly as can be ascertained, there is no *Narn*. What Tolkien is creating here is his fictive version of the old "lost original" theory used by scholars to explain relationships between apparently separately arising, variant versions of a single story. Shippey cites a Norse example in his discussion of Tolkien and depth. This rationale is proposed by some scholars to account for the resemblance between no less than three of Chrétien de Troyes' romances—*Erec, Yvain,* and *Perceval*—and their Welsh counterparts *Gereint, Owein,* and *Peredur.* Arthurian literature is exceptionally rich in such instances, and Tolkien's application of the theory to his own mythos is a distinct Arthurian echo. The non-existent *Narn* adds what Shippey calls depth to a fictive manuscript tradition meant to be the work of successive authors, scribes, and reader/reciters, thus allowing texts to be constantly recast and rewritten in many variants. The fact that the successive authors, scribes, and reader/reciters (even of the ghostly Elvish *Narn*) were all Tolkien himself does not alter the fictional picture; it merely demonstrates once again, that art and life imitate one another.

Another example of the process is *The Lay of Leithian,* of which an early fragment appears in the alliterative Túrin, sung to Túrin by Halog (*LB* 107). The *Lay* was begun in 1925 (*LB* 150), well before Tolkien's prose retelling, which Christopher Tolkien says was "finally completed" by the end of 1937 (*LR* 295). Like the Arthurian romances of Chrétien de Troyes, the *Lay* is composed in a verse form that has all the hallmarks of written composition, the difficult, demanding rhymed octosyllabic couplet. But just as Chrétien drew on earlier sources for his romances (and he states this explicitly in at least two cases) the fictive poet of the *Lay* must be supposed to have drawn on earlier and probably oral versions of the story, while his own version became the basis for the subsequent prose rewritings. As Shippey points out (277), there are no less than eight extant versions, ranging from two to two hundred pages in length. Christopher Tolkien notes that the *Lay* is later sung by Strider to the hobbits at Weathertop, a presentation that reinforces its oral origin.

Like the Arthurian material, then, many if not all of Tolkien's texts were recast and rewritten in many variants over the years. Moreover, within their internal or fictive chronology they were consciously intended to represent "the cumulative efforts of successive and often quite different authors, scribes, and reader/reciters" such as Ælfwine, Eriol, Daeron, Pengoloð, even those lovers of poetry and old tales Sam Gamgee and Bilbo Baggins. Poems by both these last are woven into *The Lord of the Rings,* and it is clear that they are there for a purpose and that they are meant to represent quite disparate poetic traditions. Though both poems are orally presented, the folkloric structure and diction of "Troll stood alone" clearly comes from a different stratum of society than Bilbo's poetic re-telling of the story of Eärendil. It is worth noting that both Sam and Bilbo are presented as the authors of their respective songs, that both have obviously composed them orally, and that both are implicitly building on already familiar material.

While I am arguing for a similarity between the Arthurian and the Tolkienian mythologies at both the micro level of swords and ship departures and the macro level of textual history, I am not proposing any one-to-one correlation between specific stories in Tolkien's mythos and those in the corpus of medieval Arthurian material. I do not suggest any direct Tolkienian counterparts to, for example, the *Mabinogion*'s "Culhwch and Olwen" (though both "Culhwch and Olwen" and the story of Beren and Lúthien fit the tale-type of The Giant's Daughter), or to Chrétien's *Perceval* or his *Yvain* or *Lancelot.* Furthermore, I don't wish to claim that all the similarities I have pointed out between the Arthurian cycle and Tolkien's myth were necessarily deliberate and conscious on his part. The tangled and overlapping chronology of his composition, especially, was simply a part of his creative process.

It seems clear, however, that Arthur was in the back of his mind. I would go further, and say that in Tolkien's early, tentative beginnings Arthur, along with other fragments of England's history, was at or near the front of his mind and only later retired to the back. Tolkien's process of naming, the very root and process of his invented languages, offers examples of both front and back positions. There is not just the shift from the early Broceliande to the later Beleriand, but from the early Avallon to the later Avalloné to the still later Tol Eressëa, all names for what remained throughout the naming process the "Lonely Isle." Not everyone recognizes the name Broceliande or would hear its echo in the later Beleriand, but breathes there a reader of Tolkien who has not also heard of Avalon, the mysterious and isolated (not to say lonely) Isle to which the wounded Arthur was taken to be healed? I doubt it.

What I am proposing is both a specific and a familial resemblance between the two bodies of work that is closer than random chance and pure accident, a likeness of motif and episode, of overall shape and size, and also of internal and external textual history. I'll wrap up my argument by offering for consideration my conclusion. It is that Tolkien was not just familiar with the medieval Arthurian corpus; he was, despite his protestation, using it both intentionally and involuntarily. He was re-working the Arthurian material to remove or re-invent those things he found objectionable and at the same time to fold what he felt was important into his own mythos. He consciously used Arthurian themes, motifs, and even names (of which I have cited only the most obvious examples), and wove them deep into the fabric of his own legendarium.

Moreover, his own painstaking, perfectionist habits of composition, his tendency to work and re-work the same material in different forms and over many years, became an involuntary and unconscious replication of the historical circumstances which gave the Matter of Britain its present shape. Thus partly by design and partly by force of circumstance, Tolkien's legendarium, over the course of its long development, took on the loose but aggregate and overlapping Arthurian textual structure. Taken all together these similarities qualify the Matter of Middle-earth not as a rival to Arthur, but as a consort venture more deeply influenced and shaped by the Matter of Britain than Tolkien was apparently willing to acknowledge or that we have heretofore been willing to see.

I want to go beyond mere resemblance and association, however, to propose that the Arthurian model gives *The Silmarillion* something it would otherwise not have. By resonating against the Arthurian corpus, the atmosphere, shape, and structure of Tolkien's mythos have acquired an added level of validity, if not veracity, and have in addition substantially increased the density and richness of its mythic texture. And as new information has come out about *The Silmarillion* manuscripts and we have learned more about the complex and complicated history of the mythology's growth, the resemblance between the Arthurian cycle and Tolkien's own has grown even closer. It can indeed, stand next to the three great Matters as a legitimate and valid fourth—the Matter of Middle-earth.

Like the Arthurian myth *The Silmarillion* is a vast and conglomerate body of literature, a believable, many-layered collection of stories in all shapes, sizes, and voices. While being wholly itself it is yet evocative in its quality and history, in its innumerable echoes and reverberations, of the Arthurian legend. And like the Arthurian legend—in fact substantially because of its influence—*The Silmarillion* does indeed qualify as a mythology which could be dedicated, if only he were still here to do it, to England.

Frodo and Aragorn

The Concept of the Hero

J.R.R. Tolkien once said that his typical response to the reading of a medieval work was the desire not so much to make a critical or philological study of it as to write a modern work in the same tradition. In *The Lord of the Rings* he has done exactly that. The book is a modern work, but in style and content it is certainly in the medieval tradition described by Richard West in his essay on "The Interlace Structure of *The Lord of the Rings* (Lobdell 80). I do not propose to assign *The Lord of the Rings* to a particular genre, such as fairy tale, epic, or romance. The book quite clearly derives from all three, and to see it as belonging only to one category is to miss the essential elements it shares with the others. More to the point is the way in which Tolkien has used these elements.

What precisely is the appeal of a modern work in a medieval tradition? What is the value of such a book to the common reader? Why not offer him a bona fide medieval work, *Beowulf* or *Sir Gawain and the Green Knight,* and leave the twentieth century to the modern novel? An answer may be found in Tolkien's essay "On Fairy-Stories." Borrowing a term from G.W. Dasent, Tolkien speaks in this essay of the "soup" of story (*MC* 120), that rich mixture which has been simmering since man first told tales, from which tales have been ladled out to nourish the imagination in every age, including our own. Although the soup is a blend of many morsels, certain elements, certain flavors, stand out and evoke immediate response. These are the basics, the raw stuff of myth out of which folktale, fairy tale, epic, and romance are fashioned. They are the motifs which recur in all mythologies and which tale-tellers have used time out of mind—the hero, the quest, the struggle with monstrous forces of evil, the ordeal and its outcome. They recur because they work, because they move readers and put them in touch with what is timeless. A modern use of these motifs reaffirms their value as a vital part of literature in an age when only scholars and children (and too few of those) read the story of King Arthur, or of Jack the Giant-Killer, or the adventures of Sigurd dragon-slayer.

The conventional medieval story, whether epic, romance, fairy tale, or some combination of these, most often focuses on one figure—the hero of the tale. If it is romance or epic the hero will be of great stature, a larger-than-life Beowulf, or Galahad, or Arthur, or Sigurd. If it is a fairy tale he may be a common man like ourselves, the unlikely hero who stumbles into heroic adventure and does the best he can—Jack, who trades a cow for beans, or the miller's youngest son who inherits only Puss-in-Boots. Larger-than-life heroes are rare in twentieth-century literature; they do not fit comfortably in an age which seems preoccupied with the ordinary. But the little man is always with us, as alive in the films of Chaplin as he is in Chaucer.

In *The Lord of the Rings* Tolkien has written a medieval story and given it both kinds of hero, the extraordinary man to give the epic sweep of great events, and the common man who has the immediate, poignant appeal of someone with whom the reader can identify. Aragorn is a traditional epic/romance hero, larger than life, a leader, fighter, lover, healer. He is an extraordinary hero who combines Northrop Frye's romance and high mimetic modes. He is above the common herd. We expect him to be equal to any situation. We are not like him, and we know it. We admire him, but we do not identify with him.

Frodo, on the other hand, is a fairy-tale hero. He is both literally and figuratively a little man, and we recognize ourselves in him. He is utterly ordinary, and this is his great value. He has the characteristics also of Frye's low mimetic hero, the hero of realistic fiction. He has doubts, feels fear, falters, makes mistakes; he experiences, in short, the same emotions we experience. He is a low mimetic hero thrown by circumstances not of his making into high mimetic action. The ways in which he deals with that action—coping with burdens that are too great, events that move too swiftly, trials that are too terrible—draw readers into the narrative, so that we live it with Frodo as we never could with Aragorn.

A look at the two side by side shows that each throws the other into greater relief, providing contrast and enriching and expanding the dimensions of the story. Having provided his book with an essentially epic hero and an essentially fairy-tale hero, Tolkien combines, and sometimes crosses, the characteristic motifs of each. Each hero has an extraordinary beginning. Each undertakes a dangerous quest and undergoes ordeals. But the parallels serve to heighten the contrast between the two. Aragorn's is a true quest to win a kingdom and a princess. Frodo's is rather an anti-quest. He goes not to win something but to throw something away, and in the process to lose all that he holds dear. In simplest terms, Aragorn's is a journey from darkness into light, while Frodo's is a journey from light into darkness—and (maybe) out again. Aragorn derives from the pattern of the youthful hero, while Frodo has the characteristics of the hero come to the end of his adventures. Tolkien gives Aragorn the fairy-tale happy ending, the princess and the kingdom. To Frodo come defeat and disillusionment—the stark, tragic ending typical of the *Iliad, Beowulf, The Morte D'Arthur.*

This crossing of motifs is not uniform, since Tolkien allows each hero enough of his typical characteristics to be recognizable. The motifs do cross, however, at crucial points in the narrative and at psychologically important moments in the unfolding of each character. I hope to show that this crossing of motifs adds an appeal which few modern readers find in conventional medieval literature, and that by exalting and refining the figure of the common man, Tolkien succeeds in giving new values to a medieval story.

Let us begin with Aragorn, the larger-than-life hero. William Ready calls him "almost too good to be human" (Ready 101), implying that his goodness somehow impairs his believability. The fact is that many readers lack the background to appreciate an Aragorn. Strider—silent, watchful, road weary—is an attractive figure. His steely presence, his air of being someone dangerous to cross, his resourcefulness in crisis, evoke a character out of the mythic American West—the stranger in town—cool, alert, alone. He has that quiet toughness we associate with our folk heroes. But in the transition from Strider to Aragorn much of that folk-hero quality is lost, and with it his hold on our imagination. Paradoxically, the more we know him, the less familiar he becomes.

He is in fact the traditional disguised hero, the rightful king, in medieval romance terms the "fair unknown" who steps from the shadows into the limelight when his moment comes. He is in the tradition of the young Beowulf, the young Galahad, the boy Arthur, all the heroes whose early years are spent in obscurity but who are destined for greatness and whose birth or origin foreshadows that destiny. A few examples will clarify the point. The medieval account of the hero frequently includes his *compert,* or conception. The conception episode almost always involves some element of magic or the supernatural. Precedent for this comes from classical myth, where the hero usually has one human and one divine or semidivine parent. Achilles, Heracles, Theseus, and even so demonstrably real a figure as Alexander the Great have divine heritage.

The best-known story of the hero's *compert* is undoubtedly that of Arthur in Malory's retelling of the Arthurian legend, wherein Merlin by his magic gives King Uther the shape of Igraine's husband Gorlois, thereby gaining him access to her bed. From this meeting Arthur is conceived. Thus the supernatural plays a part in Arthur's conception, even though both his parents are mortal. The conception of Galahad, later in the same book, involves the same bed-trick. The sorceress Brusen contrives to enchant Lancelot (apparently by getting him drunk, which doesn't take much magic) and bring him to the bed of King Pelles's daughter, Elaine, in the belief that she is Guenevere. Here again immortal ancestry is replaced by the use of magic (or trickery) in the conception of the hero.

The immortal father convention appears in Celtic and Scandinavian myth. The Irish hero Cuchulainn was fathered on a mortal woman by the god Lugh. The Norse heroes Sigmund and Sigurd were descended from the god Odin. And on a more mundane level, the genealogies of kings in the Anglo-Saxon Chronicle begin with Woden, the Germanic counterpart of Odin. We will look in vain for any similar episode in Tolkien's account of Aragorn. No god's intervention, no magic, enchantment, or supernatural events are to be found. But Aragorn does have immortal ancestry. He is of the line of the Half-Elven. It is not immediate, as in the medieval narratives, but must be traced back through many generations to an early union of Elves and Men. In Appendix A at the end of *The Lord of the Rings*, "Annals of the Kings and Rulers," Tolkien makes the following statement: "There were three unions of the Eldar [elves] and the Edain [men]: Lúthien and Beren; Idril and Tuor; Aragorn and Arwen. By the last the long-sundered branches of the Half-elven were reunited and their line was restored" (*RK* Appendix A, 314). It is clear that Aragon and Arwen each represent a branch of the half-elven. They are descended from two brothers, Elrond and Elros, grandsons of the aforementioned Idril, an elf, and Tuor, a man. Elrond, the father of Arwen, elected to remain with the elves. Elros chose to go with men, and became the first king of Numenor. His descendants, through many generations, were Elendil and Isildur, whose descendant and heir is Aragorn. In Tolkien's cosmology Aragorn's half-elven ancestry supplies him with the immortal or supernatural origin necessary to the hero figure.

The fact that Aragorn's immortal ancestry is played down—indeed so successfully buried that one has to look hard in order to find it—is consonant with Tolkien's practice throughout the book of providing realistic bases for what in a true medieval narrative would be frankly supernatural, marvelous, or miraculous. His goal is the one he outlines in his essay "On Fairy-Stories," that is, "the realisation . . . of imagined wonder" (*MC* 116). By "realisation" he means just what the word implies, making real. To make the wonderful as real as possible to his twentieth-century reader, Tolkien surrounds it with the ordinary. We meet Strider; he is gradually revealed as Aragorn, and his immortal ancestry is buried in supplemental records and appendixes so only after we believe him as a character are we allowed to make the heroic associations that enrich him and rank him with his predecessors in myth, epic, and romance.

Another element, almost a necessity in the medieval hero pattern, is obscurity until the right moment. Shadow provides contrast to light. Time after time we read in medieval stories of the hero whose origins are hidden, sometimes even from himself. He is buried in obscurity until the moment comes for him to step forward and announce himself by word or deed. Often the obscurity of the hero is linked with his upbringing in a home not his own, in circumstances that train him for his future role but offer no recognition. Arthur is removed from his mother at birth by Merlin and brought up in the household of Sir Ector, ignorant, like everyone around him, of his royal lineage. The withdrawal of the sword from the anvil signals his emergence from obscurity and proclaims him as the rightful king. Galahad, likewise, is raised in obscurity. Not until it is time for him to begin the Grail Quest is he introduced to Arthur's court. The event that announces his emergence as a hero is his withdrawal of the sword from the stone floating in the river below Camelot.

Germanic literature follows the same pattern. Sinfjotli, child of the incestuous union of Sigmund the Völsung and his sister Signy, is brought up by Sigmund in a secret woodland hideout until he is ready to avenge the slaying of his Volsung kin. Sinfjotli is fostered out to his own father, although both are ignorant of the relationship. A hero who fits the pattern rather more loosely is Beowulf. He is not precisely raised in obscurity, but he is brought up in a home not his own, the court of his uncle Hygelac. We meet him first as a hero, and only after his killing of Grendel and Grendel's dam and his return in triumph to Hygelac's court do we learn of his unpromising beginnings.

> *Hēan wæs lange*
> *swā hyne Gēata bearn gōdne ne tealdon*
> *nē hyne on medo-bence micles wyrðne*
> *drihten Wedera gēdon wolde;*
> *swyðe wēndon þæt hē slēac wære,*
> *æðeling unfrom.*

> . . . he long seemed sluggish to the Geatish court . . .
> they thought him no good; he got little honor,

no gifts on the mead-bench   from the lord of the Weders.
They were all convinced   he was slow, or lazy,
a coward of a noble   (Chickering ll. 2184–88)

In accordance with the established pattern, Aragorn comes from obscurity to recognition. Strider the Ranger is looked on with suspicion by even so good-hearted a man as Butterbur, the innkeeper at Bree. His true identity is concealed from all but a few until the time comes for him to reveal himself.

Humphrey Carpenter has pointed out that in the first draft of the scene in the common room of the Prancing Pony the mysterious stranger was not a man but a "queerlooking brown-faced hobbit" and his name was Trotter (Carpenter 188). I suggest that such a character could not develop into the kind of figure that Strider was eventually to become. A disguised hobbit-prince would not fit into Tolkien's world and would be utterly out of place among the middle-class Boffins, Bolgers, Tooks, Proudfoots, and even the Sackville-Bagginses. The change from hobbit to man materially alters the possibilities for the character. The change of name, too, seems to signal the development of a more serious tone to the story. Although Tolkien quite probably knew that "Trotter" is a legitimate Scottish-English Border surname belonging to a family in the East March of Scotland, few of his non-Scottish readers would be likely share that knowledge, and the name could bring up unlooked-for associations with animals and beast fable. Carpenter remarks that in writing the preliminary chapters "Tolkien was bending his tale away from the jolly style of *The Hobbit* towards something darker and grander, and closer in concept to *The Silmarillion*" (Carpenter 186). The alteration of the mysterious figure in the common room is certainly part of this change.

When he himself wrote of this first period of composition, Tolkien said, ápropos the scene at Bree, "I had then no more notion than [the hobbits] had of what had become of Gandalf, or who Strider was; and I had begun to despair of ever finding out" (*TL* 188). This provocative statement invites comment. Paul Kocher suggests that we can find in it part of the reason why Aragorn is difficult for readers. He simply has not been prepared for (Kocher 131). Daniel Hughes goes further and suggests that it is just here, when Tolkien discovers who Strider is and what can be done with him, that the story begins to develop its epic side (Hillegas 91).

If we take Tolkien's statement at face value, we find him describing a situation not unfamiliar to writers: his narrative had somehow got ahead of him. That unconscious process which often accompanies the conscious activity of the creative mind unexpectedly introduced new material. To be sure, this attitude suggests the traditional convention of authorial modesty: "I didn't write

it; it wrote itself." But knowing as we do Tolkien's background in medieval literature, it seems reasonable to suppose that he did have a stockpile of literary
raw material waiting to be used. We can perhaps credit his statement with a
little less coyness and a little more honesty than is usual in such cases.

What seems to have happened in the creative process to translate Trotter
into Strider and Strider into Aragorn is that Tolkien realized he had ready to
his hand in this mysterious figure the makings of an authentic mythic hero,
a medieval disguised prince. In the historical framework of Middle-earth,
Aragorn is the lineal descendant of Elendil, founder of the kingdoms of Ar-
nor and Gondor, and of Elendil's son Isildur, who took the Ring from Sauron
after defeating him in the Second Age. Aragorn is therefore not only the
rightful king of Gondor but the rightful owner of the Ring. True to epic convention, and also true to the circumstances of the world that Tolkien creates, his identity is concealed, with good reason. He is the son of Arathorn, a
chieftain of the northern line of his house, killed when Aragorn is a child of
two. Aragorn is then taken by his mother to Rivendell, where he is brought
up in the House of Elrond with Elrond's two sons. Aragorn is twenty years
old before Elrond tells him his true identity and gives him the broken pieces
of Elendil's sword, Narsil, to keep until they can be reforged.

The giving and receiving of the sword calls up another medieval motif—
the hero and his weapon. They are inextricably linked, for the association of
sword and hero is more than a medieval convention: it is a necessity in a literature which exalts heroism and deeds of arms. Beowulf may slay Grendel
with his bare hands, but it takes a sword to kill Grendel's mother, a sword,
moreover, of no ordinary kind—"ealdsweord eotenisc"—an ancient sword,
made by giants. Medieval literature is filled with swords as famous and for-
midable as those who wield them. Many who know no more of Arthur know
of his sword, Excalibur, and those of other heroes are just as worthy of note.
Beowulf's sword, Nægling, breaks in his death struggle with the dragon. The
dying Roland tries to break his sword, Durendal, so that none other shall
ever use it. We have seen that for both Arthur and Galahad the withdrawing
of a sword heralds the emergence of a hero.

The same motif occurs elsewhere. In the Norse Völsungasaga Sigmund
the Völsung pulls from a tree the sword thrust into it by Odin, after others
have tried and failed. He carries it for the rest of his life. It plays a curious role at the end of his adventures, when it is broken, apparently deliberately, by Odin in Sigmund's last battle. After the breaking of the sword the
battle goes against Sigmund, and he is killed. The fates of sword and man
are linked, and the destruction of one signals the end of the other. The fragments of Sigmund's sword are saved for his son Sigurd and reforged for the

slaying of the dragon Fáfnir. The reforging of the sword and the slaying of the dragon with it mark Sigurd's beginning as a hero.

Tolkien reworks this motif in fitting it to Aragorn. At the Council of Elrond, where the decision is made to take the Ring to Mordor, Aragorn stands before those assembled and makes his declaration:

> He cast his sword upon the table that stood before Elrond, and the blade was in two pieces. "Here is the Sword that was Broken!" he said.
>
> "And who are you, and what have you to do with Minas Tirith?" asked Boromir, looking in wonder at the lean face of the Ranger and his weather-stained cloak.
>
> "He is Aragorn son of Arathorn," said Elrond; "and he is descended through many fathers from Isildur Elendil's son of Minas Ithil. He is the Chief of the Dúnedain in the North, and few are now left of that folk." (*FR* II, ii, 259–60)

With the casting of the sword upon the table Aragorn publicly puts off Strider, assuming his rightful identity and all it implies. The sword proclaims the emergence of the hero. Arthur, Galahad, Sigmund, Sigurd all stand behind Aragorn in that moment. Tolkien is careful, however, to keep Aragorn separate from them, so that memories of the earlier heroes do not overpower his narrative. Avoiding, then, the too-familiar motif of the pulling out of the sword, Tolkien uses instead the broken sword that is to be reforged. Defined strictly, Aragorn is closer to Arthur or Sigmund than to Sigurd, since he is a king, not a dragon-slayer. The unexpected combination of king-hero with dragon-slayer's sword motif allows Aragorn to stand as a hero in his own right, in his own narrative. We remember other heroes, and other swords, but we add a new figure to the line.

What gives Aragorn his most clear-cut romance characteristics is the part of the story that treats his love for Arwen. The tradition of romantic love, which requires the knight to endure hardships and perform great deeds for the love of a lady, is necessary to the characterization of Aragorn, for all that it is subordinate to the epic side of the narrative and remains very much in the background.

As with his treatment of Aragorn's lineage, Tolkien buries much of the material relating to Aragorn and Arwen in his appendices, where the reader, if he looks, will find the "Tale of Aragorn and Arwen." A few scattered references in the story proper relate them as romantic lovers; most of them do not even mention Arwen by name. The clearest is, perhaps, a sly remark by Bilbo at Rivendell, surprised at Aragorn's absence from the feast, since "the Lady Arwen was there" (*FR* II, i, 245).

The romance element is secondary to the epic struggle—the sweep of battle and great deeds. We know that Aragorn is grimly engaged in winning his kingdom, but we know almost nothing of his love for the half-elven princess for whom he wins it, nor do we realize until it is all over that in winning the kingdom he is also winning Arwen, and that one was a condition for the other. Nonetheless a full understanding of Aragorn as a medieval hero must encompass knowledge of his love story as well as of his epic characteristics. Aragorn's is not simply a political or national or even a personal epic trial. It is also a trial of love, and in the light of the love story, which we come to know only at the end, the struggle and the battles take on a more specific and personal meaning. The love story, too, is the perfect vehicle for the fairy-tale happy ending, almost Elizabethan in its rounding off of the story with celebrations and marriages, of which Aragorn's and Arwen's is the chief.

The romance element is manifest, too, in Aragorn's capacity to heal and to renew. It has been plain from the beginning of the story that Aragorn is a healer, for his skill and knowledge of herb lore pull Frodo through in the first hours after he is wounded at Weathertop. But at that point Aragorn is still Strider to the reader, and his ability to heal could well appear as practical knowledge of the road gained as a Ranger. Only much later, when he has healed Eowyn and Faramir and Merry, when the old wife Ioreth has told everyone who will listen, "The hands of the king are the hands of a healer" (*RK* VI, v, 244), does the reader recognize that Aragorn as healer and as king is what he has always been.

The concept of the king as healer derives from the early Celtic principle of sacral kingship, whereby the health and fertility of the land are dependent on the coming of the rightful king. Where there is no king, or where the king is infirm, the land also will be barren. This idea is most explicit in the Grail legend, with its association of the Waste Land with the Maimed King whose wound, sometimes specifically located in the thighs, is a wounding of virility extending from him to his kingdom. The Maimed King in the Grail stories is counterposed to the Healing King, the Grail Knight. In the French sources and Malory's Arthurian story this is Galahad, whose healing of the Maimed King restores the land to fruitfulness. Tolkien makes full use of both these figures as the wasted lands of Middle-earth are restored to fruitfulness; Aragorn's is the positive role of healer and renewer, whose presence works to restore the land. Frodo, as I will subsequently show, becomes a kind of Maimed King figure, without whose sacrifice the efforts of the Healing King would be in vain.

All of the positive, glad-hearted, youthful elements of myth, epic, and romance cluster around the man we meet as Strider, whom we come to know as Aragorn. He is the recognized, acclaimed victor in the battle against evil, the king coming into his kingdom. He is warrior, lover, healer, renewer, a hero worthy of the heroic aspects of *The Lord of the Rings,* whose presence in the story at once contributes to, and justifies, those aspects.

Frodo is quite another thing. He is no Aragorn, no obscure hero awaiting his chance to be great. He is no warrior. And far from feeling destined for greatness, he reacts to being thrust into epic events with the cry of the common man—"Why me?" He knows, or thinks he knows, his own limitations and tells Gandalf, "I am not made for perilous quests" (*FR* I, ii, 70). He accepts an intolerable burden not from any sense that he is the proper one to bear it but simply because no one else volunteers. It is worth noting, by the way, that another "little man"—Bilbo—does volunteer, and is gently refused. The heroic figures all hang back, and the common man shoulders the burden. The point is voiced in the narrative by Elrond, who says: "Yet such is oft the course of deeds that move the wheels of the world: small hands do them because they must, while the eyes of the great are elsewhere" (*FR* II, ii, 283). This is almost a paraphrase of something Tolkien himself once said, recorded by Carpenter: "the hobbits represent the combination of small imagination with great courage which (as Tolkien had seen in the trenches during the First World War) often led to survival against all chances. 'I've always been impressed' he once said, 'that we are here, surviving, because of the indomitable courage of quite small people against impossible odds' (Carpenter 176).

Yet in spite of this surface appearance, Frodo like Aragorn embodies mythic and heroic elements which supply much of the strength of Tolkien's story. And there stretches behind Frodo too a long line of mythic figures. He is linked unmistakably to the dying Arthur, the dying Beowulf, the semi-mythical Scyld Scefing of the opening lines of Beowulf, and the highly symbolic figure of the Maimed King. Frodo becomes more than himself, But it is Tolkien's great gift that in enlarging Frodo he keeps him consistent with his beginnings. Frodo is changed, but he is yet the same. That which is universal and symbolic is condensed into the particular and literal. Frodo evokes the greater figures who stand behind him, but he is not engulfed by them. He remains Frodo. In putting their burdens on his shoulders Tolkien has succeeded in synthesizing the medieval and the modern, creating a character who conforms to mythic patterns and yet evokes the identification and empathy which the modern reader has come to expect from fiction.

Frodo's beginnings are plain enough. He is the only son of a middle-class hobbit couple, in no way unusual except for the manner of their death—drowning in a boating accident. But this is important, since Tolkien emphasizes the fact that hobbits are as a rule shy of boats and the water. They are inland people, hole-builders, earthdwellers. "Most Hobbits regarded even rivers and small boats with deep misgivings, and not many of them could swim" (*FR* Prologue, 16). The drowning of Frodo's parents is the key to one of his mythic functions, for it is thematically important that Frodo should be orphaned, and that his coming to Hobbiton be somehow associated with water.

An outstanding figure in the mythologies of the world is the child of mysterious or unknown origin who arrives, sometimes in a boat, but always associated in some way with water, and who brings with him extraordinary benefits. Perhaps the figure of this type most familiar to the Western reader is the child Moses. But to connect the mysterious child figure with Tolkien's story we need go back no further than northern European myth and literature. The opening lines of *Beowulf* tell of Scyld Scefing, the eponymous founder of the Scyldings, Hrothgar's line, who led his people to victory in battle and brought them unparalleled prosperity. He arrived as an unknown child from the sea, and the poem describes the elaborate ship burial that sends him back over the water. Scyld is one avatar of a fertility figure ubiquitous in northern mythology who appears under various names—Scyld, Sheaf, Ing, Freyr, Frodi. They all have the same value as bringers of peace and fertility, and they are more or less connected—some remotely, some, like Scyld, specifically—with water, with death, and with ships and funeral ceremonies.

Frodo's association with the mysterious or orphan child motif is evident, and the linking of that motif with Scyld and Frodi as fertility figures suggests that Tolkien wished to invest Frodo with the mythic significance of a bringer of peace, prosperity, and fruitfulness. The name Frodo, a variant of Frodi, is surely no accident, no random choice to fit a furry-footed hobbit, but one consciously chosen to state a connection Tolkien wished to make. Carpenter's biography of Tolkien reveals that Frodo's name was originally Bingo, but Tolkien, as he wrote, grew more and more dissatisfied with that name, and with good reason. Aside from its more frivolous associations, it is phonetically too close to Bilbo. The name remained Bingo, however, until Tolkien found his story turning increasingly away from *The Hobbit* and in the direction of the older and darker subject matter of *The Silmarillion.* It was not until what Christopher Tolkien has called the "Third Phase," a second starting-over after carrying the story (once) as far as Bree (and again) as far as Weathertop, that he changed his hero's name to Frodo.[1]

Frodo, the orphan associated with water, brings peace, prosperity, and fruitfulness to the Shire, though he himself can no longer benefit from them. In the end he is committed again to the water, and like Scyld, is sent over the waves to an unknown bourne. Frodo, like Aragorn, like Arthur, Galahad, Beowulf, is brought up in a home not his own, Bilbo's home. And here another medieval motif enters, for Frodo is Bilbo's nephew. The relationship of uncle and nephew, specifically uncle and sister's son, is prominent in medieval narrative from Beowulf to Malory. Jessie Weston calls it a relationship "obviously required by tradition" (Weston 191–92), and cites uncle-nephew pairs in both early and late medieval epic and romance, Weston's list includes Cuchulainn and Conchobar, Diarmid and Finn, Tristan and Mark, Roland and Charlemagne, and Gawain and Arthur. To these we might add Mordred and Arthur, Sinfjotli and Sigmund (these last two are incestuous, being son and father as well), and Beowulf and Hygelac. What all these pairs have in common is that some action initiated by the uncle is brought to its conclusion, whether for good or ill, by the nephew. In any case, the relationship is a well-established and well-recognized literary motif. We may be sure that Tolkien is giving us important information when he makes Frodo Bilbo's nephew.

The information is given obliquely, however, for, as with Aragorn, Tolkien avoids a one-to-one correlation between Frodo and earlier medieval heroes. Rather he awakens echoes of the earlier stories which will enrich his own narrative without defining it too narrowly. Thus he does not introduce Frodo into the story as a nephew but as a cousin, and he employs a comic figure—the Gaffer—to explain the relationship. "Mr. Drogo, he married poor Miss Primula Brandybuck. She was our Mr. Bilbo's first cousin on the mother's side (her mother being the youngest of the Old Took's daughters); and Mr. Drogo was his second cousin. So Mr. Frodo is his [Bilbo's] first *and* second cousin, once removed either way, as the saying is, if you follow me" (*FR* I, i, 31). It is noteworthy that Frodo's mother is closest to Bilbo, being his first cousin, while Drogo is his second cousin. The female side is stressed, and the sister's son relationship is thus obliquely alluded to.

A more specific linking of Frodo with Bilbo is given in the Prologue, where Frodo is plainly called Bilbo's "favourite 'nephew'" (*FR* I Prologue, 20). What is clear, then, is that Tolkien is adding something important to his story by so carefully underlining the relationship. Action initiated earlier by Bilbo—the finding of the Ring—will be completed by Frodo, who accepts the responsibility of throwing it away. This is the thematic basis for Elrond's gentle rejection of Bilbo's offer to carry the Ring to Mordor. The task has passed from uncle to nephew. Bilbo cannot complete the action. It is Frodo in the role of nephew who must carry it to an end.

Early in the narrative Frodo joins forces with Strider, who is all that Frodo appears not to be—big, tough, experienced, a fighter and a doer, where Frodo is small, sheltered, and unaccustomed to adventure. Beneath this surface disparity, however, Tolkien links his heroes by providing each with a variant of the same epic motif. We have already noted Tolkien's restructuring of the medieval sword motif to enrich the figure of Aragorn and give him epic associations: Similar epic associations are given to Frodo as well, but they are scaled down to hobbit dimensions and pass all but unnoticed in the narrative.

As the Fellowship prepares to leave Rivendell with the Ring there is a homely farewell scene between Bilbo and Frodo:

"Here is your sword," [Bilbo] said. "But it was broken, you know. . . . I've forgotten to ask if the smiths could mend it. No time now. So I thought, perhaps, you would care to have this, don't you know?"

He took from the box a small sword in an old shabby leathern scabbard. Then he drew it, and its polished and well-tended blade glittered suddenly, cold and bright. "This is Sting," he said, and thrust it with little effort deep into a wooden beam. "Take it, if you like. I shan't want it again, I expect."

Frodo accepted it gratefully. (*FR* II, iii, 290)

More important than the sword itself is the manner of its giving. Bilbo thrusts it into a wooden beam, repeating in unobtrusive fashion Odin's thrusting of the sword into the tree for Sigmund. Frodo "accepts" it. Tolkien does not say how. But to take it he must pull it out of the beam in a repetition of Sigmund's withdrawal of his sword from the tree, Arthur's taking of the sword from the anvil, and Galahad's withdrawal of his sword from the stone floating in the river.

A mythic pattern underlies the giving and receiving of the sword, but it has been displaced and fragmented in *The Lord of the Rings*. What in the Volsung-asaga was one sword, broken with Sigmund and reforged for Sigurd, is here two swords, and the order of events is reversed. Frodo's old sword is broken and is replaced by Sting. Sting is thrust into the beam by Bilbo and withdrawn by Frodo. The tone here is anything but epic. Instead of a supernatural event we have a quiet conversation between old friends. The speech is familiar and colloquial—"don't you know," "if you like," "I expect." The sword is small, the scabbard shabby. Bilbo fumbles in bringing it out. The gesture of thrusting it into the wooden beam is almost thrown away. The whole character of the scene is touching rather than heroic. The surface structure of this scene makes it clear that the torch has passed. Bilbo's part in the story of the Ring is over; Ring and sword have been handed on to his nephew, who must undertake the quest. The underlying mythic pattern—the sword and the method of its transfer—aligns Frodo with his epic forebears, and with Aragorn as well.

Tolkien brings his two heroes together almost, it would seem, in order to have them part. Having established each clearly, and put them side by side, he then sends them in opposite directions—Aragorn west, expanding the scope and epic action of the story, Frodo east, intensifying our focus on the perilous nature of his quest and its effect on him. The journey into Mordor is, of course, Frodo's final test, the ultimate ordeal through which he must pass to his eventual apotheosis. For it is on the journey to Mordor and in the final moments at the Cracks of Doom that the crucial event in the medieval hero story, the confrontation and struggle with the monstrous foe, embodiment of all the forces of darkness, takes place.

To see this clearly we must first look at the thesis of Tolkien's landmark essay "*Beowulf:* The Monsters and the Critics." It is undoubtedly his best-known scholarly work. It is one of the few and certainly one of the first critical essays that values *Beowulf* as a poem rather than as a historical, or philological, or sociocultural artifact. *Beowulf,* says Tolkien, is a poem about a man fighting with monsters—a manlike monster, Grendel, who preys on men and eats them, and a dragon who guards a hoard of gold. As such, the poem reflects the northern imagination, whose vision is of "man at war with the hostile world, and his inevitable overthrow in Time" (*MC* 18). The monsters are all the forces of darkness against which men have always struggled, and by which they are always defeated. The poet's phrases "heroes under heaven" or "mighty men upon earth" evokes for Tolkien "*eormengrund,* the great earth, ringed with *garsecg,* the shoreless sea, beneath the sky's inaccessible roof; whereon, as in a little circle of light about their halls, men with courage as their stay went forward to that battle with the hostile world and the offspring of the dark which ends for all, even the kings and champions, in defeat" (*MC* 18).

Clearly, for Tolkien, the monster figure is at the heart of the matter. And, important as it is, we would expect to find that he had placed such a figure at the heart of *The Lord of the Rings.* As a story in the medieval tradition, it should depend for its force as much on the monster as on the hero. And where is there a monster who confronts and battles with the hero? There are monstrous beings, to be sure, but in no case do they directly do battle with either hero. Aragorn fights orcs, but not in single combat, and only as part of a larger battle. Sam fights Shelob; Gandalf fights the Balrog. The greatest evil is Sauron, the Enemy, the Dark Lord for whom all the forces of darkness work. But he is never seen. Aragorn and Gandalf do contend with him, but at a distance and indirectly. Furthermore, while he is all evil, he is not concrete enough to fit Tolkien's criteria for monsters. For him they must be "mortal denizens of the material world, in it and of it" (*MC* 20).

I suggest that Tolkien's central monster-figure is so natural a part of the material world that he goes largely unrecognized as such. He is Gollum, the twisted, broken, outcast hobbit whose manlike shape and dragonlike greed combine both the *Beowulf* kinds of monster in one figure. To see Gollum as a manlike monster we must first accept his relationship to humanity. Tolkien makes it plain that Gollum is some kind of hobbit, "akin," says Gandalf, "to the fathers of the fathers of the Stoors." He goes on.

> . . . even Bilbo's story suggests their kinship. There was a great deal in
> the background of their minds and memories that was very similar. They
> understood one another remarkably well, very much better than a hobbit

would understand, say, a Dwarf, or an Orc, or even an Elf. Think of the riddles they both knew, for one thing. (*FR* I, ii, 63–64).

And though warped and grotesque, Gollum is not yet entirely lost to humanity:

> There was a little corner of his mind that was still his own, and light came through it, as through a chink in the dark: light out of the past. It was actually pleasant, I think, to hear a kindly voice again, bringing up memories of wind, and trees, and sun on the grass, and such forgotten things.
>
> But that, of course, would only make the evil part of him angrier in the end. (*FR* I, ii, 64)

There we have him, of hobbit kind, murderer, outcast, maddened by reminders of joys he cannot share. He is even cannibalistic, for we learn in *The Hobbit* that he eats goblins when he can't get fish, and would have eaten Bilbo if he had defeated him in the riddle game. The parallel with Grendel, the man-eating monster of *Beowulf*, is unmistakable. Grendel is outcast, a wanderer in the waste, of the race of Cain, the first murderer, and he cannot bear the sound of the harp and the song of creation.[2]

Gollum's dragon features are not so apparent. His most obvious characteristic is greed for a treasure. Dragons are traditionally associated with hoards of gold, whereas Gollum wants only the one Ring, but the difference is quantitative, not qualitative. The most famous dragon in northern literature, Fáfnir, transformed himself from man to dragon so he could guard his gold, of which the crucial portion was a ring. So Gollum, once a hobbit, has been transformed by his desire for the Ring into a creeping thing. His name, Smeágol, is related to an Anglo-Saxon word *smeáh* whose first definition in Bosworth-Toller's *An Anglo-Saxon Dictionary* is "creeping in, penetrating," with the example "Wið smeógan wyrme," descriptive of a dragon. A related word, *smeágung*, is glossed as "search, inquiry, investigation *where something is lost*" [my emphasis], which could stand as a direct description of Gollum's activities in search of the Ring. Gollum's very word for the Ring, "precious," is one translation of the Anglo-Saxon word *maðum*, glossed by Bosworth-Toller as "A precious or valuable thing (often refers to gifts), a treasure." In *Beowulf* it is glossed as "precious, or treasure," and on several occasions refers specifically to the dragon's hoard.

Gollum is a combination, then, of manlike and dragonlike monster. But a monster figure must be defined not just by what he is but by what he does. The function of the monster in medieval narrative is to oppose the hero, to body forth tangibly the evil to be overcome, to be the force against which the hero's strength and courage are tested. It is typical of what I call Tolkien's modern medievalism that having given his story a monster in the person of Gollum, he chooses for the monster's opponent not the epic hero Aragorn but Frodo, the little man who feels he is not a hero and does not want to be one.

The battle between this hero and this monster is central to a reading of *The Lord of the Rings* as a modern work in the medieval tradition. For the battle is psychological, not physical, and the battleground is Frodo himself. To explicate this we must look carefully at the special relationship of Frodo and Gollum. As early as 1957 Douglass Parker called Gollum "Frodo's corrupted counterpart" (*Hudson Review* 605). Rose Zimbardo called him Frodo's "dark counterpart" (Zimbardo and Isaacs 68). George Thomson put the relationship in perspective: "It is a well-known fact of the romance tradition that because the principal characters are simple types, the complexities of human nature must be projected into the external world. The disruptive forces of darkness and inner conflict must be represented by persons or objects outside the heroic characters" (Thomson 51–53). Thus, Gollum as Frodo's "double in darkness is more than a potentiality of his own nature. His double is truly his, an actual and developing darkness in his own character.

Fiction abounds in dualities of this kind. Dr. Jekyll and Mr. Hyde, Victor Frankenstein and his monster, Poe's William Wilson and his double are all examples of what psychology calls the "self" and the "other," that is, the overt personality and its opposite, the light and dark sides of one's nature. Jung calls this other side of mankind the "shadow" as contrasted with the overt and recognized "ego." Often this duality is presented as two aspects of one nature, as with David Lindsay's Maskull and Nightspore in *A Voyage to Arcturus,* or as E. M. Forster suggests may be the case with Virginia Woolf's life-loving Mrs. Dalloway and the young suicide Septimus Smith in *Mrs. Dalloway.*

Frodo and Gollum can fit the same pattern, Frodo as the self, Gollum as the other. Frodo is the overt, recognized character. Gollum is his dark side, the embodiment of his growing, overpowering desire for the Ring, the desire which at last becomes all-consuming and sweeps away (if only for a moment) the Frodo who has endured so much to destroy the Ring. Gollum represents precisely that "disruptive force of darkness and inner conflict" which Thomson says must be shown to the reader outside the heroic character. Gollum is what Frodo must fight within himself as the Ring increases its hold. I do not mean to present Gollum as an allegorical personification. He is not simply an abstract quality or a projection of a state of mind. Any careful reader of *The Lord of the Rings* knows that Tolkien detested allegory, and to impose it on his book is to do violence to his intention. Gollum is a fully realized character in his own right, with a considerable part to play in the story. But he can suggest these other things as well.

Today's reader of a modern narrative, however medieval its spirit, may be reluctant to accept a truly medieval monster—a dragon or a fiend—but he is accustomed to accepting internal conflict, man warring with himself, for that is what much of modern fiction deals with. Frodo monster-queller might not be credible. But Frodo tortured by growing evil in his own nature, fighting his great battle not against darkness without but against darkness within, is believable and compelling. In fighting those dark elements within himself which Gollum externalizes, Frodo fights the most insidious and powerful monster of all—and loses. Tolkien's picture of the battle, although not literal, is very much in the spirit of the northern imagination he describes in the Beowulf essay. It is that battle against "the offspring of the dark which ends for all, even the kings and champions, in defeat."

In the final moment, standing at the Cracks of Doom, Frodo succumbs to the darkness within him. He puts the Ring on his finger, claimed by it even as he claims it. The end is inevitable. For man always loses to the monster at last. Frodo is defeated just as surely as Beowulf is. It is characteristic of Tolkien, however, that he does not end on this note. Frodo loses, but in losing he wins a greater victory. The climax is designed to show that just as surely as Frodo's action is inevitable, so is Gollum's. Frodo will put on the Ring, and Gollum will be driven to seize it. In so doing he saves Frodo and destroys the Ring. Frodo's dark side, externalized as Gollum, destroys the actual dark within him, and the maddened Gollum, exulting in possession, falls with the Ring into the fire. Evil destroys itself.

Although Frodo recovers from the battle, he can no longer be what he was. He is wounded by sword, sting, and tooth, and cannot find healing. He now evokes the Maimed King of the Grail legend. The loss of his finger, seen by some critics as symbolic castration, could legitimately be interpreted as a version of the archetypal fertility wound of the Maimed King. Frodo is maimed, his loss of the Ring makes possible the renewal of the land, and, as in many versions of the Grail story, he is associated with and finally committed to water. His departure from Middle-earth to be healed of his wounds unmistakably evokes yet another wounded figure, the wounded Arthur, and his departure by ship to be healed of his wounds. It rounds off the association of Frodo with the mysterious child, with Scyld Scefing, and with those fertility figures mentioned earlier, who bring prosperity and peace. The fairy-tale hero, inconspicuous and unassuming, has been made to suffer the bitterness and loss of the medieval epic hero. Like Beowulf, like Arthur, he loses the last battle and pays a heavy price for his struggle. Such an end is dreadfully inappropriate. If he is not given half the kingdom and the princess's hand in marriage he ought at least to be able to live happily ever after. He should get some recognition, some recompense. It is not fair.

And that, of course, is just Tolkien's point. It is not meant to be fair. We are beyond the epic now, beyond romance and beyond the fairy-tale ending. In the real world things seldom turn out as we would like them to, and the little man is as subject to tragedy as the great one. For Beowulf to die, for Arthur to lose Camelot, these are, in their way, great endings to great lives. They come at the end of brave days and brave deeds. Their stories end not happily but fittingly, and that is as it should be. To take the epic ending and give it to the fairy-tale hero is to reveal new values in the old pattern. The sacrifice is all the greater for being made by one so small.

But the story must have Aragorn to give it point. Without the two heroes much of the impact would be lost. Frodo is the passing of the old, Aragorn the emergence of the new. Both happen at the same time, and each because of the other.

Tolkien read *Beowulf* as a poem of balance, the opposition of ends and beginnings. He says of it: "In its simplest terms it is a contrasted description of two moments in a great life, rising and setting; an elaboration of the ancient and intensely moving contrast between youth and age, first achievement and final death" (*MC* 28). He has built these same values, this same balance and opposition, into *The Lord of the Rings* in a synchronous rather than sequential pattern. By giving us both Aragorn and Frodo he has used the contrast between them to widen and deepen the meaning of his story.

Bilbo's Neck Riddle

On 16 January 1938 the *Observer* published a letter from "Habit" to the editor of the newspaper inquiring about literary sources and analogues for J.R.R. Tolkien's recently published *The Hobbit*. "Habit" was interested in sources for the idea of hobbits in general and, in particular, in the possibility of a Beowulfian analogue for the episode of the dragon's cup. Tolkien's reply, printed on 20 February, not only gave some answers but suggested another line of inquiry: "And what about the Riddles?" he wrote. "There is work to be done here on the sources and analogues. I should not be at all surprised to learn that both the hobbit and Gollum will find their claims to have invented any of them disallowed" (*Letters* 32). There is indeed work to be done in tracing the riddles posed by Bilbo and Gollum in their life-or-death contest, and since Tolkien's letter was written, some work has been done, not least by Tolkien himself (see *Letters* 123). One riddle, however, has not received the kind of attention it deserves. This is Bilbo's stumper, "What have I got in my pocket?" (*H* 74), the riddle that ends the game.

Recall the situation. In "Riddles in the Dark," chapter 5 of *The Hobbit*, the desperate Bilbo, lost underground and coerced into the riddle game by Gollum, is in danger of not only being beaten but possibly also being eaten by his opponent. Having run out of conventional riddles, he thrusts his hand into his pocket, encounters the ring he found on the floor of the tunnel, and asks aloud, "What have I got in my pocket?" Mistaking this personal interrogation for a riddle, Gollum (with some justice) objects that it is "Not fair, not fair . . . to ask us what it's got in its nasty little pockets" (73). Many readers would agree with Gollum. Even the narrator acknowledges that "that last question had not been a genuine riddle according to the ancient laws" (74). The pseudo-editor of the Prologue to *The Lord of the Rings,* however, takes a broader view, conceding only that "The Authorities, it is true, differ whether this last question was a mere 'question' and not a 'riddle' according to the strict rules of the Game; but all agree that, after accepting it and trying to guess the answer, Gollum was bound by his promise" (*FR* Prologue, 21). Just who these "Authorities" are is not made clear, but we may assume that they have the same status as modern authorities, that is, that they are experts in the field whose judgment is to be relied upon. We will encounter comparable modern Authorities as the argument progresses.

Without recourse to Authority and choosing expedience over ethics, Bilbo, on trial for his life and "having nothing better to ask" (*H* 73), sticks by his question, insisting that since Gollum has accepted it as a riddle, he is obliged to answer it as one. Authorities aside (for the moment) and Bilbo's insistence notwithstanding, this is the crux. Is "What have I got in my pocket?" a proper riddle or isn't it? And who decides? Failing to guess the answer after three tries, Gollum forfeits the game and is required by the "ancient laws" to lead Bilbo out of the tunnel. But is Bilbo creating his own laws? Is our hero guilty of cheating? Is it fair to ask a question to which only the questioner knows the answer? Obviously not to Gollum or the narrator, and probably not to the modern audience reading the book.

But how about to Tolkien himself? He was, after all, the one to raise the question of "disallowing" some riddles, and we may assume that, as author, he is in a position to know more about what he wrote than either Bilbo or the narrative voice. Although we must acknowledge that in a strict sense Bilbo did "invent" his last question, there is evidence to show that he did not originate the strategy behind it. Nevertheless, even if we are not being strict, his question might still be disallowed on the following grounds: (1) It is not a riddle in form, for the form conventionally disguises one thing by identifying or describing it as another; (2) it is not a riddle in intent, since it is unpremeditated and addressed by Bilbo to himself, not to Gollum; (3) it is not a question to which the contestant can by rational process arrive at an answer; therefore it is not a riddle in any sense, since a riddle, by definition, must have a viable solution.

We may presume that at some point in his dreary life Gollum had pockets, for his answers, worthy of Tom Sawyer, are predicated on that knowledge and based on a reasonable expectation or experience of what people (especially boys) are likely to have in their pockets—first "Handses!" then "Knife!" and finally "String or nothing!" (*H* 73–74). But Gollum's guesses are set up to fail, since intelligence, experience, and reasonable expectation have nothing to do with the answer or the ability to guess it. Even Bilbo did not know what he had in his pocket, which is why he asked the question in the first place.

Although to a modern jury, and to Gollum as well, such objections are both logical and persuasive, literary precedent provides a surprise verdict. According to those "ancient laws" of custom and tradition cited by the narrator (and well known to the author), Bilbo's question is an allowable riddle. Even though by modern standards and rules of fair play Bilbo is cheating, since he knows (albeit after the fact) that Gollum cannot possibly know the answer to his question, such cheating is fair (i.e., permissible) according to the precedents of the riddle game, which permit an unanswerable question in a life-threatening situation. Despite the fact that it is contrary to custom, and that the story's narrator disallows it, despite the fact that the asker himself is unaware of it, Bilbo's last question is a legitimate though very special kind of riddle. It is a neck riddle.

What is a neck riddle?

As Tolkien's narrator says of hobbits (an equally arcane field of study), neck riddles may need some description nowadays, since they are part of an ancient tradition of immense antiquity that has become rare in the modern world. But they are recognized and acknowledged by the "Authorities," experts in the field whose business it is to be familiar with antiquity and ancient traditions, and whose judgment may be relied upon. I will cite three such Authorities (Craig Williamson, Archer Taylor, and Hilda Ellis Davison), reserving J.R.R. Tolkien as an implicit fourth. In *A Feast of Creatures*, Craig Williamson's translation of Anglo-Saxon riddles from *The Exeter Book*, Williamson cites Archer Taylor's classification of Anglo-Saxon riddles into groups by type. Group 8 is the Neck Riddle Group, questions that are unanswerable except by the asker, who thus "saves his neck by the riddle, for the judge or executioner has promised release in exchange for a riddle that cannot be guessed" (Williamson 21).

Now you know enough to go on with.

Hilda Ellis Davidson's article on "Insults and Riddles in the *Edda* Poems" in *Edda: A Collection of Essays* notes that "the theme of the 'neck riddle,' as it has been called, is a very popular one, found in folktales over a large part of the world" (31). She offers two examples from her particular area of specialty— which was also one of Tolkien's—medieval Norse myth and literature. One example is from the fourteenth-century Norse *Heiðreks saga*, the other from the Eddic poem "Vafþrúðnismal." *Heiðreks saga*, very likely written in the latter half of the thirteenth century, is almost certainly a compilation of more ancient, undoubtedly oral, and therefore traditional poems. The "Vafþrúðnismal" is dated by some scholars to as early as the tenth century, but its earliest written form is in Snorri Sturluson's thirteenth-century *Edda*, recorded in two fourteenth-century manuscripts, *Codex Regius* and *Hauksbok*.

Both examples offer valid evidence that a neck riddle not only was permitted by those "ancient laws" Tolkien claimed for the fictive world of *The Hobbit* but was recognized in the no less fictive but much more traditional world of Scandinavian mythology. In "Vafþrúðnismal" the Norse god Óðinn engages the giant Vafþruðnir in a contest of *orð-speki*, verbal wit in which the loser's life is forfeit. Since for most of the contest the giant is easily able to answer every question the god poses to him, for his final throw Óðinn asks an unanswerable question: *Hvat mælti Óðinn, áðr á bal stigi, sialfr í eyra syni?* ("What did Óðinn whisper in his son's ear before he mounted the pyre?") Since no one could know what Óðinn whispered except Óðinn (his son, Baldr, being dead, presumably does not count), this is a neck riddle if there ever was one. Defeated fair and square, Vafþrúðnir concedes the match, telling Óðinn, *Nú ek við Óðinn deildak mina orð-speki. þu ert æ vísastr vera!* ("Now have I striven in word-skill with Óðinn. Thou shalt ever be wisest of all!" [*Edda Essays* 30].)

In the more complex plot of *Heiðreks saga*, Óðinn, here disguised as Gestumblindi ("Blind Stranger"), takes the place of a man standing trial who is given a chance to go free if he can ask a riddle that King Heiðrek cannot solve. As before, at stake is the loser's life. As before, Heiðrek answers every question. And as before, Óðinn resorts to a neck riddle. In fact, he resorts to the very same neck riddle: *Hvat mælti Óðinn í eyra Baldri / aðr hann vas á bál um borinn?* ("What spake Óðinn into the ear of Baldr ere he was laid on the funeral pyre?"). King Heiðrek, unlike Vafþrúðnir a sore loser, accuses Óðinn of *Undr ok argakap ok alla bleythi!* ("Wonder and wickedness and all sorts of lewdness!") and strikes at the god with his magic sword Tyrfin. The ever-elusive Óðinn flies away in the shape of a hawk, but the sword cuts off his tail feathers.

It scarcely needs pointing out that in the judgment of the Authorities, the questions asked by Óðinn, Gestumblindi, and Bilbo qualify as neck riddles, first by Taylor's classification and second by Davidson's critical certification. In each case the question is one to which only the asker knows the answer. In each case, its purpose is to rescue the questioner from a life-threatening situation. In each case it does, in fact, do just that. Given his familiarity with Old Norse poetry and prose, it would be strange if Tolkien were not familiar with the Norse examples, and equally strange if he were not aware that his own riddle game, following the precedent set by his exemplars, could legitimately employ the same strategy for the same reason and with the same outcome.

Interestingly enough, Óðinn, Gestumblindi, and Bilbo are not the only examples with which Tolkien was acquainted. A third exemplar, this one from real life rather than fiction, was J.R.R. Tolkien himself. Among the Tolkien papers archived at the Bodleian Library in Oxford is the draft of a talk given in 1947 to the Dante Society of Oxford, of which Tolkien was a member. It is titled "A neck-verse" and begins with the quotation from the Book of Psalms, verse 1 of Psalm 51.

Miserere mei Deus secundum magnam misericordiam tuam. Et secundum multitudinem miserationum tuarum dele iniquitatem meam.

Have mercy upon me O God, according to Thy lovingkindness. According unto the multitude of thy tender mercies blot out my transgressions.

In the Middle Ages a condemned prisoner could, by the proper recitation of this verse, be given a reprieve from the hangman through benefit of clergy. Though designed to show familiarity with Christian orthodoxy rather than pagan myth, it would, like the neck riddle and by the same device, save his neck.

The implicit parallel between Tolkien and the putative condemned prisoner (and, I would add, between Tolkien and Óðinn) is that the modestly apologetic Tolkien, culturally unfit to speak to Dante-lovers about their southern poet since he is, as he declares *"northern man,"* is a condemned prisoner risking his neck by addressing an expert on a subject and thus is likely to be hanged, if not reprieved. Similar to openings in other Tolkien talks, this neck-verse is intended to buy him his pardon before he begins.[1] There is no record of whether he got it, but there is reason to conjecture that his talk, the theme of which he said was *lusinga* ("undeserved praise, flattery"), may have been the germ of his later article "Middle English 'Losenger,'" published in *Essais de Philologie Moderne* in 1953. We may conclude, then, that he survived the ordeal.

Tolkien's jocular comparison of his situation with that of a prisoner in the dock getting off because of special knowledge, and that of Óðinn or Gestumblindi on trial before Vafðrúðnir or King Heiðrek and buying his life with special knowledge, is too close to be accidental. The phrases "neck-verse" and "neck riddle," while not identical, are near enough and are clearly descriptive of the same situation and the same strategy. There can be no question that Tolkien knew of the strategy and knew how to use it. There is also no question, I submit, that he bestowed it on Bilbo for use in the riddle game with Gollum.

It would not be the first instance in which Tolkien transferred an episode from medieval literature to his own modern fiction, indeed, specifically to this same modern mock-heroic little figure. As noted by the correspondent to the *Observer*, Bilbo's theft of the cup from Smaug's lair and the waking of the dragon to wrath and ruin are motifs recognizably borrowed from an incomplete and corrupt passage in *Beowulf*. Likewise, the parallels among the situations of Óðinn with Vafþrúðnir, Gestumblindi with King Heiðrek, Tolkien before the Dante Society, and Bilbo Baggins faced with Gollum are too close to be accidental. The similarity in tactic between "What did Óðinn whisper?" and "What have I got in my pocket?" is equally too close to be unintended.

I must return here to the distinction between *The Hobbit*'s narrator and its author. The narrator is a nameless fictive persona, a playful storytelling voice, while the author is an actual and established scholar of the literature that lies behind the story. Thus, although the narrator dismisses Bilbo's question as "not a genuine riddle according to ancient laws" (225), Tolkien the author is well aware that there is, de facto if not de jure, a loophole in those ancient laws and has no qualms about having his hero take advantage of it. In view of this distinction, and in answer to the concerns expressed in Tolkien's letter quoted in the opening paragraph, most of all in light of the evidence submitted here, we may safely conclude the following. Bilbo's last riddle should be allowed on the grounds that (1) an unanswerable question is legitimate in some circumstances; (2) it is a riddle in form, though the form itself is exceptional; and (3) it becomes a riddle in intent by both literary precedent and ancient custom.

Beyond these technicalities, the strategy inherent in "What have I got in my pocket?" has special literary importance, since it offers to the knowledgeable reader a clear analogue in earlier and similar stories. In addition, it serves to move *The Hobbit* beyond the realm of fairy tale and closer to the territory of myth. Bilbo is no Óðinn, it must be granted. Nevertheless, by taking the self-same stratagem used by Óðinn against his magical and death-dealing opponents, and giving it to the little hobbit Bilbo for use against the less magical but similarly murderous Gollum, Tolkien puts his small hero firmly in the tradition of older and bigger heroes (including Tolkien himself) who were not above invoking private knowledge to get themselves out of a tight spot. Tolkien the author, who is also Tolkien the scholar, makes his story's riddle game even more literary, even more traditional, even more sacrosanct than the storytelling narrator of *The Hobbit* seems to be aware.

Allegory Versus Bounce

Tolkien's Smith of Wootton Major

An academic debate between Verlyn Flieger and Tom Shippey

VERLYN FLIEGER

The issue of allegory and *Smith of Wootton Major* resides not so much in whether there is allegory to be found in the story (for there are at least demonstrable leftovers of an original allegorical intent) as in whether a reading on that level comes closest to Tolkien's final intent and best serves the story as a work of art. In *The Road to Middle-Earth* Professor Shippey asserts that "[*Smith*'s] mode is allegorical and its subject is the author himself, especially the relations between his job and his private sources of 'inspiration'" (*Road* 203). Here Shippey reads the first Cook as a "philologist-figure," the crass and materialistic Nokes as a "Critic-figure," and Smith himself as "a Tolkien-figure" (242–43). He is equally positive in his later *J.R.R. Tolkien: Author of the Century*, where he heads his discussion of the story "Autobiographical allegory: 2 *Smith of Wootton Major*" (*Author* 296). Shippey's autobiographical allegory 1 is *Farmer Giles of Ham*, though he concedes that *Farmer Giles* "makes too much sense in its own right to need an allegorical reading" (289). The implication is that *Smith* does *not* make such sense in its own right and thus benefits from a reading as allegory.

I yield to none in my admiration for Professor Shippey as a scholar, a critic, and a fellow lover of Tolkien. Nevertheless, with regard to *Smith,* I must respectfully disagree on all counts.

(1) The story's mode is fairy tale, not allegory, as Tolkien himself made clear. "This short tale is not 'allegory,'" he declared in his notes, "though it is capable of course of allegorical interpretation at certain points. *It is a 'Fairy*

Story' [my emphasis] of the kind in which beings that may be called 'fairies' or 'elves' play a part and are associated in action with human people, and are regarded as having a 'real' existence, that is one in their own right and independent of human imagination and invention" (*SWM* Extended Edition, 84).

(2) Its subject is the experience of a human in the Faery world, not "the author himself," though the reader is free to speculate that Tolkien may have had such experience.

(3) The characters are believable in their roles within the fiction and require no reference to philology, critics, or Tolkien's supposed conflict between art and life in order to be understood.

(4) The purpose of fairy tales is not to make sense but to give the reader a glimpse of the perilous realm that Tolkien called Faery (or Faërie; his spellings of the word vary).

As he himself put it, "Faërie cannot be caught in a net of words; for it is one of its qualities to be indescribable, though not imperceptible. It has many ingredients, but analysis will not necessarily discover the secret of the whole" (*MC* 114). Even more to the purpose are Tolkien's words about *Beowulf* and against its interpretation by critics as a philological, archaeological, or historical document rather than, as he chose to read it, a poem. "The significance of a myth is not easily to be pinned on paper by analytical reasoning. It is at its best when it is presented by a poet who feels rather than makes explicit what his theme portends" (*MC* 15); for "myth is alive at once and in all its parts, and dies before it can be dissected" (*MC* 15).

Shippey's interpretation of the story as autobiographical allegory of Tolkien's struggle with the opposing forces of fantasy and philology, or fantasy and faith, is precisely the kind of analysis Tolkien argues against. It may be plausible and persuasive if one is searching for biographical information about the author, though Shippey produces no external evidence that Tolkien intended such a conflict. It may conceivably tell us something about Tolkien and perhaps about Professor Shippey (as my argument here will say something about me), but it tells us nothing about what happens to Smith— not Tolkien—in Faery.

As Tolkien declared of his reading of *Beowulf*, "it is the mood of the author, the essential cast of his imaginative apprehension of the world, that is my concern" (*MC* 20), not the author's history for its own sake. Making the first Cook a philologist-figure does not improve understanding of Tolkien's imaginative apprehension of the world. However, the Cook can easily be understood in the context of the other Elf-friends in Tolkien's fiction, such as Eriol, Ælfwine, Edwin Lowdham, and Bilbo Baggins, who leave Middle-earth for the Faery realm. Making Smith a Tolkien-figure takes him right out of the story and puts him in Oxford in the twentieth century. The story's association of craft with art and art with Faery is understandable without allegorizing it, and Smith as a character works better in juxtaposition to Nokes than to Tolkien. Nokes is also a craftsman, though not a very inventive one since he largely depends on old recipes, and his unimaginative cooking, especially his over-sweetening of the cake, brands him as a journeyman.[1] He is never, like Smith, the master of his craft.

Shippey's imposition of allegorical meaning on *Smith* does not simply devalue the story as a story; it is necessarily based on the presumption that Tolkien was engaged in an interior struggle of which *Smith* is the coded expression. There is no hard evidence for this. The fact that Tolkien spent the majority of his daily life in teaching and scholarship and wrote fantasy and mythology in his spare time (and largely at night) does not necessarily mean that he felt the two areas were at war in himself. On the contrary, they worked very well together. His poetic gift enriches the most memorable of his critical essays, "*Beowulf:* The Monsters and the Critics" and "On Fairy-Stories," while his lifetime study of Old and Middle English and his reading in Norse, Welsh, and Finnish languages and mythology add authority to his fiction.

Roger Lancelyn Green's early review of *Smith of Wootton Major* warned against looking too hard for a message in what was essentially a fairy tale, writing that, "To seek for the meaning is to cut open the ball in search of its bounce" (Tolkien *Letters* 388 headnote). Green's caution has not stopped others from searching for the bounce, and in the process making some fairly bounce-deadening cuts in the fabric of the ball. Professor Shippey's extension of Green's metaphor of ball and bounce into a contention that the ball "bounces better" after it has been cut into, and that the story "makes more sense" when read as allegory is itself open to question. Balls do not bounce well after they have been cut open, if indeed they bounce at all. Moreover, the function of art is not to make "sense," but to give a glimpse of the wider realm to which art is the gateway.

Nevertheless, *Smith* is undeniably a perplexing narrative, of all Tolkien's works the most uncompromising in its presentation of the experience of mortals in the faery realm, and the opacity of the story invites interpretation. Whether it benefits from it is another issue altogether. What allegory there is in the story can be addressed and disposed of fairly easily. Tolkien has said that *Smith* began as an allegorical response to the (to him) common misconception of the word *fairy*, correlating the writer who would sweeten and prettify the notion for children to a cook baking an over-sweet cake on the assumption that all children liked sugar.

The story outgrew this concept, but the remnants can still be found in his notes, although his concern had apparently moved from the meaning of fairy to the state of organized religion. The notes show that he had thought of the shabby Great Hall, no longer properly tended, as the village church, of the Cook Nokes with his sugary misconception of Faery as the parson, of the craft or occupation of cooking as "personal religion and prayer." However, those same notes go on to make it clear that he vacillated widely between allegory and no allegory, obviously uncertain himself of how much meaning he should impose on the reader (Extended ed. 99–100).

On the model of Tolkien's argument for the centrality of the monsters to *Beowulf*, I would suggest that the Faery—the actual experience of enchantment by Smith—is at the center of *Smith*, while any leftover allegory is at the edges—the beginning and the end. This is all to the good. If the residual allegorical elements—the cake, the Cook, the Great Hall—comprised the major thrust of the narrative as published, *Smith* might be a good allegory but it would be a very dull story. It is not a dull story, though it is a surprisingly severe one—certainly not "sweet" in any respect. If we take Tolkien at his word that there is (or was) allegory in *Smith*, we would do well also to remember his words descriptive of another story, that "the tale grew in the telling." In that process the focus moved from the cake (in draft the story was titled "The Great Cake") to the central character in the story, the smith named Smith, who while still a boy swallows a magic star embedded in his slice of cake. The star functions as his entry visa into Faery, which Tolkien called "the perilous land," and of which he wrote that it has both beauty and "an ever-present peril" (*MC* 109).

The heart of *Smith of Wootton Major* lies not so much in the village machinery of Great Hall, Cook, and Parson, as in Smith's wanderings in Faery and in the reader's participation in his enchantment, bewilderment, and acceptance of that which he cannot understand. In his total lack of any key to the meaning of the phenomena to which he is witness Smith is in the position of the reader, or rather, the reader is in the position of Smith and both are in the position described by Tolkien in his opening to "On Fairy-stories." "In that realm [Faery] a man may, perhaps, count himself fortunate to have wandered, but its very richness and strangeness tie the tongue of a traveller who would report them" (*MC* 109). I suggest that this is precisely Tolkien's intention. To assume that Tolkien intended the Faery of the story to stand for something outside itself would subordinate that very richness and strangeness to some extra-literary agenda. One could no longer read it as itself, then, but only use it as a guide to another and presumably more important story. Readers would be subject to just what Tolkien objected to in allegory, "the purposed domination of the author" (*FR* I, Foreword, 7), rather than being left free, like Smith, to find their own way and make their own associations.

As a wanderer in Faery, Smith is witness to scenes and events he cannot understand and that are never explained. He sees "things of both beauty and terror that he [can] not clearly remember or report to his friends." He stands beside the Sea of Windless Storm where blue waves bear "the white ships that return from battles on the Dark Marches of which men know nothing"; he sees a "great ship cast high upon the land. . . . elven mariners" who pass over him and go "away into the echoing hills" (Extended ed. 26–28). Most mysterious of all, he comes to a lake "harder than stone and sleeker than glass." When he steps on the surface and falls, its ringing boom wakes the Wild Wind which drives him up the slopes "whirling and falling like a dead leaf" (Extended ed. 29). He clings for safety to a young birch tree, and when the Wind has passed he sees that the birch, now stripped of all its leaves, is weeping. Setting his hands on its white bark, he asks what he can do to make amends or give thanks. The trees answer is both unequivocal and puzzling. "Nothing," it says. "Go away! The Wind is hunting you. You do not belong here. Go away and never return" (Extended ed. 30).

The power of this episode, its bounce, resides in its mystery. Smith does not understand the action of the Wind or the words of the birch. He is not meant to. Nor is the reader. Smith asks for no explanation, and none is forthcoming. I suggest that in reading the episode it would be well to remember Tolkien's own caution about the realm of Faërie: that while "in that realm a man may, perhaps, count himself fortunate to have wandered," nevertheless, "it is dangerous for him to ask too many questions, lest the gates be shut and the keys be lost" (*MC* 109).

Shippey asks questions. "What is the birch that saves, the wind that threatens?" (*Road* 244). His citation of sources and analogues in Tolkien's poem "Éadig béo þu," in the Child ballad "The Wife of Usher's Well," and in Walter Scott's anecdote of the birch as protection against the wind of the world, supply his answers, but tell us nothing about Smith. His speculation that "Smith's Wind could be the world," as in Scott, "the birch its traditional opponent, scholarly study," as in "Éadig béo þu" (*Road* 245), allows him to ask more questions, now based entirely on his own interpretation.

"Did Tolkien feel he had *exploited* philology for his fiction?" "Did he feel, perhaps, that in writing his fiction he was trespassing in a 'perilous country' against some unstated law?" (*Road* 246). There is no evidence to support this, and to allow this kind of speculation to override Tolkien's own treatment is to do the story a disservice. Such a reading removes the mystery and power from the episode and replaces them with one-to-one correlations, thereby cutting open the ball and effectively removing the bounce. The mystery is not just explained—it is explained away.

In sum, the reading *Smith of Wootton Major* as allegory goes counter to Tolkien's own artistic principles. Granted, the story began as allegory. Granted, the remnants still lurk around the edges. But the story transcends its own beginnings and the allegorical leftovers add nothing to the reader's understanding of its particular and unexplainable magic. To illustrate the point, I will close with Tolkien's own best-known use of outright allegory, the allegory of the tower in "*Beowulf:* The Monsters and the Critics." After carefully implying one-to-one correspondences between contemporary critical interpretations of the poem and the field of old stone, the older hall, the present house, and the tower, he abandons allegory for art in his conclusion, which is that, "from that tower the man had been able to look out upon the sea" (*MC* 8).

There is no allegorical correlative to the sea, and the vision implied cannot be tied down to a specific meaning. The same is true of *Smith of Wootton Major.*

T.A. SHIPPEY

My comments take off from the statement made by Roger Lancelyn Green in a review of *Smith* shortly after its publication—a statement endorsed by Tolkien and quoted with approval by Dr. Flieger, and others.[2] Dr. Flieger's paraphrase of Green runs as follows:

> Green observed that the effect of the story transcends any explicit reference and warned against looking too hard for a specific message. He wrote of it that "To seek for the meaning is to cut open the ball in search of its bounce." This may prove to be the best summation of the story's appeal. The bounce is clearly there, but to search for it is to defeat its effect; to allegorize it is to deaden the bounce completely. (*A Question of Time* 233)

I accept Flieger's paraphrase, but I reject Green's metaphor. More important, if "the bounce" here is "whatever it is that makes reading the story pleasurable," then I can testify that as far as I am concerned Flieger's last phrase, "to allegorize it is to deaden the bounce completely," is not true of my experience at all. Much of the pleasure I take in the story comes from searching out allegory. This does not go away, but increases with re-reading, and re-searching. Green's metaphor, to use another metaphor, seems to me like saying "put that ball on the mantelpiece, and for goodness' sake don't bounce it, it will break!" But it doesn't break—or not when I bounce it.

I have no wish, accordingly, to try to confute Dr. Flieger's reading, but I do have to record that my experience is not hers. We are clearly reading the same text (and I do not believe that either of us has much patience with mystical notions that there is no such thing as "the same text"), but we are not reading it the same way. Is this the result of different initial presuppositions? Different areas of knowledge? Or perhaps we are reading it differently on a purely mechanical level, in the way our eyes move and we take in words?

I begin with a simple possibility: perhaps we have different views about allegory. What is an "allegory"? This question, like almost all matters of definition, has been put to the Four Wise Men of Oxenford,[3] and as with "blunderbuss" their answer is not especially helpful: the core of it runs "a figurative narrative . . . in which properties and circumstances attributed to the apparent subject really refer to the subject they are meant to suggest," a definition which leaves one wondering about words like "really" and "meant." I find it more useful to look at Tolkien's own theory and practice, and these are on the face of it incompatible. Tolkien wrote, for instance, in the Foreword to the second edition of *The Lord of the Rings*, "I cordially dislike allegory in all its manifestations, and always have done so since I grew old and wary enough to detect its presence."[4] I hesitate to say that this is not true (as stated above, you cannot tell people what they like or dislike), but the fact is that Tolkien was something of a serial allegorist. Much of the force of the opening of his famous lecture "*Beowulf:* The Monsters and the Critics" comes from three short allegories in sequence: *Beowulf* seen as a child to whose christening one fairy (Poesis) has not been invited; the criticism of *Beowulf* viewed as a Babel of tongues; and most important and most extensive, the allegory of *Beowulf* as a tower. Tolkien explicitly identifies this long paragraph as "yet another allegory," and says at the end of it, "I hope I shall show that that allegory is just."[5]

The idea of "just-ness" seems to me important, and perhaps explains the contradiction indicated above. In Tolkien's view, allegory is essentially a set of equations. Each item in the surface narrative has to correspond to an item in the unstated meaning, and those items have to fit together in closely similar ways. It was this view that led him to reject the idea that *The Lord of the Rings* was an allegory of World War II (with the Ring implicitly as atomic power). If this had been the case, he pointed out in a scornful paragraph in the Foreword already cited, the Ring would not have been destroyed, it would have been used; Saruman would have been enabled to make his own Ring; and so on. Amateur allegorists of his work, Tolkien felt, did not know their own business. Their allegory was not "just."

By contrast, though, Tolkien in the *Beowulf* lecture did know his own business. Every item in the "tower" allegory makes perfect sense if translated into the world of *Beowulf*-criticism, and so (I believe) does every item in the "Babel" allegory.[6] The point of the allegories is also perfectly clear. They function as *reductio ad absurdum:* the image of the busy critics destroying the tower, then complaining what a mess it is in, and saying it was a silly idea to build it anyway, is evidently absurd, but bears a strong resemblance to what German critics of the poem actually did. They did not think what they did was absurd, but Tolkien's allegory tries to persuade one that it was. Allegory used this way, one can see, is a simplifying and argumentative mode.

This has made it unpopular in modern critical terms. Nowadays what is valued is complexity, diversity, dialogism, multiple meanings, freedom to interpret the inexhaustible text (etc.); and allegory, with its one-to-one correspondences and its strict discipline, is viewed as limited and pedantic. In the Foreword already mentioned, Tolkien opposes it to "applicability," notes that many confuse the two, and expresses the distinction as, "the one [applicability] resides in the freedom of the reader, and the other [allegory] in the purposed domination of the author." It would be possible for me to avoid contradicting Tolkien by saying that I seek only for "applicability" in *Smith,* not "allegory." But I would point out, first, that there is an extensive scale between perfect freedom and perfect domination; and second, that several major works of English literature (including ones which Tolkien respected, and ones he probably did not) are commonly taken to be allegories, which demand interpretation and will not work without it, but where the "domination of the author" has certainly not led to a final, deadened solution.

I mean works like Langland's *Piers Plowman,* Spenser's *Faerie Queene,* Bunyan's *Pilgrim's Progress,* but, perhaps most strikingly in modern times, also Orwell's *Animal Farm.* It would be an extremely unambitious and unproductive procedure to read any of the three just mentioned "just for the story," though I can imagine there are some people who do so. Children, for instance, might read the Orwell story just as a sort of joke, though even they, I think, would feel some sense of fear, some awareness that this story is not just about animals. But in such cases the story, the attractive surface narrative, is there partly though not entirely to provoke a quest for a further meaning, clearly intended and sometimes indicated by the author; and no-one suggests that this quest should be abandoned, for fear of losing a hypothetical "bounce."[7] It is in this category of allegorical work that I would put *Smith.*

There are then two points that I would add. One is that I would put "Leaf by Niggle" in the same, or a similar category. I think this is quite clearly an allegory, and an autobiographical one, and one of the signs of this is the work's extreme "just-ness." Many of the details in it, just as with Tolkien's allegory of the tower, can be given one-to-one correspondences with reality (in my view, Niggle's house, garden, paintings, potatoes, shed, journey, temperament, and much else). These details (rightly interpreted) make the story both funnier and more threatening—they add to the bounce.[8] But the second point is that, obviously with *The Faerie Queene* and even with the much shorter and clearer "Leaf by Niggle," no-one is ever going to catch every detail. Probably the authors themselves could not have done so. Allegories of an extended kind have a habit of getting away from their authors, as the surface narrative imposes its own logic. They are also clearly used by many authors (Langland and Bunyan prominent among them) as a way of trying to understand their own feelings and their own situation, as an investigative mode as well as an explanatory one. In only the shortest and simplest allegories does the author "dominate" the reader (as Tolkien said) or even (and this is my addition) his/her own text. The advantage of all this is that it is quite possible to read an extended allegory, like *Smith,* or "Leaf by Niggle," or *Piers Plowman,* and find something new every time—but still something allegorical. Like tennis balls, they bounce higher the more you warm them up, and the way you warm them up is by playing with them.

To abandon metaphor and turn to reading *Smith,* it seems to me that my readings of the story depend on identifying details. It is amazing how easy these are to miss. Thus (and I owe the following identifications to Dr. Flieger, who has had the advantage of reading Tolkien's own commentary on his text, from which I now quote): "The Great Hall is evidently in a way an 'allegory' of the village church; the Master Cook . . . is plainly the Parson and the priesthood." Cooking meanwhile equates to "personal religion and prayer."[9] Tolkien here uses the words "evidently" and "plainly," but I do not think I made these equations on first or even later reading. What the account of the Great Hall and its festivities told me was that I was reading an allegory of some kind: social behavior in Wootton Major was too far removed from real-life behavior at any period of English history for me to accept it as just surface narrative. However, once the equations between Hall and church, etc., have been made, several other details take on meaning.

Rather late on in the tale, for instance, we are told that once Alf takes over as Master Cook from Nokes, the Hall was "re-glazed and re-painted." Some called this "new-fangled," but "some with more knowledge knew that it was a return to old custom." It is important to note that these sentences have no further narrative point. It makes no difference to the rest of the story what the Hall looks like. This rather extensive description is "narratively redundant." In an allegory, though, what is narratively redundant is likely to be allegorically especially significant. Here it seems to me that Tolkien is expressing approval of changes in church fashion in his own day, away from the careful sobriety, the "Sunday suit" style of Victorian devotion, and towards a more cheerful and more dramatic attitude to worship, seen by many as disrespectful and modernistic, but by Tolkien as a return to the medieval integration of religion with everyday life and with imaginative richness (as in the carving and painting of gargoyles, which he mentions particularly).

The Hall/church identification may make one wonder, further, about the place Smith lives, Wootton Major. Why Wootton? Why Major? Here I agree with Dr. Flieger that Wootton means, philologically, Wood-town, the town in the wood; and the wood is a highly significant image. Dr. Flieger suggests that woods are gateways to the other world, as in Dante, and this is so.[10] To it I would add that woods are for Tolkien ambiguous places.[11] He loved them as much as anyone, but he also saw them as places where travellers easily become confused, "bewildered," lose sight of the stars, lose their (physical and moral) bearings. They represent the world of reality, the mundane world, because in them it is so easy to forget that there is a world outside them, and to despair. Smith, of course, is above all the character with an available exit from Wootton, or the wood of the world, into Faerie. Meanwhile, why Major? Does the story need a Minor, and a Walton? In view of Tolkien's Catholicism, it is tempting to see the Church of Wootton Major as the Catholic Church, with Wootton Minor perhaps as its Anglican offshoot. An interesting detail here is that Nokes, not liked and not accepted as an apprentice by the previous Master Cook (so outside the "apostolic succession," so to speak) is "a solid sort of man with a wife and children." If he is "plainly" a parson, then, as Tolkien declared, he must be a Protestant one. Possibly the Major/Minor suggestion made just above is the wrong way round—as, in purely English terms, would be the case.

The question of names is especially relevant to allegory because, in normal life, names do not mean anything: surnames especially, as we all know, are not chosen but come by accident of birth; most people do not in fact know what their names "mean" (i.e., what they used to mean long ago, before they became just names). In a story, though, the author chooses the names. In realistic stories they will be chosen to sound random, as in reality. In an allegory they are likely once again to have strong suggestion. Here, and speaking entirely for myself, I cannot get over the choice of the name "Nokes." There is a Noakes in *The Lord of the Rings*, "Old Noakes of Bywater," and in his "Guide

to the Names in *The Lord of the Rings*" Tolkien noted the derivation from
Middle English *atten oke(s)*, "at the oak(s)," and added, for the benefit of his
translators, "since this is no longer recognized, this need not be considered.
The name is in the tale unimportant."[12] It is just a label, in other words, like
most names; but that is in *The Lord of the Rings*, which is not an allegory, and
which has hundreds of names without narrative meaning.

What I cannot forget, reading *Smith*, is that for Tolkien "oak" had a clear
private meaning, several times recalled.[13] "Oak" in Old English is *ác*, and
it is also the name for the rune representing "A." The name for "B" in the
Old English runic alphabet is *beorc*, or "birch." In the syllabus Tolkien devised at Leeds University, and which he tried unsuccessfully to transplant
to Oxford,[14] the "B-scheme" was the one he controlled, the language-and-
medieval scheme of study, and the "A-scheme" was the one controlled by his
colleague the Professor of Literature. These two schemes existed on terms
of strong mutual ideological hostility, which it would take many pages to explain. I can only say here that to me (the inheritor of many of Tolkien's feuds),
Alf Prentice's sharp rebuke to Nokes almost at the end has many resonances.
"You are a vain old fraud," he says, "fat, idle, and sly. I did most of your work.
Without thanks you learned all that you could from me—except respect for
Faery, and a little courtesy." Ignoring the first sentence, which is just rude,
the next two seem to me to represent reasonably well the relationship between philology (the "B-scheme") and literary studies (the "A-scheme" represented by Nokes): English departments in universities were established by
philologists, who created a discipline of vernacular literary study, and were
then ungratefully pushed aside by critics who, notoriously, had no time for
fantasy, or Faery, whether medieval or modern. If Tolkien did not intend this
equation, why choose the names "Nokes" rather than one of the many thousand neutral names available?

I have to accept, of course, that this is very largely a private symbolism,
which Tolkien could not have expected more than a few of his readers to
notice. Most of his readers, though, could still get the point, or most of the
point: Nokes is annoying not just because he has only a feeble image of
Faerie himself, but because he insists that that is the only one there is. He
is indeed absolutely precisely one of those "professional persons" who "suppose their dullness and ignorance to be a human norm," and whom Tolkien
picked out for special assault in his "Valedictory Address to the University of Oxford," clearly meaning in that context to indicate professors of
literature.[15] And then we have the strange scene in which Smith is protected
from the Wind by the weeping birch. I have said what I think about this
elsewhere, and have clearly failed to convince Dr. Flieger;[16] but this perhaps

brings us close to one reason for our disagreements. It seems to me, as said above, that my readings depend above all on details, and on "just-ness." I can accept that I miss details, and equations, like the very obvious Hall/church one. One reason why the "bounce" does not weaken, in my opinion, is that I hope to catch or identify a few more details on every new reading. What I do not think is that I am supposed just not to wonder about them, to accept them as part of surface narrative, as I might in a realistic novel.

Dr. Flieger, in a word, takes *Smith* holistically, while I take it bit by bit. There is no doubt that her way fits modern critical taste better than mine, as does a liking for dialogism, multiple meanings, freedom to interpret the inexhaustible text (etc.), as said above. Whether modern critical taste has much to do with Tolkien may, however, be doubted. I note also, in Dr. Flieger's analysis, a conviction that the whole text is somehow too fragile to be rudely disassembled. My "oak-and-birch" theory is not rejected outright, but is felt to "place a heavy burden on a story whose effect depends not a little on its lightness of touch." Elsewhere—and also in the context of rejecting auto-biographical and allegorical elements—we hear of its "gossamer appeal," its "unpretentious air," and "effortless ability to imply without stating."[17] Light, gossamer, effortless: this is an image of Faerie, but I have a feeling that this is a Shakespearean one rather than a Tolkienian one. As I have said elsewhere, Tolkien was in a technical sense one of the most "tough-minded" of authors, not a holistic person at all.[18]

One does, of course, in the end have to consider the story as a whole, the story "in its own terms," as Dr. Flieger insists, though for me one has to go through the bit-by-bit stage of considering details first: things like names are for me quite literally the story's carefully selected "own terms." I can only say here that for me the critical facts about the story are that it is double-stranded; that it is about succession; and that Smith himself appears to fail, or to enjoy only temporary success, along both strands. The one strand is cooking. The succession of Master Cooks goes Rider/Nokes/Alf Prentice/Harper. The other is possession of the star, and its succession goes Rider/Smith/Nokes's Tim. According to Tolkien's own statement, the Hall, the Master Cooks, and cooking in general, are all to be equated with religion; while it seems obvious that the star which gives entry into Faerie stands for something like Tolkien's own inspiration, a quality essentially literary and imaginative.

This basic separation seems to me, however, hard to maintain in detail. For one thing, Nokes the Cook shows a revealingly shallow attitude to Faerie, which seems to have more to do with literature than with religion. For another, it is hard for me to see Alf, the elf-king (elves are proverbially soulless) simply as a parson, a representative of the Church. I conclude, therefore, that as one might expect these two strands are not readily separable, but relate to each other. The theme of *Smith* is the integration of fantasy with belief; the question it resolves is whether fantasy—the deliberate, imaginative, literary creation of myth by individuals—is compatible with belief in the myth created by God (the Christian myth). Strict views have long insisted that this is not the case. Tolkien took such strict views seriously, but he very much did not want to accept them. *Smith* works out that debate, and also makes the case for the autonomy of fantasy against the beef-witted, rigorously practical, "stands to reason" attitude of Nokes (so often repeated since by "modernist" critics).

Uncertainty is conveyed once more by redundancy, this time by "redundant characters." These are the characters introduced, it seems, so as to be excluded from both sequences of succession: Smith's son Ned, and his grandson Tomling. Neither becomes Cook, neither receives the star. Indeed, in one of the least expected strokes of the narrative, the star goes to a descendant of Nokes, Nokes of Townsend's Tim. These surprising introductions seem to me to be capable of interpretation, but perhaps the point to make here is that they seem to me to demand it. Surely Tolkien here is saying something at once pessimistic (no-one can control the future) and optimistic (inspiration may appear to be lost, but will return in some entirely unpredicted form): it reminds me of the debate between Legolas and Gimli in Minas Tirith, Gimli taking the pessimistic view (human works all fail), Legolas the optimistic one (but their seed does not fail).[19]

My essential point about allegory and its "bounciness" is however this: a full reading of *Smith*, for me, would look like a long edited text, with footnoted commentary on several score, or several hundred separate points. To name a very small selection of them, the character Rider, the Fairy Queen doll, and the contrast between it and the real Fairy Queen, the "old books of recipes" which Nokes can barely read, the strange sequence in Smith's family of Nokes-like names (Nell, Nan, Ned), the King's Tree, the Living Flower which *is* inherited by Smith's kin, the scented bell-flowers which go to Tomling, the story's forty-eight year time-span, the character Harper who "comes from your own village," the name Townsend (Nokes of Townsend is "quite different"), the word "nimble," almost the last word of the story and one marked like Ned, Nan, Nell, and Nokes by the philological feature of "nunnation." What do all these mean? In some cases, I think I know, but it would take a long and separate comment to explain; in others I do not know, but am still thinking about it (which means that there is still "bounce" in reserve). But it seems to me that that is the way complex allegories work. Their life is in detail. Their texture is not "gossamer," but surprisingly tough. The fear that their charm may be destroyed by too close an analysis is misplaced. They ask for careful thought, not just emotional response, because they have something serious and complex to express. This is emphatically not to say, however, that what they have to express can be reduced to some (once decoded) much simpler meaning. It is perhaps this last mistaken belief which has created the modern reaction against the allegorical mode. But that is not the way that medieval allegorists worked, nor necessarily modern ones.

A Mythology for Finland

Tolkien and Lönnrot as Mythmakers

J.R.R. Tolkien's stated ambition to dedicate a mythology to England is now generally accepted as the original and primary motive behind his fiction. The motive behind the ambition, however, has not been interrogated as to its rationale. England had survived for many centuries without a mythology. What impulse, at a particular point in history, made Tolkien suddenly decide it needed one? What besides his own literary ambition might have impelled a young, unpublished writer to attempt such an enormous undertaking? In at least partial answer, I offer two quotes. Here is the first:

> Why has not England a great mythology? Our folklore has never advanced beyond daintiness, and the greater melodies about our country-side have all issued through the pipes of Greece. Deep and true as the native imagination can be, it seems to have failed here. It has stopped with the witches and the fairies. It cannot vivify one fraction of a summer field, or give names to half a dozen stars. England still waits for the supreme moment of her literature—for the great poet who shall voice her, or, better still, for the thousand little poets whose voices shall pass into our common talk (*Howards End* 279).

And here is the second.

> I was from early days grieved by the poverty of my own beloved country: it had no stories of its own (bound up with its tongue and soil), not of the quality that I sought, and found (as an ingredient) in legends of other lands. There was Greek, and Celtic, and Romance, Germanic, Scandinavian, and

Finnish (which greatly affected me); but nothing English, save impoverished
chap-book stuff. . . . I had in mind to make a body of more or less connected
legend . . . which I could dedicate simply to: to England. . . . (*Letters* 144)

The second quote seems so clearly both a paraphrase of and a response to
the first that it is next to impossible to read the two in conjunction without
hearing the same voice in both, or imagining at least an ongoing conversation between like-minded individuals. "Witches and fairies" (from quote
number one) could certainly qualify as "impoverished chap-book stuff"
(from quote number two), and the plea of the first that "England still waits
for . . . the great poet who shall voice her" is answered in the second by the
stated intent to make "a body of more or less connected legend" and dedicate it to England.

Similar as these sentiments appear, they were expressed by two very different writers at two widely separated times. The first quote is from E. M.
Forster's *Howards End,* first published in 1910, where Forster put the sentiments in the mouth of Margaret Schlegel, an English woman of Germanic
heritage who is trying to find a home. The second is from J.R.R. Tolkien's
1951 letter to Milton Waldman of Collins Publishing explaining the rationale behind the Silmarillion. That they are so close in expression of national
sentiment and desire for cultural heritage is for one good reason. Both were
responding to the same stimulus, and the same climate of thought.

This stimulating climate was the folklore movement, the great surge of collecting and cataloguing of myth and folklore which swept Western Europe
in the nineteenth and early twentieth centuries. National mythologies were
being discovered or re-discovered at an astounding rate, and studies of their
languages and lore were the focus of new scholarship. In this movement, Finland was and remained for many years the leader. This was largely because of
the impact on the Finns in particular and on the emerging European nationalistic spirit in general of the newly formulated Finnish national epic, *Kalevala.*
Francis Magoun, who translated *Kalevala* into English in 1963, states that,

Appearing at a time when there was little or no truly bellelettristic Finnish
literature, the *Kalevala* unquestionably—and most understandably—became a source of great satisfaction and pride to the national consciousness then fast developing among the Finns, who had been growing restive
under their [then] Russian masters. To some extent the *Kalevala* became
a rallying point for these feelings, and permitted and in a measure justified
such exultant statements as "Finland can [now] say for itself: I, too, have
a history!" (Magoun xiv)

More specifically and more personally, the Finns themselves said of Elias Lönnrot, the man who compiled and published *Kalevala,* "A single man, by scurrying about, has created a heritage for us" (*Kalevala* 342).

Lönnrot in effect gave Finland its own myth and mythic identity equal to that of Greece or Scandinavia. He gave it its own pre-history and its own cultural individuality apart from the overlordships of Russia and Sweden, both of which had annexed Finland at one time or another. *Kalevala* became a kind of extended rallying cry in Finland's struggle for nationhood, which struggle culminated in its Declaration of Independence in December of 1917.

The work's effect on Finnish art and culture was equally profound. It became the instant inspiration for all kinds of artistic expression. In music, it inspired Jan Sibelius, the great Finnish composer, first to write the nationalistic *Finlandia,* and then to interpret a number of stories from *Kalevala.* His *Lemmenkäinen Suite,* the *Tapiola Suite,* the *Kullervo* Symphony, the *Swan of Tuonela,* all owe their inspiration to *Kalevala,* as does Sibelius's contemporary Robert Kajanus's *Aino* Symphony. As part of the same Finnish arts movement, the Finnish painter Akseli Gallen-Kallela executed a series of powerful pieces illustrating scenes from *Kalevala* and giving a new energy to Finnish visual art.

How did this affect Forster and inspire Tolkien? It gave them both an example. A simple sequence of dates will show a clear temporal, if not necessarily causal, sequence leading from *Kalevala* to the Forster passage and thence to Tolkien's burgeoning ambition to provide a mythology for England. In 1907, the earliest English translation of *Kalevala* direct from the Finnish, W.F. Kirby's Everyman edition, was published. In 1910, Forster's *Howards End,* with Margaret Schlegel's lament for an English mythology, appeared and was widely read. In 1914, Tolkien's first effort at intentional myth-making, "The Voyage of Eärendil," was written. Until more of his correspondence with the members of his earliest literary circle, the TCBS becomes available, we have no way of ascertaining if Tolkien had read *Howards End,* although the striking similarity in the paragraphs quoted above certainly encourages such an assumption. We do know, however, that he had read *Kalevala,* at that time the most recent and most visible evidence of the value of myth to a society in need of a voice.

Tolkien's published letters make it clear that his interest in *Kalevala* dated back to the period in his life outlined by these dates. Recall his statement quoted above that the Finnish "greatly affected" him. Similar comments in less mythically descriptive letters specifically attribute much of his immediate inspiration to *Kalevala.* In October of 1914, he wrote to his wife Edith that he was trying to turn one of the stories of *Kalevala* "into a short story somewhat on the lines of Morris' romances with chunks of poetry in between" (*Letters* 7). In 1944, he wrote to his son Christopher that, "Finnish nearly ruined my Hon. Mods and was the original germ of the Silmarillion" (*Letters* 87). In 1955, he wrote to W.H. Auden that *Kalevala* "set the rocket off in story," and that his legendarium was "an attempt to reorganize some of the Kalevala, especially the tale of Kullervo the hapless, into a form of my own" (*Letters* 214).

Although he was not yet published in any field scholarly or artistic when he launched his dream in 1914, Tolkien's knowledge of mythology, especially the mythologies of Northern Europe and the British Isles was both deep and wide. He was familiar with the Icelandic *Eddas* and sagas; with the Germanic history-cum myth of the Huns and Burgundians; with the Irish hero tales, the Welsh *Mabinogion,* and the complex and comprehensive Arthurian "Matter of Britain." With such an array of national stories to draw on, what was it about this mythology for Finland that spurred him first to imitate it, and then to invent one of his own for England? I suggest that as much or more than the stories themselves, the specific example of *Kalevala*'s compiler, Elias Lönnrot, was what inspired Tolkien.

What had Lönnrot done? He had "scurried about," roaming over the backwoods and rural areas of Finland and the Russo-Finnish Karelian border collecting and transcribing from unlettered peasants their *runos,* their orally performed songs. His project stretched over twenty years and resulted first in his university thesis on Väinämöinen in 1827, published as the Proto-*Kalevala* in 1928, then the Old *Kalevala,* the name given to the 1835 edition after publication of the much longer version of 1849, *Kalevala* as we have it today. Lönnrot compiled, selected, and put into narrative order songs of creation and heroism, incantations and shamanism and the vagaries of ordinary human life. In so doing, he gave Finland, for two hundred years the fief alternately of Sweden and Russia, its own mythic and literary heritage—its own national identity. He reconstructed for Finland a world of magic and mystery, a heroic age of story that may never have existed in precisely the form he gave it, but nevertheless fired Finland with a sense of its own independent worth.

I propose that Tolkien envisioned himself doing exactly that, constructing a world of magic and mystery, creating a heroic age that, although it might never have existed, would give England a storial sense of its own mythic identity. But with this difference—that his work, unlike Lönnrot's, which for all his selection and arrangement was made of original oral material, would be a fictive construct. Unlike Lönnrot, Tolkien would not be "scurrying about." He was a writer, not a collector. He would invent, and by connecting his invented myths to England's extant history he would interweave a whole tapestry where before had been only disconnected scraps of information. He would be, in Forster's words, both the "great poet" who would give England her voice, and the "thousand little poets" whose voices would "pass into our common talk." Tolkien would follow the Lönnrot model in having an auditor (ultimately a series of auditors) who heard, transcribed, and passed on the songs of his fictive race of Elves, but he would be at once the singer and the scribe, the performer and the audience.

Several factors related only tangentially to *Kalevala* added impetus to Tolkien's developing ambition. As a student at King Edward's School in Birmingham, he had added to his growing store of languages excursions into Old English, reading the sparse remnants of early English mythic poetry, among them the *Crist, Beowulf,* and *Sir Gawain and the Green Knight.* Each in its separate way fired his imagination—the *Crist* which gave him the name Eärendel which he co-opted and wove into his own myth, *Beowulf,* whose tragedy gave him a model for heroic struggle, *Sir Gawain* whose combination of myth and chivalry with a flawed hero intrigued him. Nevertheless, while these were certainly mythic, and certainly in English, they were not what Tolkien wanted as a mythology for England. None could be England's *Kalevala.* The *Crist* is overtly Christian, which he found too explicit for an invented myth; *Beowulf* is an English poem but not an English myth, having as its subject matter the exploits of a northern Scandinavian who goes to Denmark, and *Sir Gawain and the Green Knight* is directly connected to Arthur and his court, therefore Celtic or British rather than English.

Growing out of this as a related factor may have been Tolkien's perception of the deleterious effect on English language and culture of the Norman Conquest, an event in English history which he regarded as an unmitigated catastrophe and which he heartily condemned. At some time in the school year of 1909–10 the eighteen-year-old Tolkien made a speech to the School Debating Society on the motion—"probably," says his biographer Humphrey Carpenter, "of his own devising" (Carpenter 40)—"That this house deplores the occurrence of the Norman Conquest." Here he attacked "the influx of polysyllabic barbarities which ousted the more honest if humbler native words" (Carpenter 40).

It seems safe to suppose that in addition to the ouster of language in the wake of the Conquest, Tolkien might also have mourned the ouster of a presumed pre-Conquest mythology for which the Old English language, now suppressed by "the influx of polysyllabic barbarities" had been the vehicle. Nor is it unreasonable to speculate that his imagination could make an analogy between the plight of Finnish lore and language overrun by the Swedes and Russians and that of Old English lore and language overrun by the Normans. In restoring, or newly creating his mythology dedicated to England, he created as well a language to be its vehicle, Quenya, which he called "Elven-Latin" and said he intended it to be a language of lore, whose phonology is directly and intentionally modeled on the phonology of Finnish.

A further comment by Tolkien in his description of his projected mythology invites another comparison with *Kalevala*. He wrote that, "[t]he cycles should be linked to a majestic whole and yet leave scope for other minds and hands, wielding paint and music and drama" (*Letters* 145). We need look no further than the paintings of Axel Gallen-Kallela and the music of Jan Sibelius to see what inspired that statement, nor is it a great stretch of imagination to speculate that Tolkien might have hoped for artists of that calibre to continue and elaborate his own work. In fact, although not necessarily always of that calibre, and perhaps not quite in the arenas he would have wanted, he has been granted his wish. Operas and concert pieces inspired, if not by *The Silmarillion* at least by *The Lord of the Rings*, abound, while pseudo-folk settings of the poems from that book, chiefly on guitar, are legion. Painting, too, has taken Tolkien's work for inspiration. Tolkien calendars and illustrated volumes of all his works continue to appear, not a few of them by reputable and able artists like Ted Nasmith and Alan Lee and Michael Hague. And as for drama, there have been several BBC radio productions of *The Hobbit* and *The Lord of the Rings* as well as any number of amateur productions. As well, there have been to date three attempts to translate his books into film, the latest being Peter Jackson's. Whether Tolkien would have approved of any of the results remains a matter for speculation and debate.

What, finally, can we conclude from this concatenation of mythic impulses? Did Tolkien answer Forster's call? Did he succeed, like Lönnrot, in giving England a mythology all its own? While the answer to the first question is "yes," the answer to the second must be, "no, he did not succeed," not, at least, in any nationalistic sense. Neither *The Silmarillion* nor its offshoot, *The Lord of the Rings* will ever inspire patriotic emotion in the English breast, or culturally distinguish any English person from the rest of the world. But he did give England—and the rest of the world—a work of mythic quality and mythic proportions and, we may safely suppose by this time, a kind of mythic endurance. And for that, our thanks must go in large measure to Elias Lönnrot.

Tolkien, *Kalevala,* and "The Story of Kullervo"

Although we have known since Humphrey Carpenter's 1977 biography of Tolkien that the Finnish *Kalevala* was a major influence on Tolkien's legendarium,[1] we have until recently lacked access to one important piece of supporting evidence, and that lack has hindered our full understanding of his mythology's relationship to its source. "The Story of Kullervo," his retelling in prose and verse of an episode from *Kalevala,* published for the first time in *Tolkien Studies* in 2010, should be recognized as an essential step along the road from adaptation to invention that resulted in the Silmarillion. There are other reasons as well why it should take its place in the spectrum of Tolkien's work. For one thing, it was, as far as we know, his earliest reuse of existing material from a real-world mythology. For another, it was the forerunner and inspiration for the tragic epic of Túrin Turambar, one of the three Great Tales of the fictive mythology of Middle-earth. Without the story itself to fit into the sequence, we have had only the beginning (*Kalevala*) and the end (Túrin) of the process, but not the middle. Moreover, much of our information has of necessity been acquired secondhand, either through Carpenter's biography or Tolkien's *Letters,* which itself constituted Carpenter's evidence for much of what he tells us. And some of the information from either of these sources has been at the least confusing, if not contradictory.

For example, Carpenter's statement that Tolkien said of *Kalevala* as a whole that he wanted "something of the same sort that belonged to the English" (59) is straightforward and easy to understand. The comment, made in a 1915 talk to an undergraduate society while Tolkien was a student at Oxford, was his response to the myth and nationalism movement that spread through Western Europe and the Isles in the nineteenth and early twentieth centuries but was brought to a halt by the 1914 war. Out of that movement came Wilhelm Grimm's *Kinder- und Hausmärchen,* Jacob Grimm's *Deutsche Mythologie,* Jeremiah Curtin's *Myths and Folklore of Ireland,* Moe and As- bjørnsen's *Norske Folkeeventyr,* and Lady Guest's translation of the Welsh *Mabinogion,* in addition to Elias Lönnrot's *Old Kalevala* (1835) and expanded *Kalevala* (1849) and a host of other myth and folklore collections. "There was Greek, and Celtic," Tolkien wrote later, "and Romance, Germanic, Scandina- vian, and Finnish (which greatly affected me); but nothing English" (*Letters* 144). If these nation-cultures could have their own mythologies, he felt, Eng- land should not be left behind.

And that led to the Simarillion, Tolkien's fictive, wholly invented mythol- ogy, which he envisioned as "a body of more or less connected legend . . . which I could dedicate . . . to England; to my country" (*Letters* 144). So far, so good. But after this, the picture becomes muddled. Carpenter's specific dec- laration that episodes in Tolkien's tale of Túrin Turambar were "derived quite consciously from the story of Kullervo in the *Kalevala*" (96) was a useful bit of information, yet it seemed in conflict with his judgment in the same para- graph that the influence of *Kalevala* on the Túrin story was "only superfi- cial" (96). With due respect to Carpenter, I disagree. I propose that Kullervo's story in *Kalevala,* far from being a "superficial" influence, is a profound one, the root and source of the story of Túrin, though as we shall see, it has been filtered through Tolkien's interim adaptation. Publication, in the same year as the Carpenter biography, of Christopher Tolkien's edition of *The Silmarillion* finally gave us the saga of Túrin to compare with the Kullervo story in *runos* 31–36 of *Kalevala.*

One of the earliest scholars to seize the opportunity for comparison was Randel Helms, whose 1981 *Tolkien and the Silmarils* suggested that the story in *Kalevala* "is a tale that begs to be transformed." But without access to "The Story of Kullervo," Helms could only see Tolkien "learning to outgrow an in- fluence, transform a source," from the "lustful and murderous" Kullervo of *Ka- levala* to the heroic but doomed Túrin Turambar of his own legendarium (6). Interest grew slowly, with critical commentary of necessity jumping straight from *Kalevala* to the Tale of Túrin, with the result that so distinguished a Tolkien scholar as Tom Shippey could declare that "the basic outline of the tale (of Túrin) owes much to the 'Story of Kullervo' in the *Kalevala*" (*Road* 232) and venture no further.

The pace picked up as the twentieth century turned to the twenty-first. Charles Noad conceded that "insofar as Kullervo served as the germ for Túrin, this was in one sense the beginning of the *legendarium,* but only as a model for future work" (*Legendarium* 35). Given the lack of other evidence, that, perforce, was all that scholars could conclude. Richard West, in general agreement with Carpenter and Helms, observed that "the story of Túrin did not remain a retelling of the story of Kullervo," adding that "if we had the earliest version we would undoubtedly see that Tolkien started out that way, as he said, but at some point he diverged to tell a new story in the old tradition" (*Legendarium* 238). In her much-later article, "Identifying England's Lönnrot," Anne Petty compared Elias Lönnrot, the compiler of *Kalevala,* with Tolkien, calling attention to the way in which both myth-makers drew on earlier sources in applying their own organization and textualization to the story elements, Lönnrot's sources being actual rune-singers as well as earlier folklore collectors, and Tolkien's being limited (to her knowledge) to the invented bards, scribes, and translators within his fiction (Tolkien Studies I, 69–82). What Helms and Shippey and West and Petty did not and could not know was that in Tolkien's case an extra-mythological transitional story and transitional character contributed substantially to the transformation.

The appearance in 1981 of Tolkien's *Letters* gave us more information but little clarification, for the letters gave mixed signals, or at least showed Tolkien's mixed feelings about the relative importance of *Kalevala* to his own mythology. His disclaimer that as "The Children of Húrin" the Kullervo story was "entirely changed except in the tragic ending" (*Letters* 345) probably influenced Carpenter's comment about it being "only superficial." But while it is understandable that Tolkien would want to privilege his own invention and establish his story's independence from its source, other more positive references to *Kalevala* in his letters tell a different story. The mythology "greatly affected" him (144); the language was like "an amazing wine" (214); "Finnish nearly ruined [his] Hon. Mods" (87); *Kalevala* "set the rocket off in story" (214); it was "the original germ of the Silmarillion" (87). There is no question that Túrin Turambar is a fully realized character in his own right, far richer and better developed than the Kullervo of *Kalevala,* and set in an entirely different context. In that respect, it could truthfully be said that the story was "entirely changed." But an essential step was omitted. The figure of Kullervo passed through a formative middle stage between the two. "The Story of Kullervo" is the missing link in the chain of transmission. It is the bridge over which Tolkien crossed from Finland to Middle-earth. How he made that crossing and what he took with him are the subjects of my discussion.

Tolkien first read *Kalevala* in the English translation of W.F. Kirby in 1911 when he was at King Edward's School in Birmingham. Though the work itself made a powerful impression on him, Kirby's translation got a mixed reaction. He referred to it as "Kirby's poor translation" (*Letters* 214) yet observed that in some respects it was "funnier than the original" (*Letters* 87). Both opinions

may have motivated him to check out from the Exeter College library in November 1911 a copy of Eliot's *A Finnish Grammar,* in an effort to learn enough
Finnish to read *Kalevala* in the original. Although both Carpenter (Bodleian
Library MS Tolkien B 64/6, folio 1, pencil note; *Tolkien* 73) and Scull and
Hammond (*Chronology* 55; *Guide* 440) date "The Story of Kullervo" to 1914,
according to Tolkien's own account it was sometime in 1912 that he began the
project. A 1955 letter to W. H. Auden dated his attempt to "reorganize some
of the Kalevala, especially the tale of Kullervo the hapless, into a form of my
own" to "the Honour Mods period. . . . Say 1912 to 1913" (*Letters* 214–15).

Tolkien's memory for dates is not always reliable. Witness his dating of
The Lord of the Rings in the Foreword to the second edition to "the years
1936 to 1949" (*LotR* xvi), when *The Hobbit* itself was not published until September of 1937, and *The Lord of the Rings*—begun as a sequel to and initially
called "the new '*Hobbit*'"—not launched until December of that year. And
the letter to Auden was written some forty-three years after the "period"
referred to. Nevertheless, the two references to "Hon. Mods" (Honour Moderations—a set of written papers comprising the first of two examinations
taken by a degree candidate) are explicit and identify a specific phase and
time in Tolkien's education. He sat for his Honour Moderations at the end
of February 1913 (Carpenter 62). The Hon. Mods "period" would thus be the
time leading up to that, at the latest January 1913 (during which time he was
also re-wooing Edith and persuading her to marry him), and more probably
also the later months of the preceding year. He was also at that time apparently in the early stages of inventing Qenya (Hostetter), and some of the
story's invented names, imitatively Finnish in shape and phonology, have
also a noticeable resemblance to early Qenya vocabulary.

Such a convergence of extracurricular interests—learning Finnish, "reor-
ganizing" Kullervo, and inventing Qenya—would surely be enough to explain
Tolkien's confession to Auden that he "came very near having my exhibition
[scholarship] taken off me if not being sent down" (*Letters* 214). Nevertheless, this first practical union of "lit. and lang." embodied the principle Tolkien was to spend the rest of his life upholding, his staunchly maintained belief that "Mythology is language and language is mythology" (*TOFS* 181), that
the two are not opposite poles but opposite sides of the same coin. It was a
period in Tolkien's life rich with discoveries that fueled and fed each other.
Much later he wrote to a reader of *The Lord of the Rings,* "It was just as the
1914 war burst on me that I made the discovery that 'legends' depend on the
language to which they belong; but a living language depends equally on the
'legends' which it conveys by tradition" (*Letters* 231). In the event, he did pass
his Hon. Mods., though with a Second, not the hoped-for First; consequently
did not have his exhibition taken off; and, thankfully, was not sent down,

though he was persuaded to change from Classics to English Language and Literature. And in the long run it was "lit. and lang." that triumphed, for *Kalevala* and Finnish generated Qenya and "The Story of Kullervo," and Tolkien's "Kullervo" led to his Túrin, to the Silmarillion, and by way of *The Hobbit* to *The Lord of the Rings*.

The sole existing manuscript of "The Story of Kullervo," in the Bodleian Library, is a legible but heavily emended text written in pencil on lined foolscap, plus jotted notes and outlines on smaller sheets of paper. Humphrey Carpenter's dating of the manuscript to 1914 is probably based on Tolkien's statement in a letter to Edith dated to October 1914 that he was "trying to turn one of the stories [of *Kalevala*]—which is really a very great story and most tragic—into a short story somewhat on the line of Morris' romances with chunks of poetry in between" (*Letters* 7). But the creative spark is hard to pin down. When and where and how does the impulse to tell a story begin? With an "I can do that" moment when reading a text? With a mental lightbulb in the middle of the night? A note on the back of an envelope? A sentence scribbled on a napkin? Tolkien recognized the quotidian nature of inspiration, writing years later (1956), "I think a lot of this kind of work goes on at other (to say lower, or deeper, or higher introduces a false gradation) levels, when one is saying how-do-you-do, or even 'sleeping'" (*Letters* 231). In the case of "The Story of Kullervo" (unlike the opening of *The Hobbit*, famously written on the back of an exam), we will probably never know precisely.

Taking some time perhaps late in 1912 as a presumptive starting date, and Carpenter's 1914 as the terminus ad quem, we can see "The Story of Kullervo" as the work of a very young man—twenty or so when he started, twenty-two at the most when he broke off. Whatever Tolkien's immediate intent for the story, and whatever its contribution to his later work, it is best understood in retrospect as a trial piece, that of a writer learning his craft and consciously imitating existing material. As Carpenter points out, and as Tolkien was at pains to acknowledge, the style is heavily indebted to William Morris, especially *The House of the Wulfings*, itself a stylistic mixture in which narrative prose frequently gives way to "chunks" of poetic speech. Like its model, Tolkien's story is deliberately antiquated, filed with poetic inversions—verbs before nouns, and archaisms: "hath" for "has," "doth" for "does," "him thought" instead of "he thought," "entreated" in place of "treated," as well as increasingly lengthy interpolations of verse spoken by various characters. Much of this style carries over to the earliest stories of Tolkien's own mythology, such as "The Cottage of Lost Play" in *The Book of Lost Tales*.

When we fit this period into the whole arc of Tolkien's creative life, a pattern takes shape of successive stages of development, all of them showing the same interests and methods but each having its own individual character. It is important to our understanding of each text that "The Story of Kullervo" was written by an undergraduate, *The Lord of the Rings* by a man in middle life—his forties and fifties—and it was a man in his early seventies who wrote *Smith of Wootton Major*. A similar arc of changes over time marks the revisions of the Silmarillion material from the earliest phase of "The Cottage of Lost Play" to the middle period of "Akallabêth" and "The Notion Club Papers" and "The Fall of Númenor" to the late and deeply philosophical meditations of the "Athrabeth Finrod ah Andreth" and "Laws and Customs among the Eldar."

"The Story of Kullervo" belongs firmly to the pre-Silmarillion period. It was written well before Tolkien's service in France in 1916, and three years before his 1917–18 creative burst that led to the earliest versions of the Great Tales in those school notebooks. Though it lacks the markers of "The Shores of Faëry" or "The Voyage of Eärendil"—two contemporary poems (both published in *The Book of Lost Tales* 2) that Tolkien flagged as forerunners of his mythology—it should nevertheless be credited as an equally significant precursor. Tolkien may not have had the Silmarillion in mind when he wrote "The Story of Kullervo," but he certainly had "The Story of Kullervo" in mind when he began the Silmarillion. It contributed substantially to the 1917 "Turambar and the Foalókë" and later versions of that story, as well as to the 1917 "Tale of Tinúviel" and its later versions, for which it somewhat surprisingly provided a significant character. This early narrative was an essential step in Tolkien's progress as a writer. It was a creative pivot, swinging between its *Kalevala* source and the legendarium for which it was itself a source.

But what was it about this particular story that so powerfully called to him? John Garth calls it "a strange story to have captured the imagination of a fervent Roman Catholic" (26). Tolkien clearly did not find it strange ("great" and "tragic" were his words) and seems to have felt no conflict with his Catholicism, which at that point was not very "fervent" anyway. Carpenter cites Tolkien's acknowledgment that his first terms at Oxford "had passed 'with practically none or very little practice of religion'" (58) and notes his "lapses of the previous year [1912]" (66). Connecting Tolkien's attraction to the Kullervo story to his Father Francis–enforced separation from Edith, Garth proposes that its appeal may have lain "partly in the brew of maverick heroism, young romance, and despair" (26). Without discounting Garth's connection of the story to Tolkien's immediate situation, I suggest that the story of Kullervo also resonated deeply with the circumstances of his very early life. Kullervo's description of himself as "fatherless beneath the heavens" and "from the first without a mother" (Kirby II, 101, ll. 59–60) cannot be overlooked, still less two lines of verse, stark and explicit, transferred unchanged from the Kirby *Kalevala*, wherein Kullervo bewails his fate, to one of the "chunks of poetry" in Tolkien's own story:

I was small and lost my ~~mother~~ father
I was young (weak) and lost my mother. (Tolkien Studies VII, 231)

The fact that he first included and then crossed out these lines is significant. They may have been at once right on the mark and too close for comfort to the tragedy of his own life. Like Kullervo, Tolkien was fatherless and without a mother. When he was small (a child of four) he lost his father; when he was young (a boy of twelve) he lost his mother.

Let us look at the narrative that Tolkien called "most tragic." Strife between brothers leads to the killing of Kullervo's father, Kalervo, by his uncle Untamo, who lays waste his family home and abducts Kullervo's unnamed mother, identified in the poem only as "one girl and she was pregnant" (Runo XXI, l. 72). Kullervo is born into captivity and as an infant swears revenge on Untamo, who, after three attempts to kill the precocious boy, plus failure to get any work out of him, sells him as a bondslave to the smith Ilmarinen. The smith's wife sets him to herding the cattle but cruelly and capriciously bakes a stone into his bread. When he cuts into the bread, his knife, his only memento of his father, strikes the stone and the point breaks. Kullervo's revenge is to enchant bears and wolves into cow-shapes and drive them into the barnyard at milking time. When the smith's wife tries to milk these bogus cattle they attack and kill her. Kullervo then flees but, being told by the Blue-Robed Lady of the Forest that his family is alive, decides to go home, vowing again to kill Untamo. He is deflected from his vengeance by a chance encounter with a girl whom he either seduces or rapes (the story is equivocal on this point). Upon disclosing their parentage to each other, the two discover that they are brother and sister. In despair, the girl throws herself over a waterfall. Consumed with guilt, Kullervo fulfills his vengeance, returning to Untamo's homestead to kill him and burn all his farm buildings, then asks his sword if it will kill him. The sword agrees, and Kullervo finds "the death he sought for" (Runo XXXVI, l. 341).

I do not propose a one-to-one equation between Kullervo and Tolkien, nor do I claim autobiographical intent on Tolkien's part. Parallels there certainly are, but Father Francis Morgan was not Untamo (though he did separate John Ronald from the girl he loved). Beatrice Suffield, the aunt in whose care Tolkien and his brother were temporarily put after their mother died, was not the smith's wife—though Carpenter notes that she was "deficient in affection" (33). Tolkien was neither a cowherd nor a magician, though he did become a fantasist. Nor did he engage in revenge killing or commit incest. And though, unlike Kullervo, he was not mistreated and abused, like Kullervo, he was not in control of his own life. There was undeniably something in Kullervo's story that touched him deeply and made him want to

"reorganize" it into "a form of [his] own." And that something stayed viable
as his legendarium took shape.

Garth is right about one thing, however. It is certainly a "strange story,"
as even a cursory synopsis shows: a perplexing jumble of loosely connected
episodes in which people do things for mysterious reasons or for the wrong
reason or for no reason at all. With the exception of Kullervo, the characters
are one dimensional—the wicked uncle, the cruel foster mother, the wronged
girl—and Kullervo himself, while more fleshed out, is an enigma both to himself and to those he meets. The story is not so strange, however, in Tolkien's
version, which carefully connects cause, effect, motivation, and outcome. Already a certain pattern is in place, the effort to adapt a traditional story to his
own liking, to fill in the gaps in an existing story and tidy up the loose ends.
The best-known example is *The Hobbit*, in which Bilbo's theft of a cup from
the dragon's hoard is, for those who've read *Beowulf*, a hard-to-miss reworking of a problem passage in that poem where, because the manuscript is damaged, the text is full of holes, with words, phrases, and whole lines missing or
indecipherable, rendering the entire episode an unsolvable puzzle.

In *Beowulf* (ll. 2214–31), an unidentified man driven by unknown necessity creeps into the dragon's lair and steals a cup, which wakens the dragon
and leads to Beowulf's death. Too much is missing for us to know anything
more about the circumstances. Though he denied any conscious intent,
Tolkien fills in the holes and answers the questions in a major scene in *The
Hobbit*. The unknown thief is Bilbo; his necessity is to prove himself as a
burglar. He steals the cup to demonstrate his prowess to Thorin and the
dwarves, and flees up the tunnel, leaving behind him a wrathful Smaug, who
wreaks vengeance on Laketown. Tolkien did much the same kind of thing,
though more poetically, in his *Sigurd and Gudrún* poems, straightening out
the tangle of Old Norse, Icelandic, and Germanic legends that make up the
story of Sigurd and the Völsungs (there are, for example—and for unex-
plained reasons—two Brynhilds, one a valkyrie, the other the very human
daughter of King Buthli), and filling in the missing eight pages in the Eddic
manuscript (for more on this, see Tom Shippey's excellent review article on
The Legend of Sigurd and Gudrún in *Tolkien Studies* VII).

Returning now to *Kalevala* and "The Story of Kullervo," let us consider
what Tolkien chose to keep, what he left out, what he changed, and how he
changed it in this earliest attempt at rewriting myth. The major items are:

1) Kullervo's family
2) His sister
3) His personality

4) His dog
5) His weapons
6) His incest
7) His ending

I'll finish with a brief look (brief because it will be obvious to anyone who has read the Silmarillion) at the effect this transitional piece had on his subsequent work, smoothing rough edges and deepening the emotional level of this "strange story."

First, Kullervo's family. One of the problem points in the *Kalevala* story is that Kullervo has two families and becomes an orphan twice. His first family is destroyed by Untamo in the raid that captures Kullervo's mother. The narrative is clear at this early point in the story that this is a complete wipeout, leaving the newborn boy with no home, no father, and no living relatives beside his mother. It is thus confusing to most readers when, much later in the story, the family turns up alive and well, before the incest but after Kullervo kills the smith's wife. He is then told, to his and the reader's surprise, that his family is alive. The thematic justification for this second appearance is that it gives him relatives—another father and a newfound brother and sister—who can tell him in elaborate verse how much they don't care whether he lives or dies, thus reinforcing his feelings of alienation and the rejection he's already gotten from Untamo and the smith's wife. The plot function is to provide Kullervo a sister he has never seen and so set the stage for the incest.

The two-family mix-up is the result of Lönnrot's combining into one sequence several songs originally independent of one another, according to Domenico Comparetti, one of the earliest scholars to write on *Kalevala*. Comparetti pointed out that "Kullervo's finding his family alive at home after they were said to have been killed by Untamo, is a contradiction that betrays the joining together of several runes" (148), runes not even from the same localities, and with differing variants (145). The confusion is not unlike the two-Brynhilds mix-up. Lönnrot may have been juggling his material, but he had precedents. In these versions, the hero's name is not always Kullervo; in Ingria it is Turo or Tuirikkinen, in Archangel and Karelia it is Tuiretuinen (Comparetti 148). There is no hard evidence that Tolkien had read Comparetti, though it seems probable, given his fascination with *Kalevala*. But it was the effect of *Kalevala* as is, not its history of composition or its component parts, that so engaged Tolkien. His quote from George Dasent that "We must be satisfied with the soup that is set before us, and not desire to see the bones of the ox out of which it has been boiled" (*MC* 120) was as applicable to Finnish mythology as to fairy-stories.

Tolkien ignored the bones, eliminating the second family altogether and giving the first family its extra children, an older brother and sister already in place before Untamo's raid. Their mother, pregnant again at the time Untamo attacks, gives birth to twins after she is abducted by Untamo. These are a boy, whom she names Kullervo, or "Wrath," and a girl she names Wānōna, or "Weeping." The pre- and post-Untamo sets of children are not close in either age or temperament, and the older set is hostile to the younger, paving the way for their later rejection of Kullervo. When he is sold into slavery, his older brother and sister both tell him—in long lines of verse—how much they won't miss him. His exile separates him both geographically and emotionally from his mother and sister, so that when he meets Wānōna again we can reasonably believe that he does not recognize her.

Second, Kullervo's relationship with his sister. In *Kalevala* he has none, and because of the two-family combination, he meets her for the first time on the occasion of the incest. Tolkien considerably expands and complicates this relationship, building up the childhood closeness of the twins and emphasizing their alienation from their older siblings and their consequent reliance on one another. Kullervo and Wānōna spend more time with each other than with anyone else. They are neglected "wild" children who roam the woodlands, their only friend the hound Musti, a dog with supernatural powers who acts as both companion and protector. When Kullervo is sold into slavery by Untamo, he is followed by Musti, but cut off from his family. He declares that he will miss no one but Wānōna, yet in his exile he forgets her entirely and fails to recognize her when, by accident, they meet again, with fatal consequences.

Third, Kullervo's personality. Again, in *Kalevala* he has none, or very little. His characteristics are precocious strength and an aptitude for magic. Barely three days old, he kicks his cradle to splinters. Set to rock an infant not long afterward, he breaks the baby's bones, gouges out his eyes, and burns his cradle. In addition, he is apparently indestructible, for Untamo has three tries at killing him, first by drowning, next by burning, and finally by hanging. Nothing works. He survives the drowning and measures the sea. He escapes the burning and plays in the ashes. He is found on the hanging tree carving pictures in the bark. Set to clear a field, he creates a wasteland; told to build a fence, he makes an impenetrable enclosure with no way in or out; assigned to threshing grain, he reduces it to dust. No reason or motive, except that he was rocked too hard as a baby, is given for this extreme behavior. It's just the way he is. You can't take him anywhere. Rather oddly, he is also handsome and a bit of a dandy, described as having "finest locks of yellow colour," "blue-dyed stockings," and "shoes of best of leather" (Runo XXII, ll. 2–4).

Tolkien's Kullervo is equally strong, but far from handsome or fashionable. He is "swart" and "ill-favoured and crooked," low in stature, and "broad and knotty and unrestrained and unsoftened" (Tolkien Studies VII 221, 222). Yet we come to understand him and even feel sympathy. The big difference between Tolkien's Kullervo and the one in *Kalevala* is that while their actions are the same (he does all the weird things I've described), Tolkien's Kullervo is clearly marked by early trauma. He is scarred by his father's murder and embittered by his and his mother's enslavement and cruel treatment by Untamo. He grows crooked for lack of a mother's care. Tolkien portrays him as sullen, resentful, angry, and alienated, close only to his sister Wānōna and the hound Musti. "No tender feelings would he let his heart cherish for his folk afar" (222). He nurses grudges, he's lonely and a loner, a perpetual outsider, one of those people forever on the fringe of society, unable or unwilling to fit in.

Fourth, his dog. There is no such supernatural animal as the great hound Musti in this part of *Kalevala*, though there is a black dog called Musti (which simply means "Blackie" in Finnish) that, after the second family has all died, follows Kullervo into the forest where he kills himself. Tolkien's Musti is a significant character in the story and plays an active part in several episodes. He initially belongs to Kalervo and early in the story returns to the homestead to find it destroyed, his master killed, and the lone survivor captured. He follows her but stays in the wild, where he befriends the children Kullervo and Wānōna, and is associated with the dog of Tuoni, Lord of Death. Tolkien is tapping in to a standard mythological convention here, the connections among dogs and death and the underworld, which, although Musti is not the dog of Tuoni, nevertheless foreshadows the tragedy to come. While not of the underworld, Musti is described as "a dog of fell might and strength and of great knowledge." He is a shape-changer and a practitioner of magic, which he apparently teaches to Kullervo, instructing him in "things darker and dimmer and farther back even . . . before their magic days" (217).

Musti becomes a kind of tutelary figure to Kullervo and gives him magic talismans, three hairs from his coat with which to summon or invoke the hound in time of danger. These hairs save Kullervo from Untamo's three attempts to kill him, explicitly with the first (drowning), by implication in the second (burning), and again explicitly in the third (hanging), where "this magic that had saved Kullervo's life was the last hair of Musti" (218). Musti's magic is "about" Kullervo from then on. Musti follows him when he is sold into slavery and teaches him the magic that later enables him to use the wolves and bears to kill the smith's wife. In Tolkien's notes for the uncompleted ending of the story Musti appears twice, once when he is killed in Kullervo's raid on Untamo's homestead, and at the scene of the suicide, where Kullervo stumbles over the "body of dead Musti" (235).

Fifth, his weapons. Like his *Kalevala* counterpart, Tolkien's Kullervo has both a knife and a sword. In *Kalevala* Kullervo laments the breaking of his knife, "this iron . . . heirloom from my father" (Runo XXXI, ll. 91–92), and explains to the smith's wife while she is being gnawed by bears and wolves that this is her punishment for causing him to break his knife. In Tolkien's story the knife has a greater history. It is given to the infant Kullervo when his mother first tells him of the "Death of Kalervo" (capitalized as if it were a story in itself). It is described as "a great knife curious wrought" that his mother had "caught from the wall" (Tolkien Studies VII 216) when Untamo descended on the homestead but had no chance to use, so swift was the attack. The knife has a name, Sikki, and is instrumental (together with the hair of Musti) in saving Kullervo from being hanged. It is this knife with which the boy carves pictures on the tree, wolves and bears and a huge hound, as well as great fish said to be "Kalervo's sign of old" (218). The breaking of his knife on the stone in the cake causes Kullervo to lament its loss in verse, addressing the knife by name, calling it his only comrade and "thou iron of Kalervo" (228). The sword makes its appearance late in the story, after Kullervo has met Wānōna again, and their tragedy has happened. He takes the sword to kill Untamo and makes it the willing instrument of his death.

Sixth, the incest, which is the story's emotional climax. As noted previously, in *Kalevala* this episode is a conflation of disparate *runos* from Ingria, Karelia, and Archangel featuring different heroes with different names. Lönnrot smoothed the edges and regularized the hero's name to conform to the existing *runos* in his compilation. His Kullervo, on his way home after paying the taxes, accosts a succession of girls, inviting each into his sleigh. The third girl is the one he scores with, and theirs is a brief encounter quickly followed by the exchange of family information revealing the incest, which results in her suicide. The scene is potentially tragic, but handled so quickly and tersely that it's over almost before you know it.

Tolkien makes much more of the event and builds up to it carefully. His Kullervo, after his murder by proxy of the smith's wife, on the run and on his way to settle his score with Untamo, is met by the Lady of the Forest, who tells him the path he should follow and counsels him to avoid the wooded mountain, where ill will finds him. Of course he ignores her advice and goes to "drink the sunlight" (232) on the mountain. Here, in a clearing on the mountain, he sees a maiden who tells him she is "lost in the evil woods" (232). At the sight of her he forgets his quest and asks her to be his "comrade." She is frightened, telling him that "Death walketh with thee," and "Little does thy look consort with maidens" (232). Angry that she has made fun of his ugliness and hurt that she has rejected him, he pursues her through the woods and carries her off. Though at first she rejects his advances, she does not long resist him, and they live together in apparent happiness in the wild until the fatal day when she asks him to tell her who his kinfolk are.

His reply that he is the son of Kalervo is the revelation that leads to her realization that she and her lover are brother and sister. In Tolkien's treatment it becomes one of the most dramatic moments in the story. She says no word of her discovery but stands gazing at him "with outstretched hand," crying out that her path has led her "deeper deeper into darkness / Deeper deeper into sorrow / Into woe and into horror. . . . For I go in dark and terror / Down to Tuoni to the River" (234). Running away from Kullervo "like a shivering ray in the dawn light" (234), she comes to the waterfall and throws herself over the brink. But this is all we are told about her at this point. Though she recounts her own story, she does not reveal her parentage. No does Tolkien reveal it directly, letting her subsequent suicide and Kullervo's awakened memory, his "old knowledge" (234) of her speech and manner and the violence of her reaction, underscore, without explaining, the tragedy of the situation. Only at the end of the story is Kullervo made to understand who she is and realize what he has done.

Sixth and last, the ending. Lönnrot's conflated and ill-assorted version takes Kullervo back to his second family, then to war against Untamo, then home to find that all his second family are now dead, and finally to his decision to end his life by asking his sword if it is willing to kill him. It is and it does and he dies, still alienated, isolated, and alone. Tolkien left his version unfinished, breaking it off at the point where Kullervo, horrified in dawning suspicion of who the maiden is, and witness to her suicide, takes his sword and rushes blindly into the dark. But Tolkien had the end in mind, and a clear sense of how he wanted to treat it. Jotted outline notes have Kullervo go back to Untamo's home, kill him and lay it waste, then be visited in a dream by his mother's ghost, who says that she has met her daughter in the underworld and confirms that she is the maiden who killed herself. It seems clear that Tolkien intended this to be the delayed moment of dyscatastrophe for which there is no upward turn, the hitherto-withheld information that he has violated his sister. Waking in terror from this overload of shame and sorrow, the anguished Kullervo rushes into the woods wailing, "Kivutar" (an alternate name for his sister), and comes to the glade where they first met. It is here that he asks his sword if it will kill him. It is more than willing, and he dies on its point.

Both Tolkien's reworking of his source and his story's relation to his subsequent work are clear. His Kullervo is the hinge between the rather weird

Kullervo of *Kalevala* and the tragic, mixed-up Túrin Turambar of the Sil-marillion, providing Túrin with all family trauma, all the pent-up anger and resentment, all the negative emotions that fuel that character's bad decisions and make him so memorable. The geeky misfit of *Kalevala* becomes the angry, alienated, grudge-nursing outsider of "The Story of Kullervo," who in turn develops into the fuller, more psychologically developed, self-isolating figure of Túrin Turambar, clearly related to his precursors but given a more coherent world and clearer framework within which to act out his tragedy.

Tolkien smoothes the *Kalevala*'s awkward two-family structure into one family with several siblings, and this becomes the war-torn and disastrously reunited family of Túrin. The unknown and unnamed sister of *Kalevala* becomes Wānōna ("Weeping"), in "The Story of Kullervo," Kullervo's twin and companion in hardship, and Wānōna in turn contributes to Túrin's dearly loved and missed sister Lalaith ("Laughter") as well as the never-seen Nienor ("Mourning"), who becomes Niniel ("Tear-maiden"). All these meanings are significant, but the one for Wānōna is an unmistakable precursor of the names for Túrin's never-before-seen sister/wife. It is worth noting that in Tolkien's outline for the story's ending, his Kullervo cries out to his sister, calling her "Kivutar" ("Pain"). In *Kalevala* Kivutar is the goddess of Pain and Suffering. While Edith was clearly wife, not sister, their romance and enforced separation and what Tolkien called "the dreadful sufferings of our childhoods, from which we rescued one another" (*Letters* 421) are strong reminders of the loneliness of Kullervo and Wanona as children, and Kullervo's anguish when she leaves him in death.

Kullervo's knife Sikki, all that he has of his father, finds a prominent place in the *Unfinished Tales* version of the "Narn i Hîn Húrin," where "curious wrought" becomes "Elf-wrought," and the knife, here not an heirloom but a birthday present, is given to Túrin on his eighth birthday by his father, who describes it as "a bitter blade" (*UT* 64). Túrin gives the knife to the serving-man, Sador, but later misses it and mourns its loss. It seems clear, however, that the knife is a tool rather than a weapon, unlike the grim and foreboding sword that becomes Kullervo's death. Its multiple identities, first as Anglachel then Gurthang then Mormegil, give Túrin an equal identity and a name and eventually the sword takes his life. However, as Richard West has pointed out, Tolkien developed the weapon "far beyond what he found in his Finnish source," making it "an embodiment of the ill fate that besets the hero" (*Legandarium* 239).

Since the sword is the efficient cause of the hero's death, it is worth comparing the three instances, first in *Kalevala*, then in "The Story of Kullervo," and finally in the story of Túrin, that distinguish it from other swords belonging to other heroes: the fact that it speaks and interacts with the hero. Here is the speech in *Kalevala:*

> Wherefore at thy heart's desire
> Should I not thy flesh devour,
> And drink up the blood so evil?
> I who guiltless flesh have eaten,
> Drank the blood of those who sinned not? (Runo XXXVI, ll. 330–34)

Here is "The Story of Kullervo" version in Tolkien's plot notes in the Bodleian Library:

> The sword says if it had joy in the death of Untamo how much in death of even wickeder Kullervoinen. And it had slaid many an innocent person, even his mother, so it would not boggle over K[ullervo]. (Tolkien Studies VII, 235)

And here is the sword to Túrin in the version in *The Silmarillion:*

> Yea, I will drink thy blood gladly, that so I may forget the blood of Beleg my master, and the blood of Brandir slain unjustly. I will slay thee swiftly. (*Silm* 225)

While there is not a great deal of difference among the three versions (though the second is reportage rather than direct speech), the last two are closer to one another than either is to the first. In place of the more general "guiltless flesh" and "those who sinned not" of the primary *Kalevala* source, the other two passages cite specific names of people whom the sword has killed, in Tolkien's note associating wicked Untamo with wickeder Kullervo, and in *The Silmarillion* contrasting guilty Kullervo with innocent Beleg and Brandir. Both of Tolkien's swords are more judgmental, have more knowledge, more personality, and more dramatic impact, than their *Kalevala* model. Worth notice is that in his essay "On the Kalevala" Tolkien described the voice of Kullervo's sword as that of "a cruel and cynical ruffian" (Tolkien Studies VII 253), foreshadowing the darker aspects he later gave to his own sword, Anglachel, in the story of Túrin.

An unexpected carryover from this early story to the Silmarillion material is the episode of Kullervo's return, crying aloud his sister's name, to the waterfall where she killed herself. It reappears in "Of Tuor and His Coming to Gondolin" in *Unfinished Tales*, where it becomes a vivid, briefly flashed moment in which Tuor and Voronnwë at the Falls of Ivrin hear "a cry in the woods" and glimpse "a tall Man, armed, clad in black, with a long sword drawn," crying aloud in grief the name "Ivrin, Faelivrin!" Minimal explanation is given. "They knew not," says the narrative, "that . . . this was Túrin son of Húrin," and never again "did the paths of those kinsman . . . draw together" (*UT* 37–38). Curiously, Túrin's anguish and loss are not for his sister/wife Niniel, as we might expect, but for Finduilas, the elf-maiden who loves him and for whose death he is somehow responsible. The intrusion of this moment into "Of Tuor" is a clear borrowing from Tolkien's note outline where Kullervo, returning to the falls where she has killed herself, cries aloud for Kivutar. In "Of Tuor" it is grief witnessed from the outside by an audience ignorant of the circumstances and thus unable to comprehend the anguish and loss. The scene is disturbing, intentionally dislocated, an interlace gesture from one story to another. The fact that both stories gesture toward the even earlier story is eloquent testimony to the hold that Tolkien's Kullervo had on his imagination.

The most surprising revelation is that Huan the Hound, the supernatural helper of Beren and Lúthien, did not spring fully formed from Tolkien's brow but has a clear forerunner in Musti. Musti is perhaps Tolkien's most noteworthy addition to his *Kalevala* source, and Huan is, after Túrin himself, the clearest avatar carried over from the earlier story to the world of the legendarium. Talking (and helping) animals are not unknown in the world of Middle-earth. The fox (though he is an anomaly) in Book 1 of *The Fellowship of the Ring,* the talking thrush, and the raven Roäc son of Carc in *The Hobbit,* the eagles in both *The Hobbit* and *The Lord of the Rings,* and the dog Garm from *Farmer Giles* are the best examples—that is, unless you count talking dragons such as Smaug and Glaurung, who have solid precursors in Icelandic mythology. Glaurung is plainly derived from the Fáfnir of the *Poetic Edda,* where Smaug and *Farmer Giles*'s Chrysophylax are comic examples, but nearer in type to Kenneth Grahame's Reluctant Dragon than to Icelandic mythology, and Garm belongs in that same parodic category.

Musti is a bit different; he is Tolkien's best example of a particular fairy-tale archetype, the animal helper, a type that includes Puss-in-Boots, the talking horse Falada of the Grimms' "The Goose-Girl," the Firebird in the story of Prince Ivan, the Little Humpbacked Horse, and various shape-changing bears and wolves in Norse and Icelandic folktales. In Tolkien's own work, Beorn of *The Hobbit* comes close, but he is nearer in type to the shape-changers of the sagas than to the animals of fairy tale, and his own animals, though they walk on their hind legs and wait table, are not magical helpers but mere circus performers. Huan is a far better representative of the archetype. Nevertheless, he does not derive immediately from his fairy-tale predecessors but is in direct descent from Musti, whose obvious inheritor he is. In both stories the loyal, supernatural hound is a powerful character in his own right, and in both stories the hound is a victim of his own loyalty, following the hero to his death in a climactic and violent episode late in the narrative.

"The Story of Kullervo," then, was the spark that "set the rocket off in story" (*Letters* 214), as Tolkien wrote to Auden. He was not exaggerating. This very early narrative, incomplete and derivative as it is, ignited his imagination and was his earliest prefiguration of some of the most memorable literary figures and moments in the Silmarillion. Moreover, it is not beyond conjecture that without the former, we might not have the latter, at least not in the form in which we know it. The hapless orphan, the unknown sister, the heirloom knife, the broken family and its psychological results, the forbidden love between lonely young people, the despair and self-destruction on the point of a sword—all transfer into "The Tale of the Children of Húrin" not direct from *Kalevala* but filtered through "The Story of Kullervo." We can now see where these elements came from, and how they got to be what they are. Most telling, paradoxically because perhaps least necessary is the move from Musti to Huan—a figure almost unchanged save for his name. It seems clear that Tolkien found Musti simply too good to waste and recycled him from the unfinished early story to the later and more fully realized fairy-tale context of the romance of Beren and Lúthien.

"The Story of Kullervo" was Tolkien's earliest attempt at retelling—and, in the process, "reorganising"—an existing tale. As such, it occupies an important place in his canon. Furthermore, it is a significant step on the winding road from imitation to invention, a trial piece by the orphan boy who loved *Kalevala,* resonated with Kullervo, and wanted to create "something of the same sort that belonged to the English."

Brittany and Wales in Middle-earth

Describing to a potential publisher his fictive mythology of *The Lord of the Rings* and the Silmarillion, J.R.R. Tolkien wrote that, among other things, "It should . . . be redolent of our 'air' (the clime and soil of the North West, meaning Britain and the hither parts of Europe) . . . possessing the fair elusive beauty that some call Celtic" (*Letters* 144). Taking Tolkien at his word, I intend to look at the Celtic influence on two separate aspects of his work. For the "hither parts of Europe," I have chosen Brittany through which to explore his treatment of the Otherworld and its inhabitants, and for Britain, Wales as the inspiration for one of his invented languages. I'll begin with the Otherworld. Tolkien's own term was *Faërie*, of which he said, "*Faërie* contains many things besides elves and fays, and besides dwarfs, witches, trolls, giants, or dragons: it holds the seas, the sun, the moon, the sky; and the earth, and all things that are in it: tree and bird, water and stone, wine and bread, and ourselves, mortal men, when we are enchanted" (*MC* 113). This description has all the earmarks of the Celtic Otherworlds, which Proinsias MacCana describes as being "filled with enchanting music from bright-plumaged birds, from the swaying branches of the otherworld tree. . . . it has abundance of exquisite food and drink, and magic vessels of inexhaustible plenty. . . . This world transcends the limitations of human time. . . . It also transcends all spatial definition" (124). Both Otherworlds have their dark sides as well. MacCana calls the Celtic Otherworld "a region of perilous adventure and of fearsome, malignant beings" (126). Tolkien called his *Faërie* "the Perilous Realm" (*MC* 109). Both are pictured as within or just the other side of observable reality, as present to the perceiving senses as is the "real" world, and geographically contiguous with it. There is a sense, of course, in which Tolkien's whole fictive creation is an Otherworld, but within that world are specific places—generally Elven strongholds or forests, such as Rivendell, Lothlórien, the Old Forest, Mirkwood, Fangorn—that are more explicitly adapted from the Otherworlds of Celtic myth.

Even before these appeared, however, Tolkien had borrowed outright from Brittany the Otherworld forest of Broceliande. Tolkien's Broceliande appears in his long narrative poem "The Lay of Aotrou and Itroun," published in the *Welsh Review* in 1945 (though written earlier). The poem itself is a Breton borrowing, bearing a distinct resemblance to the folk ballad "Aotrou Nann Hag ar Gorrigan" ("Lord Nann and the Corrigan") in Théodore Hersart de la Villemarqué's collection *Barzaz Breiz: Chants Populaires de la Bretagne.*

Tolkien's poem tells of a childless lord who rides into Broceliande to seek a Corrigan.

> In the homeless hills was her hollow dale,
> black was its bowl, its brink was pale;
> there silent on a seat of stone
> before her cave she sat alone. (Welsh Review 255)

The crone, who can read his thoughts, gives him a crystal phial containing a magic potion that will enable his wife to conceive. She will take no payment, saying she will ask for her reward at a time of her own choosing. The lord's wife subsequently bears twin children, and in his joy he offers to bring her anything her heart desires. She asks for "venison of the greenwood deer" and "waters crystal-clear and cold." His pursuit of a white deer to satisfy his wife's request leads the lord again deep into the forest. Instead of a deer he finds the Corrigan waiting for him by a crystal fountain, no longer a crone, but a young and beautiful fairy woman.

> In the dell
> deep in the forest silence fell.
> No sign or slot of doe he found
> but roots of trees upon the ground,
> and trees like shadows waiting stood
> for night to come upon the wood.
>
> The sun was lost, all green was grey.
> There twinkled the fountain of the fay,
> *   *   *   *   *

Soft was the grass and clear the pool;
He laved his face in water cool.
He saw her then, on silver chair
before her cavern, pale her hair,
slow was her smile, and white her hand
beckoning in Broceliande.

The moonlight falling clear and cold
Her long hair lit; through comb of gold
She drew each lock, and down it fell
Like fountain falling in the dell.

The Corrigan now tells him her price—his love or, if he refuses her, his life.

"For this at least I claim my fee,
if ever thou wouldst wander free.
With love thou shalt me here requite,
for here is long and sweet the night;
in druery dear thou here shalt deal,
in bliss more deep than mortals feel." (261)

Of course he refuses her, and of course he dies. In the familiar pattern of "Lord Randal" and a dozen other folk ballads, he rides home to tell his steward, "Make my bed! / My heart doth swell; / my limbs are numb with heavy sleep, / and drowsy poisons in them creep" (263).

The theme of the Otherworld woman who enchants a mortal man is common in folktale and myth and appears in a number of variants, such as "Tam Lin," "Thomas Rymer," and "Clerk Colville." Another and related motif concerns the hunter who inadvertently crosses into the Otherworld in pursuit of a deer that is also a supernatural manifestation. In the First Branch of *The Mabinogion*, Pwyll, Prince of Dyfed, pursues a deer and finds himself suddenly in the Otherworld domain of the Lord of Annwvn. The Breton lai of *Graelent* tells of a man who follows a white hind through the wood to a place where fairy maidens are bathing in a fountain. The enchanted bride of Fionn mac Cumhaill appeared to him in the shape of a deer. And Lord Nann of the Breton ballad hunts a deer that leads him to the fay. As in these episodes, Tolkien's Lord rides unaware into just such an Otherworld in pursuit of just such an animal that becomes a woman.

While all the examples I've cited follow the pattern to a greater or lesser degree, the Breton ballad of Lord Nann comes closest to Tolkien's poem. Scholars such as Jessica Yates and Tom Shippey have noted the poem's general conformation to type, but more particularly its close resemblance to the ballad in Villemarqué's folk collection. There are, to be sure, some differences between the two works. The Lord's desire for a child, his bargain with the fay, her crystal phial, and the potion are Tolkien's additions. His poem is a good deal longer than the ballad, the setting and episodes are amplified, and the character of the Lord is more developed. In other respects, however, especially the Lord's bewitchment by the fay and his death, "The Lay of Aotrou and Itroun" follows "Aotrou Nann Hag Ar Gorrigan" pretty closely. In addition to the plot, we can count the setting in Broceliande, the figures of the white deer and the fairy woman, and the deliberate use of Breton words such as *aotrou* and *corrigan*, all of which suggest that Tolkien's was in a sense paying homage to his Breton source.

Interestingly, a related Welsh example can be found in W. Jenkyn Thomas's *Welsh Fairy Book*, illustrated by Willy Pogány and published in 1907 by Unwin, later to become Tolkien's own publisher. A story in that volume, called "The Lady of the Lake," tells of a widow's son who is beguiled by a fairy woman at a lake. A facing page illustration shows a fairy maiden standing in a pool and combing out her long hair. In Tolkien's poem, the ballad, and the folktale, the Corrigan is explicitly pictured near water, seductively combing out her long hair with a golden comb. More than surface similarity, however, connects Tolkien's poem to these sources. Not only did he own a first edition of *Welsh Fairy Tales* (with the illustration), but he also owned the 1846 two-volume edition of *Barzaz Breiz*, inscribed on the flyleaf with his name and the date 1922.[1] It seems reasonable to conclude, then, that both played a part in the creation of "The Lay of Aotrou and Itroun."

The real significance of this evidence, however, does not reside simply in what it can tell us about Tolkien's use of sources. The greater but less obvious contribution lies in how Tolkien became his own source, for he translated the Breton ballad through his poem into the imagined world of *The Lord of the Rings*. The fairy Corrigan of Broceliande in "The Lay of Aotrou and Itroun" is the clear precursor to Tolkien's golden-haired Elven queen Galadriel of Lothlórien, who gives a phial filled with a magic essence to the hero, Frodo. Galadriel is a more fully developed character, but the familiar figurations—a fairy woman with luxuriant hair dwelling in an Otherworld forest, a magic fountain or pool, the gift to a wayfarer of a crystal vessel—all are immediately recognizable once we have identified the sources.

A little background here, for those who have not read *The Lord of the Rings*. In pursuit of their quest, Frodo and his companions are led into the hidden stronghold of Lothlórien, a place with all the earmarks of a Celtic Otherworld. Lórien is an unknown forest, referred to by those who do not live there as "the secret woods" and the "perilous land" (*FR* II, iii, 297; vi,

352). It is inhabited by Tolkien's Elves, a clearly Celtic fairy folk. It is part of the world of Middle-earth, within ordinary space and time, yet outside the laws of either. Characterized as "a timeless land" (*FR* II, vi, 365) that no one can enter except at the will of the inhabitants, it follows MacCana's description of the Celtic Otherworld that transcends time and space.

This Otherworld is ruled by Galadriel, who shares a number of similarities with the Corrigan of Tolkien's poem. For one thing, though it is a small detail, Tolkien makes a special point of Galadriel's hair. He doesn't have her comb it, but he does have one of the Fellowship, Gimli, fall in love with her and ask for a strand of her hair as a remembrance. It is clearly part of her attraction. Another similarity is that the members of the Fellowship feel that Galadriel can read their minds, and that she offers to give each his heart's desire, as did the Corrigan with the Breton Lord. Moreover, to some, at least, she appears evil. One man, Boromir, openly suspects her of evil designs, remarking, "I do not feel too sure of this Elvish Lady and her purposes" (*FR* II, vii, 373). Others share his suspicion. "Then there is a Lady in the Golden Wood, as old tales tell," says Éomer skeptically. "Few escape her nets, they say. . . . But if you have her favour, then you also are net-weavers and sorcerers, maybe" (*TT* III, ii, 35). It seems clear that Tolkien is deliberately playing the figure of Galadriel off the far darker and more ominous figure of the Corrigan.

The likeness goes beyond character to setting. In one scene Galadriel leads Frodo and Sam to "a deep green hollow, through which ran murmuring the silver stream that issued from the fountain on the hill. At the bottom, upon a low pedestal carved like a branching tree, stood a basin of silver, wide and shallow, and beside it stood a silver ewer" (*FR* II, vii, 376). The similarity of this setting to the one described in the poem is clear—the deep hollow, the fountain stream, the basin or pool. Tolkien carries the resemblance as far as it will go in this scene, for Galadriel toys with the idea of becoming a sorceress in truth by succumbing to the power of the One Ring. When Frodo offers her the Ring, she replies, "'In place of the Dark Lord you will set up a Queen. And I shall not be dark, but beautiful and terrible as the Morning and the Night! Fair as the Sea and the Sun and the Snow upon the Mountain! Dreadful as the Storm and the Lightning! Stronger than the foundations of the earth. All shall love me and despair!' . . . [She seemed] tall beyond measurement, and beautiful beyond enduring, terrible and worshipful" (*FR* II, vii, 381). Tolkien's purpose is to show that good may be mistaken for evil by those who do not understand it, or whose hearts are themselves susceptible to evil, as is the heart of the Lord in the poem.

The parallels to Tolkien's poem and the Breton ballad are obvious, but just as obvious are the differences. Where the Corrigan really is an evil sorceress, Galadriel turns out to be a beneficent, even a blessed, figure—as close to a goddess as Tolkien allowed himself to get in *The Lord of the Rings*. Her momentary surrender to the power of the One Ring reveals her dark side, but she overcomes it, as the Lord in the poem does not. Where the Corrigan's phial and potion, which seem to bring his desire to the Lord, are actually the cause of his death, Galadriel's phial, filled with light, will be the saving of Frodo on more than one occasion. The fact that Galadriel is in every way the obverse of the Corrigan, light where the Corrigan is dark, giving where the Corrigan is possessive, a bringer of life, not an agent of death, simply puts in high relief their generic relationship to one another. I suggest that without the Breton ballad we would not have Tolkien's Corrigan, and without his Corrigan, we would not have his Galadriel—not, at least, as she finally appears.

My second area of Celtic influence, this from Wales, concerns language. Two major invented languages are spoken in Middle-earth—Quenya and Sindarin. Both these languages were based on real-world languages, Quenya on Finnish and Sindarin on Welsh. We can forget about Quenya, or High-elven, the older of the two languages. Tolkien called it "Elven Latin" and made it, like Latin or Sanskrit, a language of learning and lore rather than everyday speech. Most of the Elvish spoken or quoted or sung in *The Lord of The Rings* is Sindarin, the language of the Sindar, the Grey-elves.[2] In 1955 Tolkien wrote to his publisher Houghton Mifflin that Sindarin "is in fact constructed deliberately to resemble Welsh phonologically and to have a relation to High-elven similar to that existing between British (properly so-called, sc. the Celtic languages spoken in this island at the time of the Roman Invasion) and Latin" (*Letters* 219). The answer to the reasonable question "Why Welsh particularly?" comes in a letter written in 1954 to Naomi Mitchison, where he explains that Sindarin was given "a linguistic character very like (though not identical with) British-Welsh: because that character is one I find, in some linguistic moods, very attractive, and because it seems to fit the rather 'Celtic' type of legends and stories of its speakers" (*Letters* 176).

We have already learned from Tolkien that he wanted his legends to have "the fair elusive beauty that some call Celtic." "I began with language," he said, and "found myself involved in inventing 'legends' of the same 'taste'" (*Letters* 231). But if he "began" with language, what led him from vocabulary and grammar to the invention of legend? The clue is his statement that the "stories were made rather to provide a world for the languages than the reverse" (*Letters* 219). He came to realize that just as people need language, so language, if it is to live and thrive, needs people, and both need a world. "[L]egends depend," he said, "on the language to which they belong; but a living language depends equally on the 'legends' it conveys by tradition" (*Letters* 231).

But how, exactly, does Welsh influence Sindarin? How closely does Sindarin resemble Welsh, even medieval British-Welsh? A little history is necessary here. In 1951 Tolkien wrote, "[T]o those creatures which in English I call . . . Elves are assigned two related languages . . . whose history is written, and whose forms . . . are deduced scientifically from a common origin" (*Letters* 143). The "common origin" is noteworthy. Tolkien followed accepted linguistic theory in creating a parent language for Quenya, and Sindarin, a sort of Proto-Indo-Elvish. The word "phonologically" is the key. The resemblance does not lie in the lexicons of the two languages (which in fact have almost nothing in common) but in the *phonological development* of each. It is in the regular systems of sound changes over time that Sindarin and Welsh show striking similarities.

I want to look at two phonological changes shared by Welsh and Sindarin that had far-reaching and characteristic consequences on the resultant grammars of each. But first I must enter a caveat. While I have studied Middle Welsh and done my obligatory translations of *Pwyll* and *Branwen*, I am sadly out of practice in that language. And though I am familiar with Tolkien's languages and can translate a few phrases, I am not a Tolkien linguist. In preparing this part of my paper I called on my colleague Carl Hostetter, who is not just a linguist but an expert in the history and development of Tolkien's invented languages. The following information all comes from him.

Now to those phonological changes. The first is *vowel affection.* In the development of both Welsh and Sindarin from parent languages, all words of those parent languages having two or more syllables and ending in a final vowel lost the final vowel. Where this lost vowel was a long *í* or a long *á*, however, before being lost, it caused certain regular and characteristic changes, called *affections*, in certain preceding vowels. The most significant of these in both languages is that caused by the loss of original final long *í*, since *í* was a prevalent element in plural formations in both Primitive Celtic and Proto-Elvish. As a result, a prevalent means of forming plurals in both Welsh and Sindarin is by *internal vowel changes* conditioned ultimately by *i*-affection, as, for example, in Welsh *bardd* ("bard"), plural *beirdd*, or Sindarin *adan* ("man"), plural *edain*. This will be familiar to English speakers from such pairs as *foot/feet, mouse/mice*, and so forth. But while such plurals are small in number and no longer productive in English, they are exceedingly common in both Welsh and Sindarin. Furthermore, the specific patterns of such internal vowel changes in Sindarin and Welsh are strikingly similar. Here are a few further examples:

Welsh
brân ("crow"), plural *brain*

ffon ("stick"), plural *ffyn*

Sindarin
tâl ("foot"), plural *tail*
hên ("child"), plural *hîn*
orod ("mountain"), plural *eryd* (also *ered*)

The second change is *lenition* of intervocalic stops. In the development of both Welsh and Sindarin from their parent languages, certain classes of consonants were subject to *lenition*, or "softening," when they came between two vowels. The largest such class was the *stops*, consonants like *p* and *d* characterized by the "stopping" of the flow of air during their pronunciation. Stop consonants occur in two varieties, *voiced* and *voiceless*. In the Proto-Elvish parent language of Sindarin, as in Primitive Celtic, the voiceless stops were *p, t, k*, and the corresponding voiced stops were *b, d, g*.

When these stop consonants came between two vowels in the parent languages, they underwent a regular and characteristic phonetic change. The voiceless stops became voiced (*p > b, t > d*, and *k > g*), while the voiced stops became spirantized (*b > v, d > ð, g > g*). Besides the stop consonants, the voiced nasal *m* was also subject to lenition, becoming spirantized to *v* (spelled *f* in Welsh). Comparing Sindarin with the older Quenya (in which intervocalic stops were unchanged), we see such pairs as Quenya *opele* ("town"), Sindarin *obel;* Quenya *atan* ("man"), Sindarin *adan;* and Quenya *Heka!* ("Be gone!"), Sindarin *Ego!* In Welsh, we find such exemplars as *cybydd* ("miser") from original Latin *Cupidus;* Welsh *Cyndaf* ("proper name"), from British *Cunotam(os);* and Welsh *deg* ("ten") from British **dekan*.

In the development of both Welsh (and all the Celtic languages) and Sindarin, a grammatical extension of this dictated that when a word in the ancestral language ended in a vowel and preceded another word that began with a stop consonant, and when this pair of words was united by some close grammatical relationship, for example, article and noun, or verb and direct object, the initial stop consonant of the second word of the pair underwent soft mutation whether or not it was between two vowels. This lenition was preserved in the descendant languages even when the original vowel that had conditioned the lenition was not preserved, and lenition was extended as a grammatical marker to environments where there had been no original conditioning vowel at all.

One example will suffice. In both Sindarin and Welsh, a noun beginning with a stop consonant, when immediately following a verb of which it is the direct object, shows lenition. Thus in the sentence *Lasto beth lammen* ("Listen to the word of my voice"), the Sindarin noun *peth,* meaning "word" (related to the verb *pedo,* "speak"), is lenited from *peth* to *beth* because it is the direct object of the imperative verb *Lasto,* "Listen!"

Technical as all this might seem, a memorable plot moment in *The Lord of the Rings* hinges on the principle of lenition. On their journey with the Ring, the Fellowship find their way blocked at the entrance to Moria, an underground city. The doors are closed and can only be opened by the right spell. The wizard Gandalf, who can read Sindarin, deciphers the Elvish inscription on the doors as *Pedo mellon a minno* and translates it as "Speak, friend, and enter," interpreting *mellon* ("friend") as the subject of the verb *pedo* ("speak"). This is reasonable, since in Sindarin, as in Welsh, the subject of a verb (as opposed to the object), when immediately following the verb, does not show lenition. The *m* in the word *mellon* is not lenited; if it were, it would be *vellon*, not *mellon*. Since the sentence on the doors clearly reads, "mellon," Gandalf assumes that *mellon*, "friend," is the subject of the sentence, addressed to the reader of the inscription. Accordingly, he speaks every spell he can think of, but the doors do not open. Here is why. The phrase *pedo mellon* is not direct address ("Speak, friend"). Instead, it is an instruction as to what word will open the gate—the word *mellon*. Thus even though *mellon* is grammatically the subject of the verb *pedo* and therefore would normally be lenited, the word is semantically independent of the sentence, and so not subject to the rule. It therefore appears in its unlenited form. When Gandalf realizes this, he correctly reinterprets *pedo mellon* as "Say 'Friend'" and speaks the word *Mellon,* and the doors open.

Now, this is pretty esoteric, and no one but Tolkien was likely to get the full import when the book was published. Even now, a bare handful of non-Welsh will know enough about language in general and Sindarin in particular to appreciate the subtlety of Tolkien's word play. It remains the most inside of inside jokes—one for the benefit of the author alone. But it is more than a joke. It also says something important about the history of Middle-earth and gives Tolkien a way not just to illustrate but to use his concept of the interdependence of language and people and the world they live in. The Elves who originally wrote the inscription were a friendlier people living in a more open and trusting world than Gandalf, in the dark days of Middle-earth, has come to expect, and their use of language reflects this. Tolkien makes sure the reader gets this point at least, by having Gandalf say, "I had only to speak the Elvish word for *friend* and the doors opened. Quite simple. Too simple for a learned loremaster in these suspicious days. Those were happier times" (*FR* II, iii, 322). By revising his grammar to fit that of the Elves of an earlier age, Gandalf arrives at an understanding not just of what they said but of who they were.

These are rather limited examples of the influence of two Celtic cultures on Tolkien's work, all that time and space allow. Much remains to be explored of the "fair elusive beauty that some call Celtic" that Tolkien meant to be so much a part of his creation.

The Green Knight, the Green Man, and Treebeard

Scholarship and Invention in Tolkien's Fiction

Imagination and scholarship are so closely interwoven in Tolkien's work that they are almost impossible to disentangle. Just as each informed the other, so each drew from the other. Tolkien's scholarship put his fiction on solid ground, as the world of Middle-earth bears witness. Likewise, his imagination often imbued his scholarship with a markedly poetic quality, as his essay on *"Beowulf:* The Monsters and the Critics" demonstrates. The intersection of imagination and scholarship was the flashpoint at which his creativity ignited. The result in *The Lord of the Rings* is a work deeply rooted in medieval tradition and at the same time newly created, wholly fresh and original.

While this intersection occurs in all Tolkien's work, it is nowhere more true that in the case of one of his most memorable characters, Treebeard the Ent, the slow-speaking, orc-abhorring tree shepherd who befriends Merry and Pippin, and with his fellow-Ents wreaks such well-deserved havoc on Isengard. Treebeard's personification of wild nature, his ponderous, strangely musical language, and his long-sighted world-view—as well as his sense of humor—make him one of the most remarkable creations in a book full of remarkable creations. At first read, he would seem to be entirely original, new-sprung out of Tolkien's forehead. A closer look show him to derive from an old tradition, one as old as, if not older than almost anything else in the story.

So engaging is Treebeard as a character, and so attractive are the Ents as a concept, that many readers of *The Lord of the Rings* wrote to Tolkien seeking more information about them. What Tolkien wrote in reply says much about the relationship between scholarship and invention. In one letter to a reader he commented: "though I knew for years that Frodo would run into a tree-adventure somewhere far down the Great River, I have no recollection of inventing Ents. I came at last to the point, and wrote the "Treebeard" chapter without any recollection of any previous thought, just as it now is" (*Letters* 231). He had more to say on the subject to W.H. Auden.

> Take the Ents for instance. I did not consciously invent them at all. . . . I daresay something had been going on in the "unconscious" for some time. . . . But looking back analytically I should say that the Ents are composed of philology, literature, and life. They owe their name to the *eald enta geweorc* [old creations of giants] of Anglo-Saxon, and their connexion with stone. Their part in the story is due, I think, to my bitter disappointment and disgust from schooldays with the shabby use made in Shakespeare of the coming of "Great Birnam Wood to high Dunsinane hill": I longed to devise a setting in which the trees might really march to war. (*Letters* 211–12 n)

Such comments make it appear that on one hand Tolkien is vigorously rejecting invention and on the other blithely citing its sources, but this is not as contradictory as it first seems. There is truth in both assertions, since each describes a separate operation of the conscious and unconscious mind. Disgust with Shakespeare may explain the Battle of Isengard, but it does not explain Ents, nor does it account for the particular character of Treebeard. High Birnam Wood may have been the match, but there had to be something already present from which it could strike fire. Tolkien might well have had no conscious awareness of inventing Ents, yet "looking back analytically" he could see that something had "been going on in the unconscious for some time," and that three elements—philology, literature, and life—were at hand for him to draw upon.

   Ready at hand they certainly were, but with marked differences in quality and kind, coming from different sources and speaking to different areas of the mind. Philology and literature are specific and interconnected disciplines, but "life" is so general a term it is hard to know exactly what Tolkien meant by it. For the purpose of my argument, I will apply it to his own life and specifically to his well-known love for trees. A poignant anecdote included in his Introductory Note to *Tree and Leaf,* and recounted in his *Letters* as well, tells the of the sad fate of "a great tree—a huge poplar with vast limbs—visible through my window even as I lay in bed. I loved it," he says, "and was anxious about it." With good reason, for as he tells the story, "it was suddenly lopped and mutilated by its owner, I do not know why. It is cut down now, a less barbarous punishment for any crimes it may have been accused of, such as being large and alive" (*TL* viii). While this account of the loss is in the context of his writing of "Leaf by Niggle," with its central image of a tree, the feeling behind the anecdote of love and respect for trees, for things "large and alive," has also a clear relationship to the Ents.

Philology and literature are easier to document. Tom Shippey's *The Road to Middle-earth* cites Tolkien's fascination with the power of philology to "resurrect from the dead a society long since vanished" (Shippey 37). The reference is to an article in *Essays and Studies* (1929) on "*Ancrene Wisse and Hali Meiðhad*" in which Tolkien made use of a minute distinction in verb-endings to postulate the existence of a society whose dialect of English was in direct descent from Anglo-Saxon, without interruption by the Conquest. This same power of philology to resurrect is also at work in Tolkien's creation of the Ents, in his impulse to resurrect a tradition if not "long since vanished," at least less recognized today than in former times.

In the case of the Ents, philology had not just a generative or resurrective role, but a nominative and philosophical one as well. Shortly after the publication of *The Two Towers* Tolkien wrote to a reader that the Ents "grew rather out of their name than the other way about," that he had always felt something should be done "about the peculiar A. Saxon word *ent* for 'giant' or mighty person of long ago" (*Letters* 208). He added that "If [the word] had a slightly philosophical tone" though in "ordinary philology . . . quite unconnected . . . with . . . the verb to be," that was also of interest to him. The Ents grew out of their name. What's in a name? Let us begin with philology. Treebeard says that "Real names tell you the story of the things they belong to in my language, in the Old Entish, as you might say" (*TT* III, iv, 68). Tolkien named his Ents in playful echo of actual Anglo-Saxon, but since as yet there is no full dictionary of Old Entish, let us try a dictionary of Anglo-Saxon. Bosworth-Toller gives *ent,* "giant," and *entisc,* "belonging to or made by a giant." The more general *OED* gives a second definition for *ent* (listed as "*metaph. rare*") as "the ent, or existent."

While nominally the Ents owe their origin to the primary dictionary meaning of the word, Tolkien's comment about the slightly philosophical tone suggests that he may also have had in mind the metaphysical and rare meaning, from which the Ents may derive something of their ancient, enduring, and tree-ish nature. Although he conceded that "ordinary philology" ruled it out, Tolkien seemed to want to reconnect the word *ent* to the verb "to be," that is, to the primal notion of "being" in the sense in which he described the poor lopped poplar as "being large and alive." We can see from these references that while Treebeard, like many another character in *The Lord of the Rings,* went through changes, one idea behind his creation may be at least as old as nature itself. He is something large and alive, a being from that vast, nonhuman forest world whose power and wildness antedate civilization and have both fascinated and frightened humanity since people first lived in houses.

His character as such did not develop all at once, however, for as originally conceived, Treebeard was more ent-as-giant than ent-as-tree. An early draft of *The Lord of the Rings* has Gandalf tell Frodo at Rivendell that he was "caught in Fangorn and spent many weary days as a prisoner of the giant Treebeard" (*RS* 363). This giant Treebeard was not yet the character he was to become, as Tolkien's notes here make clear: "Frodo meets the Giant Treebeard in the Forest of Neldoreth . . . he is deceived by the giant, who pretends to be friendly, but is really in league with the Enemy" (*RS* 384). A subsequently discarded scene describes the meeting thus:

> Frodo . . . looked up, but he could see nothing through the thick entangled branches. Suddenly he felt a quiver in the gnarled tree-trunk against which he was leaning, and before he could spring away he was pushed, or kicked, forward onto his knees. Picking himself up he looked at the tree, and even as he looked it took a stride toward him. He scrambled out of the way, and a deep rumbling chuckle came down out of the tree-top. "Where are you, little beetle?" said the voice. (*RS* 382)

"Little beetle" is the clue, and the ensuing dialogue makes the point that if Frodo is so small that Treebeard cannot see him, Treebeard is so huge that Frodo likewise cannot see him, and that what he took to be a forest is really Treebeard's "garden." When he looks closer, he sees that "what he had taken for smooth tree-stems were the stalks of gigantic flowers—and what he had thought was the stem of a monstrous oaktree was really a thick gnarled leg with a rootlike foot and many branching toes" (*RS* 384).

Though the potential is clearly already there, Treebeard is at this point in his development an ent in the "giant" sense, but not yet in the "existent" sense. There is no hint as yet of his great age, of his enduring "being." He is in the forest, but he is not yet an integral part of it. What changed this giant into the Treebeard we know was not so much philology as literature. Fresh creation though he is, his descent can be traced from ancient literary ancestors. One ancestral branch is that of the original *enta* or *eótena*, the giant figures whose mention in Anglo-Saxon poems such as *Beowulf* and *The Wanderer* and *The Ruin* inspired Tolkien, as he says to "do something" with them.

Another branch derives from the literary and folk tradition of the Green World, the untameable world of nature. The wood as a place of mystery and otherness has been a standard topos for English writers from the Middle Ages to the present. Kenneth Grahame's Wild Wood that so frightens Rat and Mole in *The Wind in the Willows* and the enchanted woods to which Shakespeare's world-weary dukes and rebellious lovers flee from the trammels of society are modern and Renaissance examples. The greenwood is a world celebrated in Britain to this day in folk festivals and mummers' plays whose pagan origins predate Christianity. Perhaps the wood's clearest embodiment is to be found in the fourteenth-century Middle English poem of *Sir Gawain and the Green Knight*, most obviously in the character of the Green Knight himself. And it is in direct descent from that literary branch in general, and from the Green Knight in particular, that Tolkien has derived Treebeard.

Tolkien had a long and fruitful association with *Sir Gawain and the Green Knight*. He first read this most famous of Middle English poems while he was still a student at King Edward's School in Birmingham. In 1925, while he was at Leeds University, he published a scholarly edition of the poem with E.V. Gordon which, while it has been updated several times, remains a standard on English school syllabuses, and is still cited in scholarly references. It was one of the texts he taught at Leeds and later at Oxford. Sometime in the 1930s or 40s he wrote his own translation of the poem, dramatized and broadcast in 1953 by the BBC, and published together with his translations of *Pearl* and *Sir Orfeo* by Christopher Tolkien in 1975. It was the subject of Tolkien's W.P. Ker Memorial Lecture at the University of Glasgow in 1953. Though the critical focus of Tolkien's lecture was what he called "the great third Fit," the Temptation of Sir Gawain, Tolkien's analysis of the poem shows that he was well acquainted with the figure the poet called *þat grene gome*, "that green man," and *þe gome in þe grene*, "the man in the green," and well aware of the faërie quality which that figure brought to the story. His creative imagination could not have remained unaffected by a powerful presence like that of the Green Knight.

While the poem in which the Green Knight plays so large a part is overtly Christian, the Knight himself has long been recognized as having a decidedly pagan air. Although his specific function in the plot is to test the hero's Christian virtues, the power of his presence transcends the didacticism of the text to evoke an ancient, archetypal response. His entry into King Arthur's court during the New Year celebration, a green giant with green hair and green beard, clothed all in green-ho, riding a green horse, carrying a green holly branch in one hand and a green axe in the other, stops conversation dead and no wonder. The poet describes him as *þe most on þe molde on mesure hyghe* (l. 137), "the largest on earth in measured height," and as *Half etayn in erde* (l. 140), "half a giant upon earth." (Tolkien's verse translation gives "Half troll" for *Half etayn*.) And with this we are back again to philology, for *etayn* is the Middle English equivalent of Anglo-Saxon *eóten*, like *ent*, a word meaning "giant."

Surpassing the knights of Arthur's court not just in stature but in age, the Green Knight has no hesitation in insulting the King. When Arthur tells the Knight he has come to the right place if he is looking for a fight, the Knight contemptuously tells the King he doesn't fight with children.

> *Nay, frayst I no fyȝt, in fayth I þe telle,*
> *Hit arn aboute on þis bench bot berdlez chylder*
> Nay, I wish for no battle, in faith I tell thee.
> Here about on this bench are but beardless children. (ll. 279–80)

Arthur may be young, and some of his knights likewise (depending on which of the many Arthurian traditions you choose), but the Green Knight's oh so superior put-down makes it clear that he comes not just from a wilder, but an infinitely older world than the one they know.

"Children" is bad enough, but "beardless" is a particularly low blow, especially coming from someone who is most uncivilizedly hairy.

> *A much berd as a busk ouer his brest henges,*
> *þat wyth his hiȝlich here þat of his hed reches*
> *Watȝ euesed al vmbetorne abof his elbowes* (ll. 182–84)

> A beard as big as a bush hangs over his breast
> That with his splendid hair fell from his head
> In a circle to just above as his elbows.

The same characteristics can be observed in Treebeard, described in *The Lord of the Rings* as "almost Troll-like," adding that whether "it was clad in stuff like green and grey bark or whether that was its hide was difficult to say." A prominent feature is the "sweeping . . . beard, bushy, almost twiggy" (*TT* III, iv, 66). Particular words are worth noting. Tolkien's use of the word "troll" for both the Green Knight and Treebeard, and "bushy" seems very close to "as big as a bush." "Bushy beard" is a mere figure of speech, a dead metaphor, but like all metaphors it has its roots (no pun intended) in real perception. A full beard can look like a bush, as Edward Lear's well-known limerick attests:

> There was an old man of Liskeard
> Who said, "It is just as I feared,
> A cock and a hen, four larks and a wren
> Have all built their nests in my beard."

Both the limerick and the metaphor it relies on show the power of words to establish reality. With remarkable economy, Tolkien has brought it all together in one portmanteau word—*Treebeard*—which is at once his character's description, his metaphor, and his name.

In a parallel to the Green Knight's patronizing attitude toward the "beardless children" of Arthur's court, Treebeard treats the beardless hobbit Merry and Pippin like children. Talking to them, he tells them, makes him feel as if he is talking to young Entings. His addition of Hobbits immediately after Ents in the mnemonic Long List explicitly calls them "children."

> *Ents the earthborn, old as mountains*
> *the wide-walkers, water drinking:*
> *and hungry as hunters, the Hobbit children,*
> *the laughing folk, the little people. (TT III, x, 191)*

Then too, there is the matter of color. Controversy has simmered for years over the significance of the Green Knight's color, and shows no sign of letting up. The focus of the conflict is precisely the validity or invalidity of the vegetation aspect which connects the Green Knight to Treebeard. Arguing against the view of the Green Knight as a nature figure, Roger Sherman Loomis stoutly insisted that the *Gawain* poet was too good a Christian to think of making the Knight a "vegetation spirit." In order to make this convincing, Loomis had to replace the Knight's green with grey and play up his affinity with non-vegetation myth-figures. Thus Loomis connects him with Cu Roi, the churl in dark grey who plays the Irish version of *Sir Gawain and the Green Knight*'s Beheading Game (Loomis 59), and with Arawn, the grey-clad Otherworld chieftain of the Temptation episode in "Pwyll," the First Branch of the Welsh *Mabinogion.*

In contrast, John Speirs unequivocally identifies the Green Knight as a vegetation figure, as "the Green Man—the Jack in the Green of the village festivals of England and Europe. He is the descendant of the Vegetation or Nature god of . . . almost immemorial tradition whose death and resurrection mythologizes the annual death and rebirth of nature" (cited in Moorman, *The Works of the Gawain Poet* 295). The *Gawain* poet explicitly uses both these terms, calling the knight a "green man," a *grene gome,* and "the man in the green," *þe gome in þe grene.* Whatever the Knight's function in the Christian poem, it does not seem unlikely that the poet was aware of the figure's pagan identity, that he may have been using as description familiar titles out of English folklore. The best evidence for this, directly connected to his green color, is the holly branch which the knight carries in his hand.

Bot in his on honde he hade a holyn bobbe,
þat is grattest in grene when greueʒ ar bare (ll. 206–7)

But in his one hand he had a holly branch,
That is greatest in green when groves are bare

As John Williamson points out in his book *The Oak King, the Hollt King,*
and the Unicorn, the holly is the most outstanding evergreen in the winter
forest, a verdant contrast to the deadness of the leafless trees. The significance of holly in medieval Europe is apparent in the familar English carol
"The Holly and the Ivy."

The holly and the ivy
When they are both full grown,
Of all the trees that are in the wood,
The holly bears the crown.

In Christian Europe the holly crown was identified with Christ's crown of
thorns, but Williamson cites an older and wilder significance, noting that in
the south of Europe and particularly in the Mediterranean region,

there is an indigenous type of evergreen oak called the *kermes,* or holly
oak. This holly oak bears a leaf that is almost identical to the foliage of
the northern European true holly. In classical times and long thereafter,
the Mediterranean peoples revered the holly oak because—unlike the deciduous oak—it remained green during the winter months. From this pre-
Christian sanctity of the Mediterranean holly oak came a diffusion of influences from the south, resulting in the same reverence for the look-alike
hollies of northern Europe. The people there, however, did not differentiate between the holly and the evergreen oak, but considered the holly to
be the winter counterpart of the deciduous, summer oak (Williamson 62).

Behind the seasonal cycle and the veneration for both the holly and the
oak was an ancient European religion that focused much of its symbolism
upon fertility. (64)

Both the oak and the holly, then, were seen as embodiments of the spirit of
the forest, of wild nature, and the Oak King and the Holly King personified
that spirit.

It does not take a great leap of imagination to see the *Gawain* poet's Green
Knight bearing his holly bobbe as just such a personification. Recall that

Frodo mistook Treebeard's leg for "the stem of a monstrous oak tree." It does not then demand much effort to recognize the oak-associated Treebeard and the holly-bearing Green Knight as linked and similar presentations of the same powerful primitive figure, the Green Man—one of the oldest and most pervasive images in the art and iconography of northern Europe, woven in tapestry, word-pictured in poems and ballads, memorialized in folktales and celebrated in folk festivals.

In his most mysterious representation of all, he appears carved in stone or wood as the foliate head, with leaves for hair and vines growing from nose and mouth, which decorates the portals and architraves and pediments of medieval churches and cathedrals. In his book *Green Man: The Archetype of Our Oneness with the Earth,* William Anderson cites three main forms.

> In the first and oldest form he is a male head formed out of a leaf mask; his hair, features, and physiognomy are all made either of a single leaf or many leaves. In the second form he is a male head disgorging vegetation from his mouth and often from his ears and eyes; the vegetation may curl round to form his hair, beard, eyebrows and moustaches. The third form . . . the head is the fruit or flower of vegetation. (Anderson 14)

Here there is no text, no plot, or character to illuminate meaning. The image itself is the text, and must be compared with other kinds of texts for clues to its meaning. Fortunately, we have such a text in *Sir Gawain and the Green Knight.* The carved heads in church and cathedral recall the most extraordinary image in that poem, the Green Knight's head severed from his body, tucked under its owner's arm, and still speaking as the decapitated Knight rides away. The foliage as hair, especially facial hair, recalls not just the Green Knight's hair and beard, but the twiggy, mossy facial hair which gives Treebeard his name and character.

There are hundreds of these mysterious heads adorning churches and cathedrals from the west of Ireland to east of Moscow, appearing over a period beginning as early as the eighth century of the Common Era and continuing into modern times. What are they doing in church? On a visit to Peru in 1999 I was delighted to find foliate heads adorning the carved wooden altar of the Cathedral at Cuzco. The Green Man had made it to the New World. But how has he transcended his pagan origin to become part of the very structure of Christianity? Does his appearance testify to the ability of Christianity to absorb and use elements of other religions? Is it evidence of syncretism, an instinctive transfer of imagery from one belief system to another, its greenery recalling the Tree of the Garden and the Tree of the

Cross? There is no answer, only the silent face, enigmatic, untamed, a little frightening to the human eyes whose glances they return. Saying nothing, they can mean anything. We are free to make of them what we will.

Much has been made of them. They have been interpreted as symbols of Christ, as portraits of the Horned God of Celtic mythology, as emblems of Natural Law. They may be any or all of these. The mysterious leaf-enfolded visage, a pagan image in a Christian environment, is old wine in a new bottle still retaining its flavor. It is an ancient motif in a new text, still retaining its mystery like the Green Knight in the Christian poem or the character of Treebeard in a modern fantasy. Each is a message from an older world, all are avatars of the same energy, the force that recreates itself in yearly rhythm. Whatever his epithet, call him the Green Man, the Green Knight, or Treebeard, he is the archetype of the green world and he speaks for the spirit of wild, uncultivated life.

But what makes Tolkien's Treebeard so vivid a character? What makes him so singularly himself and not just another Green Man? We have seen that he is derived from old tradition, and Tolkien seems at first to make him more so, giving his antiquity, indeed his very being a philological basis, even allowing the "metaphysical, rare" second meaning to supersede the first, so that the ent, the existent, replaces the giant. It is just here that creativity intersects scholarship, for the existent Treebeard is, in Tolkien's world, also the pre-existent. He is "the oldest of all living things" (*TT* III, viii, 164), whose long slow years have seen the others arrive one by one.

Tolkien's linguistic invention, wholly imagined, yet linguistically consistent, puts those slow years into words and gives them a voice. As much a part of Treebeard as his giant size and his vegetative nature is his language, the measured, holophrastic Entish locutions that make a sentence out of a word like "hill" and take half a day to say "good morning." "It is a lovely language, says the old Ent, "but it takes a very long time to say anything in it, because we do not say anything in it, unless it is worth taking a long time to say, and to listen to" (*TT* III, iv, 68). Tolkien has taken a metaphor, the poetry of nature, made it a living reality, and given it a voice we cannot help but listen to.

Moreover, it is a conscious voice, for a clear addition to the metaphor is Tolkien's unique concept of the Ents not as tree but as shepherds of trees. His careful distinction between the two allows him to endow the latter with an un-vegetative self-consciousness. Treebeard has memory of the past, awareness of the present, and most especially a foreboding of the future not granted the old vegetation gods, nor the Green Man, nor the Green Knight. Here is fresh invention, manifest first in Treebeard's recollection of the past when the Ents were young and the Entwives still a part of their lives. "Those were the broad days!" the old Ent tells Merry and Pippin. "Time was when I could walk and sing all day and hear no more than the echo of my own voice in the hollow hills" (*TT* III, iv, 72).

Invention is manifest also in Treebeard's awareness of the present, for the word "shepherd" invests him with the role of guardian of nature, and thus conveys Tolkien's point that the flora of the natural world, like its fauna, have predators, and need protection against their enemies. "[N]obody cares for the woods as I care for them," the Ent tells the hobbits (*TT* III, iv, 75). The voice of Treebeard reminds a world whose Cartesian world-view has effectively divorced it from nature that it may be losing—and indeed destroying—something irreplaceable. It is a voice both archetypal and individual, and implicit in it is a criticism of the "hastiness" of a humanity that can cut down what has taken years to grow and leaves a wasteland in its place. "[T]he Ents loved the great trees," says this voice, "and the wild woods, and the slopes of the high hills; and they drank of the mountain-streams, and ate only such fruit as the trees let fall in their path" (*TT* III, iv, 79). The use of the past tense drives home the point that Treebeard's world is fast disappearing, and that he knows it.

And this is Tolkien's point. For above all, Tolkien's invention is manifest in Treebeard's foreboding of the future. The Ents and the world they care for— in both senses of that expression—are dying out. The invention that Tolkien brings to the old pattern is not just personification of the force that through the green fuse drives the flower, but also a modern depiction of ecological loss, a wholly contemporary protest against depredation of a kind unknown to the world in which Treebeard and his predecessors dwelt so naturally. The image of the Green Man is powerful in all his guises, but it is his modern avatar, it is Treebeard the Ent who makes the most forceful statement. The Green Man stares out silently from the stone, his message the green leaf itself. The Green Knight, despite his color, speaks less for the green world than for a man-made chivalric code with little relation to nature. It is Treebeard, at once the oldest and the newest of the type, who speaks out against the ruination of the environment, who speaks from and for the natural world. It is Treebeard who convenes Entmoot, and leads the Ents to war against the machine.

The Ents primal energy is the very essence of the wild, and it is that wildness which is doomed. It is not just orcs that will destroy them, not just axes, nor fire, nor the inevitable destruction wrought by war. It is civilization which by its very nature will eventually kill off the wild. Not just the industrializing of Saruman but the industrious gardening of the Entwives will bring an end to the Ents and their world. The tame, by its very desire for order, will edge out the wilderness. Tolkien's wild trees are making their last stand. The time of the Ents is over, and the Fourth Age, the Age of Men the predators of trees, is about to begin. And so, at the end of the chapter which bears his name, Treebeard speaks the epitaph for himself and his world.

> "Of course it is likely enough, my friends," he said slowly, "likely enough that we are going to *our* doom: the last march of the Ents. But if we stayed at home and did nothing, doom would find us anyway, sooner or later. That thought has long been growing in our hearts; and that is why we are marching now." (*TT* III, iv, 90)

That thought could not have grown in Treebeard's heart had it not grown in Tolkien's heart first, had not life finally overtaken philology and literature. The coming of high Birnam Wood to Dunsinane may have been the match, the fuse the intertwisted strands of Anglo-Saxon giants and pagan fertility figures, but the point of ignition was the heart of a man who loved and mourned a huge poplar with vast limbs whose only crime was being large and alive.

Missing Person

While the fictive mythology of J.R.R. Tolkien, especially *The Lord of the Rings,* owes a clear debt to Celtic and Germanic myth and fairy tale, it has also been proposed that it and its parent mythology as published in *The Silmarillion* and *Unfinished Tales* seem to have clear Judeo-Christian references. His mythic cosmos has what at first glance looks like the familiar Judeo-Christian God (Eru/Ilúvatar), angels (the Valar), a rebel angel (Melkor/Morgoth), and the traditional Judeo-Christian elements of temptation, transgression, sin, and salvation. One important element, however, is missing from this list—the chief actor in the Christian drama and the central event in the Christian mythos. There is no Christ. And therefore, there is no single moment when his history turns a corner, no one act which makes everything which comes after different from what came before.

I have said there is salvation, but a necessary distinction must be made here between salvation and redemption, between a savior and a redeemer. For while Tolkien's myth has a number of saviours, it has no one redeemer. *Redeem,* according to *The American Heritage Dictionary,* comes from Latin *redimere,* "to buy back," that is, to regain, by paying a price, what has been lost or sold. *Save,* from Latin *salvare, salvus,* "safe," means "to rescue from harm, to bring to a safe condition." There are a number of saviour-figures in Tolkien's work, who rescue or make safe their world or their companions, but there is no one character who buys back for all time what has been lost.

This is deliberate. Tolkien's stated intention was to omit from his work any overt reference to religion or religious practices in his imaginary world (*Letters* 172). For he said: "Myth and fairy-story must, as all art, reflect and contain in solution elements of moral and religious truth (or error), but not explicit, not in the known form of the primary 'real' world" (*Letters* 144). To point up the effect of this omission, let me contrast Tolkien with someone to whom he is often compared, C.S. Lewis. Lewis and Tolkien—friends, fellow-Christians, writers of mythic fantasy—approach the question of religious reference in their fiction differently, and the difference is characteristic of each. Two of Lewis's mythological fantasies—*The Lion, the Witch, and the Wardrobe*, and *Perelandra*, have—each in its own way—a central event which is consciously and deliberately modeled on Christianity. In *The Lion, the Witch, and the Wardrobe*, the lion, Aslan, sacrifices himself by offering to die in the place of Edmund, a sinning mortal enticed into evil by a tempting female, Jadis the White Witch, who offers him a forbidden comestible. When Aslan dies for Edmund, the stone table breaks, Edmund is redeemed, death runs backward and Aslan is resurrected. The reference is obvious, as Lewis certainly intended that it should be. He is a little more oblique in *Perelandra*, but not much. Here, the Green Lady is subjected to considerable rhetoric by the un-man, whose persuasive efforts are to get her to disobey Maleldil's prohibition and sleep on the fixed land. She is saved from this error by Ransom (his name a fairly obvious pun) who, in this case, prevents the Fall rather than redeeming humanity after it.

We will search in vain through Tolkien's mythology for any such specificity. Lewis comes close to allegory; Tolkien stays nearer to metaphor. Tolkien's work is informed with Christian meaning, but devoid of any re-use of specific Christian events, and especially The Event. This is deliberate. To Robert Murray Tolkien wrote that he had "not put in, or [had] cut out, practically all references to anything like 'religion'" (*Letters* 172), and his letter to Milton Waldman explicitly faulted the "Arthurian world" for its unequivocal involvement with Christian religion (*Letters* 144).

A more artistic, less technical reason for Tolkien's omission has to do with the nature of the world which Tolkien has created, and the way in which its elements interact. He explained this in a letter to a reader:

> I suppose a difference between this Myth and what may be perhaps called Christian mythology is this. In the latter the Fall of Man is subsequent to and a consequence (though not a necessary consequence) of the 'Fall of the Angels': a rebellion of created free-will at a higher level than Man; but it is not clearly held (and in many versions is not held at all) that this affected the 'World' in its nature: evil was brought in from outside, by Satan. In this Myth the rebellion of created free-will precedes the creation of the world (Eä); and Eä has in it, subcreatively introduced, evil, rebellions, discordant elements of its own nature already when the *Let It Be* was spoken.

The Fall or corruption, therefore, of all things in it and all inhabitants of it, was a possibility if not inevitable (*Letters* 286–87).

Thus the nature of Tolkien's world derives directly from the rebellion and the discord which preceded and in large measure shaped it. The strife is already in the Music which is the blueprint for creation, but there by Melkor's defiance of Eru's theme and his insistence on introducing a theme of his own. The Fall occurs before history begins.

Tolkien's approach is to build on this first Fall a series of lesser Falls, each the consequence in some way of the one before it, each of which brings evil, but none of which wreaks irreparable damage on humanity—that is, all of the Free Peoples—as a whole. First of the lesser Falls is that of Fëanor, the elven smith who refuses to give back the light. Next is that of his people, the Noldor, who, as a consequence of his refusal, defy the angelic powers to leave Aman, the holy place, for darkened Middle-earth. The only Fall which in any way resembles the Judeo-Christian one is the Fall of the Men of Númenor, well along in Tolkien's history, when they defy a prohibition, the Ban of the Valar, and set foot in the Undying Lands. But unlike the Judeo-Christian sequence, this is a consequence of evil rather than the genesis of it, and occurs toward the end of the myth, not at the beginning.

Corollary to these lesser Falls is a series of lesser salvations, partial rescues in which humanity, or a portion thereof, is saved from evil, but in each case only temporarily. These are important episodes in Tolkien's story, but it is clear that each is a momentary reprieve, the winning of a battle, but not of the war. Analysis of four examples of such lesser salvation will show to what degree each approximates the Christian model, and how and why each departs from it.

The first of the saviours is Eärendil, whose coming is adumbrated through much of *The Silmarillion*. Eärendil is half-elven, a blend of Tolkien's two major races, son of an elven princess, Idril, and a mortal man, Tuor. Tolkien's half-elven are a deliberate intermixture of the natural and the supernatural, and evoke all those heroes of myth and literature from Theseus to Achilles who are the products of a union between a god or goddess and a mortal. The Christian hero is, of course, Christ, begotten of God, born to Mary.

Eärendil's part in the mythology is to intercede with the Valar on behalf of Men and Elves. He is a petitioner pleading pardon for the Noldor and forgiveness and mercy for both of Tolkien's races. He is described as "the looked for that cometh at unawares, the longed for that cometh beyond hope" (*Silm* 248–49). When his mission is successfully completed, he is lifted up "even into the oceans of heaven" (*Silm* 250). Abstracted from the story he looks remarkably Christlike. He is of natural and supernatural parentage; his coming has been prophesied; he comes unexpectedly; his mission is to save humanity; and finally, he is lifted up into the heavens where he and the jewel he wears, the Silmaril, become a light unto men.

But in the context of the story these allusions to Christ recede, while the events and background surrounding them provide a different perspective. The intercession of the Valar is temporary, and does not work for all time. Unlike Jesus, Eärendil marries, and when he voyages through the heavens, his wife, Elwing, waits for him. By "heavens" Tolkien plainly means the sky as seen from earth, not the abode of God. Eärendil, like similar figures in Native American and northern European myth and legend, is the personification of a celestial body, the evening and morning star which even our un-mythic culture identifies as the planet Venus, named after a Greco-Roman goddess. And while the light of a particular bright star readily translates into a spiritual metaphor (as it did for the Anglo-Saxon poem which probably gave Tolkien the concept (Carpenter 64), it has other associations as well. The Norse form of the name is Örvandil, and Örvandils-tâ is Örvandil's frozen toe, broken off by the god Thor and flung into the sky, where it remained as a star (Grimm I, 375). Thus the name and therefore the figure, have as much a pagan as a Christian aspect. It seems clear that Tolkien is deliberately mingling pagan and Christian elements so that neither will predominate. Both contribute something to his story, but the meld of the two makes Tolkien's Eärendil into something new which can still remind the reader of something old.

Another character whose actions and attributes seem to fit the role of saviour is Gandalf. Considered only in the context of *The Lord of the Rings,* he would at first seem to conform to the pattern beautifully. But we must acknowledge both his prior introduction in *The Hobbit* and his subsequent assimilation into the mythic pattern of the Silmarillion. In *The Hobbit* he is simply the wizard and wise old man who traditionally aids the hero of the fairy tale. In writing *The Lord of the Rings* Tolkien wove him into the fabric of his cosmology as one of the Istari, an order of wizards. His character is most vivid in *The Lord of the Rings,* where his most dramatic act is the willing sacrifice of himself to save his companions on the Bridge of Khazad Dum. His ordeal with the Balrog includes a journey into the underworld, a death, and a resurrection. Moreover, Tolkien's narrative makes it clear that he knew what was in store for him and went deliberately to meet it. When he returns transformed from Grey to White, he appears first to his followers and they do not recognize him. The sequence is familiar to any reader of the Gospels.

His name, too, is evocative. Tolkien borrowed it from the catalogue of dwarfs in Snorri Sturluson's *Edda* (Faulkes 16). Philologist that he was, Tolkien certainly knew the meanings and resonances of the name. The usual translation of Gandalf is "sorcerer elf." The "sorcerer" fits well enough with "wizard" to let it pass, although sorcery is most often linked with black magic where wizardry is not. But it is the *alf*, not the *Gand* that is of interest here. Jacob Grimm points out that the Elder Edda several times associates âlfar (that is, elves) with æsir (that is, gods) "as though they were a compendium of higher beings." (Grimm II, 443). He also associates alf with Latin albus, "white or light colored" (444). *The American Heritage Dictionary* traces alf back to Indo-European al bho-, "white." We can safely assume that Tolkien, well aware of this trail of meanings, knew what was built into the name he chose for the figure, and that even if he made no use of these connotations in *The Hobbit* he knowingly used them in *The Lord of the Rings.*

The sum of this evidence points persuasively to an interpretation of Gandalf as a kind of Christ. He is a being of light, associated with, or comparable to a god; he is aware of his end before it happens, and accepts it; he dies, is resurrected, transformed, appears to his followers on the road (in this case Fangorn Forest), and at the end of the book, leaves bodily for the Undying Lands.

But again, a larger context blurs the edges of the pattern. To begin with, he is wholly supernatural, not a mortal man, and therefore the one character in the book for whom this concatenation of events and circumstances will seem least miraculous. His return from the dead, far from being trumpeted as a resurrection, is so well hidden that many readers remain unaware that he has died. Moreover, his function within the story is not to save, but to arouse, to galvanize into action. Gandalf Stormcrow brings news of trouble where he goes; he is an alarm, not a salvation. In Tolkien's cosmology he is a kind of demigod, one of the Maiar, or lesser Valar. His true name is Olórin, for which Tolkien supplies no clear meaning. But he glosses the name Gandalf as "the Elf of the Wand," and cites it as the name by which Olórin is called among men (*UT* 391). Gandalf is thus specifically fitted into the mythology within the angelic hierarchy, below Eru (the creator) and the Valar, but above men and elves, and outside any pattern which would encompass the God made man who is Christ.

Next, let us consider Aragorn, certainly a saviour, and one who in many respects fits the pattern better than Gandalf. He is mortal, a man, albeit of a very high order. Like Eärendil, he is of the half-elven, and thus of both natural and supernatural lineage. He is a king coming to claim his kingdom. He is a healer, as his actions on Weathertop and in the Houses of Healing demonstrate. He can raise the dead, or the apparently dead, for he brings Eowyn, Merry, and Faramir back from the threshold of· death by calling them. His coming ushers in a new era of peace.

In the case of Aragorn, the distinctions between him and Christ are as much of degree as of kind, and can obliquely allude to Christ. Tolkien has (I think deliberately) chosen for Aragorn a pattern into which he and Christ both fit, but which has a wider context than the mythology of either. This is the pattern of the sacral king, a vital element of the mythologies of the ancient world, appearing in Greek, Germanic, and Celtic myth as well as the Christian. In the ancient mythologies such a figure has a role far more physical than spiritual, for his charge and his responsibility are the physical well-being of his kingdom. Sacral kingship is built explicitly on the relationship between the king and his kingdom, and in ancient cultures is manifest chiefly through fertility. The king is the husband of his country, and on his virility and his potency depends its fertility. Such a motif is most manifest in the Celtic ideal of the Waste Land, the barrenness that follows the wounding or the illness of the king. The ancient figure of the maimed king or wounded king which develops from Celtic legend and is assimilated into the grail story is the sacral king robbed of his potency. Aragorn, like Galahad, like Arthur at the start of his reign, is the positive of this figure, the healing king who restores the waste land and brings renewed vitality with his reign.

Little effort is needed to understand how this motif was translated from the material and physical renewal of the Celtic myth to the spiritual rebirth heralded by Christ in Christian mythology. Knowing this pattern, Tolkien fit Aragorn into it, but held him to the physical realm so that he would evoke the lesser figures of Arthur and Galahad, and through them gesture toward Christ rather than directly presenting him. Aragorn's renewal is largely on the physical and material level, and has less to do with spiritual salvation than with the practical aspects of governing, marrying, having children, providing the country with a structure and a direction. Aragorn's re-planting of the White Tree, his union with Arwen, the establishment of a lawful succession, the renewal through his office of the whole of Middle-earth, are in the old tradition of the sacral king, as Christ is the bringer of the new.

Without doubt, the likeliest saviour candidate is Frodo, whose appointed mission is to destroy the Ring and thus save Middle-earth and its inhabitants. And here the parallels to Christ, the allusions to the story of the Gospels, are clear, and probably deliberate. There is no doubt that the experiences which Frodo undergoes, the trials, the torments—all of which contribute thematically to his function in the story—are reminders of the experiences and ordeals of Christ. Abstracted from the narrative, the list is impressive: Although Frodo voluntarily assumes the burden of the Ring, he feels as if "some other will" is using him (*FR* II, ii, 284). He has a last supper with his followers before setting out on his journey. He suffers five wounds, one a blow in the side with a spear, one a laceration with thorns. He has a moment in a garden where he tries to relinquish his burden and be released from his destiny. He undergoes temptation in the wilderness. He is betrayed by one of his followers. His way is dolorous, his ascent of the mountain painful; he carries a heavy load. His surrender of himself at the end is total.

Beyond these specifics, the character Tolkien has given Frodo fits the paradigm of Christ; he is certainly the most Christlike of all Tolkien's saviour figures. He is a beloved master, patient in suffering, stern in righteousness, forgiving of his enemies, or at least of the closest enemy—Gollum. He is a willing sacrifice. Both in terms of event and in terms of character, Frodo's story would seem to fit perfectly into the larger, Christian story. But herein lies Tolkien's strength as a myth maker and as a weaver of tales. For the events and the character cannot be divided from the narrative without doing damage to both the character and the story. Tolkien means to remind the reader, through Frodo, of Christ. But he just as surely means for his reader to be able to tell the difference between them. This is the strength of the narrative, and its poignance.

For the underlying purpose of the parallels is to underscore the fact that Frodo is not Christ, that he is (literally) too small for the burden he has to carry, that in the end he fails. By deliberately placing the burdens of Christ on the shoulders of someone who is not big enough to bear them, Tolkien makes his story immensely moving, resonant in its implications, and considerably more modern than we might at first expect. Unlike Earendil, unlike Gandalf, unlike Aragorn, Frodo is a failed hero, and as such he speaks directly to an age immersed in doubt, an age which wants belief but cannot trust it, an age which stumbles into disbelief at every turn of modern life.

But like Aragorn, Frodo fits a larger pattern, one which allies him with Christ but just as much with other, similar figures in the mythic past. For he too derives from the ancient hero tradition, and has significant similarities with the figure of the wounded king. Frodo's size and hobbit origins camouflage his archetypal characteristics, but they are as much a part of him as they are of Aragorn, and for the same reasons. Like Aragorn, Frodo is of mixed ancestry; through the fabulous Belladonna Took he has a strain of fairy, and so is parallel to half-elven Eärendil, to Aragorn, indeed to all the heroes of myth and legend who are born of a natural and supernatural union.

And, like Aragorn, Frodo is an avatar of the figure of the sacral king, a bringer of peace, prosperity, and fertility. His name is even more revealing of his function than is Gandalf's of his implicit characteristics. The name Frodo or Frodi is one prominent in northern European myth and legend. It is the name of several kings and heroes, the most notable of whom appears in the Prose *Edda* as a bringer of a time of peace and prosperity known as "Frodi's Peace," a time when men were so ungreedy and unwarlike that a gold ring lay unprotected on Gnita heath and no one presumed to take it. This King Frodi seems to be a counterpart of the Norse god Freyr, one of the oldest of the pagan fertility gods of northern Europe. One of Freyr's epithets is *inn froði* "the fruitful," and both figures may be aspects of the same principle (Ellis Davidson 103–4). The Norse word *froðr* usually translated "fruitful," or "wise," probably derives from the Indo-European root prăt-, "wise, well-traveled" (Walde-Pokorny II, 86) but during the Middle Ages was also associated with the principles expressed in the Indo-European root prī-, "to love," and both were associated with Freyr and Frodi.

It seems clear that Tolkien's choice of Frodo as the name of his hobbit-hero was deliberate and intended to associate Frodo with all these figures. But it is just as clear that the association is negative rather than positive, intended to bring poignance to Frodo's failure. For he is that most moving of hero types, one whose sacrifice benefits everyone but himself, one who, in saving the world (as Frodo does through Sam and Gollum) loses it. Aragorn the healer, Frodo the wounded figure, both evocative of Christ, share between them the renewal of Middle-earth.

Of all Tolkien's saviours, Frodo alone loses everything. He undergoes a spiritual death with no promise of rebirth. The parallel with Christ so movingly suggested breaks down at this point. Both Frodo and Christ offer themselves and are used. Christ emerges whole and transfigured. Frodo does not. He loses himself, loses his shadow, loses the Ring at the climactic moment at the Cracks of Doom where he succumbs to temptation (but after how long and desperate a struggle), and suddenly becomes sinning Adam, not redeeming Christ. Nothing is promised him in recompense, nothing given. He is mortal man who will die, not knowing what comes next.

Each of these figures falls short of the paradigm in some way, but precisely because they fall short, because they are part of Tolkien's own story and not of the Christian story, they can suggest the latter and enhance its meaning and largeness. The central event only happens once. And ultimately, Tolkien's mythology is not, as Lewis's emphatically is, a re-telling of the Judeo-Christian mythos. It is intended to complement Christianity, to translate its meaning but not its plot, into an imaginative world.

Tolkien seems to be suggesting that, Christ or no Christ, the light is there if one wants to find it. In his world the Fall, the separation from God, from the light, is a gradual process. It is a sequence of many individual decisions, each with its consequences, none irreversible. The process is continual, encompassing both fall and redemption as parts of a whole. We might say that

Tolkien's world is falling rather than fallen, that it is dynamic rather than static, and that, since it emphasizes transition rather than transaction, no one act will buy back all that has been lost.

Thus, by not retelling the events of the Christian story, Tolkien leaves his reader free to find them at will, free to make associations, apply interpretations, bring to bear on the story whatever seems personally most vital and immediate. Tolkien's mythos is a mirror, reflecting at a distance the themes and actions of many mythologies, but leaving at the center a space for his audience to see itself, and thus to participate in the story.

Part Three

Tolkien and His Century

Part Three, Tolkien and His Century, strives to bring mythology popularly viewed as medieval (or pseudo-medieval, if you dislike that sort of thing) into the twentieth century in which he lived and worked. "A Cautionary Tale" assesses the mythological value for a country torn by the two greatest wars of his century of Tolkien's dark and doom-laden "mythology for England" with its Elven wars and stories of unrelenting strife and suffering. "The Mind, the Tongue, and the Tale" puts Tolkien in the context of twentieth century developing language theory. "A Post-modern Medievalist" shows Tolkien using in *The Lord of the Rings* some surprisingly post-modern literary techniques such as archetypal displacement, self-referentiality, and meta-fiction which connect him (untypically) with John Fowles, and (unexpectedly) with the *Beowulf* poet. "Taking the Part of Trees" looks at Tolkien the ecologist, who turns out to be not quite as green as everybody would like him to be.

"Gilson, Smith, and Baggins" looks at Tolkien's life as well as his fiction, and the influence on *The Lord of the Rings* of his King Edward's School fellowship of the TCBS, and his experience of the loss of two of that fellowship in World War I. The next essay, "The Body in Question," continues along the same lines with a more focused look at the war-torn body of Frodo Baggins, pierced by a Morgul knife, poisoned by a giant spider, amputated by a crazed alter ego, and faded to the edge of transparency by the prolonged wearing of the Ring. Tolkien puts his hobbit hero through one physically and psychologically punishing ordeal after another but stubbornly refuses to ameliorate his pain, console him for his loss, or reward him for his sacrifice.

And finally, my foray into the world of Tolkien film, "A Distant Mirror," posits the circularity through which Tolkien's *The Lord of the Rings* led directly to George Lucas's *Star Wars* which led directly to Peter Jackson's *The Lord of the Rings* which now leads a new generation of readers back to the amazing and enduring book that started it all.

A Cautionary Tale

Tolkien's Mythology for England

With the considerable increase in published work by J.R.R. Tolkien subsequent to his death in 1973 and now augmented for good or ill by the popularity of the films based on his work, a fair amount of critical attention has been paid to his stated ambition to write what he intended to be a "mythology for England."[1] Both the extent to which his work actually qualifies as a mythology, and the ways in which it connects with English myth, legend, and history[2] have been subject to scrutiny. Taking as given both its status as an invented mythology and its connections, direct or oblique, with Tolkien's England, I want to explore what that mythology might reveal about how Tolkien saw his England at a particular moment in history, and what he might have wanted to tell it in mythological terms.

For all his reputation as a fantasist, Tolkien was a writer whose work was grounded in the upheavals, the confusions, and the uncertainties of the twentieth century in which he lived and wrote. It was a century torn by the two most widespread wars in history, haunted by both long after the fighting ceased. The first war, in which Tolkien saw service and lost within the space of a few weeks all but one of his closest friends, came perilously close to wiping out his generation. Certainly, it changed irrevocably the world in which he had grown up. Yet for all its disruption of a way of life, World War I accomplished surprisingly little except to pave the way for World War II.

Both wars, together with the uneasy peace that interrupted them, were the immediate external context for Tolkien's fiction, and it is in this context that I propose to consider it.[3] His major work, the Silmarillion—by which I mean the legendarium as a whole, including *The Lord of the Rings*[4]—was bracketed by these wars. It was conceived as the first one was getting under way, written largely in the period between the two, and for all practical purposes brought to a close not long after the finish of the second.[5] It reflects its time and circumstances in many ways, but chiefly because it is all about war. The last third of *The Hobbit* concerns the Battle of Five Armies and describes in remarkable political detail for a children's book the uneasy coalitions and alliances that make up both sides. *The Lord of the Rings* shows a world preparing for and engaging in major battles. *The Silmarillion* is focused on warfare of all kinds, from sustained campaigns to pitched battles to guerilla fighting.

If this is a mythology for England, it presents a picture of a culture in decline, torn by dissension and split by factions, a society perpetually at war with itself. Read in this light, Tolkien's work seems more like Orwell's *1984* than the furry-footed fantasy its detractors never cease to categorize and deride. Tracing an arc from the "Ainulindalë," or song of creation, to the destruction of the One Ring, the Scouring of the Shire, and the end of the Third Age of Middle-earth, Tolkien's history begins in imperfection and ends (or rather stops, for Tolkien never fully reached the end) with a decisive yet admittedly temporary defeat of the forces of evil. Along the way, much that is fair and wonderful passes forever, as Theoden says, out of Middle-earth.

The primary function of any mythology, real or feigned, is to mirror a culture to itself, giving its world a history and its people an identity, as well as connecting both to the supernatural or transcendent. The stories of gods and heroes that make up the bulk of any primary mythology reflect the worldview of the society that generates them, and interpret the contending forces that society perceives as governing its world. True of any primary mythos, this is no less true of Tolkien's secondary, invented mythology. What, then, is the worldview of this mythology and how do the contending forces play out? Who are the gods and heroes of his invented world, and how do they enact its story?

Tolkien borrowed from the myths of northwestern Europe for the flavor of his stories, and much has been written about his debt to existing mythologies from Scandinavia to Sumer. Nevertheless, he wrote to Father Robert Murray that *The Lord of the Rings* was "a fundamentally religious and Catholic work" (*Letters* 172), and one might assume that nothing in the legendarium as a whole would contradict that. Rather surprisingly, a quick comparison between the two reveals some fundamental differences, and not just on the level of doctrine or creed. Tolkien's is a far darker world than that envisioned by Christianity, and falls short of the promise and the hope that the older story holds out. Unlike the Judeo-Christian mythos with which it is so often compared, and which tells of a world fallen through human willfulness and saved by sacrifice, Tolkien's mythos as a whole begins with a fall long before humanity comes on the scene. He wrote of his story:

I suppose a difference between this Myth and what may be perhaps called Christian mythology is this. In the latter the Fall of Man is subsequent to and a consequence (thought not a necessary consequence) of the 'Fall of the Angels': a rebellion of created free will at a higher level than Man; but it is not clearly held (and in many versions not held at all) that this affected the 'World' in its nature: evil was brought in from outside, by Satan. In this [i.e., Tolkien's own] Myth the rebellion of created free-will precedes creation of the world (Eä); and Eä has in it, subcreatively introduced, evil, rebellions, discordant elements of its own nature already when the *Let it Be* was spoken. The Fall, or corruption, therefore, of all things in it and all inhabitants of it, was a possibility if not inevitable. (*Letters* 286–87)

Thus original sin (if one may borrow that term) enters the world in the very process of its coming to be, when the melodic theme that is the metaphor for creation is distorted by the clamorous and discordant counter-theme of the rebel demiurge Melkor. The resultant Music sets the tone for all that is to follow.

The supreme godhead, Eru/Ilúvatar, who both proposes the theme and conducts the Music, is neither the Judaic God of Hosts who alternately punishes and rewards his people, nor the traditional Christian God of love and forgiveness. Rather, he is a curiously remote and for the most part inactive figure, uninvolved, with the exception of one cataclysmic moment, in the world he has conceived. The lesser demiurgic powers, the Valar, have only partial comprehension of the world they have helped to make. The primary heroes, the Elves, are gifted beings caught in a web of pride, power, and deceit—largely of their own weaving—that hampers and constrains every effort they make to get free of it. The secondary heroes, Men, are courageous but shortsighted blunderers with but little sense of history and even less comprehension of their place in the larger scheme of things.

The whole narrative of the Silmarillion is a story of enterprise and creativity gone disastrously wrong. From the first rebellious theme of Melkor, Tolkien's invented world is characterized by strife and dissension wherever there should be peace and harmony. Melkor's intervention in the Music results in contending themes whose two interactive forces of discord and harmony thereafter operate together as Fate. Within this fate, the greatest of the Elves, the craftsman-figure Fëanor, achieves a transcendent creation, the Silmarils, yet his very creativity leads directly to his downfall. These great gems, housing the last of the light, are stolen by Melkor to become the Jewels in the Crown. Instead of shedding light, they engender darkness. They are the proximate causes of pride, possessiveness, and lust. Obsessive desire for them leads Fëanor to the Oath which binds him and his sons to pursue anyone who holds a Silmaril. This is the Fall of the Elves, resulting in theft, betrayal, kinslaying, and war; and finally, in the death—without ever regaining the Silmarils—of Fëanor himself.

Even after Fëanor's death, the story of the Elves in Middle-earth is a history of contention centering on the establishment and defense of beleaguered strongholds such as Gondolin and Doriath and Nargothrond. It is an account of successive battles—Dagor-nuin-Giliath, The Battle under Stars, Dagor Aglareb, The Glorious Battle, Dagor Bragollach, The Battle of Sudden Flame, and Nirnaeth Arnoediad, The Battle of Unnumbered Tears. These battle-names are strung on Elven history like beads on a string. Some of the battles they win and some they lose, but there is never a decisive victory, and all are part of the struggle that shapes their lives in Middle-earth.

Tolkien's Men fare little better than his Elves. Of their major heroes, one—Beren—loses his hand in obtaining a Silmaril for the Elven king Thingol, who in his turn is first corrupted and then killed by his desire to possess it. The price Beren pays for the Silmaril seems to have bought little more in the end than the price paid by the thousands of Tolkien's generation who lost their lives on the Somme in 1916 in "the war to end all wars." Another of his fictive heroes—and in terms of characterization one far more memorable than Beren—is the hapless Túrin Turambar, "Master of Fate, by Fate Mastered," a man of good intentions who careens from disaster to disaster and bad choice to bad choice, finally killed by his own sword after his belated realization of all the havoc his actions have wrought. The story of Túrin was one of the earliest to take shape in Tolkien's legendarium, and his desire to write it goes back to his discovery while still in school of Kullervo, the equally hapless and doomed hero from the Finnish epic *Kalevala*. That he gave Kullervo a formative role in his mythology for England may very well say something about Tolkien's notion of what England might need to know about itself, but it does not suggest that he had much hope for the future of his country.

And finally, there is the hero most typical of the twentieth century, the little man Frodo Baggins, struggling his slow, painful way to Mordor, falling more and more under the spell of the Ring, and finally losing himself to it utterly at the Cracks of Doom. What Tolkien does to Frodo provides the bleakest outcome of the entire history. Frodo is infected with the darkness of the Morgul knife, stung by Shelob, and maimed by Gollum in cruel and even less rewarded replication of Beren's lost hand. The peace he has won for Middle-earth is not his to enjoy, and he gets no recognition of his achievement on his return to the Shire he saved. He is like the thousands of returning servicemen from both wars—from any war, really—who come back to a world that has no way to understand where they have been or what they have experienced.

In Tolkien's war and for decades after it was called "shell shock." Now we call it "post traumatic stress syndrome" and we still have no remedy for it. Frodo loses his finger, his home, and his innocence. Worst of all, he loses the Ring he carried for so long and which has left its ineradicable mark on him, no less indelible even for having been destroyed. "It is gone forever," he tells Sam. "and now all is dark and empty" (*RK* VI, ix, 304). This greatest loss—a deprivation at once emotional, psychological, metaphoric, and symbolic—cannot be made up, and Frodo is bereft of more than a finger.

If through his mythology Tolkien was trying to show his country something (and I think he was) what was it he wanted the England of the twentieth century, a country battered by two disastrous wars, marked by post-war austerity, ultimately bereft of its imperial possessions, to know about itself? I have called this essay "A Cautionary Tale" on the model of Hilaire Belloc's *Cautionary Verses,* one of which advises children to "always keep a-hold of Nurse, for fear of finding something worse" (Belbe, 12). Tolkien's advice, put more dramatically, though somewhat less poetically, would have been not to keep a-hold, but be able to let go. It is the advice of Ulmo the Vala to Turgon the Elf, "Love not too well the work of thy hands and the devices of thy heart" (*Silm* 125). It is just what Frodo cannot not do, nor Fëanor, nor Thingol, nor the Elven kingdoms of Middle-earth. It is advice no nation is likely voluntarily to take to heart and put into practice. Nevertheless, it is good advice to any nation at any time.

The Mind, the Tongue, and the Tale

A brief statement in Manuscript A, the 1939 first draft of Tolkien's essay "On Fairy-stories," declares unequivocally that "Mythology is language and language is mythology" (*TOFS* 181). If I ever put a bumper sticker on my car, it's going to say that. No modifiers, no explanations, just seven words that convey Tolkien's bedrock belief about words and what they do. Mythology does not *use* language; it *is* language—in shape and sound and meaning. Language does not *express* mythology; it *is* mythology—on the hoof, in action, alive, and moving. In this sense, the whole text of "On Fairy-stories" is an extended gloss on that statement. The next sentence in the draft, "The mind, and the tongue, and the tale, are coeval" (181), adds what is implicit in the bumper sticker, the perceiving human consciousness that is the necessary link between mythology and language. The 1934 B draft, which became the published essay, dropped the bumper sticker but kept the mind, the tongue, and the tale (221) and addressed the implied question: "To ask what is the origin of stories, is to ask what is the origin of the mind, and of language" (218).

Taking "language" to mean words in a meaningful pattern and "mythology" to mean the worldview of a culture carried by its stories of gods and heroes, we can read these statements as variations on the theme that language, stories, and storytellers together make up an interlocking, interdependent system. There is no story without a teller, no teller without a language, no language without something to talk about. Without a world to report on, and without the people who live in that world to do the reporting, language has no use. Tolkien's description in the same essay of Faërie as containing "the seas, the sun, the moon, the sky; and the earth, and all things that are in it: tree and bird, water and stone, wine and bread, and ourselves, mortal men" (32) illustrates the process. The listed items are the phenomena of a world, brought into being by the words that name them.

Though it is one of the bases of his creative method, the idea did not originate with Tolkien. It comes from a particular school of linguistic thought that developed out of nineteenth-century German romanticism, found a home in comparative philology and mythology, and was expressed in the ideas of Owen Barfield, a philosopher of language and part of the circle of Oxford friends that included Tolkien and called itself the Inklings. Barfield's seminal work, *Poetic Diction*, was the outgrowth of his exploration into the function of language as developing human consciousness from a primal unity in which one word could express a cluster of interrelated perceptions—what we might now call metaphoric—to an increasingly fragmented but commensurately more precise vocabulary in which each narrower word further refined and isolated meaning. A development, we might say, from the language of poetry to the language of science.

Barfield was part of a current of thought taking shape in the early and mid-twentieth century. In 1925 the German philosopher Ernst Cassirer posited in *Sprache und Mythos,* translated into English as *Language and Myth,* that "[a]ll theoretical cognition takes its departure from a world already preformed by language" (28), and that "[t]he difference between . . . languages . . . is not a matter of different sounds and marks, but of different world conceptions" (31). "[E]ach language" he said, "draws a magic circle round the people to whom it belongs, a circle from which there is no escape save by stepping out of it into another" (9).

In the late twenties, thirties, and forties of the twentieth century the idea was further explored by Edward Sapir and Benjamin Lee Whorf, both of them linguists, anthropologists, and philosophers, who over the course of those decades developed what has come to be known as the Sapir-Whorf hypothesis: the proposition that the traditional stories of a culture—its history, percepts, and concepts as encoded in its language—determine the speakers' cognition of their experienced world. We know our environment through the words that create our perceptions of it. From this it followed logically that different languages containing different words for the "same" things encode different perceptions and thus create different realities, different worlds.

All these men, Barfield, Cassirer, Sapir, Whorf, and Tolkien, were pursuing the same line of thought, that language is as much the creator of phenomena as it is the response to them. It was Tolkien, however, who put these ideas to work by using them to create his world of Middle-earth. Closest to him in time and place, Barfield's work had the most influence on Tolkien, who said of Barfield's concept of original semantic unity that it modified his whole outlook on language (Carpenter *Inklings,* 42). Not redirected it, let us note, but modified, perhaps refined, it. Tolkien was already going in the same direction, but Barfield gave him a push. In his later years Tolkien was a philosopher of language, as his more explicitly theoretical post–*Lord of the Rings* writings from the sixties show. In those years he was moving, we might say, from the language of poetry to the language of science. But in his creative period, the years that gave us *The Silmarillion* and *The Hobbit* and *The Lord of the Rings,* he worked on the principle that poetry and science are not "opposite poles" but parts of the same thing. What he called his "scientifically deduced" invented languages were integrally related to his passion for myth and fairy tale (*Letters* 143).

The fairy-story essay, of course, enters fairly late in the game, for by 1939 Tolkien had already been putting these principles to work in his fiction for twenty years, beginning with the "Lost Tales" that became *The Silmarillion* and continuing into *The Hobbit* and *The Lord of the Rings.* He began with a paradigm somewhat more robust than Sapir-Whorf (but still open to question), the hypothesis that a Proto-Indo-European language was the ancestor of a dispersed and divergent family of modern and archaic Indo-European languages (excluding Finnish and Hungarian). This gave him the model for his Elves and their primitive Proto-Elvish language, from which descended a dozen or so Elven languages, chief of which are Quenya and Sindarin.

But Tolkien did more than model the Indo-European language theory; he dramatized it. Starting with proto-Elven Qenya ("speech") he divided his Quendi ("Speakers") and their languages by a linguistic and geographic and ultimately political fragmentation and dispersal into linguistic and cultural/political subgroups. Out of the original Quendi, set off by prefixes, came the Calaquendi ("Light-elves") and the Moriquendi ("Dark-elves"); from the Calaquendi came the Vanyar ("Fair-elves"), the Noldor ("Wise-elves"), and the Teleri ("Late-comers"), while the Moriquendi acquired a variety of sub-names such as Avari ("Unwilling"), Úmanyar ("Non-Aman"), and Sindar ("Grey-elves"). These are all names for perceptions of and by self and other, and as those perceptions grew and changed through experience, so did the names.

Elven migration is a macro rather than a micro example. A closer look at some individual names and experiences from the many Tolkien scattered so lavishly throughout *The Lord of the Rings* will show how he intended the name-thing partnership to work. I'll cite examples of different ways Tolkien saw it working, examples that trace an arc from a preverbal period through the development, decline, and even disappearance of words over time. My first example will illustrate how the nature of the thing imposes limitations on the word. My second example will show how experience and word interconnect and develop each other. The third example will demonstrate how changed experience can keep the word but obscure the usage. My fourth example will show how time can shorten both shape and sound and in so doing erode the meaning. And the last example will illustrate dramatically how the disappearance of the thing can deprive the language of the word.

I'll start with some lines of dialogue I think everyone will recognize. In chapter 7 of *The Lord of the Rings*, "In the House of Tom Bombadil," Frodo, apologizing for what he fears might be a "foolish" question, asks Goldberry, "Who is Tom Bombadil?" (*FR* I, vii, 135). Now this is not a foolish question at all. It is in fact a very good question both within the fiction, where the hobbits are understandably puzzled by the appearance of this extraordinary creature, and external to it, where readers are equally puzzled. It is one of the most frequently asked questions on *Lord of the Rings* chat rooms and posts, and one that my students have been asking me for thirty years. Goldberry's answer to Frodo's question, "He is," has misled many readers to relate her two words to the Biblical "I am" and take them for an allusion to God. Careful reading and observance of the comma after "is" show that they are not, for both Goldberry and the sentence continue with what Tolkien explained in a letter was "the correct answer." This is "He is, as you have seen him." Tom is *sui generis*. He is a noun that does not take a modifier. Goldberry adds ("as a concession," says Tolkien [*Letters* 192]) a statement of *what* Tom is. "He is the Master of wood, water, and hill." Tolkien's word "concession" suggests Goldberry can see that Frodo is not quite up to the metaphysic of unique existence.

Not only that, but he misunderstands her use of the word "Master," confusing it with domination and possession. "Then all this strange land belongs to him?" he asks. "No indeed!" she answers emphatically. "The trees and the grasses and all things growing or living in the land belong each to themselves. Tom Bombadil is the Master" (135). She does not explain what she means; she simply repeats the key word, *Master*. For clarification we must go again to Tolkien's *Letters*, where he writes that "He [Tom] is *master* in a peculiar way: he has no fear and no desire of possession or domination at all" (192). It seems clear that Tolkien is using the word in the sense of "authority" or "'teacher," its original Latin usage (definition 10 in the *OED:* "a teacher, a tutor, preceptor"). That says *what* but not *who* and doesn't answer Frodo's question.

A few pages on in that same chapter, Frodo, trying again to get a straight answer, asks Tom directly, "Who are you, Master?" Like many good teachers, Tom answers the question with a question: "Don't you know my name yet? That's the only answer" (142). Tolkien explained in a letter that "Goldberry and Tom are referring to the mystery of *names*" (*Letters* 191), though we must admit that referring to something as a "mystery" is not much of an explanation. The mystery deepens at the Council of Elrond, where Tom acquires several additional names that also say *what* but not *who* he is (*FR* II, ii, 278). Elrond calls him "Iarwain Ben-adar," oldest and fatherless, a literal translation of Noldorin/Sindarin *iarwain,* "old-young" (Hammond and Scull 128), and *pen/ben,* "without," + *adar,* "father." The Dwarves call him "Forn," which is an actual Icelandic word: *forn,* meaning "old" in the sense of ancient past (*An Icelandic-English Dictionary*). Men of the North call him "Orald" (cp. German *uralt,* "immemorial, hoary, very old"). In his "Guide to the Names in *The Lord of the Rings*" (first published in Jared Lobdell's *A Tolkien Compass* in 1975, and republished in Hammond and Scull's *The Lord of the Rings: A Reader's Companion* in 2005), Tolkien noted that "*Forn* is actually the Scandinavian word for "(belonging to) ancient (days)," and *Orald* is an Old English word for "very ancient" (Lobdell 171; Hammond and Scull, 761).

Since all these words express essentially the same idea, it seems clear that Tom's additional names add only a common acknowledgment of age to our knowledge of who he is. But "is," as in Goldberry's initial statement, is the operative word. As the oldest being, Tom comes before history and therefore cannot be related to or associated with anything but himself, his own existence. Tom is pre-language and therefore not formed by language, saying of himself, "Tom was here before the river and the trees; Tom remembers the first raindrop and the first acorn. He made paths before the Big People, and saw the little People arriving. . . . He knew the dark under the stars when it was fearless—before the Dark Lord [not Sauron, but Melkor] came from Outside" (*FR* I, vii, 142). Like Väinämöinen, the "eternal singer" of the Finnish *Kalevala,* Tom is his world's oldest sentient being. He is fatherless, self-begotten, preexistent. He simply "is."

Having given an answer that penetrates the mystery but does not explain it, Tom then turns Frodo's own question back on him. "Tell me, who are you, alone, yourself and nameless?" (*FR* I, vii, 142). Without his name Frodo is not just "nameless"; he is "alone," solitary, lacking any point of reference. For contrast we can look at Bilbo's introduction of himself to Smaug in *The Hobbit* as he recites his multiple identity-conferring names: clue-finder, web-cutter, stinging fly, and (moving to uppercase) Ringwinner, Luckwearer, and Barrel-rider (*H* 190). It is clear to the reader that in his own estimation Bilbo has come a long way from what Gloin described as a "little fellow bobbing and puffing on the mat" back in Bag End (*H* 24). These names are performative, describing actions arising out of specific situations. Bilbo's new names are what he is, and that is not who he used to be. They are what he *does*. While Smaug cautions the cocky, self-promoting hobbit not to let his imagination (we might say his developing ego) run away with him, the idea seems to be that there is an umbilical connection between word and thing (or person), and that each in a sense creates the other.

My second example comes from Treebeard the Ent, one of Tolkien's most profound commentators on language, who carries the interconnection of name and experience several steps further. First he tells Merry and Pippin to be more cautious about letting out their "own right names" (*TT* III, iv, 68). This follows the ancient notion that the connection between the name and the thing means that possession of one brings with it power over the other (which is Bilbo's real reason for all those hyphenated epithets in his conversation with Smaug). Next the old Ent announces that he is not going to tell the hobbits *his* name because it would take too long. His name is "growing all the time," he says, because it is "like a story" (*TT* III, iv, 68). In fact, it is a story and as such is a perfect illustration of the idea that language, mind, and storytelling are parts of the same whole. The Entish language is agglutinative, meaning that words, which are actually long phrases and whole sentences, can be formed by adding a cluster of affixes to a base word. We have only a few examples, one of which is *a-lalla-lalla-rumba-kamanda-lind-or-burúmë,* which Treebeard explains (it is not really a translation) as "the thing we are on, where I stand and look out on fine mornings, and think about the Sun, and the grass beyond the wood, and the horses, and the clouds, and the unfolding of the world" (*TT* III, iv, 68–69).

Pippin's zippy one-word translation, "hill," and Merry's suggestions of "shelf" and "step" are good for a laugh in the dynamic of the scene, but they underscore the difference in perception that for Tolkien is the basis of differences in language. The hobbits are "hasty" folk, little in stature, quick in speech, and their language (for all that Tolkien explained their vocabulary as translation into the Common Speech) matches their personality. "Frightfully treeish" is Merry's two-word description of Fangorn Forest. Treebeard's extended term encompasses a world of perception over time, his experience of the hill, the weather, his response to sun, grass, horses, clouds, and the "unfolding of the world" to his perceiving eyes. We can say with some truth that Ents and hobbits live in different worlds, or that the world "unfolds" to their eyes in different ways. The Ents' language, like the trees themselves, is slow growing, developing over time; it has a core like a tree's heartwood to which rings are added year by year as the tree grows.

But the process has its opposite in the history of the world of Middle-earth, for language can diminish as well as grow, it can cast off as well as accumulate. This leads me and Treebeard to my third example, which involves the original full name for what readers of *The Lord of the Rings* know as

Lórien or Lothlórien, *Laurelindórenan lindelorendor malinorélion ornema-*
lin (TT, IV, iv, 70). Tolkien's linguistic treatment of the name and its relation
to its referent, the Elven stronghold of Galadriel and Celeborn, illustrate
both the agglutinative linguistic principle and its opposite process, an ongoing shortening and limitation of expression, removal rather than accre-
tion. The full name means "the valley where the trees in a golden light sing
musically, a land of music and dreams, there are yellow trees there, it is a
tree-yellow land" (*Letters* 308). Unlike the word for "hill," it is Entish only in
structure and perception; the words themselves are Quenya. The shortened
form, *Laurelinórenan*, means "Land of the Valley of the Singing Gold," while
the even shorter name, *Lóthlorien*, a Quenya-Sindarin hybrid, translates as
"Dreamflower." *Lórien*, the name by which it is best known and most often
referred to in *The Lord of the Rings*, is shorter still. It means simply "Dream,"
the proper name of Lórien the Vala of dreams, and as such is inevitably opposed to "waking," which we can read as "reality."

This progressive shrinking of the name becomes an indicator of Lórien's
regressively receding relationship to Time and Change. Lórien is out of time
in both senses of that expression. Its proper time has run out so that in the
natural course of history it would have decayed. But it has not; it is outside Time, artificially preserved, the experience of time slowed almost to a
standstill by Galadriel's elven ring. "Perhaps they are right," says Treebeard.
"Maybe it is fading, not growing." He adds, "They are falling rather behind
the world in there, I guess" (*TT* III, iv, 70). He is correct. Lórien is falling behind the times, slipping backward into the past. From his perspective on the
Great River of time, Frodo sees it "like a bright ship masted with enchanted
trees" (*FR* II, viii 393), a "living vision of that which has already been left far
behind by the flowing streams of Time" (*FR* II, viii, 389).

Looking forward rather than backward, Appendix F of *The Lord of the
Rings* supplies the literal translation of another of Treebeard's names for
Lórien: Quenya *Taurelilómëa-tumbalemorna Tumbaletaurëa Lómëanor,*
which Tolkien translates literally as "Forestmanyshadowed-deepvalleyblack
Deepvalleyforested Gloomyland" and paraphrases loosely as "there is a
black shadow in the deep dales of the forest" (*RK*, Appendix F 409). Here
the process of naming becomes almost predictive, a foreshadowing of what
will become of Lórien in the course of time. Worth noting here are the comments Tolkien made in his letters about the Elves and Lórien. He called his
Elves "embalmers" trying to stop change (*Letters* 197), "as if a man were to
hate a very long book still going on, and wished to settle down in a favourite
chapter" (*Letters* 236).

The operative—and damning—term, of course, is "embalmers," with its
clear connotations of preserving the appearance of life in the face of death,

holding on to something when its time has passed. It is significant, I think, that these explanations are not within the work itself, but external to it. While they are derived from it, they are subsequent to it and in a completely different mode. They cannot be part of it, for they would destroy what they explained. My point is that the most dramatic conveyance of what time is doing to Lórien comes through the succession of words Tolkien used to describe, not to explain, it—words intended to show process, to picture time in action.

My fourth example involves the somewhat puzzling episode in which Gandalf misinterprets the inscription on the Doors of Moria, *pedo mellon a minno*, as "Speak, friend, and enter" (*FR* II, iv, 318). After faithfully and fruitlessly following these instructions, he suddenly arrives at the correct reading, "Say 'Friend' and enter," without any visible clue, his only explanation being that "Merry, of all people, was on the right track" (*FR* II, iv, 321). Merry was the only one of the company to ask what the words meant, and the key is that the same sentence can be susceptible of different meanings, an insight that anticipates Derrida and deconstruction by several decades. In Gandalf's two successive Common Speech (English) translations, this difference is conveyed by changes in punctuation, the commas surrounding the word "friend" in the first translation suggesting that it is direct address, their removal in the second turning the word "friend" into a password. The attendant shift from "Speak" to "Say" (words often interchangeable) underscores the slipperiness of language and its dependence on context for meaning. "Those were happier times," says Gandalf, contrasting the past, when the words were inscribed and Dwarves and Elves were on better terms, with the story's present "suspicious days" (*FR* II, iv, 322).

My final example comes from *The Hobbit* and gives us another illustration of Tolkien's philosophy of language, that loss of the thing leads to loss of the experience of the thing, and consequently to loss of the words for both thing and experience. Tolkien actually referred to this example (again obliquely and without explanation) in a letter to C. A. Furth of Allen & Unwin. "The only philological remark (I think) in *The Hobbit* is . . . an odd mythological way of referring to linguistic philosophy, and a point that will (happily) be missed by any who have not read Barfield (few have) and probably by those who have" (*Letters* 22). This occurs in chapter 12 of *The Hobbit*, "Inside Information," and describes Bilbo's reaction, both emotional and physical, to his first sight of the dragon. "To say that Bilbo's breath was taken away is no description at all. There are no words left to express his staggerment, since Men changed the language that they learned of Elves in the days when all the world was wonderful" (*H* 184).

The reference to Barfield is explicit evidence that Tolkien had taken Barfield's ideas to heart and to paper. Moreover, it is worth noting that Tolkien has had to invent a new word, *staggerment,* to express what there are "no words left to express." Both the nonce-word and the linguistic deficiency for which it cannot compensate result from the fact that what produced the lost words—the visceral shock engendered by catching sight of a dragon in all his fearsome glory—is no longer available to the dragon-deprived experience of Men in these degenerate modern times.

In his groundbreaking essay *"Beowulf:* The Monsters and the Critics," Tolkien wrote that "The significance of a myth is not easily to be pinned on paper by analytical reasoning [*pace* Sapir, Whorf, Cassirer, even Barfield]. It is at its best when it is presented by a poet who feels rather than makes explicit what his theme portends; who presents it incarnate in the world of history and geography, as our poet has done" (*MC* 15). What Tolkien praised the poet for doing in *Beowulf* he has himself done in *The Lord of the Rings* and *The Hobbit.* Rather than make explicit, he has felt, and in so doing has made his audience feel, the significance of his myth, illustrating rather than explaining what his theme portends and presenting it incarnate with its own history and geography in his world of Middle-earth.

To sum up: in Tolkien's work mythology is language and language is mythology and both are dynamic and ongoing processes. He was a practitioner, not a theorist. Tom Bombadil, Treebeard the Ent, Lórien/Lothlórien, Merry Brandybuck, and Bilbo Baggins, each in a different way practices language as process, showing (1) how the thing imposes limitations on the word (Tom); (2) how words and meanings assemble themselves over time (Treebeard); (3) how both word and meaning can disassemble themselves over time, shrinking as things change (or, in the case of Lórien, resist change); (4) how the same words in the same order can convey different meanings (Merry); and (5) how loss of the thing results in loss of the word (Bilbo). Many more examples can be found throughout the books, but I hope these have provided evidence that in the end, Tolkien's philosophy was grounded in his practice, in his words, just as his practice, his words, was the vehicle for his philosophy.

A Post-modern Medievalist

Like so many words we take for granted, the word *medieval* can mean different things to different people and in different contexts. If we say, "the stained glass is medieval," that evokes one image. If we say, "the plumbing is medieval," that evokes quite another. Just so, in the context of the work of J.R.R. Tolkien, and in particular of *The Lord of the Rings,* we should be both cautious and careful about what we mean by *medieval* and where and how we apply it to so rich and various a work. Tolkien's book is something of a chameleon; it will take on whatever literary hue best blends with its readers' assumptions. If you want fantasy, it is fantasy, replete with wizards and dungeons and dragons and fantastical invented creatures such as hobbits. If you want epic, it's epic, with battles galore, banners flying, and swords flashing, not to mention axes and spears and bows and arrows. If your taste is for romance, this is a classic journey into faery lands forlorn, and you can hear the horns of elfland faintly blowing. If your preferred genre is fairy tale, that is what you get: a brave and modest little hero, a magical ring of invisibility, supernatural helpers, spells, and incantations. If you see the book from any one of a number of the conventional medieval literary perspectives, you can find material in the text to support your view.

I am my own worst example, for over the course of nearly fifty years I have seen it as all of the above and more. When I first discovered *The Lord of the Rings* in the winter of 1957, before I ever knew who J.R.R. Tolkien was, what he taught, or where he taught it, I was struck by what seemed to me then its strongly medieval flavor. I had recently taken a course in translating *Beowulf,* and the correspondences I saw between the Anglo-Saxon language, customs, architecture, and verse forms—especially the verse forms—occurring in that poem and those of the culture of Rohan were unmistakable. A decade and a half later, as part of a course in modern fantasy I began to teach *The Lord of the Rings*. I made it my purpose in life to educate the untutored general reader in the medieval and mythic aspects of Tolkien's work, its epic and romance and fairy tale underpinnings.

Thus, the Rohirrim were simply Anglo-Saxons transplanted straight from *Beowulf* to Middle-earth; Isengard and Mordor were obviously the Tolkienian versions of Celtic Waste Lands; Gandalf was a combination Merlin/Odin figure; Sting recalled Excalibur, and Narsil/Anduril recalled Gram, the broken and re-forged sword of the Völsungs. Boromir was an epic hero; Aragorn a Healing King; while Eowyn's crush on him was a clear echo of Malory's Maid of Astolat and her infatuation with Lancelot. The Woses of Druadan forest were typical medieval Wild Men; and my Frodo staggered under the combined burden of being a fairy tale hero, a Miraculous Child, and a fertility figure. I wasn't wrong. But I was only partly right.

What I was not seeing, because at the time it didn't suit my purpose, was the demonstrably non-medieval forest that surrounded without obscuring these undeniably medieval trees, the great stone city of Gondor; the nostalgic Shire of Tolkien's own Warwickshire childhood with its Hardyesque inhabitants good and bad; the 1920's reference slipped in with the hyphenate Sackville-Bagginses, carrying echoes of Vita Sackville-West and the modernist literary lights of Bloomsbury. (Okay, this last is a joke, but it is a modern joke, and it puts a spin on the Sackville-Bagginses that no medieval author would recognize.) Nor was I sufficiently willing to acknowledge that Isengard was a twentieth-century military-industrial complex, nor that Saruman used some ominously modern political rhetoric, or that there was a perceptible whiff of Nazi-like annexation in the takeover of the Shire by Sharkey and his gang. And when Tolkien's *Letters* were published in 1981, I read with considerable surprise what he wrote to a correspondent, Rhona Beare, in 1958, "[t]he Númenorians of Gondor [are] . . . best pictured in Egyptian terms" (*Letters*, 281). He illustrated this with a sketch that depicts something remarkably like the high-peaked white war crown of Upper Egypt under the pharaohs. That's one I suspect few readers imagined when they first tried to picture Gondor.

Nonetheless, such eclecticism is typical of Tolkien's sweeping approach to history and to the cultures of his Middle-earth. His Elves may use longbows, and his Dwarves protect themselves with chain mail and fight with axes, but his orcs make use of explosives, and they use flame-throwers against their enemies. To underscore this and make sure we get the point that Saruman is waging technological war, Tolkien has Pippin vividly describe one of the most horrific deaths in *The Lord of the Rings,* that of the "very tall handsome Ent" Beechbone at the Battle of Isengard, who, "got caught in a spray of some liquid fire and burned like a torch: a horrible sight" (*TT* III, ix, 173). To be sure, both explosives and liquid fire were used in the ancient world, most specifically by the Romans, but the use of both died out before the Middle Ages.

To most modern readers the spray of liquid fire would evoke recognizably modern technology, and typically destructive technology at that. The effect achieved in the scene Pippin describes is shockingly realistic, deriving as it surely does not wholly from Tolkien's knowledge of history, but also from his personal knowledge of World War I. There is a bizarre hybrid touch here, a deliberate mix of the realistic and the fantastic, each supporting the other. This inhuman weapon is used on a *tree,* something made of wood and therefore conventionally suitable for burning, but a tree which at the same time is a *person,* a "tall handsome" sentient being with a proper name, for whom burning "like a torch" is a hideous death. The combination adds both dreadful realism and weird fantasy to the scene; hence, Pippin's feeling comment that it is "a horrible sight."

When all these elements, not just collectively un-medieval but chronologically disparate among themselves, are acknowledged as being part of the fabric of *The Lord of the Rings* it becomes more difficult to characterize the book as being of any period except its own, the Third Age of Tolkien's distinctive Middle-earth. Even the thematic elements we most confidently label "medieval," the doomed-warrior heroism, the quest, the sacrifice, even the great Ring itself, have correspondences in the mythologies of the ancient world that antedate the Middle Ages, and transcend their medieval versions to be at once more archaic and more modern. A contemporary, retro-pre-Raphaelite, nouveau William Morris kind of fascination with medievalism may have had some hand in beguiling us into a tendency to lump all aspects of Tolkien's Middle-earth together under the umbrella-term "medieval" or "pseudo-medieval."

It is my belief that Tolkien would have disapproved of such lumping. As evidence, I offer that same 1958 letter to Rhona Beare wherein, speaking in terms of costume, he stated unequivocally, "The Rohirrim were not 'mediaeval', in our sense. The styles of the Bayeux Tapestry . . . fit them well enough" (*Letters,* 280–81). Granted, we do not know exactly the precise sense in which Ms. Beare was using the term (perhaps asking what kind of battle dress the Men of Rohan wore), but we can infer from Tolkien's denial that he was correcting her. Given that the language, customs, and culture of the Rohirrim are not just generalized medieval Anglo-Saxon but are particularized and localized as Mercian[1], and that the central kingdom of medieval Anglo-Saxon

England was known as Mercia, we might legitimately ask what he meant by "our sense" of medieval.

He gives a fair answer in the same letter, where he calls Pauline Baynes's illustrated knights in *Farmer Giles of Ham* "King-Arthurish," explaining that he means by that term belonging to "our 'mythological' Middle Ages which blends unhistorically styles and details ranging over 500 years, and most of which did not of course exist in the Dark Ages of c. 500 A.D." (*Letters*, 280n.). At the very least, he seems to be suggesting, we ought to subdivide *medieval* into "early," middle," and "late," or even "high." The "ish" suffix pejoratively appended to "King Arthur" suggests that he meant to refer to the kind of a-chronological treatment the Arthur story has received from some of its modern re-tellers and illustrators, a vague pastiche of styles and times, a Middle Ages not just mythologized but stretched and pulled into some sort of "one size fits all" blanket concept. Perhaps in calling *The Lord of the Rings* "medieval," not just Rhona Beare, but other readers as well are unhistorically blending styles and details ranging over 500 years. Or more.

I would say yes, we are doing just that. I would go even further to maintain that in addition we are confusing the author with the work to the detriment of both. Because we know that Tolkien was a scholar of medieval literature and language, because we have his learned essays on two of the great medieval poems, *Beowulf* and *Sir Gawain and the Green Knight* (poems themselves possibly separated by more than Tolkien's "500 years"), as well as his great essay "On Fairy-stories," we assume that he must necessarily have written his fiction in the same mode in which he studied and taught. We are partly right. He did say on more than one occasion that his typical response to reading a myth or a fairy story was to try to write something of his own in the same mode.

Thus, he wrote in modern English language and Old English alliterative metre a "Fall of Arthur." Thus, he wrote a Völsung cycle based on poems in the Icelandic Elder *Edda*, again using modern English but cast in fornyrðislag, a meter used in the Eddaic poems. His last-published story, *Smith of Wootton Major*, is a fairy story in the truest sense of that term. Yes, there is a clearly "medieval" (in the most general sense) flavour to certain aspects of the *Lord of the Rings*. Yet even in that massive work, he was not always recreating a particular past in subject matter or style or tone. He was no more stuck in the Middle Ages than he was stuck in the twentieth century, and to be fair to him and his work, we have to see him situated in both.

Let us start with subject matter. His book prominently features a Quest, described by some enthusiasts as an "anti-Grail" quest, though that only tells what it isn't, not what it is. But the book's closest analogue to the Queste of the Sankgreal in Sir Thomas Malory's Arthurian story (published in 1485 and

that is Renaissance, not by any stretch the Middle Ages) is the journey of Sam
and Frodo in Mordor, which is different in important respects from that para-
digmatic quest. Tolkien's quest (we should probably call it "journey") features
ordinary people, not knights, as does Malory's; his heroes fight reality, not
visions; they are beset with mud, dust, thirst, hunger, and despair rather than
the Grail Quest's demonic temptations that vanish in a puff of smoke. The
only temptation Frodo has to battle is the one he carries with him—the Ring.

Certainly the book has aspects of Romance in the medieval tradition of
Chrétien de Troyes and Marie de France, standard plots in which lovers separated by cruel circumstances are forced to go through a series of trials before
being reunited. Still, it must be acknowledged that what Romance there is
exists largely by implication in the barely hinted-at love story of Aragorn and
Arwen and their long wait to be together. So submerged is this in the larger
story that the appearance of Arwen at the end of the action and her marriage
with Aragorn may come as a surprise to many reading the book for the first
time. The details of their romance are almost totally buried in the narrative
proper, and the full treatment of the story is relegated to the Appendix. Moreover, that particular Romance motif has a distinctly modern analogue in Tolkien's own life, his guardian-enforced three-year separation from Edith Bratt.

Then there is style. The book is cast in two distinct prose styles. One is
the high or epic style. It is conventionally medieval in the pre-Raphaelite or
William Morris sense of the word, but it borrows also from Malory, with
paratactic constructions hung on a string of "ands." Here is an example.

> And so they [Eowyn and Faramir] stood on the walls of the City of Gon-
> dor, and a great wind rose and blew, and their hair, raven and golden,
> streamed out mingling in the air. And the Shadow departed, and the Sun
> was unveiled, and the light leaped forth; and the waters of Anduin shone
> like silver, and in all the houses of the city men sang for the joy that welled
> up in their hearts from what source they could not tell. (*RK* VI, v, 241)

There are epic inversions like, "Very bright was that sword" (*FR* II, iii, 290),
and declamations such as, "Aragorn son of Arathorn was going to war upon
the marches" (290), and archaisms such as "Forth the Three Hunters!" (*TT*
III, i, 22). This is the kind of thing the critics always single out for derision
when they talk about Tolkien's style.

The other is the "low" style, or ordinary English (which the critics never
seem to notice). In the narrative itself this is called the Common Speech, and
is used for the non-epic portions of the story (by far the major portion) and
in particular for the Hobbit episodes and the actual speech of the Hobbits.
Of the two styles, call them high and low or epic and common, the Common

Speech is the dominant one, and sets the tone for the entire book. It's hard to imagine anyone in a medieval work saying, "I shall have to brush up my toes," as Merry remarks to Pippin after their escape from the orcs in Book Three (*TT* III, iii, 62). Or anyone, even in thought, referring to another character as "old Strider," as Pippin does after his capture by the Uruk-hai (*TT* III, iii, 47). Or describing a forest as "frightfully tree-ish," as Merry characterizes Fangorn (*TT* III, iv, 65). Nor can I imagine a medieval writer—even Chaucer in "The Reeve's Tale"—having characters talk like Tolkien's orcs. "You've no guts outside your own sties," sneers Uglúk to Grishnákh (*TT* III, iii, 49). "I'll put red maggot-holes in your belly," Shagrat snarls to Snaga (*RK* VI, i, 182). And the anonymous soldier and tracker orcs who follow Sam and Frodo in Mordor are capable of such non-medieval locutions as "Nar!" and "Garn," and "I'll stick you, if you don't shut it [your mouth] down!" (*RK* VI, ii, 202).

This kind of gutter language is more typical of John Osborne than John Gower. Nevertheless, the exchanges among the orcs, rough-edged, rude, and colloquial-laden as they are, present some of the most immediate and realistic passages of conversation in the book. The orc dialogues—quarrelsome, contentious, abusive—have the ring of authentic speech. This is how some strata of hoi polloi talk among themselves. Somewhere, somehow (at a guess, in the war), Tolkien, with his ear attuned to languages of all kinds, overheard real people using such salty vernacular, appropriated it to his invented world, and made it into a sort of Tolkienian Vulgate, a direct translation of the Black Speech.

Finally and most important of all, there is tone, manifest in the attitude of the author toward the narrative. Tolkien's tone, his attitude toward his narrative and characters, is more complex and multi-valent than at first appears. *The Lord of the Rings* subverts (we might even say deconstructs) itself by looking like a medieval, or pseudo-medieval, or imitatively medieval fantasy epic/romance/fairy tale, while in specific places in the narrative sounding like—in spirit, in character, and (most important but least noticed) in tone—a surprisingly contemporary twentieth-century novel, very much in and typical of its time. And here Tolkien is not only not medieval, he is emphatically modern, or—dare I say it?—post-modern.

Even its adherents often find it difficult to say, succinctly, just what postmodernism is, but one of its hallmarks is the intentional questioning of strategies of representation. On the literary plane this is called meta-narrative, and characterizes a level at which the narrative refers to or reflects on itself, or deconstructs itself, or interrogates itself. John Fowles's *The French Lieutenant's Woman* (published, let us not forget, in 1969, fifteen years after *The Lord of the Rings*) is a classic example of this technique. Having considered and rejected the possibility of suicide for his heroine, Sarah, Fowles's narrator, who is and is not himself, inquires portentously at the close of Chapter 12, "Who is Sarah? Out of what shadows does she come?" (Fowles, 94). The mystery thus set up is solved only with the introduction of a deeper mystery, that of the imagination, as Fowles opens the following Chapter 13 by answering literally his own rhetorical question.

> I do not know. This story I am telling is all imagination. These characters I create never existed outside my own mind. If I have pretended until now to know my characters' minds and innermost thoughts, it is because I am writing in . . . a convention universally accepted at the time of my story . . . (Fowles 95)

Fowles has not just set up a mystery, he has set up his audience as well. We have been forcibly ejected from the story and made to feel a little foolish in the process. We may even be a bit abashed, as if we have been caught doing something we shouldn't—believing in the story, participating in the fiction.

Not content with this, Fowles goes on to use his authorial power to play with our minds. The time of his story—that is, the time in which the story is set—is 1867. So he is writing a Victorian novel. But the time of the story, as he very well knows, is also the time when he is writing it, the middle sixties of the twentieth century, and further, of course, whatever time after that a reader is engaged in reading it. What convention, then, is "universally accepted" and at what time? Fowles is reminding us that it is we who accept the conventions and allow them to operate, and by that reminder intentionally breaking the willing suspension of disbelief so beloved of Coleridge. He forces us as readers to see that the "time" of the story is any time it collaborates in the reader-text bargain that is the re-creative reading process, and that we as readers are in league with the author in whatever he does.

Fowles was hot stuff in the late sixties, when *The Lord of the Rings*, considered "popular" in the negative sense, was being hooted at by the critical heirs of Edmund Wilson,[2] scorned as "boys' adventure" with no sex, and its swift demise predicted on that basis. How times have changed. The "boys' adventure" has been steadily in print for over fifty years, enjoyed by readers of all ages, with the demand displaying no signs of a slacking-off. Defying the predictions, *The Lord of the Rings*, far from being a short-lived phenomenon in the literary landscape, is an enduring and important twentieth-century landmark. In addition, critical attitudes have slowly come round to the recognition that Tolkien was when he wrote and is now as modern an author as his contemporaries. The critics are starting to see what has always been there.

Evidence of Tolkien's post-modernity is both obvious and unobtrusive in *The Lord of the Rings*, in such plain sight that it is easy to overlook. The most critically interesting, theory-oriented passage in the book is also one of the quietest, calling no attention to itself yet accomplishing much the same thing as does Fowles in the passage from *The French Lieutenant's Woman* quoted above. The only difference is that Tolkien does it better, using greater narrative skill, more authorial subtlety, and more courtesy toward his reader. The passage in question is from *The Two Towers*, Book Four, and records the conversation between Sam and Frodo on the Stairs of Cirith Ungol. As an episode, it is structurally unnecessary, contributing nothing to plot or character. Indeed, it is a kind of "time out" from the action, a breathing space for its exhausted characters, and is used by Tolkien as a "time out" from the whole fictive process. It says a great deal about Tolkien's own awareness of literary conventions and how their spotlight can be turned on the reader as easily as on the fiction.

Stranded by Gollum at the very entrance to Mordor, and enjoying a brief respite from their ordeal, Frodo and Sam wander into distinctly post-modern territory by idly (at first) kicking around the self-reflexive idea that they are in a story. Sam remarks that stories are not nearly as much fun to be in as they are to read about. He wonders what kind of story he and Frodo are in, and how it will end. Note that Tolkien, unlike Fowles, has not broken through the confines of his narrative. We are still within the Secondary World. This kind of imaginative speculation is right in character for Sam, who, as we have been told repeatedly, loves stories and is always talking about them. Here he talks himself through one of his favorites, the story of Beren and Lúthien, only to realize as he gets to the end that it is not the end, for that story goes on into another story, that of Eärendil. It is at this point that Sam finally comes to the realization that he and Frodo are part of the same ongoing story, that they are, in fact, in *The Silmarillion*.

This is an interesting conceit, but it's hardly anything new, or it would not be if Sam, or Tolkien, didn't take the concept to the next level. Sam says he wants to be in a tale "put into word" that is, "told by the fireside," (and by implication told by someone other than Sam), or even better, *read* out of:

> a great big book with red and black letters, years and years afterwards. And people will say: "Let's hear about Frodo and the Ring!" And they'll say: "Yes, that's one of my favourite stories. Frodo was very brave, wasn't he, dad?" "Yes, my boy, the famousest of the hobbits, and that's saying a lot." (*TT* IV, iv, 321)

Sam's little flight of fancy cheers the doomed and despairing Frodo, who laughs in genuine enjoyment and declares, "Why Sam . . . to hear you somehow makes me as merry as if the story was already written" (*TT*, IV, vii, 322).

Tolkien is here being post-modern with a vengeance, cocking a knowing eye at his reader as if to say, "If you haven't got it yet, here it is." For the story *is* already written. And it *is* read out of a book, the very book we are holding in our hands as Frodo speaks. Perhaps even, if the reader chances to have the Collector's Edition, a great big book with red and black letters. At the same time, it has not yet been written because Sam and Frodo are in the middle of their adventure and it is not yet over, nor do they know how it will come out. By forcing the reader to be in two places at once, inside the story on the stairs with Sam and Frodo, and outside the story reading the already-written book that puts them there, Tolkien enters the world of post-modern theory (and quantum physics, to which, especially Heisenberg's Indeterminacy Principle, post-modern theory owes a great deal).

That scene on the Stairs of Cirith Ungol is itself an image of post-modern indeterminacy. Sam and Frodo are poised on the threshold of Mordor, neither in nor out. The reader is in precisely the same position, neither wholly in the narrative (for we have been reminded that we are reading a book) nor wholly outside it (for as long as we are reading it, the book we are reading has not yet been finished). Tolkien's deft handling of this whole episode is the measure of his skill and modernity as a writer. For where Fowles blatantly and rather crudely has his narrator reflect on his own process of narration, Tolkien far more subtly has his characters reflect on their own function as characters. Where Fowles intentionally and abruptly breaks the illusion to kick his readers away from the narrative and shock them into self-consciousness, Tolkien intentionally but unobtrusively allows Frodo and Sam to conduct his readers outside the narrative before they have noticed the transition, and usher them into readerly self-awareness before they realize it.

This is not as innovative a technique as it might seem. It was used by the *Beowulf* poet twelve hundred or so years ago when, as a scop singing of Beowulf's victory over Grendel, he sang of a scop singing of Beowulf's victory over Grendel. The poem (and indeed the poet) are thus as self-reflexive and self-referential as is John Fowles. Or J.R.R. Tolkien. Well then, is the *Beowulf* poet anachronistically post-modern? Or is the technique actually surprisingly medieval? What exactly do these terms refer to, and how should we use them? It seems clear that for a start, we should use them more cautiously and with a fuller awareness of their resonance than heretofore.

My last example will examine Tolkien as an influence on an author usually regarded as an exemplar of post-modern technique, but also one who, like Tolkien, was a scholar and teacher of medieval literature. I mean John Gardner, the author of *Grendel,* one of the most meta-textual works to come out of the late twentieth century. Sam's final speech in that conversation on the Stairs of Cirith Ungol is the link. Musing on the nature of story, he reflects, "Why, even Gollum might be good in a tale . . . and he used to like tales himself once, by his own account. I wonder if he thinks he's the hero or the villain?" And then Tolkien rams the conceit home. "Gollum!" [Sam] called. "Would you like to be the hero?" (*TT* IV, viii, 322). The direct address brings out the obvious but generally unstated truth that we are all the heroes of our own stories, and that it is only the point of view that privileges one hero over another. In 1971, Gardner took Gollum and made him (by way of his medieval/post-modern equivalent) the hero of his own story in *Grendel,* and not just the hero, but the narrator as well.

In Gardner's hands this once-medieval monster has become Sam's post-modern step-child and Gollum's foster-brother. No longer the inarticulate, shadowy monster villain of the tale of *Beowulf,* Grendel becomes the highly articulate, self-pitying, self-mocking, self-dramatizing, hyper-self-conscious hero of his own tale told in his own words. Giving him the starring role in his own story is Gardner's inevitable and predictable post-modern answer to the challenge of Sam's question, "Gollum! Would you like to be the hero?" The answer is obvious. Of course he would. In fact, he probably thinks he is. And Frodo and Sam are supporting players in his story, only elevated to starring roles by a shift in perspective, like Tom Stoppard's Rosencrantz and Guildenstern.

Gardner's Grendel and Tolkien's Gollum, however, both owe a debt to the Grendel of the original poem. Gardner's character owes it directly, Tolkien's more obliquely but no less plainly, as his second edition revisions to the Gollum chapter of *The Hobbit* reveal.[3] Moreover, our understanding of the "medieval" Grendel is inevitably colored by our familiarity with his twentieth-century avatars. We read him by their light. Such a round dance, with characters reflecting one another and giving voice to one another, shows a continuity of literature and literary themes that transcends periods and terms and labels.

What this all means is that we must abandon our preconceptions and start seeing and reading Tolkien as we have always seen and read Fowles and Gardner and their peers, as a man of his time. We must take him out of the medieval box in which he has languished for too long, and set him solidly in the context of the twentieth century that shaped him and produced his work. We will have to abandon our conventional understanding of words like *medieval* and *post-modern,* and instead start regarding Tolkien afresh and as he is and has always been.

He himself had a word for this necessary process. He called it *Recovery,* and declared it to be one of the essential uses of fairy-story. In "On Fairy-stories" he defined Recovery as the regaining of a clear view, "so that the things seen clearly may be freed from the drab blur of triteness or familiarity." This drab blur of triteness, the familiarity that takes things for granted, Tolkien sees as the product of a kind of appropriation of things seen but not looked at. "We say we know them," he goes on. "They have become like the things which once attracted us by their glitter, or their colour, or their shape, and we laid hands on them, and then locked them in our hoard, acquired them, and acquiring, ceased to look at them" (*MC* 146).

It is exactly this, I suggest, that we have done with and to Tolkien for the past fifty years. We have said we "know" him, and his work, which attracts us so powerfully by its glitter and colour and shape. And assuming that we "know" both, we have then all too often laid hands on them and locked them in our hoard and ceased to look at either. (I do not mean we have ceased to read; but "reading" and "looking at" are not necessarily the same thing.) We have appropriated Tolkien, pronounced his work to be "medieval," and continued for too long to read both book and author by that light. It is time for a change.

Now that we have the advantage of fifty years of hindsight, we can put *The Lord of the Rings* in clearer perspective. We can look at it from a distance that far from lending enchantment, removes it, and allows us to more easily see Tolkien in his time—as an essentially modern author using all the authorial tools and techniques available from whatever period—writing to, and for, and about any audience from his own time and beyond it that can appreciate his story.

Taking the Part of Trees

Eco-conflict in Middle-earth

> In all my works I take the part of trees as against all their enemies. Loth-
> lórien is beautiful because there the trees were loved; elsewhere forests
> are represented as awakening to consciousness of themselves. The Old
> Forest was hostile to two-legged creatures because of the memory of
> many injuries. Fangorn Forest was old and beautiful, but at the time of the
> story tense with hostility because it was threatened by a machine-loving
> enemy. . . . The savage sound of the electric saw is never silent wherever
> trees are still found growing.
>
> —(*Letters* 419–20)

So wrote J. R. R. Tolkien in a letter to the *Daily Telegraph* in 1972. Readers of
his works will undoubtedly recognize and almost certainly applaud the sentiments he expresses. In the years since *The Lord of the Rings* was published,
Tolkien has come more and more to be viewed as a kind of advance-man
for the Green Movement. Patrick Curry's recent *Defending Middle-earth:
Tolkien, Myth and Modernity* is only the most recent of a number of eco-
conscious works which have elected Tolkien banner-bearer for a kind of
whole-earth ideology. A recent BBC television program on Tolkien and his
work called *The Lord of the Rings* "the epic of the Green Movement."[1]

It is clear that in seeing and protesting the destruction by humanity of
the world it inhabits and of which it is a part, in recognizing that the natural
world was an endangered enclave in need of protection against encroach-
ing civilization, Tolkien was years ahead of his time. While there may still
be some industrial apologists who will deride him as a 'tree-hugger,' there
are more and more ecologically conscious readers who will applaud him
for being just that, since his fiction seems to stand foursquare in defense
of trees against their human (or orcish) predators. The names and descrip-

tions of trees in his fiction constitute a catalogue any reader will recognize—
Laurelin, Teleperion, the White Tree, Niggle's Tree, the Party Tree, the mal-
lorns of Lothlórien, Finglas, Fladrif, Fimbrethil, Bregalad, Treebeard (these
last more properly tree-herds, but for all practical purposes walking, talking
trees), and even the avenging Huorns who after the Battle of Helm's Deep so
thoroughly requite their axed and incinerated kindred.

The many book-jacket photographs of Tolkien posed in juxtaposition to a
tree, preferably a large and ancient one, are inconographic representations of
his relationship to these and other trees that spread their branches throughout his fiction. The real picture, however, is not that simple. It is complicated,
contradictory, and deserves more careful scrutiny that it has received up to
now. Since unexamined praise is as useless as unexamined censure, I wish respectfully to suggest that Tolkien, his ecological stance in regard to Middle-
earth, and that stance's too-often uncritical characterization and acceptance
by his admirers, all warrant a closer look.

In the context of his letter to the *Telegraph,* and with the memory of
so many trees to support the position maintained therein, it may come as
something of a shock to be reminded that the first real villain to be met
with in *The Lord of the Rings* is a tree. I except the Black Riders, since at this
point in the narrative we have not met, but only seen and heard them. We
don't know who or what they are or what they want. But we know more
than enough about Old Man Willow. Huge, hostile, malicious, his trapping
of Merry and Pippin in his willowy toils, his attempt to drown Frodo, give
the hobbits their first major setback, and come uncomfortably close to ending their journey before it has properly started. As if a tree-villain were not
enough, the villain's habitat, the Old Forest, which on the strength of Tolkien's letter should qualify as venerated Tolkienian ground, is equally malevolent. Not just dark and mysterious and filled with little-understood magic
like the Mirkwood of *The Hobbit,* the Old Forest is consciously menacing,
consciously ill-intentioned toward those humans who invade it. The hobbits' encounter with the Old Forest is the first really dangerous, frightening
adventure that they experience in *The Lord of the Rings.*

This can hardly be placed under the heading of taking the part of trees,
and we are forced to acknowledge a noticeable disjunction between Tolkien's treatment of trees in this early episode—indeed between his portrait of
Old Man Willow and those of all his other trees—and the position he takes
in his letter, which is very much more what we should expect of him. His
assertion in 1972 that the Old Forest's hostility was caused by "the memory
of many injuries," is certainly not clear in the Old Forest episode written in

1938 (*The Return of the Shadow* 110), and the discrepancy suggests the possibility, indeed the likelihood that his protective stance had codified in the
intervening years, gaining strength and solidity as he reflected on it.

It cannot be denied that as the reader and the hobbits encounter them,
the Old Forest and Old Man Willow are negative forces. They are working
against the hobbits, and without the timely appearance of Tom Bombadil,
the journey of the Ring would be over almost before it started. The Forest,
we are told, has long had a bad reputation in the Shire. According to Fatty
Bolger, who won't go in it, "stories about it are a nightmare," and it is "quite
as dangerous as Black Riders" (*The Fellowship of the Ring* 117, 118). In the
course of the hobbits' journey through its tangled pathways the Old Forest trips them, traps them, throws branches at them, blocks their progress,
forces them to go where it wants rather than where they want, and does
everything in its not inconsiderable power to make them feel unwanted,
unwelcomed, and unliked. Pippin's protest that he is "not going to do anything" only antagonizes the Forest, while Merry feels obliged to point out
to Frodo that the burden of his little song that "east or west all woods must
fail" offends it even further (122, 123). What we are shown at this point in
the narrative is Tolkien's version of the standard fairy-tale dark wood on the
order of those in "Snow White" and "Hansel and Gretel."

If the Forest is presented as dangerous and threatening, Old Man Willow is shown as worse, for he is beyond threat; he is simply evil. He sings
the hobbits into an enchanted sleep, throws Frodo in the water and holds
him under, nearly cuts Pippin in half, and swallows Merry whole. Frodo and
Sam seriously consider chopping him down or burning him up, and there
is no suggestion in the text that either action is ecologically insensitive. Old
Man Willow is an enemy, plain and simple. Frodo calls him "a beastly tree"
(128), and when Tom Bombadil tells the hobbits that "his heart is rotten,"
the reader has no reason to disagree (141). This picture of Willow-man simply does not fit with Tolkien's vision of other trees, nor does the Old Forest
as here presented fit with his other forests, let alone with his declaration
in the letter to the *Telegraph*. Indeed, in a later episode, after the battle of
Helms Deep, the Huorns do to the orcs exactly what the Old Forest here
tries to do to the hobbits. We must recognize at least a double standard
here, if not a fundamental contradiction, which, I suggest, is emblematic of
a larger contradiction running throughout the book, a contradiction, which
Tolkien's admirers may be reluctant to see.

Most readers have accepted both Huorns and Willow-man at face value
without stopping to interrogate the apparent contradiction. Jane Chance,
for example, compared Willow Man to the Barrow-wight rather than to the

Huorns, finding both tree and wight to be death figures, and linking roots (for Willow-man) with graves (for the Barrow-wight). (Chance 106). She stated unequivocally in *Tolkien's Art* that "Old Man Willow and his malice represent the living embodiment of the parent Tree of Death" presumably in Eden. While Chance's reading was consciously Christian, more than a little allegorical, and a great deal more than a little overstated, I think it is safe to say that a large portion of Tolkien's audience would at least go with her as far as seeing in Willow Man the embodiment of some kind of evil, if not necessarily the primal Biblical one.

It is worth noting that Paul Kocher's *Master of Middle-Earth,* one of the earliest critical books on Tolkien (and perhaps the first to display on its cover a photo of Tolkien in conjunction with a huge tree) was also one of the few with good words for Willow-man. Kocher described Willow-man's hostility as "natural hatred for destructive mankind" (Kocher 71). While this legitimate defense of Willow-man is in harmony with Tolkien's letter to the *Telegraph* (and indeed with later passages in the book) it is out of kilter with the episode itself, and highlights the contradiction mentioned above, which Tolkien's seems never fully to have reconciled. Moreover, the "destructive mankind" which Kocher cites must be extended to encompass destructive hobbit-kind—and this cannot mean just Ted Sandyman and the gang that terrorizes the Shire in the last chapters. It must mean all the hobbits, the good ones as well as the bad ones, all our favorite characters, including Merry and Pippin and Frodo and Sam and his Gaffer.

This is not comfortable for hobbit-lovers to see, let alone to acknowledge. For all their exasperating parochialism, the hobbits are by and large and with a few exceptions an endearing bunch, and their Shire is an appealingly nostalgic rural enclave. The Prologue to *The Lord of the Rings* tells us that "[Hobbits] love peace and quiet and good tilled earth," and that "a well-ordered and well-farmed countryside was their favourite haunt" (*The Fellowship of the Ring* 10). Saruman's attempt to convert this countryside to an industrial state is presented and understood as abhorrent and unacceptable. When the Shire is restored to its former beauty as a peaceful farming community of kitchen gardens, fields, hedgerows, and comfortable pockets of wood and stream for camping out, readers are reassured and comforted that the world is once again as it should be.

It is easy to buy this vision of an idyllic rural world and an ecologically responsible species (the phrases "well-ordered" and "well-farmed" are value-laden) without pausing to consider that tilled earth by its nature can have no trees, and that farms must necessarily replace wilderness, which in the Europe on which Tolkien's Middle-earth is based was very likely to be forest. A thoughtful reader would have to acknowledge that much of this well-ordered, well-farmed countryside that is the hobbits' "favourite haunt," even Frodo's peaceful sunlit garden with the sound of Sam's shears in the background, must at some earlier time have been wrested from what Tom Bombadil calls the "vast forgotten woods" (*The Fellowship of the Ring* 141) of which the Old Forest is the sole survivor.[3]

In fact or in fiction, where there are people, trees are in danger—not just from farmers clearing land for crops, but from loggers cutting timber, home-builders replacing trees with houses, road-builders laying tracks. The sound of the electric saw which Tolkien finds so savage is merely the by-product of a technological advance over the less noisy but equally tree-destructive hand-operated saw that was undoubtedly wielded by the hobbits and their predecessors. Here is the sticking-point: wild nature and the human community do not co-exist easily. Perhaps in an ideal world they should, but in the real world they simply don't. And in Tolkien's fiction, this sticking point leads to an unreconcilable contradiction that puts his much-loved Shire-folk in this one respect on a par with his orcs, and in the same respect makes the villainous Old Man Willow and his Forest no more villainous than Tree-beard and his Ents. Tolkien's own words are the evidence, as the following passages will show.

1. [Saruman] and his foul folk are making havoc now. Down on the borders they are felling trees—good trees. . . . hewn up and carried off to feed the fires of Orthanc. . . . Many of those trees were my friends, creatures I had known from nut and acorn; many had voices of their own that are lost forever now. (*TT* III, iv, 77)

2. the hobbits came and cut down hundreds of trees, and burned all the ground in a long strip east of the Hedge. . . . After that the trees gave up the attack, but they became very unfriendly. (*FR* I, vi, 121)

3. Tom's words laid bare the hearts of trees and their thoughts, which were often dark and strange, and filled with a hatred of things that go free upon the earth, gnawing, biting, breaking, hacking, burning: destroyers and usurpers. It was not called the Old Forest without reason, for it was indeed ancient. . . . filled with pride and rooted wisdom and with malice. But none were more dangerous than the Great Willow: his heart was rot-ten, but his strength was green. . . . (*FR* I, vii, 141)

All three passages should be familiar to lovers of Tolkien's world. The first is Treebeard's indignant description of the activities of Saruman and his orcs. The second is Merry's account of how the hobbits secured Buckland against the attack of the Old Forest. And the third is Tom Bombadil's revelation of the nature of the Old Forest, its feelings, and a little of its history. Careful consideration of all three is at once confusing and enlightening. The first quotation is both sorrowful and indignant, expressing outrage against destruction and irreparable loss. The second, in contrast, is unemotional—a simple, declarative sentence. It describes the normal (not necessarily "natural") activity of any community in keeping its land cleared for human use. But it fudges the issue, since it does not acknowledge that this activity—that is the felling and burning of trees—is exactly the same as that described so indignantly in the first quote. Nowadays we call it clear-cutting of old-growth forest, and hard-core conservationists are pretty unanimously against it.

The third quotation is the key to the confusion, and a close reading will show that while the first two passages are in conflict with one another, the third passage is in conflict with itself. In critical terms it deconstructs itself, as careful examination of its language and structure will demonstrate. In the voice of Tom Bombadil, who understands the Old Forest if anyone does, Tolkien begins by telling the hobbits (and us) that the thoughts of trees like Old Man Willow are often "dark and strange," and "filled with hatred." But almost immediately we are given a legitimate reason for these dark thoughts, this hatred; they are engendered by the activities of "things that go free upon the earth." As used here, "free" is a loaded word, for we are not accustomed to thinking of trees as "unfree," or indeed, connecting them with any concept of freedom versus restraint. We are being reminded of something so obvious that it's easy to overlook—trees cannot run away. If someone starts hacking at a tree with an axe, the rooted tree has to stand and take the blows.

Next we are told in no uncertain terms why things that "go free" fill unfree trees with hatred. This is because of the kinds of things they are free to do. An ascending scale of present participles, increasing in intensity from the merely unpleasant "gnawing, biting," through the destructive "breaking" to the harsh and violent "hacking, burning," describes just what things that go free are free to do to trees that cannot escape them. The sentence is brought to a climax and a close with two nouns carrying unmistakable condemnation: "destroyers" and "usurpers." *Destroyers* is a negative word; nobody likes destroyers. But the word *usurpers* is just as negative if not more so. As employed by an author who believed in hereditary kingship and thought the Norman Conquest was a disaster, it cannot but suggest the unjust, unlawful, hegemonic occupation of territory by those to whom it does not rightfully belong.

But then we are told that that the Forest is "filled with pride and malice," and that Willow Man's heart is "rotten." A paragraph that began by describing to its escaped victims a tree's dark, strange thoughts filled with hatred, has doubled on itself to explain that hatred as a reaction (which now seems quite justified) against attack, against the violent usurpation of territory that rightfully belongs to the trees, and has then re-doubled to assert that those trees are filled with pride and malice. The narrative voice seems to be arguing both sides of the question. Now revisit the second quote cited above, Merry's matter-of-fact account of how the hobbits cut down "hundreds of trees and burned all the ground in a long strip," and see how that matches with the "hacking" and "burning" of the third quote. The two passages describe the same activities in very nearly the same terms. Who, then, are the destroyers and usurpers? We cannot escape the conclusion that some of them, at least, are hobbits. Pursuing this line of argument, we can see in their actions a provocation at least for the malice and hatred of the Forest, if not for the rottenness of Willow Man's heart.

What the hobbits do to the old Forest—cutting down and burning hundreds of trees—is no less than what Saruman's Orcs do to Fangorn. Moreover, what the Old Forest tried but failed to do to the Shire is no more than what the Ents succeed in doing to Orthanc. As Merry describes the trees at Orthanc, "Their fingers, and their toes, just freeze onto rock; and they tear it up like bread-crust. It was like watching the work of great tree-roots in a hundred years, all packed into a few moments" (*The Two Towers* 172). Merry is dramatizing and speeding-up the natural activity of trees, but he is not underestimating its effects. What happens at Orthanc is not merely *like* the work of great tree roots, it *is* the work of great tree roots. The result of that work is the transformation of Saruman's military-industrial complex into forest, into the Treegarth of Orthanc. Treebeard's domain has now overrun and replaced Saruman's.

To accept Fangorn Forest as somehow different in quality from the Old Forest, to see the Ents as heroes while at the same time seeing Willow-man as a villain filled with pride and malice, we must ignore the motivation specifically accorded the trees by Tom Bombadil, and close our eyes to the identical actions taken in their own defense by the two forests. These parallels, which I am neither inventing nor exaggerating but simply abstracting from their emotional context, make it plain that Tolkien is sending mixed signals here, or at the very least that he is making it more difficult to distinguish the good guys from the bad guys than one might wish.

Why did the hobbits cut down hundreds of trees and burn the ground? Because, as Merry tells it, the trees "attacked the Hedge: they came and planted themselves right by it and leaned over it" (*FR* I, vi, 121). By "planting" themselves, the trees are by natural means extending their domain into the Shire, or at least into Buckland, in the same way the Ents overrun Orthanc.

Both forests are doing essentially the same thing, and that is only what it is the nature of forests to do—to "plant" themselves, to reproduce and grow and in so doing to extend their territory. This is arbitrarily characterized as a good action when done by the Ents and their army of trees, and a bad action when done—for the very same reasons—by the trees of the Old Forest. Treebeard nostalgically describes to Merry and Pippin the results of unhampered growth by trees.

> Aye, aye, there was all wood once upon a time from here to the Mountains of Lune, and this was just the East End. Those were the broad days! Time was when I could walk and sing all day and hear no more than the echo of my own voice in the hollow hills. The woods were like the woods of Lothlórien, only thicker, stronger, younger. (*TT* III, iv, 72)

Sounds wonderful, doesn't it? A huge, unspoiled, old-growth forest never touched by the hand of man. Treebeard is describing exactly the kind of "vast forgotten woods" of which Tom Bombadil says the Old Forest is the survivor. What we have here is not just an unreconciled contradiction; it is essentially a double standard: the chopping and burning of trees is presented as villainous when done by orcs in Fangorn, but when done by hobbits in the Old Forest the same activities are not only made acceptable, they are necessary for "a well-ordered and well-farmed countryside."

The temptation for readers anxious to smooth away such discrepancies—if indeed they notice them at all—is to substitute motives for results. Orthanc is an engine of war fueled by the trees that the orcs chop and Saruman burns, and so the Ents are justified in attacking it. The Shire is an agrarian community threatened by the encroachment of the Old Forest, and so the hobbits are justified in clearing the ground along the Hedge. What is overlooked in such reasoning is that no matter who is doing the chopping, or for what purpose, the effect on the trees—which grow according to nature rather than operating from motives in the human sense—will be the same, and it will be destructive. "I am not altogether on anybody's *side*," Treebeard tells Merry and Pippin, "because nobody is altogether on my *side*" (*TT* III, iv, 75). He is more right than the romantic reader would like to think.

Conversely, no matter which forest is expanding—whether it is Fangorn or the Old Forest—trees will take possession, and the effect on the countryside will be the same. If we accepted at face value Tolkien's presentation of both cases, we would have to conclude that what is right for Fangorn is wrong for the Old Forest, or that what is bad for the Ents is good for the Shire; whereas an alternate view of the situation might be that what Fangorn does to the orcs is just what the Old Forest tries to do to the hobbits. Or to put it yet another way, the only real difference between Treebeard and Old Man Willow is that one is fond of the hobbits and the other tries to eliminate them.

Before we come to such a conclusion, however, we should look again, and carefully, at a tale that grew in the telling, and acknowledge in Tolkien's defense that these apparently competing episodes were developed at very different times in the chronology of composition, and out of very different parts of their author's imagination. With the pursuing Black Riders transformed from what was originally to have been the pursuing Gandalf into a shadowy, ill-defined menace, the story needed a more palpable, perhaps less obviously supernatural, obstacle for his heroes to confront. Moreover (and this, I think, is crucial to the apparent contradiction), when Tolkien created Old Man Willow and the Old Forest, Treebeard and Fangorn did not yet exist.

Willow Man and the Old Forest belong to what Christopher Tolkien characterizes in *The Return of the Shadow* as the "first phase" of his father's laborious re-writing process, whereas Fangorn and Treebeard began to take shape in the "third phase," during which the character of Treebeard altered drastically. Both Fangorn and Treebeard make their first appearance in Gandalf's account to Frodo, when the latter awakes in the house of Elrond, of the reasons for his disappearance. "I was caught in Fangorn," says Gandalf, "and spent many weary days as a prisoner of the Giant Treebeard" (*RS* 363). Neither a tree nor a good guy as yet, this Treebeard is unmistakably a villain whose imprisonment of Gandalf adumbrates the more purposeful imprisonment by Saruman that eventually replaced it. Treebeard's next appearance is in "a scrap" of narrative in "ornamental script," which began as a letter dated July 27–29 1939, but which chiefly describes Treebeard as Frodo first encounters him. Here, according to Tolkien's notes, "Frodo meets the Giant Treebeard in the Forest of Neldoreth . . . he is deceived by the giant who pretends to be friendly, but is really in league with the Enemy" (*RS* 384). Treebeard speaks "out of the treetop," and has a "thick gnarled leg with a rootlike foot and many branching toes" (*RS* 383, 384). Tree-*like* he may be (or be becoming), but he is still a giant, while Fangorn has been at least temporarily replaced by the forest of Neldoreth.

By the time Merry and Pippin escape the Orcs and arrive at Fangorn Forest in what Christopher Tolkien calls the "fourth phase," many things had changed. Tolkien's comment in a letter to W. H. Auden that "Fangorn Forest was an unforeseen adventure" (*Letters* 216–17) almost certainly refers to the hobbits encounter with a Treebeard now not only completely tree-ified, but radically re-imagined. Indeed, it is tempting to speculate that the apparently self-contradictory speech of Tom Bombadil quoted above may have been one cause, at least, of the change in his character. The shift in consciousness that comes halfway through the Bombadil paragraph may have led to the development of a tree-guardian who speaks for the trees in their own voice. We can grant, then, that perhaps not only the tale but also its author's consciousness did indeed grow in the telling, and that during that telling some inconsistencies were left unattended, as is not unimaginable in so long and complex a narrative as *The Lord of the Rings*.

Nevertheless, the evidence I have cited shows plainly that Tolkien had written himself into what, when it is divorced from the undeniable spell of the story, is clearly an untenable position. He was espousing two unreconcilable attitudes with regard to nature wild and nature tamed—by which I mean nature cultivated according to human standards. The first response of Merry and Pippin to Fangorn Forest is revealing in this regard. Merry calls it "frightfully tree-ish." Pippin finds the forest "dim and stuffy," calls it "untidy" and "shaggy," and compares it to the Old Took and his old room at Tuckborough, "where the furniture had never been moved or changed for generations," and where both the Old Took and his old room "got older and shabbier together." He cannot imagine what spring would look like, "still less a spring cleaning." (*TT* III, iv, 64–65). The parallels between Treebeard and the shabby Old Took and between the Took's old room and the shabby old Fangorn Forest are inescapable and intentional. But we must remember that the spring cleaning that Pippin finds so hard to imagine is a human concept and a human activity. It is not the nature of trees to tidy up.

The obvious contrast is with Lórien, where the trees are neither untidy nor shaggy, but columnar—tall and shapely, with branches high above the ground. There is no underbrush. The smooth trunks of the trees are silver, their unfading leaves gold. They are the habitat of people, of Elves, who build dwelling-places among their spreading branches. Caras Galadon is a city of tree-trunks standing orderly and harmonious. It is as much a garden as a forest, or better yet, a city that is its own garden. The flet where Celeborn and Galadriel meet the Fellowship is built around the central trunk, the central column, of a great tree, and Tolkien's description of it recalls the Party Tree built into the tent at Bilbo's farewell gathering. (Both images recall the Barnstokk, the great tree at one end of King Völsung's hall in the Norse *Völsunga Saga*, a story with which Tolkien was well-acquainted.) The whole effect of Lórien is aesthetically pleasing. It is civilized, cultivated in all senses of that word, as different a world from Fangorn Forest as can be imagined and still be called a wood.

One vision, that of Fangorn, is of nature let alone, existing in a state of wildness entirely untouched by the destructive "two-legged creatures" that Tom Bombadil talks about. The other vision, that of Lórien, is of nature transcended. Lorien is a faery forest that is unlikely to be found in a natural state on earth. It is an enchanted and enchanting correlative of the Ent-wives and their ordered, tended gardens. Tolkien admired both visions. He wanted both visions. But he was honest enough to acknowledge—or to have Treebeard acknowledge for him—that the latter vision was bound to over-whelm and replace the former.

> 'Of course it is likely enough, my friends,' [Treebeard] said slowly, 'likely enough that we are going to *our* doom: the last march of the Ents. But if we stayed at home and did nothing, doom would find us anyway, sooner or later. That thought has long been growing in our hearts; and that is why we are marching now.' (*TT* III, iv, 90)

The paradox may be expressed briefly as follows: civilization and nature are at undeclared war with one another. To make a place for itself, humankind will tame a wilderness whose destruction and eventual eradication, however gradual, is at once an inevitable consequence and an irreparable loss. I be-lieve that Tolkien agreed with each of these positions at one time or another, but that he also felt too many of them at the same time for his own peace of mind or for the inner consistency of *The Lord of the Rings*.

Taking the *Lord of the Rings* entire and as it stands, we will be less than honest readers if we allow ourselves to gloss over the undeniable similarities between Willow-man and Treebeard in both motivation and action, and the similarities in consequences between the tree-chopping of orcs and the tree-chopping of hobbits, activity for which one group is blamed while the other is commended. We have been a little too ready to want it both ways, to stay in the narrative moment and allow the narrator the benefit of the doubt, and in so doing forget what it may be inconvenient or uncomfortable to remember.

There are, to be sure, one or two places in which Tolkien does directly address both the problem and his own ambivalence, but even then he offers no convincing final answer. One instance is in *The Silmarillion*. There, in the chapter titled "Of Aulë and Yavanna" Tolkien imagined a conversation between Aulë, the smith-Vala and creator of the axe-wielding Dwarves, and his spouse Yavanna, the mistress of the trees and "the lover of all things that grow in the earth" (*The Silmarillion* 27).

> I hold trees dear [says Yavanna, who fears the axes that her husband makes for his Dwarves]. Long in the growing, swift shall they be in the felling. . . . Would that the trees might speak on behalf of all things that have roots, and punish those that wrong them! (Silm. 45).

In answer to her prayer Manwë apparently solves the problem by creating the Shepherds of the Trees, the Ents. "Now let thy children beware!" Yavanna tells Aulë. "For there shall walk a power in the forests whose wrath they will arouse at their peril." Aulë's response is typical. "Nevertheless they will have need of wood," he says, and goes on sharpening axes (Silm. 46).

The other instance occurs in the posthumously-published fragment "The New Shadow," which Tolkien said he abandoned because "it proved both sinister and depressing," and showed "Gondorian boys playing at being Orcs and going round doing damage" (*Letters* 344). Part of the damage the Gondorian boys do is to steal unripe apples to play with. An argument over the morality or immorality of this arises between Borlas, the owner of the apple-trees, who describes "pulling down unripe apples to break or cast away" as "Orcs' work," and Saelon, the apple-stealer, who points out with some logic that "If it [is] wrong for a boy to steal an apple to eat then it is wrong to steal one to play with. But not more wrong " (*Peoples* 412). Borlas replies that,

> fruit is fruit, and does not reach its full being until it is ripe; so that to misuse it unripe is to do worse than just to rob the man that has tended it; it robs the world, hinders a good thing from fulfilment. Those who do so join forces with all that is amiss, with the blights and the cankers and the ill winds. And that was the way of Orcs. (*Peoples* 413)

Saelon points out the obvious—that Borlas's answer is entirely human-centered, and thus fails to take into account the feelings of the trees in question.

> And is the way of Men too. . . . To trees all Men are Orcs. Do Men consider the fulfilment of the life-story of a tree before they cut it down? For whatever purpose: to have its room for tilth, to use its flesh as timber or as fuel, or merely to open the view? If trees were the judges, would they set Men above Orcs, or indeed above the cankers and blights? What more right, they might ask, have Men to feed on their juices than blights? (*Peoples* 413)

A judicious reader would have to concede that Saelon has a point. In his even-handed treatment of the debate thus far, Tolkien seems to be fairly representing both sides of the question. To humans, waste (picking unripe apples) is wrong, while to trees "all Men are Orcs."

The debate becomes lopsided, however, with Borlas's reply, that "if a man eats [a tree's] fruit he does it no injury" for "it produces fruit more abundantly than it needs for its own purpose: the continuing of its kind" (413). This begs the question, since by the same token—the over-abundance of the fruit—a boy who steals some of it to play with does the tree no injury either. Moreover, Borlas's ensuing argument that "the proudest tree is not wronged, if it is bidden to surrender its flesh to warm [a] child with fire" (413), again substitutes motives for results, as was the case with the parallel situation of Orcs and Ents. The tree is going to die whether it is proud or humble (and the man who chops it down to burn will not know which it is), while to warm a child is not necessarily more virtuous than to warm an adult.

I do not mean to suggest that Tolkien was exceptional in falling into inconsistency in this matter. He was not. But his own excellence betrays him. Because of the very believability, the "inner consistency of reality" of the world he created, he has always been and continues to be held to a higher standard than most authors. We require of fiction that it be consistent, a demand we rarely make of real life and would not get if we did demand it. We have especially required of Tolkien that his sub-creation—so vivid and convincing that many of his readers pretend to live there—stick to its own norms, when the wonder is that he managed to achieve as much consistency within it as he did. The problem of how to live on earth without changing it, of how to answer growing human needs without sacrificing to them some portion of the natural environment, is unsolvable. If we live and work and eat and build, even if we plant and prune and tend and cherish, it is inevitable that we alter nature, and in that alteration it is also inevitable that some of the things we would wish to preserve will be irretrievably lost. Tolkien recognized this when he spoke in the voices of both Merry and Treebeard, of both Aulë and Yavanna, of both Borlas and Saelon, and most poignantly in the voice of Theoden, who upon first seeing the Ents, comments ruefully to Gandalf: "May it [the war] not so end that much that was fair and wonderful shall pass forever out of Middle-earth?" (*TT*, III, viii, 155)

Theoden was right and Tolkien knew it, and together with Theoden and Treebeard he mourned the passing of much that was fair and wonderful. Yet war is not the only destroyer, it is simply the one most obvious and most obviously evil. There are others less obvious and therefore more insidious. It is not just the orcs and their axes that will finally overcome Treebeard and eradicate Fangorn. It is also the Entwives and their human counterparts—the gardeners and tillers of the soil—who will ultimately crowd out the wilderness.

The poignant duet between Ents and Entwives that Treebeard sings to Merry and Pippin, the debate between wild and tamed nature over whose "land is best" with its beautiful descriptions of each, ends with the argument unresolved, with winter come, darkness fallen, the bough broken, and labour past. The promise that the song holds out of a land in the West "where both our hearts may rest" may be impossible of fulfillment in Middle-earth.

Gilson, Smith, and Baggins

Possibly the best-known line in *The Lord of the Rings* is "Well, I'm back," the simple declarative with which Sam Gamgee closes the book. Here is how it appears in context:

> Sam turned to Bywater, and so came back up the Hill, as day was ending once more. And he went on, and there was yellow light, and fire within; and the evening meal was ready, and he was expected. And Rose drew him in, and set him in his chair, and put little Elanor upon his lap.
> He drew a deep breath. "Well, I'm back," he said. (*RK* VI, ix, 311)

And on that quiet, domestic note the book and the story both are ended.

While thanks to Christopher Tolkien's work in *Sauron Defeated*, we now know that Tolkien had originally conceived an Epilogue tying up many of his story's loose ends, I think most would agree that he was wise to cut it, and end the story with Sam's return from the Grey Havens. Sam's statement echoes *The Hobbit*'s, "There and Back Again" and returns the story to hobbit simplicity after the captains and the kings depart. On thematic and structural levels, it works well, and it is fitting that Sam should have this last word. "Well, I'm back," seems on the face of it, to be a typically Gamgean locution—short, factual, to the point. But what exactly is the point? On the purely plot level, Sam's statement seems a bit redundant. Of course he is back, we can see that. We don't need to be told, nor do Rose and Elanor, for he is expected and the evening meal is ready. What besides announcing his return might Sam be saying by "Well, I'm back"? More important, what might Tolkien be saying?

Reserving answers to these questions for the moment (I will return to them later) let us leave Sam sitting in his chair surrounded by his family, and shift our gaze to another man, also sitting, this time alone out in a wood at night. Here there is no yellow light, no warming fire, no welcoming meal. Unlike Sam, this man, John Ronald Tolkien, is not by any means "back," not at home. He is in fact a long way from home, in France, in a catastrophic war, and he has received news of the death in battle of one of his closest friends, Rob Gilson. Most serious readers of Tolkien's work know the story, best told in John Garth's *Tolkien and the Great War,* of the Battle of the Somme, how the English soldiers came up out of their trenches on July 1, 1916, and crossed No Man's Land under a relentless fusillade from German machine guns that mowed them down in rows. They hadn't a chance. Twenty thousand English soldiers were killed that day. One of them was Rob Gilson.

Who was Rob Gilson? Two years younger than Tolkien, only twenty-two when he was killed, Rob Gilson was the son of the headmaster at Tolkien's old school, King Edwards. The names of Gilson, G.B. Smith, and Christopher Wiseman, and their relationship with one another and with Tolkien are familiar to anyone seriously interested in Tolkien (see Garth above). The "immortal four," as Smith called their fellowship, had been friends since schooldays. Core members of the boyhood fellowship they called the TCBS, they were young men with rather inchoate ambitions to change the world.

To further contrast Tolkien's lonely isolation with Sam's firelit welcome, we can go to his own words at that time, an account in a letter to Christopher Wiseman of his first response to the news of Rob's death. "I went out into the wood . . . last night and also the night before and sat and thought." Tolkien was no stranger to bereavement, having lost his father when he was barely four years old, and his mother—a deeper and more conscious loss—when he was twelve. But the loss of Gilson when he was twenty-four apparently raised more perplexing questions, or perhaps he was just old enough now to face them, to sit and think.

His letter went on:

> I cannot get away from the conclusion that it is wrong to confound the greatness which Rob has won [in his death] with the greatness which he himself doubted. . . . I now believe that if the greatness which we three [surviving members] certainly meant . . . is really the lot of the TCBS, then the death of any of its members is but a bitter winnowing of those who were not meant to be great—at least directly (*Letters* 9).

Why was the nature of Rob's "greatness" or lack thereof an important question in Tolkien's mind? He went on to elaborate:

The greatness I meant was that of a great instrument in God's hands—a mover, a doer, even an achiever of great things. . . . [Rob's] greatness . . . touches the TCBS on that . . . side which perhaps . . . was the only one that Rob really felt—"Friendship to the Nth power." What I meant . . . was that the TCBS had been granted some spark of fire—certainly as a body if not singly—that was destined to kindle a new light. . . . (*Letters* 9).

Unlike Tolkien and G.B. Smith, both of whom had ambitions to be poets, or Christopher Wiseman, who was an accomplished amateur musician, Gilson seems to have felt less intensely the "spark of fire" to which Tolkien refers. Although by all accounts Rob Gilson was much loved by those who knew him, and though he had a keen interest in architecture and design, he was apparently regarded by the other TCBS-ites as perhaps the least artistically ambitious of the four. His great value, at least as Tolkien felt it, writing to Wiseman, was "Friendship to the Nth power." Rob Gilson was valuable for what he was in himself, not for any ambition to "kindle a new light," not for what he might or might not have wanted to accomplish.

We must keep in mind that the man who sat in the wood that night, the man who wrote the letter, was not the comfortable, pipe-smoking professor of philology and world-famous writer of fantasy whose photograph is on the book covers. He was a deeply devout twenty-four year old not long out of University, in the throes of extreme mental shock, sitting alone in a dark wood trying to reason his way out of a crisis at once emotional, religious, and philosophical. He was trying to find some meaning in the apparently meaningless death of a dear friend in a useless battle that achieved nothing. His letter and two additional ones to Tolkien from G.B. Smith (who was himself to die from wounds a few months later—another loss for Tolkien) are poignant records of their struggle to come to terms with death—not the inevitable dying off of the previous generation which to some degree we all take for granted—but death in their own generation, violent, unnecessary, untimely death. Tolkien's letter confronts all the difficult questions—about the purpose of life and the significance of death—and gropes desperately for some comprehensible answers. It is no wonder that he went into the woods to sit and think.

In his grief and wrestling with the angel of death we can discern a mixture of emotions and reactions. First, there is survivor's guilt—Gilson is dead, Tolkien is still alive. Why, and how? The British high command placed Tolkien behind the lines on July 1, Gilson at the front. But how did that military placement fit into the greater scheme of things? Was it destiny? Providence? The luck of the draw? The words of Gandalf to Frodo, written many years later, seem drawn out of this moment. "Many that live deserve death. And

GREEN SUNS AND FAËRIE

some that die deserve life. Can you give it to them?" (*FR* I, ii, 69). Did Tolkien, who lived, deserve death? Did Gilson, who died, deserve life? The man in the wood, who knew he could not give it to him, found no comfortable answer.

Next there is the corollary, almost desperate need to see the point in so apparently pointless an event, to put it in the personal context of the TCBS. Was Gilson not "meant to be great," therefore *meant* to die? Was he meant to die and therefore not meant to be great? And the inevitable next step— was Tolkien *meant* to live in order to be great? Again, at that moment, in those circumstances, no answer. Finally, there is a probing of the unfathomable nature of God. The phrase *bitter winnowing* carries implications not just of separating grain from chaff, but also of the hand that shakes the basket, of controlling force, perhaps even an overarching divine plan. But that is to ascribe a pretty tough attitude to the God he is struggling to understand.

It should be understood here that I am not questioning Tolkien's faith. I am not interrogating his God. I am simply trying to outline the confusion and despair out of which he was trying to puzzle his way—first while sitting in the wood and thinking, and second in writing the letter to Christopher Wiseman.

Most moving of all, however, is not Tolkien's attempt at reason, but his account of his feelings. "So far my chief impression is that something has gone crack. . . . I don't feel a member of a little complete body now . . ." (*Letters* 10). This, apparently, is the shock most deeply felt, Rob's severance from the TCBS, and the effect that will have on the fellowship. Something has "gone crack." Something is broken, so that Tolkien no longer feels part of a whole body, and is striving in loneliness and isolation to find coherence in the fragments that are left. A scant half year after that night in the wood, Tolkien was sent home from the Front with trench fever, and for him the war was effectively over. As it happened, only two of "the immortal four" survived the war, Tolkien and Christopher Wiseman. Fifty years later Tolkien would write in the Foreword to the second edition of *The Lord of the Rings*, "By 1918 all but one of my close friends were dead" (*FR* Foreword 7). G.B. Smith's death in France from shell wounds, coming only five months after Gilson's death, was a second body-blow to the fellowship, a second severe loss for Tolkien, and one he never forgot.

Tolkien and Smith had been fellow poets, and that bond brought them especially close. When the war was over, Tolkien, encouraged by Wiseman, arranged to publish Smith's slender legacy of poetry, titled *A Spring Harvest*. I don't think it is accidental that he reached for agrarian metaphors—"bitter winnowing," "spring harvest," with their images of wind-sifted separation and unripe grain reaped too early—to deal with these untimely losses. They convey a strong sense of youth painfully aware of its own apparent expendability in the eyes of powers beyond its control. It was at least partly in the context of these losses that Tolkien began to write his *Silmarillion* mythology.

Now the function of a mythology is to give meaning to existence, to put human life inside a larger frame, to address if not always to answer the fundamental questions—why are we here? What is our place in the scheme of things? Why do we live? Why do we die? As Tom Shippey has pointed out, Tolkien's concern with such questions, although superficially masked by the beauty and complexity of his invented world, links him more closely to the realistic (and pessimistic) war writers of his generation than to the later fantasists with whom he is usually grouped (Shippey, *Proceedings* 84–93). It is notable that in his invented mythology Tolkien gives his invented world one race that does not die—Elves—and another that dies but does not know why— Men. Tolkien wrote to a reader of *The Lord of the Rings* that his great story, and in this he included *The Silmarillion*, was about "death and immortality."

As Tolkien's work has ripened and his audience with it, this theme has become more and more clear. Even *The Hobbit,* the most cheerful of his books, has the two youngest dwarves, Fili and Kili, killed in battle defending Thorin Oakenshield. Moreover, they are killed uselessly since, as it turns out, Thorin himself also dies from battle wounds. The imminence of death is at the heart of Tolkien's essay on *Beowulf* and the monsters. It informs the last half of his essay "On Fairy-stories," which singles out for special mention two essentials that fairy-stories offer their readers—Escape from Death, and that Escape's corollary, Consolation, the joy of the Happy Ending when Death is overcome. Tolkien's major fictions give his readers all three. Death, Escape from Death, and the Happy Ending. But they also withhold them. *The Hobbit's* Bilbo Baggins comes home safe, but Thorin Oakenshield and Fili and Kili die in the Battle of Five Armies. The narrative momentum of *The Silmarillion* rides on a series of vivid descriptions of lost battles. There are a myriad deaths in *The Lord of the Rings,* all but one—that of Denethor—deaths in battle. Tolkien gives Sam the Happy Ending, but withholds that Consolation from Frodo.

A minor but important work, Tolkien's verse play "The Homecoming of Beorhtnoth," his riff on "The Battle of Maldon," begins with everybody dead, except Tída and Totta, who were not in the battle. Searching the field for the body of Beorhtnoth, they tell over the names of those fallen and rehearse their deeds. It is a litany of deaths, most importantly that of Beorhtnoth himself, whose "homecoming" after the battle is in a farm wagon, delivered to the monks of Ely for burial. A bitter contrast to Sam's warm welcome. The deeper we probe into *The Lord of the Rings* the more pronounced becomes the sense of passing and loss. "[H]owever the fortunes of war may go," says Theoden to Gandalf at Helm's Deep, "may it not so end that much that was fair and wonderful shall pass forever out of Middle-earth?" Gandalf's answer, "To such days we are doomed" (*TT* III, viii, 155), gives little consolation. A perceptive early comment by Douglass Parker in *The Hudson Review* notes that, "Tolkien's whole marvelous, intricate structure has been reared to be destroyed, that we may regret it. . . . as a necessary concomitant of being human" (*Hudson Review* 609). With the substitution of *mourn* for the milder word *regret,* Parker's statement seems to me a fitting commentary on Theoden's words.

The songs of Rohan, surely among the most moving poems in the book, are all about loss. Here is the first, chanted by Aragorn at the barrows of Edoras:

Where now the horse and the rider? Where is the horn that was blowing?
Where is the helm and the hauberk, and the bright hair flowing?
Where is the hand on the harpstring, and the red fire glowing?
Where is the spring and the harvest and the tall corn growing?
They have passed like rain on the mountain, like a wind in the meadow;
The days have gone down in the West behind the hills into shadow.
Who shall gather the smoke of the dead wood burning,
Or behold the flowing years from the Sea returning? (*TT,* III, vi, 112)

Never has the *ubi sunt* theme of the classical poets been given more vivid life in death. Of all the Rohan poems, the most elegiac is the song of the Mounds of Mundberg, sung by "a maker in Rohan" at some unspecified time in the a future far beyond the time of the book's action. Like "The Homecoming of Beorhtnoth," it is a litany of the names of warriors fallen in the Battle of the Pelennor Fields—Théoden, Harding, Guthláf, Dúnhere and Déorwine, Grimbold, Herefara and Herubrand, Horn and Fastred, Derufin and Duilin, Hirluin the Fair and Forlong the old. They "fought and fell there in a far country," and "Long now they sleep/under grass in Gondor by the Great River" (*RK* V, vi, 124–25).

Looking eagerly for flaws in the surface, detractors of *The Lord of the Rings* have expressed disappointment that while lots of minor characters die (which these critics apparently consider unimportant), all the main characters in the story survive. They have not read deep enough. True, Tolkien's hobbit fellowship, unlike the TCBS, does, apparently, survive the war. None of the original four dies, and all come home. They are all, at least temporarily, "back" in the sense of Sam's declaration. But here the similarity begins to fade. Frodo, of all of them the one who most deserves to be "back," is never back in the way that

Sam is. Unwelcomed, unappreciated, wounded, recurrently ill, recurrently in pain, he cannot stay in the Shire, for it no longer has any place for him.

Now Frodo, for all his courage and the high regard of Gandalf, is (and I think is intended to be) an ordinary hobbit. Tolkien himself conceded that "Frodo is not so interesting" as Sam (*Letters* 105). But that, I suggest, is the point of the story. Frodo is not meant to be an "interesting" personality. Partly because he is so continually under stress, he is of all the Fellowship the least differentiated by character or temperament. He has neither the light-hearted impulsiveness of Pippin, nor the solid practicality of Merry. He is not a poet like Bilbo, not a gardener like Sam. He is not a maker, and not by any choice of his own a "mover, a doer, an achiever of great things" or indeed any things at all. He is an ordinary person doing something extraordinary not because he wants to but because he has to.

Not unlike Rob Gilson among the TCBS, Frodo has no outstanding skills or talents except perhaps that of "Friendship to the Nth power," best exemplified in his relationship with Sam. Although he is never in a catastrophic battle like Rob Gilson, never succumbs to his injuries like G.B. Smith, Frodo's life is, in its own way, as destroyed by war as were theirs. He is irrevocably if not fatally wounded, both physically and mentally, by his ordeal. His departure oversea to Valinor offers him no redress, only the possibility of healing *"if that could be done"* [my emphasis] wrote Tolkien (*Letters* 328), and he clearly left the outcome open.

I don't want to propose that Tolkien consciously modeled Frodo on Rob Gilson, nor that Gilson was in the forefront of his mind as he wrote. But he almost certainly was in the back of it, part of the "leaf-mould of the mind" that Tolkien said was the source of all his work. I do want to suggest that a particular phrase about Gilson in Tolkien's letter, "the greatness which he himself doubted," is paraphrased in Frodo's protest to Gandalf, "I am not made for perilous quests." It is clear from Tolkien's letter that Rob Gilson did not altogether share the sense that Tolkien certainly felt and that Smith and Wiseman quite probably shared of being "a great instrument in God's hands." In giving Frodo this self-doubt, Tolkien was investing him with some of the humility that Rob Gilson apparently exemplified.

Gilson's self-doubt and Frodo's plaintive "Why was I chosen?" come from the same place in the human psyche. Gandalf's answer, "You may be sure that it was not for any merit that others do not possess" (*FR* I, ii, 71) is the precursor to Frodo's answer to Sam, many pages later. "It must often be so . . . when things are in danger: some one has to give them up, lose them, so that others may keep them" (*RK* VI, ix, 309). In their sacrifice to something greater than themselves, Frodo and Rob Gilson paid a high price for their courage.

Whether Rob Gilson's sacrifice bought anything lasting is a question Tolkien answered only by Frodo's sacrifice, which bought peace for Middle-earth.

When in grief and despair Tolkien wrote to Christopher Wiseman, "Something has gone crack. I don't feel a part of a little complete body now," he was feeling the amputation of Rob Gilson from the TCBS, the severance that so permanently and irrevocably divides the dead from the living. Those who are gone will never come back. In this world, we will never see them again. Tolkien recreated that "little complete" body in the *Lord of the Rings*, but then deliberately made it go crack again. He reared a structure "to be destroyed, that we may regret it."

Now I want to revisit my opening questions about Sam's "Well, I'm back"—what might Sam be saying, what might Tolkien be saying?—and offer an answer. I propose a revision—not of the writing but of the traditional reading of that sentence. What if instead of "Well, I'm *back*," emphasis on return, Sam said "Well, *I'm* back," in implicit evocation of those who were not back. It could just as easily have been said by Tolkien as by Sam. What might such a reading say about all those lost in Tolkien's wars—not just the war of the Ring but the war to end all wars—and the one that followed that one, when it was clear that war does not end wars? What would it say about Frodo, who came back but could not stay?[1] What would it say about Rob Gilson and G.B. Smith as well as about Fili and Kili and Thorin and Theoden and Boromir and Hama and Forlong the Old? They are not back. They will never be back. Not within Time. Not within the circles of this world. Long they sleep now under grass, their graves unvisited, their lives preserved only in a song about their deaths.

But the song is important. The tradition of song and the function of song—not just as pastime or entertainment (though these clearly have real value, especially in *The Fellowship*) but also as celebration, as history, as elegy, as eulogy—these are of central importance to Tolkien's work. Again and again the motif recurs in his story. Determined to break out from Helm's Deep in a last foray, Theoden tells Aragorn, "Maybe we shall . . . make such an end as will be worth a song—if any be left to sing of us hereafter" (*TT* III, vii, 144–45). Pursuing the orcs at Cirith Ungol Sam thinks "I wonder if any song will ever mention it: How Samwise fell in the High Pass and made a wall of bodies round his master. No, no song. . . . for the Ring'll be found and there'll be no more songs" (*TT* IV, x, 345). And it is Sam, again, who imagines hearing the song of Nine-fingered Frodo and the Ring of Doom and gets his wish at the field of Cormallen, where the unnamed minstrel of Gondor makes his imaginary song a reality.

For as everyone knows, Sam's despairing vision at Cirith Ungol is unrealized. There *is* a song. *The Lord of the Rings* is the song. And Sam's last words—whether for himself or for those who cannot come back, for Gilson, Smith, and Baggins—are the end of the song.

The Body in Question

The Unhealed Wounds of Frodo Baggins

"Alas! There are some wounds that cannot be wholly cured," said Gandalf.
—J.R.R. Tolkien, *The Return of the King*

I propose to explore Tolkien's treatment of the body of Frodo Baggins, with particular attention to the drastic physical and psychological changes that take place on and in that body over the course of Frodo's journey (a journey as much metaphorical and spiritual as geographic and physical). My argument will be that the changes that come about in various circumstances and situations are emblematic of Frodo's changing relationship to himself, to the "real" world around him, and to the quasi-metaphoric, quasi-psychological world of the Ring, which represents the dark side of the human personality.

Any reader of *The Lord of the Rings* knows what a hobbit looks like. The Prologue describes them as "a little people, smaller than Dwarves: less stout and stocky, that is, even when they are not actually much shorter," with height variable and "ranging between two and four feet of our measure." We are told that they dress "in bright colours," notably yellow and green, and have "thick curling hair" (usually brown) on heads and feet. They have "long and skilful fingers" and faces "broad, bright-eyed, red-cheeked, with mouths apt to laughter, and to eating and drinking" (*FR* Prologue 10–11). In this respect, Frodo Baggins would seem at the beginning of his adventure to be a pretty generic hobbit, though Gandalf's depiction of him as quoted by Barliman Butterbur enhances the picture somewhat. Barliman's description of "A stout little fellow with red cheeks . . . taller than some and fairer than most, and he has a cleft in his chin: perky chap with a bright eye" seems to lift Frodo a bit beyond his fellow hobbits, for example, Merry and Pippin (*FR* I, x, 178–79). They get no such individual representation (except for their Ent-draught-increased height and curling hair at the end of the story), so we can only suppose them to be as long-fingered, bright-eyed, red-cheeked, and fond of eating and drinking as their neighbors. We come to know them through their speech and behavior rather than from their looks.

With the exception of Gollum, whose wasted, aged, and scrawny appearance will have a bearing on Frodo's, we get a more complete picture of Frodo's exterior than that of any other hobbit. There is a reason for this beyond authorial realism. What happens to Frodo's body over the course of his journey is the outward manifestation of his changing inner condition. It illustrates one of the bleakest motifs in the book, that Frodo's sacrifice is physical and moral as well as spiritual, that both kinds are presented as being interdependent, and that such giving up of self and substance may or may not be rewarded. Great loss may perhaps result in great gain, but then again it may not; and neither is a foregone conclusion. The first thing to notice is a twofold circumstance: (1) that Frodo's physical self diminishes steadily and perceptibly over the course of the book and (2) that such external alteration can be seen as an index of internal change. Although this condition may be overlooked by readers more in search of plot than theme, Tolkien takes good care to note this diminution, not frequently, but pointedly.

A brief conversation among Pippin and Frodo and Strider fairly early in the journey from Bree to Weathertop says more than at first meets the eye.

> Pippin declared that Frodo was looking twice the hobbit that he had been.
>
> "Very odd," said Frodo, tightening his belt, "considering that there is actually a good deal less of me. I hope the thinning process will not go on indefinitely, or I shall become a wraith."
>
> "Do not speak of such things!" said Strider quickly, and with surprising earnestness. (*FR* I, xi, 196–97)

In spite of a "thinning process" that is as much metaphorical as actual, Frodo is on the way to being "twice the hobbit" he has been, though it is not until almost the end of the book when Saruman, leaving the Shire, speaks the final word on what this early exchange foreshadows. "You have grown, Halfling," he observes, resentful of Frodo's refusal to retaliate against his attempted stabbing. "Yes, you have grown very much." But then Saruman continues, "Do not expect me to wish you health and long life. You will have neither" (*RK* VI, viii, 299). He is right, although too few readers attend to his words, which put paid to the hopeful but careless assumption that Frodo's journey to the Undying Lands will give him eternal life. Tolkien's several statements in his letters make it clear that Frodo will die like any mortal. His journey to Valinor is, like King Arthur's to Avalon, to be healed, if he can be, of his wounds. "Frodo was sent or allowed to pass over sea to heal him—if that could be done, *before he died*" (*Letters* 328).

While Frodo's growth is psychological and spiritual, his girth, or lack of it, is physical. Yet the "thinning process" to which he refers also has a metaphorical component, and Strider, who knows more than Frodo about what is going on, is not amused. Neither we nor Frodo can understand the intensity of his reaction, for at this point we do not know that the Black Riders, who have followed the hobbits from Hobbiton and will shortly surround and ambush the travelers on Weathertop, are themselves wraiths—Ringwraiths. Nor have we yet any concept of what becoming a wraith in this sense entails—the dreadful loss of life and soul that has changed the nine kings from "mortal men doomed to die" into the deathless and bodiless servants of Sauron they have become through possession of the nine rings and submission to the One Ring.

Let us pause for a moment and consider the possible metaphoric ramifications of the Ring's one capability that we see and can measure, that of conferring invisibility. What might it mean to disappear, to lose apparent physical substance, to be seen through as if not there? I suggest that in the case of Frodo, whose bearing of the Ring carries more metaphoric meaning than anyone else's except Gollum's, Tolkien is using invisibility as the outward and visible (or invisible) sign of an inward process, a progressive fading and loss of self. This does not become manifest in Frodo, however, until after he puts on the Ring at Weathertop. No apparent ill effects accrue, for example, from his wearing the Ring in the house of Tom Bombadil and again at the Prancing Pony. At the time of Pippin's comment, we probably do not heed the portent, seeing only that in Frodo's case less is more, that his outward appearance is in inverse proportion to his actual corporal substance. He is noticeably thinner (there is "a good deal less" of him than there was when he set out from Hobbiton), yet he looks "twice the hobbit" that he was. He gains as he loses. Neither Frodo nor the reader can know at this point that the "thinning process" is both actual and metaphoric, an exterior manifestation of an interior and spiritual change that will indeed go on, if not "indefinitely," at least to the end of the journey and Frodo's departure over sea to Valinor.[1]

Following Pippin's casual observation, the next evidences of Frodo's transformation come after and as a direct result of his wounding by the Morgul-knife at Weathertop. During the subsequent journey to the Ford, his perception of reality changes as he begins to fade out of the real world while at the same time the real world begins to fade before his eyes. The first indication that this is happening to him comes first as memory and then as dream.

He lay tossing and turning and listening fearfully to the stealthy night-
noises: wind in chinks of rock, water dripping, a crack, the sudden rat-
tling fall of a loosened stone. He felt that black shapes were advancing to
smother him, but when he sat up he saw nothing but the back of Strider
sitting hunched up, smoking his pipe, and watching. He lay down again
and passed into an uneasy dream in which he walked on the grass in his
garden in the Shire, but it seemed faint and dim, less clear than the tall
black shadows that stood looking over the hedge. (*FR* I, xii, 214–15)

What begins as an apprehension of black shapes advancing, and a dream of
a dimming garden and tall black shadows, soon becomes actuality as Frodo
fades further and further out of the physical world and deeper and deeper
into the psychological and metaphorical wraith-world of the Ring. Brief
examples will illustrate the increasing effect of his weakening hold on the
world around him and the concomitant development of his perception of
and participation in the shadow world.

"The trees and rocks about him seemed shadowy and dim" (*FR* I, xii, 215).
"Frodo lay half in a dream, imagining that endless dark wings were
sweeping by above him, and that on the wings rode pursuers that sought
him in all the hollows of the hills" (216).
"[E]very now and again a mist seemed to obscure his sight, and he
passed his hands over his eyes" (216–17).
"Ever since the sun began to sink the mist before his eyes had darkened, and he felt that a shadow was coming between him and the faces of
his friends" (222).
"[D]uring the day things about him faded to shadows of ghostly grey"
(224).

Further supporting evidence comes at the Ford of Rivendell. By this time,
Frodo has not only borne (and worn) the Ring; he has been stabbed with
the Morgul-knife, which has left a part of itself in the wound. The result
of this is both physical and psychological, making the real world appear to
his eyes "shadowy and dim," while allowing the shapes of the Black Riders
at the Ford (no longer dream shapes but actual) to be "dark and solid" so
that he can see them clearly. It takes little imagination to see this physical
change as part of Frodo's increasingly precipitous slide from one world into
another—from the phenomenal world to the interior, darkly faërian world
of the Ring. It is thus no accident that in the flight to the Ford Frodo can see
the Ringwraiths clearly.

"The Riders seemed to sit upon their great steeds like threatening stat-ues upon a hill, dark and solid, while all the woods and land about them receded as if into a mist" (225). The outside world, which has increasingly faded since his wounding, is now almost beyond his perception, while the previously shadowy world of the wraiths is as clear and hard edged as it was at Weathertop. It should not be overlooked that, unlike at Weathertop, here Frodo is not wearing the Ring. He has no need to be; the wound has done its work. "He could see them clearly now: they appeared to have cast aside their hoods and black cloaks, and they were robed in white and grey. Swords were naked in their pale hands; helms were on their heads. Their cold eyes glittered, and they called to him with fell voices" (226).

Not to be overlooked in all this shadow is the fact that when he is at the Ford, Frodo can also see Glorfindel, "a white figure that shone and did not grow dim like the others" (*FR* II, i, 235) in Frodo's perception. Frodo may be well and truly in the Ring world, but that very circumstance has sharpened his perception of light as well as dark. The mundane world is dim and faded, but Frodo can see beyond the dark to Glorfindel "as he is upon the other side" (235). We may ask at this point, "The other side of what?" The phrase may refer simply to the other side of the world, to Aman/Valinor, the Land in the West at the end of the Straight Road. But it may also refer to the far edge of the Ring world, and to the possibility that by going deeply into the dark and passing through it, one can come out again into the light on the other side.

This is surely the implication behind Gandalf's perception of Frodo at Riv-endell. Although the Morgul-sliver has been removed from Frodo's shoulder, its effects remain, as shown by the appearance, the physical body, of the con-valescent Frodo.

> [To] the wizard's eye there was a faint change, just a hint as it were of transparency, about him, and especially about the left hand that lay out-side upon the coverlet.
>
> "Still that must be expected," said Gandalf to himself. "He is not half through yet, and to what he will come in the end not even Elrond can foretell. Not to evil, I think. He may become like a glass filled with clear light for eyes to see that can." (235)

The "hint . . . of transparency" seems to be the opposite of the shadow-transformation of the Black Riders, a movement into translucency rather than darkness, while the reference to a glass filled with clear light is an un-mistakable adumbration of the Phial of Galadriel that Frodo carries into Mordor. Nevertheless, Gandalf's "He may become" withholds the certain promise that such transformation will be the outcome of Frodo's ordeal. He has a long way yet to go, and to what he will come in the end no one in the story can foretell, only his creator, who is taking him deeper and deeper into the shadow side of his own heart and mind.

This becomes clearer when the Company enters Moria, where we are told that Frodo can "see further in the dark" than any of his companions, an awareness the narrative attributes to the "grim wound" of the Morgul-knife, which has made him "more aware of things that could not be seen" (325). It seems obvious that Tolkien is telling us not just that Frodo has excellent night vision, but that his perception of the darkness embodied (or disembodied) in the Ringwraiths—a darkness that is within him as well—has sharpened. It can be no accident that it is at this point in his ordeal and in the underworld of Moria that Frodo becomes aware of his own shadow, Gollum, who is both literally and figuratively shadowing him.

It is worth remembering that back in the sunlit study at Bag End, Frodo had rejected as "loathsome" Gandalf's suggestion that Gollum might be a hobbit, that there could be any relationship between himself and Gollum. "I cannot believe that Gollum was connected with hobbits, however distantly," said Frodo with some heat. "What an abominable notion!" (FR I, ii, 63).[2] Since then not only has he been stabbed by the Morgul-knife, but he has worn the Ring not just once but three times. Although two of those instances, in the house of Tom Bombadil and at the Prancing Pony, have apparently had no consequences, the episode at Weathertop has had a profound effect. A striking contrast to the "hint . . . of transparency" observed by Gandalf is Frodo's distorted perception of Bilbo when, at Rivendell, he asks to see the Ring: "a shadow seemed to have fallen between them, and through it he found himself eyeing a little wrinkled creature with a hungry face and bony groping hands." Frodo feels a desire to strike this Gollum-like apparition, and at this point it is Bilbo, not Frodo, who can say, "I understand now" (FR II, i, 244).

By the time Frodo gets to Moria, his ability to see into the dark has been deepened by experience. He still cannot "see" the real Gollum, who shadowlike is behind him, but he has been more than half in the Ring world since Weathertop, and he knows now that Gollum is there. His face-to-face meeting with Gollum in the Emyn Muil will be his first opportunity to confront his shadow, and it is not unimportant that he now makes a pact with it and agrees to rely on his shadow, his dark side, to guide him through the Dead Marshes and take him to the Black Gate. We may see this as the halfway mark in that journey when Gandalf says Frodo is not "half through yet," with the darkest part still to come. The two deadliest of his physical wounds are still ahead of him—Shelob's sting, which brings him close to death, and Gollum's bite, which robs him of both finger and Ring and leaves him with only bitter self-knowledge. The growth of Frodo's shadow side, coupled with an actual wearing-away of his physical substance, has the paradoxical effect of illuminating his inner being.

> [Sam] saw his master's face clearly, and his hands, too, lying at rest on the ground beside him. He was reminded suddenly of Frodo as he had lain, asleep in the house of Elrond, after his deadly wound. Then as he had kept watch Sam had noticed that at times a light seemed to be shining faintly within; but now the light was even clearer and stronger. Frodo's face was peaceful, the marks of fear and care had left it; but it looked old, old and beautiful, as if the chiselling of the shaping years was now revealed in the many fine lines that had before been hidden, though the identity of the face was not changed. Not that Sam Gamgee put it that way to himself. He shook his head, as if finding words useless, and murmured: "I love him. He's like that, and sometimes it shines through, somehow." (*TT* IV, iv, 260)

The two moments of translucency and inner light that show Frodo as others see him—first Gandalf and then Sam—are in stark contrast to his own self-awareness, which seems conscious of only loss and pain. Whatever healing may be ahead of him, his present state is at once better and worse than it was when he set out from Bag End. The inner light shines brighter, but only in contrast to the dark. Frodo may be "twice the hobbit he was" in terms of his spiritual and psychological growth, but he has still the potential to become a wraith, to fall completely under the domination of the Ring. This is, of course, exactly what happens. The implied similarity to Gollum— the one "an old weary hobbit, shrunken by the years that had carried him far beyond his time, beyond friends and kin, and the fields and streams of youth" (*TT* IV, iii, 324), the other old and beautiful, chiseled by the "shaping years" but, like Gollum, far beyond the fields and streams of youth—is not accidental. Frodo's ordeal is taking its toll, and it is not over.

By the time it is over, by the time Tolkien has put his small protagonist through the punishing trials that still await him, and the final, awful test that he will fail, Frodo will have been stripped of most of what he started out with. He will have lost his innocence, his self-protective ignorance, his ordinary physical and psychological self, and his home. All that on top of the greatest loss of all—the Ring. "It is gone for ever," he says on the anniversary of his capture by the orcs at Cirith Ungol, "and now all is dark and empty" (*RK* VI, ix, 304). Frodo, too, is dark and empty. The loss has saved him from wraith-hood but left him bereft and diminished. He has grown spiritually, but only by the perhaps necessary subtraction of his ordinary physical self.

Paradoxically, he may be "twice the hobbit" precisely because of all his losses. Frodo is capable of forgiving Gollum and showing mercy to Saruman. But it is worthy of notice that as the narrative draws to its close, we get no more descriptions of light from within. Gandalf's prediction, so carefully couched in the subjunctive by Tolkien, appears not to have come true. Frodo seems less like a glass filled with clear light than like a combat veteran suffering from post-traumatic stress syndrome. "There is no real going back," he tells Gandalf on the ride home. "Though I may come to the Shire, it will not seem the same, for I shall not be the same. I am wounded with knife, sting, and tooth, and a long burden. Where shall I find rest?" (*RK* VI, vii, 268).

Not in the Shire, as the rest of the story makes clear. Sam feels "vague anxiety about his master," who has no part in the great year 1420 that marks the renewal of the Shire. He is "not the same."

> Frodo dropped quietly out of all the doings of the Shire, and Sam was pained to notice how little honour he had in his own country. Few people knew or wanted to know about his deeds and adventures; their admiration and respect were given mostly to Mr. Meriadoc and Mr. Peregrin and (if Sam had known it) to himself. (*RK* VI, ix, 305)

But the shadow of "old troubles" haunts Frodo on the anniversaries of their occurrence, as Sam begins to realize.

> One evening Sam came into the study and found his master looking very strange. He was very pale and his eyes seemed to see things far away.
> "What's the matter, Mr. Frodo?" said Sam.
> "I am wounded," he answered, "wounded; it will never really heal." (*RK* VI, ix, 305)

It is not until "afterwards" that Sam recalls the date, 6 October, the two-year anniversary of Frodo's wounding on Weathertop. Moreover, "it" does not ever "really" heal. Frodo's illnesses, the year-marks of his wounds, are debilitating reminders of his ordeals—reminders to readers not just of the inescapable fact that Frodo does not recover, but that Tolkien does not want us to forget that he does not recover. Frodo at the end of the book is less "like a glass filled with clear light" than like a deeply damaged, battle-scarred veteran of war whose post-traumatic flashbacks are the psychic souvenirs of his physical injuries. Frodo's maimed body bears the marks and the memories of his experience, marks and memories he will carry with him to Valinor to be healed, *if that can be done,* but Tolkien leaves the question in doubt.

By the time he takes ship for the Undying Lands, Frodo has faded—out of view, out of life, out of common remembrance. He has been "too deeply hurt," as he tells Sam, to enjoy the Shire. "Someone has to give [things] up, lose them, so that others may keep them" (*RK* VI, ix, 309). Such bitter knowledge is hard for readers to accept. We want a Happy Ending for Frodo, while Tolkien uncompromisingly refuses to give us one. His letters paint an even bleaker picture than his fiction, like this to Eileen Elgar in 1963.

> He [Frodo] appears at first to have had no sense of guilt (III 224–5); he was restored to *sanity* and peace. But then he thought that he had given his life in sacrifice: he expected to die very soon. But he did not, and one can observe the disquiet growing in him. . . . Slowly he fades "out of the picture," saying and doing less and less. I think it is clear on reflection to an attentive reader that when the dark times came upon him and he was conscious of being "wounded by knife sting and tooth and a long burden" (III 268) it was not only nightmare memories of past horrors that afflicted him, but also unreasoning self-reproach: he saw himself and all that he had done as a broken failure. (*Letters* 327–28)

Gandalf was right when he speculated at Rivendell that Frodo would not "come to evil." But neither does he come to unalloyed good, but rather to a painful and debilitating self-realization. Frodo's greatest unhealed wound transcends his physical maiming and loss. It is the deeper, self-inflicted wound of his "unreasoning self-reproach." The hobbit who left the washing-up for Lobelia and walked away from Bag End on 22 September has been changed both externally and internally into the maimed and battered body and damaged psyche, the "broken failure" who returns to the Shire little more than a year later only to fade out of the picture and finally leave it altogether.

Of all the many bodies in Tolkien's Middle-earth, it is Frodo's body, chiseled to beauty by the shaping years yet scarred by great struggle and greater failure, that pays the highest price and gets the least reward.

A Distant Mirror

Tolkien and Jackson in the Looking-Glass

More than any other twentieth-century author, J.R.R. Tolkien has caught and for well over half a century held the public imagination. While his work is usually classed as fantasy, it derives in large measure from his long familiarity with all kinds of medieval literature from myth to epic to fairy story, and that medieval flavor is the aspect of his work most apparent to most readers. True, he put modern speech in the mouths of the Grendels and dragons of *Beowulf.* True, he had the dwarves of the *Eddas* drinking coffee, ordering ham and eggs, and conducting themselves in a distinctly corporate fashion. Nevertheless, *The Hobbit* and *The Lord of the Rings* are most often understood as taking place in a mythicized, vaguely medieval setting and society. The result is that whether Tolkien meant it to or not, his work has re-defined the period for the popular imagination. You may agree or disagree with Norman Cantor's suggestion that Tolkien and C. S. Lewis between them invented the Middle Ages, but I think it is fair to say that Tolkien re-invented them for popular culture, and validated their appeal in a world grown disaffected with its own tenets of modernist reaction.

Here's an illustration. Shortly after Peter Jackson's adaptation of *The Fellowship of the Ring* was released, a scholar of my acquaintance told me of seeing the film with a friend thirty-two times, and planning to go again. The friend, a medievalist, particularly admired Jackson's attention to detail, and singled out the armor as being authentic to the period. If, like me, your immediate response is "what period is that?" you may go on to wonder to what degree the *idea* of the Middle Ages becomes a kind of fairy tale "otherworld" sufficiently removed in time and culture to enchant and refresh jaded modern (and modernist) eyes.

Like his audience, Tolkien felt imprisoned in a time that embraced much that he hated and wanted to escape, and it is for that very reason that his work, however medieval it may appear, speaks to his own twentieth century as well. It is compelling because it is a medieval–modern hybrid, and its example has inspired other such hybrids in literature, and, most recently, in film. I am not talking now just about costume design in Peter Jackson's film, but also about George Lucas's *Star Wars* epic, an essentially medieval story complete with monsters, sword fights, and Jedi knights, re-decorated as space opera. Lucas was more than inspired by Tolkien's example; he was enabled by it. I think it is safe to say that if Tolkien hadn't written *The Lord of the Rings,* thus sparking the enormous resurgence of modern fantasy, Lucas could never have conceived and carried through a major production like *Star Wars.* Tolkien gave him a genre, an archetypal cast of characters, and an audience that was ready and waiting to embrace a myth.

Now that the *Lord of the Rings* films have appeared, we can see that the influence stretches in both directions. If Lucas brought Middle-earth to a galaxy far away, Jackson has given us *Star Wars* in Middle-earth, one epic film as father to another. The godfather of both, however, is Tolkien, and it is his example, setting the standard for the way in which all of these crafts-men mirror one another, that I want to explore. So I am going to talk about Tolkien's modern use of his medieval models and also about his modern adapters' use of Tolkien's medievalism as a model. I will begin with some lines from a great and mythic medieval story, lines that, although they deal with words rather than with pictures, both state and illustrate my case more clearly than I can.

	At times the scop,
a thane of the King,	glorying in words,
the great old stories,	who remembered them all,
one after another,	song upon song,
found new words,	bound them up truly,
began to recite	Beowulf's praise
a well-made lay,	of his glorious deed,
skillfully varied	his matter and style.
He sang all he knew	of famous Sigemund
...	[who] killed a dragon,
treasure's keeper. (Chickering ll. 867–87)	

These lines from *Beowulf,* exalting Beowulf's victory over Grendel, describe a poet composing a poem exalting Beowulf's victory over Grendel—a poem

which, since it covers the same material in the same way, may be the very one
that the *Beowulf* poet is singing. The poem is talking about mythmaking and
thus about itself, mirroring its own mythic face in a passage more modern,
more self-aware then we might expect to find in a medieval work—a passage at once intertextual and self-referential. It is my first and in many ways
my best example of the looking-glass of my title. But the lines I have quoted
do more than reflect on themselves. They also turn the mirror outward to
reflect another myth, this one about Sigemund and the dragon, thus second-
arily reflecting Beowulf's dragon-slaying at the end of the poem. The *Beowulf*
poet holds up his own performance to the mirror of the original performance
which in turn reflects back upon his own. He then turns that same mirror forward toward yet another poem to reflect thematically on the end of his story.

The effect is that of multiple poetic voices overlapping and singing together,
reminding the audience that the poets and their poems are parts of what was
once an extended tradition. Able thus to look from mirror to mirror, the audience can take in all the stories in a compound reflection. Since the *Beowulf*
poet was Tolkien's master in art, it seems appropriate to take this concept
from *Beowulf* and apply it with variations to similar intertextual references in
Tolkien's work and those filmic reconfigurations and adaptations I have cited.

Like *Beowulf*, Tolkien's stories are all about themselves as stories. This is
not just authorial self-promotion; the stories are there to affirm the importance of myth in a myth-forgetful age, from the dwarves' song of dragons
and lost treasure, and the legends of the King under the mountain in *The
Hobbit*, to Elven songs about Beren and Lúthien, and Nimrodel, and Eärendil
the Mariner in *The Lord of the Rings*. Tolkien is mirroring his own interior
mythic heritage, just as did the *Beowulf* poet. Even more like the *Beowulf*
poet, he can turn his mirror to reflect outward, as he does explicitly in one
obvious episode wherein *The Hobbit* both reflects and reflects upon *Beowulf*.

In the second half of *The Hobbit* Bilbo Baggins is sent by the dwarves into
the lair of Smaug, the dragon, where he steals a cup from the dragon's hoard.
Here is the scene.

> There he lay, a vast, red-gold dragon, fast asleep. . . . Beneath him, under
> all his limbs and his huge coiled tail, and about him on all sides stretching
> away across the unseen floors, lay countless piles of precious things, gold
> wrought and unwrought, gems and jewels, and silver red-stained in the
> ruddy light. . . . [Bilbo] gazed for what seemed an age, before, drawn almost
> against his will, he stole from the shadow of the doorway . . . to the nearest
> edge of the mounds of treasure. . . . He grasped a great two-handled cup, as
> heavy as he could carry. . . . Then Bilbo fled. . . .

the dwarves were still passing the cup from hand to hand and talking delightedly . . . when suddenly a vast rumbling awoke in the mountain underneath. . . .

Dragons may not have much use for all their wealth, but they know it to an ounce as a rule, especially after long possession. . . .

He would not forget nor forgive the theft, not if a thousand years turned him to smouldering stone. . . . (*H* 184–88)

Once wakened, Smaug issues forth from his cavern in a flaming rage, seeking revenge. He attacks Lake-town, zooming over it like a fighter plane on a strafing run, spouting fire, and burning houses.

[T]hey could see him as a spark of fire rushing toward them and growing ever huger and more bright. . . .

Fire leaped from the dragons jaws. . . . Fire leaped from thatched roofs and wooden beam-ends as he hurtled down and past and round again . . . Flames unquenchable sprang high into the night. (*H* 210–11)

With some allowances for difference between prose and poetry, and cultural disparities in audience and narrative style, the episode both reflects and offers a reflection on a passage from the second half of *Beowulf* in which an unnamed thief does exactly the same thing. The situation in the original is described as follows.

Three hundred years   that harm to the people
held one of its hoards,   dwelt in the earth,
mighty in powers,   until a lone man
kindled its fury;   he took to his master
the gold-plated flagon   . . . .
. . .   The hoard had been pilfered,
its treasure lessened   . . .
. . .   his lord looked upon
the gold of the ancients   for the first time.
By then, also,   the dragon had wakened
and with it new strife.   . . .
. . .   . . .
Cleverly, in secret,   the outlaw had stepped
past the dragon's head.   . . . . (Chickering ll. 2278–2291)

Once wakened, this dragon, too, seeks vengeance.

the barrow-snake	was swollen with rage,
wanted revenge	for that precious cup,
a payment by fire.	. . .
. . . the dragon rejoiced	. . . ,
	flew out in fire,

with shooting flames. (Chickering ll. 2304–2309)

Much like Bilbo's dragon,

The visitor began	to spew fire-flakes,
Burn the bright halls;	the glow rose high,
A horror everywhere.	The fiery terror
left nothing alive	wherever it flew.
Throughout the night sky	the burnings were visible. (Chickering ll.
2312–2316)	

It didn't take readers of *The Hobbit* long to spot the likeness. The book was published in September of 1937, and in January of 1938 a letter to the London *Observer* signed "Habit" inquired, "is the hobbit's stealing of the dragon's cup based on the cup-stealing episode in *Beowulf?*" Tolkien's reply, printed a month later was:

> *Beowulf* is among my most valued sources; though it was not consciously present to the mind in the process of writing, in which the episode of the theft arose naturally (and almost inevitably) from the circumstances. It is difficult to think of any other way of conducting the story at that point. I fancy the author of *Beowulf* would say much the same." (*Letters* 31)

Given the similarity between the two episodes, this does seem just a tad disingenuous. If *Beowulf* was not "consciously present" to his mind, it was certainly not very far away. During the period when he was writing *The Hobbit* he also wrote, delivered, and published his landmark lecture on "*Beowulf: The Monsters and the Critics.*" In his lecture–essay Tolkien talked about the *Beowulf* poet and his poem like a fellow-poet rather than a distant critic. Indeed, his comment to the *Observer* that "the author of *Beowulf* would say much the same" as Tolkien did about how to conduct the story at that point is evidence of Tolkien's strong identification with that poet. He knew the poem from the inside out; he knew what worked and what didn't work. The passage in question doesn't work.

The manuscript at this point is so corrupt, so damaged, with so many lacunae, that the lines I quoted have almost as many gaps as they have words and phrases. Missing are the identity of both thief and master, a clear motive for stealing the cup, and the circumstances surrounding the theft. These are and will remain—unless an early medieval crib turns up—unsolvable mysteries. In his own way, in his own voice, and in his own story, Tolkien offers a solution to the mystery. This is not plagiarism. It is a kind of long-distance reconstruction. He is filling in the gaps.[1]

His use of the word "circumstances" in his letter to the *Observer* is the key. By inserting the *Beowulf* episode into his own story and creating circumstances that would support it, by assigning a name, a personality, and the crucial action to his own character, Bilbo, Tolkien has brought *Beowulf* forward into *The Hobbit*. At the same time he has retro-fitted *The Hobbit* into *Beowulf* using a situation that the poet himself created. He has shone his own modern mirror on that medieval work in a way that makes sense of an otherwise puzzling passage that has both aroused and defeated the curiosity of scholars for years.

I am not suggesting that Tolkien thought he was improving on *Beowulf*, just giving it a helping hand, though as Tom Shippey has pointed out, Tolkien's essay does sometimes give the impression that he thought nobody had ever understood *Beowulf* but him. On the basis of that essay Shippey goes on to assert (and I would agree) that "Tolkien felt more than continuity with the *Beowulf*-poet. He felt a virtual identity of motive and technique." More than that, and again, I agree, Shippey says it was important to Tolkien to know the poem's "exact literary mode," and even more significant that "that literary mode was one he himself wanted!" (Shippey *Road* 44). Wanted, and felt not just competent but responsible to use.

Not to be outdone by the man whose work he is adapting, Peter Jackson uses a similar tactic in his *Fellowship of the Ring* film. In Jackson's treatment of the hobbits' arrival at Bree, the four hobbits—Frodo, Sam, Merry, and Pippin—arrive at Bree, to find a high wall towering over their halfling forms, its door closed against them. They knock, and a panel in the door opens to show the face of the gatekeeper, who looks out, then shuts the panel and opens one lower down to see the hobbits and ask them what they want. In contrast, the incident in Tolkien's book is described as follows.

> They came to the West–gate and found it shut, but at the door of the lodge beyond it, there was a man sitting. He jumped up and fetched a lantern and looked over the gate at them in surprise.
>
> "What do you want and where do you come from?" he asked gruffly. (*FR* I, ix, 163)

The differences between this scene and the one in Jackson's film are nota-ble—a shut gate, not a closed door; no wall, as the hobbits can see beyond the gate to the open door of the lodge; the gate-keeper looks *over* the gate, not through an open panel in a door.

Like Tolkien, Jackson is reaching back to a classic and bringing it into his own work. Unlike Tolkien, he is using fairy tale rather than epic, and his source is L. Frank Baum by way of Hollywood. *The Wizard of Oz* has a re-markably similar scene in which four travelers, Dorothy, the Scarecrow, the Tin Man, and the Cowardly Lion, finally get to the Emerald City. The huge doors are shut against them and they knock for entrance. A panel opens in the tall door, the doorman looks out and then slams it before re-opening it to ask them what they want. Jackson's hobbit-scene is too close to be acci-dental. Nor is it mere playfulness. It has a definite purpose.

The tradition of films visually quoting from other films is well-estab-lished, and it is clear that Jackson is choosing that tradition over Tolkien's text. Contemporary moviegoers are, I daresay, accustomed to recognizing and appreciating such filmic allusions as homage from one film-maker to another. Jackson's is explicit enough that few viewers will fail to recognize the reflection, or to see that with it he is paying homage to a classic. Some will go on to make connections (whether valid or invalid I leave to your judgment) between Bree and Oz, between Frodo and Dorothy, perhaps even between the Witch of the West and the Black Riders.

While these are predictable responses, I have a feeling that Jackson wants to do more than that. He wants his mirror quite literally to re-flect, to point to Oz and then bend the reflection back to highlight his own film. There are other, more subtly Oz-ian moments in his film as well. The long-per-spective shots of Moria's gothic receding archways, rows of pillars, and cor-ridors stretching to infinity owe their effect of immensity and distance to the pointed green archways and endless halls down which Dorothy and her friends apprehensively approach the Wizard.[2]

The Wizard of Oz is arguably the most magical fantasy film ever made. Arriving as it does at what many would see as the height of the modernist movement, the end of the nineteen-thirties, its contemporary appeal and enduring popularity might be seen in hindsight as an early sign that mod-ernism had engendered its own counter-current in popular culture. It is, in any event, a high standard for any artist working in the fantasy genre to live up to. In directing his viewers' attention through his own film to this classic and using it to reflect back upon his own work, Jackson is conferring on his fantasy the imprimatur of authority. Not, like Tolkien inserting *The Hobbit* into *Beowulf,* because he is filling in a regrettable lacuna, or making sense of a garbled passage. Rather, he is seeking like the *Beowulf* poet to establish himself as an artist working within a tradition and to establish his film as a worthy successor in that tradition. I think it is a safe bet to say that for his particular audience he has succeeded.

Staying for the moment with Jackson, I want to go now to the relationship of his film to Lucas's *Star Wars* and the triangulation of both with Tolkien's *Lord of the Rings.* I ask your indulgence while I point out the obvious. First, Lucas took some of the major personnel and episodes of Tolkien's Middle-earth and transported them to a galaxy far away. The mirroring of Gandalf in Obi Wan Kenobi and Sauron in Darth Vader is as clear as the mirroring of Beowulf's dragon in Tolkien's Smaug. Luke Skywalker's reflection of Frodo is more tenuous, but clear in Jackson's portrayal of Luke's relationship to Obi Wan and Obi Wan's knowledge and guidance of him, and concern for his safety.

By the time Jackson brought them all back to Middle-earth, they had suffered a star-change, subtly re-shaped by their sojourn in the galaxy. The mirrors are now angled instead of facing one another, and the reflection is not doubled but tripled. When Jackson filmed the episode at the earlier-mentioned Doors of Moria, for example, he bounced Tolkien's brief, spooky treatment of the assault on Frodo by the Watcher in the Water off Lucas's *Star Wars* treatment of the same incident, with Luke Skywalker as Frodo and a more visible and explicit monster. Tolkien's book has one tentacle seize Frodo by the ankle before Sam cuts him free and they run. Lucas has a full-body capture in which Luke Skywalker is enveloped in multiple tentacles and dangled upside-down. Jackson develops the Lucas version and the result is a Tolkien-Lucas-Jackson triptych with each mirror reflecting the other two.

Fight scenes in the films are also triply reflective. The fight Tolkien describes between Gandalf and the Balrog is mirrored in the fight between Obi Wan Kenobi and Darth Vader in Lucas's first film. Obi Wan's willing sacrifice of himself to save Luke replicates Gandalf's sacrifice of himself to save Frodo. His declaration that "If you strike me down I shall become more powerful than you can possibly imagine" predicts a reappearance that Tolkien recounts only after it happens, the return of Gandalf the Grey as Gandalf the White. Even Obi Wan's last line, "Run, Luke, run," is the echo of Gandalf's "Fly, you fools!" When Jackson films Tolkien he can count on his viewers' memories to supply the parallels. After viewing *The Fellowship of the Ring,* a Tolkien scholar of my acquaintance said and I quote: "Gandalf and the Balrog was everything I imagined it would be and possibly one of the great scenes in film, maybe even better than the Vader–Obi Wan light sabre fight."

The extended fight between Luke and Darth Vader at the end of *The Empire Strikes Back* takes its action from the earlier Obi Wan–Darth Vader fight, but takes Darth Vader's rhetoric about ruling together and taming the dark power from Tolkien's Saruman at his first meeting with Gandalf. And filming his more kinetic version of that first meeting, Jackson looks beyond Tolkien's book to Lucas's film treatment, multiplying Lucas to the ninth power, raising the ante, and giving Tolkien's two wizards a special-effects set piece in a duel of wizardry they never had in the book. By now the tradition has been so solidly established that when Jackson films Tolkien two generations of viewers see the movie in a George Lucas looking-glass.

Concluding now with Tolkien's book and ways in which he develops the idea of mirroring, I want to say first that such explicit reflection as his of *Beowulf* in the cup episode of *The Hobbit* is not typical of his more mature work in *The Lord of the Rings.* Here external allusion is largely replaced by an internal self-reflexivity more like that of the *Beowulf* poem's awareness of its own origins. Tolkien keeps all the references within his own framework, achieving thereby something of the same effect. From Gaffer Gamgee's first mention of Sam—"Crazy about stories of the old days he is, and he listens to all Mr. Bilbo's tales" (*FR* I, i, 32)—we are to understand that *The Lord of the Rings* will be the story of its stories.

The first explicit example of this occurs at Weathertop, where Strider tells the four hobbits stories "to keep their minds from fear," a purpose which, as Tolkien well knew, has always been one of the chief goals of story—to keep away the dark even by singing about it, as did the *Beowulf* poet. Strider tells "tales and legends of long ago" and of "the good and evil deeds of the Elder Days." The only tale of Elder Days directly quoted is "the tale of Tinúviel" which is Tolkien's own *Lay of Beren and Lúthien,* a quote from his Silmarillion mythology of which *The Lord of the Rings* is a continuation. Strider sings only a part of the *Lay,* going on to explain that his song is a rough translation into Common Speech of an Elvish original. Well and good, except there is no Elvish original. Tolkien has mirrored his own work in a non-existent reflection which has Strider as bard looking back to the earlier poet or poets who first composed out of actual events the poem he is "translating." Strider's comment that his song is a dim reflection of the original suggests the *Beowulf* poem reflecting its own beginning by singing about itself.

Another example occurs at Rivendell in Bilbo's song of Eärendil and the Silmaril. It takes up a full three pages, halts the forward flow of the narrative, and tangles Bilbo and the Elf Lindir in an argument about stylistic differences between the poetry of Hobbits and that of Men. Yet at this point readers (unless they have read *The Silmarillion*) cannot realize the significance of the song, or its place in the history of Middle-earth. That doesn't stop Tolkien. A mere 466 pages later, he tell us exactly its significance and establishes its place in the history in a conversation between Frodo and Sam on the stairs of Cirith Ungol, the most self-aware, self-reflexive, modern passage in the book.

Sam's realization as a lover of stories that it is more fun to hear a story than to be in one, leads him to a further and deeper revelation. Here is their conversation. Sam speaks first.

> "The brave things in the old tales and songs. . . . I used to think they were things the . . . folk of the stories went out and looked for. . . . But that's not the way of it with the tales that . . . stay in the mind. Folk seem to have been just landed in them. . . . I wonder what sort of a tale we've fallen into?"
>
> "I wonder," said Frodo. "But I don't know. And that's the way of a real tale. . . . You may know . . . what kind of a tale it is . . . but the people in it don't know."

Sam agrees, and cites as example Beren, the hero of the *Lay of Beren and Lúthien* already sung by Strider in Tolkien's earlier example of the self-referential technique that he learned from the *Beowulf* poet.

> "Beren, now, [says Sam] he never thought he was going to get that Silmaril from the Iron Crown . . . and yet he did. . . . and the Silmaril went on and came to Eärendil. And why, sir . . . you've got some of the light of it in the star-glass that the Lady gave you! Why, to think of it, we're in the same tale still! Don't the great tales never end?"
>
> "No, they never end as tales," said Frodo. "But the people in them come, and go when their part's ended."

Sam's belated discovery that he is in the very story he is talking about leads him to further speculation.

> "I wonder if we shall ever be put into songs or tales. We're in one, of course, but I mean: [and here Tolkien slams his message home] put into words, you know . . . read out of a great big book with red and black letters, years and years afterward." (*TT* IV viii, 320–21)

It scarcely needs pointing out that that is an exact description of *The Lord of the Rings*—it is (at least in its more elaborate hard-cover editions) a great big book with red and black letters. As in *Beowulf* but more self-consciously, the book is reflecting itself, the story describing itself, the tale predicting its own transmission, the characters in the story creating even as they comment on the story they are in.

It could be argued that Tolkien is simply re-cycling his own material, and in one sense this is true, but in a larger sense, it is part of a more romantic concept. All his tale is part of a story whose continuance stretches from *The Silmarillion* to the Red Book of Westmarch with additions made by Frodo and Sam, to whatever edition of *The Lord of the Rings* we hold in our hands as we read, the whole many times copied and re-copied throughout an indeterminate future. This is more than authorial practice or a lit. crit. concept. It is a belief, an article of faith, that stories and the telling of stories are instincts in the human psyche, that they are part of the human condition, and an essential part of our nature as users of language. We are story-telling critters. He states this clearly in his essay "On Fairy-stories," where he declares unequivocally: "To ask what is the origin of stories . . . is to ask what is the origin of language and of the mind" (*MC* 119). If saying it once is good, saying it twice is better, and Tolkien rephrases the proposition a few pages later, saying that "The incarnate mind, the tongue, and the tale are in our world coeval" (122).

But showing is always better than mere saying. Tolkien gives his best illustration of the principle to Sam to bring the audience back from the shattering and unbearable moments when Frodo claims the Ring and Gollum inadvertently saves the day and Middle-earth. At Sam's suggestion, he and Frodo have retreated from the Cracks of Doom as the mountain blows itself to bits. At that cataclysmic moment Sam steps out of the action to remind us that we are reading a story.

> What a tale we have been in, Mr. Frodo, haven't we? . . . I wish I could hear it told! Do you think they'll say: *Now comes the story of Nine-fingered Frodo and the Ring of Doom?* And then everyone will hush, like we did, when in Rivendell they told us the tale of Beren One-hand and the Great Jewel. I wish I could hear it! (*RK* VI, iv, 228–29)

And of course he does get to hear it, at the Field of Cormallen, when a minstrel of Gondor announces to Sam's delight and satisfaction, that he will sing a lay "of Frodo of the Nine Fingers and the Ring of Doom" (*RK* VI iv, 232). Tolkien cannot pass up this final *Beowulf*ian opportunity to have the story reflect its own image and sing about itself. Since the minstrel begins in high sunshine and ends his song as the shadows of the trees have lengthened, we must assume an extended performance, encompassing more than the brief moments at the Cracks of Doom and almost certainly recounting the whole story of Frodo's journey from Bag End to Mordor. He sings *The Lord of the Rings*, or an abbreviated version thereof.

If the *Beowulf* poet can use his own work as a reflector, so can Tolkien, and so he does—again and again and again. His life's work is grounded in the principle. And as Tolkien, so George Lucas, and as both of them, so Peter Jackson. Their works become a hall of mirrors reflecting one another and out of old tradition new tradition is born.

Now switching my metaphor from mirrors to roads, I will finish with a quote from my favorite author.

> The road goes ever on and on,
>   Down from the door where it began.
> Now far ahead the road has gone,
>   And [we] must follow if we can,
> Pursuing it with eager feet,
>   Until it joins some larger way
> Where many paths and errands meet.
>   And whither then? I cannot say

Permissions and Acknowledgments

"Allegory Versus Bounce: Tolkien's *Smith of Wootten Major.*" From *The Journal of the Fantastic in the Arts* 12:2 (2001). Reprinted with the permission of *The Journal of the Fantastic in the Arts.*

"A Cautionary Tale: Tolkien's Mythology for England." From *A Hidden Presence: The Catholic Imagination of J.R.R. Tolkien,* ed. Ian Boyd, C.S.B and Stratford Caldecott. South Orange, NJ: The Chesterton Press, 2003. Reprinted with the permission of Ian Boyd, C.S.B.

"The Curious Incident of the Dream at the Barrow: Memory and Reincarnation in Middle-earth." From *Tolkien Studies* 4 (2007). Reprinted with the permission of the University of West Virginia Press.

"A Distant Mirror: Tolkien and Jackson in the Looking-glass." From *Postmodern Medievalisms,* ed. Richard Utz and Jesse G. Swan. Cambridge: Boydell & Brewer, 2005. Reprinted with the permission of Boydell & Brewer.

"Fantasy and Reality: J.R.R. Tolkien's World and the Fairy-story Essay." From *Mythlore* 22: 3 (Winter 1999). Reprinted with the permission of *Mythlore.*

"The Footsteps of Ælfwine." From *Tolkien's Legendarium,* ed. Verlyn Flieger and Carl F. Hostetter. Westport, CT: Greenwood Press, 2000. Copyright © 2000 by Verlyn Flieger and Carl F. Hostetter. Reproduced with permission of ABC-CLIO, LLC.

"Frodo and Aragorn: The Concept of the Hero." From *Tolkien: New Critical Perspectives,* ed. Neil D. Isaacs and Rose A. Zimbardo. Lexington: University Press of Kentucky, 1981. Reprinted with the permission of the University Press of Kentucky.

"Gilson, Smith, and Baggins." From *Tolkien's* The Lord of the Rings: *Sources of Inspiration,* ed. Stratford Caldecott and Thomas Honneger. Zurich and Jena: Walking Tree Publishers, 2008. Reprinted with the permission of Walking Tree Publishers.

"The Green Knight, the Green Man, and Treebeard: Scholarship and Invention in Tolkien's Fiction." From *Scholarship & Fantasy: Proceedings of* The Tolkien Phenomenon, ed. Keith Battarbee, University of Turku, 1993.

"Missing Person." From *Mythlore* 12:4 (Summer 1986). Reprinted with the permission of *Mythlore*.

"The Music and the Task: Fate and Free Will in Middle-earth." From *Tolkien Studies* 6 (2009). Reprinted with the permission of the University of West Virginia Press.

"A Mythology for Finland: Tolkien and Lönnrot as Mythmakers." From *Tolkien and the Invention of Myth: A Reader*, ed. Jane Chance. Lexington: University Press of Kentucky, 2004. Reprinted with the permission of the University Press of Kentucky.

"A Postmodern Medievalist?" From *Tolkien's Modern Middle Ages*, ed. Jane Chance and Alfred K. Siewers. New York: Palgrave Macmillan, 2005. Reproduced with permission of Palgrave Macmillan.

"Taking the Part of Trees: Eco-conflict in Middle-earth." From *J.R.R. Tolkien and His Literary Resonances*, ed. George Clark and Daniel Timmons. Westport, CT: Greenwood Press, 2000. Copyright © 2000 by George Clark and Daniel Timmons. Reproduced with permission of ABC-CLIO, LLC.

"Tolkien and the Idea of the Book." From The Lord of the Rings *1954–2004: Scholarship in Honor of Richard E. Blackwelder*, ed. Wayne G. Hammond and Christina Scull. Copyright © 2006. Milwaukee, WI: Marquette University Press. Reprinted by permission of the publisher. All rights reserved. http://www.marquette.edu/mupress/.

"Tolkien and the Matter of Britain." From *Mythlore* 23: 1 (Summer/Fall 2000). Reprinted with the permission of *Mythlore*.

"Tolkien's Wild Men: From Medieval to Modern." From *Tolkien the Medievalist*, ed. Jane Chance. Copyright © 2003 by Jane Chance. New York and Oxford: Routledge. Reproduced by permission of Taylor & Francis Books UK.

"When is a Fairy-story a *Faërie* Story? *Smith of Wootton Major*." From *Myth and Magic: Art According to the Inklings*, ed. Edouardo Segura and Thomas Honegger. Walking Tree Publishers, 2007. Reprinted with the permission of Walking Tree Publishers.

"Whose Myth Is It?" From *Between Faith and Fiction: Tolkien and the Powers of His World*, proceedings of the Arda Symposium at the Second Northern Tolkien Festival, Oslo, August 1997. Reprinted with the permission of Nils Ivar Agøy.

Notes

The Music and the Task

1. This is not to say that all readers have overlooked it. See the entry for "Free Will and Fate" (pp. 324–33) in Scull and Hammond's *Reader's Guide*, vol. 2 of *The J.R.R. Tolkien Companion and Guide*. See also my own exploration in *Splintered Light: Logos and Language in Tolkien's World*, pp. 52–53.

2. It should be emphasized that the ensuing discussion is entirely literary, not theological or philosophical. I am not (nor was Tolkien), arguing the actuality or the validity of either fate or free will, merely their fictive representation as aspects of his invented world. Conceptually, of course, and semantically, each apparently independent element requires the other as its opposite corollary, as up needs down, or dark needs light for full comprehension. Free implies that from which to be free, a constraint removed or denied; while Fate, cf. the *OED*'s first definition as the unalterable predetermination of events, implies restraint of what would otherwise be free.

3. My knowledge of modern fantasy, I hasten to add, is not encyclopedic. I welcome correction by those more familiar with the subject.

4. Such readings include Boethian, as both Shaun Hughes and Kathleen Dubs proclaim (Hughes review of *Tolkien and Modernity* in *Tolkien Studies* V 25; Dubs "Providence, Fate, and Chance: Boethian Philosophy in *The Lord of the Rings*" in *Tolkien and the Invention of Myth*); Boethian and/or Manichean, both of which are considered but rejected by Tom Shippey in his *Road to Middle-earth* 128–29; Augustinian as John Houghton maintains in his article "Augustine of Hippo" in *J.R.R. Tolkien Encyclopedia*.

5. *Wyrd* is one of several words used in the poem to denote an all-powerful supernatural force, others being *Metod*, "measure," *Dryhten*, "lord or The Lord" (often translated as "God"), and *God* with specific reference to the Judeo-Christian deity. The intended meanings and appropriate translations have been and still are the focus of the ongoing debate over the amount of Christianity in the poem. My purpose here is not to enter that debate, merely to note the worldview conveyed by wyrd in its original meaning.

6. The initials stood for "Tea Club Barrovian Society," after Barrows Store in downtown Birmingham, the meeting place of the four when they were all students together at King Edward's School.

7. The phrase "what we three certainly meant" was an allusion to the "Council of London," a meeting among Tolkien, Smith, Gilson and Wiseman in Decem-

ber of 1914 that in some fashion crystallized the hopes and artistic ambitions of the four before they went off to war.

8. Although more than two decades separate Smith's words from Frodo's, that hobbit's outcry to Gandalf at Bag End, "Why was I chosen?" seems in context a direct response.

9. Though it should be noted that several critics have seen a connection between Tolkien's war experience and his fiction. Brian Rosebury links Tolkien to the "lost generation" of World War I writers (Rosebury 133–52); Tom Shippey characterizes him as a "post-war writer" in the tradition of George Orwell, William Golding, and T.H. White (*Road* 288); John Garth's *Tolkien and the Great War* sheds new biographical light on the connection, and Janet Brennan Croft's *War and the Works of J.R.R. Tolkien* gives some valuable insights into Tolkien's treatment of war in *The Hobbit* and *The Lord of the Rings*.

10. Careful reading of "Ainulindalë" shows that the Valar, who are outside— indeed are creators of—the Music, are for that reason independent of it. Indeed, Ilúvatar makes clear their autonomy when he invites them to adorn the Music "each with his own thoughts and devices, *if he will*" [my emphasis].

11. A note in Tolkien's unpublished linguistic papers is apposite here. He wrote that, "[t]he author is not in the tale in one sense, yet it all proceeds from him (and what was in him), so that he is present all the time. Now while composing the tale he may have certain general designs (the plot for instance), and he may have a clear conception of the character (independent of the particular tale) of each feigned actor. But those are the limits of his 'foreknowledge'. Many authors have recorded the feeling that one of their actors 'comes alive' as it were, and does things that were not foreseen at all at the outset and may modify in a small or even large way the process of the tale thereafter. All such unforeseen actions or events are, however, taken up to become integral parts of the tale when finally concluded. Now when that has been done, then the author's 'foreknowledge' is complete, and nothing can happen, be said, or done, that he does not know of and will/or allow to be. Even so, some of the Eldarin philosophers ventured to say, it was with Eru."

12. "Turambar and the Foalókë," *The Book of Lost Tales'* earliest version of "The Children of Hurin," Tolkien applies the word weird explicitly to Túrin: " . . . soon too had he met his death—and his weird had been the happier thereby" (*LT* II, 85).

13. It is worth noting in this context that what Tolkien called the "three Great Tales" of his legendarium, the story of Beren and Lúthien, "The Fall of Gondolin," and "The Children of Húrin" all involve the intrusion of a free-willed Man into a fated Elven stronghold with direct effect on the lives of the elves therein, as well as on the outcome of the story.

14. Considerations of space preclude examination of the greatest exemplar of the intricate interconnections of fate and free will, Túrin son of Húrin, whose chosen epithet, Turambar embodies the Quenya morpheme mbar (fate), and whose free choices bring disaster on himself and those around him, both Men and Elves.

15. The fairy tale model for the whole episode is the story of "Culhwch and Olwen" in the Welsh *Mabinogion*. The story is an exemplar of the tale-type called

by folklorists "The Giant's Daughter." Its plot hinges on the efforts of a supernatural parent whose death, it is foretold (i.e. fated), will occur when his daughter marries, to forestall the marriage by setting the suitor an impossible and deliberately lethal task. When the suitor, with the aid of magic, accomplishes the task, the parent is accordingly killed. Variants on this type can be found in the Finnish *Kalevala*'s wooing stories of two of that mythology's heroes, Ilmarinen and Lemminkainen. Ilmarinen succeeds. Lemminkainen doesn't.

16. This is not the first of such collaborations. Again and again we see Tolkien interlocking fate with free will, linking doom with choice. On what he calls "the day of choice" at the Falls of Rauros, Aragorn tells Frodo that "the choice" of where to go next will wait on him, and adds, "Such is your fate"(*FR* II, x, 412).

Tolkien and the Idea of the Book

1. The participation of Frodo and Sam in the book project was set out in the Epilogue to *The Lord of the Rings*. Since that chapter was omitted from the published text, the account of their contributions to the book appears only in chapter 11 of *Sauron Defeated* (1992), "The Epilogue."

2. This "supplement" enhances the likeness to the *Red Book of Hergest,* whose second volume (the first contains the *Mabinogion*) is the *Bruts* or *Stories of the Kings.*

3. On p. 108 of his essay "Ancrene Wisse and Hali Meiðhad," published in *Essays and Studies by Members of the English Association* 14 (1929), Tolkien had argued for "a closeness of relationship between the language and the spelling of two distinct MSS. and hands that is astonishing, if not (as I believe) unique." He proposed that the scribes of these two manuscripts had used a language and orthography so nearly identical that the Ancrene Wisse (Language A) and Hali Meiðhad (Language B) were "in fact in one language and spelling (AB)."

4. The tales therein, "The Music of the Ainur" and the earliest accounts of Valinor, the Trees, and the Noldor, "The Fall of Gondolin," "The Tale of Tinúviel," "Turambar and the Foalókë," "The Nauglafring," and "The Tale of Eärendel," are in essence the Lost Tales, the earliest versions of the central stories of the Silmarillion.

5. Heorrenda was also Tolkien's choice for the name of the *Beowulf* poet, one more indication of his early attempt to attach his mythology to English tradition.

6. The colophon survives only in the Pierpont Morgan Library Caxton, and until the discovery of the Winchester manuscript, the word "hoole" was misread as "booke" and deleted on grounds of redundancy. Vinaver reads the correct colophon as making Malory's reference "crystal clear: the 'whole book' is the series which is here concluded" (*The Works of Sir Thomas Malory,* ed. Eugene Vinaver, 3rd ed. rev. P.J.C. Field [Oxford: Clarendon Press, 1990], 1:xlv).

7. The question was whether the word hole in the phrase "hole of the tree" meant "bole of the tree" or, as Tolkien suggested when Lewis consulted him, "fork of the tree," from Old English healh = Latin angulus "fork." Vinaver apparently preferred bole, which is what his edition uses (1:255). However, the phrase

as it appears in the manuscript, "at the holy of the tre hongys a basyn [basin] of couper [copper] and latyne [brass]" (Sir Thomas Malory, *The Winchester Malory: A Facsimile* [London: Oxford University Press, 1976], f. 97) could mean either, since the initial letter in holy can be read as either h or b. Tolkien's conjecture, therefore, is plausible, and the whole incident is evidence for the high level of scholarly interest the discovery engendered in the academic community.

8. Hence the necessary colophon at the end of the last book that established all of them as comprising the "hoole book."

9. Coincidentally, this lengthy period between discovery and publication is echoed in the equally lengthy stretch between Tolkien's December 1937 start on the "new Hobbit" that became *The Lord of the Rings* and his 1951 letter to Milton Waldman making the case for dual publication.

10. It is one of the ironies of fate (or of the publishing business) that even without the Silmarillion and due entirely to the need to spread out production costs, *The Lord of the Rings*, like the *Winchester*, was first published in three volumes (though in the case of *The Lord of the Rings* this was also spread out over two years). Also like the *Winchester*, it had been written as a sequence of separate but interconnected books, six in the case of *The Lord of the Rings*, eight in the case of Malory's work. Both works were later published in one-volume editions.

11. In this context, it is worth noting that Tolkien characterized the last departure of Bilbo and Frodo by ship into the West as "an Arthurian ending" (*SD* 132).

WHEN IS A FAIRY STORY A FAËRIE STORY?

1. Tolkien's choice of the word *fay*, rather than *magic*, to characterize the star is deliberate. The word is derived from Old French faie, "one with magical powers," itself derived from Latin fātā, plural of fāftum, "fate." Although early in the essay he states that, "Faërie itself may perhaps be most nearly translated by Magic," he goes on to say that this is "magic of a peculiar mood and power, at the furthest pole from the vulgar devices of the laborious, scientific magician" (*MC* 114). His spelling of Faërie shows through its etymology that Tolkien intended the word to carry a far older and darker meaning than that conventionally carried by the word magic, with its connotations of spells and cabalistic signs on the one hand, and sleight-of-hand and illusion on the other.

2. To the continuing confusion of readers and critics alike, Tolkien's orthographic practice, while remaining fundamentally true to sound and sense, varied perceptibly, going from Faërie (in the essay) to Fayery or Fayerye (in the story's rough drafts) to Faery (in the final published version). It is worth noting, however, that he seldom, other than a few special or conventional instances, used the spelling Fairy except in a derogatory sense. I will stick to Tolkien's practice by following whatever spelling is used in the work referred to, thus Faërie when referring to the essay, and Faery when referring to the story.

3. It is only fair to note that in the earliest versions of his *Silmarillion* mythology Tolkien used the word Fairies to refer to those beings he also called Gnomes and later Elvenfolk or Elves.(see *LT* I 13, 19, 110). He was equally conventional in

assigning Bilbo Baggins a "fairy" ancestress to account for the Tookish, adventurous side of his personality.

4. So named only in the drafts of the story, but not in the published text, where it is called simply "a lake."

THE FOOTSTEPS OF ÆLFWINE

1. At times Eriol and Ælfwine were treated as separate characters. See Christopher Tolkien's account of "The History of Eriol or Ælfwine" in *The Book of Lost Tales Part Two.*

2. See Christopher Tolkien's commentary in *The Lost Road,* p. 8.

3. See Christopher Tolkien's note in *Sauron Defeated,* p. 146.

THE CURIOUS INCIDENT OF THE DREAM AT THE BARROW

1. Since I have discussed the time-travel elements in both stories at greater length in *A Question of Time,* Chapters 5 and 6, I will confine my observations here to those aspects having a direct bearing on Tolkien's handling of reincarnation.

2. As well as fictional treatment in the "Papers," Tolkien gave this idea of inherited memory of language a more scholarly handling in his 1955 O'Donnell lecture, "English and Welsh." Here he drew an even sharper distinction between a "native language" or inherent linguistic predilection, and a "cradle-tongue," the first-learned language of custom (*Angles and Britons* 36).

3. This date is one of two possible oblique and tantalizing allusions in the text to a New World mythology, the Maya creation story, *Popol Vuh.* In addition to marking the fictive discovery of "The Notion Club Papers," the date 2012 A.D. marks the end of the pre-Columbian Maya Calendar Long Count. This is a cycle of days so vast that its curve appears linear, beginning on 13 August 3114 B.C. and running until 23 December 2012. At that time a new era will begin, and with it a new Long Count. Whether Tolkien knew of this is un-demonstrable, but it is certainly true that he had read widely in scholarly studies in myth and folklore, and was familiar with the major names in this comparatively new discipline, such as Max Müller and Andrew Lang. Lang, at least, knew something of Maya mythology, and mentions *Popol Vuh,* in his Introduction to the 1884 edition of Grimm's *Household Tales,* with which, it is safe to assume, Tolkien was familiar.

The second allusion, even more oblique, occurs in a rejected, early version of the minutes for Night 66. The subject under discussion here is false, sometimes called "folk" etymology, the dangerous amateur practice of assuming that because two words in two different languages have the same shape and sound they must also have the same meaning. The example given by Lowdham is "that *popol* means 'people' or 'popular assembly' in Tamil, but has no connexion whatever with *populus* and its derivatives, and is really derived, they say, from a Tamil word for a mat for the councilors to squat on" (*SD* 300). Popol is, in fact Quiché, a meso-American Maya language in which the word for "mat" is indeed *pop,* and the word for "council" is *popol,* meaning those who sit on the mat. Hence the title of the above-mentioned Maya Quiché text, *Popol Vuh,* translated as The Book of Council. Two translations of *Popol Vuh* were available at the time Tolkien was working on "The Notion Club Papers" a Spanish translation by Carl Scherzer published in 1857, and a French translation by the Abbé Brasseur de Bourbourg published in 1861. I can find no evidence that Tolkien had read either translation though given his wide-ranging interest in and curiosity about myth it seems a reasonable possibility.

4. No explanation is offered for the switch from "bliss" to "truth," and Tolkien's intention here is unclear. The Ælfwine name is more or less continuous in form between the two time-travel stories, changing from Lombardic Alboin in *The Lost Road* to modern English Alwyn in "The Notion Club Papers" but retaining a recognizable shape and spelling. Likewise, in *The Lost Road* the Bliss-friend name shifts from Anglo-Saxon Eadwine (ead, "happiness, bliss") to Lombardic Audoin. The change to Tréowine in "The Notion Club Papers" is ill provided-for, and thus seems arbitrary.

5. Republished in 2005 by Cold Spring Press with an Introduction by Douglas A. Anderson.

6. Tyrn Gorthad. Tentative etymology: tyrn-TUN=hill, mound, gor-GOS= dread, terror), thus Dread Mound. The old name for the Barrowdowns, many built in the First Age.

7. This is in no way intended as a criticism of Merry's sensitivity or his intelligence. But Tolkien clearly presents him as the steadier, soberer hobbit—for example in his lack of curiosity about the palantír—in contrast to the impulsive, intuitive Pippin, who is not only mysteriously drawn to that crystal ball, but also on a different occasion able to read Grishnákh's mind. That Merry is the less likely of the two to have a psychic experience makes the episode at the barrow all the more effective.

Whose Myth Is It?

1. Even more like a "parody of Christianity" is Andreth's puzzling introduction of what she calls the Hope of Men that the One will "enter into Arda" and heal it, a later rewriting of original draft material—where Andreth's name is Saelon—about the Great Hope for the same possible future event (*MR* 321–22, 350). In both text and early draft this whole passage is perplexing. What seems here a clear (albeit hearsay) reference to the Incarnation of God is something that elsewhere Tolkien had explicitly abjured. "The Incarnation of God is an *infinitely* greater thing than anything I would dare to write" (*Letters* 237). We can add to this is his emphatic disqualification of the Arthurian world as England's mythology on the grounds that it is "involved in, and explicitly contains the Christian religion," which he declared seemed to him "fatal" (*Letters* 144). What are we to make of these competing voices not just in the text, but in the author himself? Christopher Tolkien's reading of this conundrum is that the Hope referred to in the "Athrabêth" is an extension of the "theology" of the sub-created world into "specifically . . . Christian belief," and a "challenge" to the views expressed in the Waldman letter (*MR* 356). Christopher's initial acknowledgement that there are "problems" in the "Athrabêth" for the interpretation of his father's

thought seems like an understatement. One can sympathize. "Problems" is putting it mildly. Either Tolkien has executed a complete about-face and is now following in the footsteps of C.S. Lewis, or he is putting the Advent of Christ on the level of King Arthur's hoped-for return from Avalon.

TOLKIEN AND THE MATTER OF BRITAIN

1. Tolkien's use of the word "stories" here discounts non-narrative evidence. Germanic-English place-names such as Wayland's Smithy, a long barrow in Warwickshire, or earthworks such as Wansdyke (corrupted from Woden's Dyke) in Hampshire and Somerset, or Grim's (a by-name for Woden) Ditch in Wiltshire, are mute evidence of an early English belief system akin to the Norse or Germanic. Whatever stories may at one time have gathered around these sites are now lost. See Brian Branston, *The Lost Gods of England,* OUP, 1974.

2. See Shippey's discussion of "depth" in *The Road to Middle-earth,* pp. 274–75.

3. Faced with an Inklings evening devoted to a reading from Tolkien's mythos, Dyson is reported to have exclaimed, "Oh fuck, not another elf!" (Wilson 217).

FRODO AND ARAGORN

1. See Christopher Tolkien's discussion of this very complicated history of composition in *The Return of the Shadow,* Volume VI of *The History of Middle-earth.*

2. For more on this see Bonniejean Christensen's excellent analysis of Tolkien's second edition revisions of Gollum in "Gollum's Character Transformation in *The Hobbit,*" in Jared Lobdell's *A Tolkien Compass.*

BILBO'S NECK RIDDLE

1. See Tolkien, "On Fairy-stories" in *Essays Presented to Charles Williams* and "English and Welsh" in *Angles and Britons* for other examples.

ALLEGORY VERSUS BOUNCE

1. Nokes far more evokes the figure of Ted Sandyman than of any critic except possibly Edmund Wilson. But then Wilson, at least in his understanding of *The Lord of the Rings,* might be said to be a Sandyman-figure.

1. See Flieger, *A Question of Time* 233, and Doughan 17.

2. I refer here to Tolkien's joke about the word "blunderbuss," in *Farmer Giles of Ham,* 16. To him "the Four Wise Clerks of Oxenford" were the editors of the *Oxford English Dictionary,* see Kocher 161. There are more than four of them now, of course.

3. See the *Oxford English Dictionary,* eds. J. Simpson and E.S.C. Weiner, 2nd ed. 1989, s.v. "allegory."

4. *The Lord of the Rings,* 2nd edition, London: George Allen & Unwin, 1966, and Boston: Houghton Mifflin, 1967.

5. See Tolkien, *The Monsters and the Critics and Other Essays* 8.

6. For an interpretation of the "tower" allegory, see Shippey, *Road* 1982: 36–37 and *Road* 1992: 43. I regret to say that both times there is a critical misprint—the "man's own descendants" question should read, "Why did not he restore the old house?" The "Babel" allegory has never been explained in detail, though most of the evidence for such an explanation is to be found in Shippey and Haarder 1998. A full edition of the early drafts of Tolkien's lecture, with commentary, is in preparation by Michael Drout for Arizona State University Press.

7. Quite a lot of people might like to argue that the quest should be turned in some other direction. The rather obvious equations of *Animal Farm* (old Major as Marx, Snowball as Trotsky, Napoleon as Stalin, Moses the raven as the clergy) have been repeatedly denied—and it is true that one wonders what happened to Lenin.

8. For my reading of this story, see Shippey, *J.R.R. Tolkien: Author of the Century* 266–77. The reading there contains significant additions of detail to the original theory as advanced in Shippey, *Road* 1982: 34–35 and *Road* 1992: 40–41.

9. For these, see Flieger, *A Question of Time* 232.

10. See once more Flieger, *A Question of Time* 250.

11. The point has also been made by Flieger in a new article, "Taking the Part of Trees."

12. See Tolkien, "Guide to the Names," 1975: 170.

13. It is most obvious in the Old English poem called "Eadig Beo þu!" in *Songs for the Philologists* 13, translated Shippey, *Road* 1982: 229.

14. See Tolkien, "The Oxford English School,"1930.

15. See Tolkien, *The Monsters and the Critics and Other Essays* 225.

16. See Shippey, *Road,* 1982: 206–7, 1992: 244–46, 320, and Flieger, *A Question of Time* 243–4.

17. See Flieger, *A Question of Time* 244, 231, 233.

18. I have to repeat that "tough-mindedness" here has a special sense, of being concerned with details, single facts, rather than systems, see Shippey, *Road* 1982: 215–16, *Road* 1992: 291–92. It is quite possible to be "tough-minded" and "tender-hearted" at once. The basic idea is William James.'

19. See *Lord of the Rings* III: 149 (start of the chapter "The Last Debate").

TOLKIEN, *KALEVALA*, AND "THE STORY OF KULLERVO"

1. For a general discussion, see Helms, *Tolkien and the Silmarils;* Noad, "On the Construction of 'The Silmarillion'"; West, "Túrin's Ofermod" and "Setting the Rocket Off in Story"; Shippey, "Tolkien and the Appeal of the Pagan"; Gay, "J.R.R. Tolkien and the Kalevala"; Petty, "Identifying England's Lönnrot"; and Himes, "What J.R.R. Tolkien Really Did with the Sampo?"

BRITTANY AND WALES IN MIDDLE-EARTH

1. The book is now in the English Faculty Library in Oxford.

2. An exception is Galadriel's lament "Ail Laurie Lantar" as the Fellowship leaves Lórien. This is in Quenya.

A Cautionary Tale

1. Strictly speaking, a misnomer, but one now so firmly entrenched in Tolkien scholarship it is too late to dislodge it. What Tolkien actually described was a mythology he could "dedicate" to England. There seems little qualitative difference between the two phrases.

2. See Carl Hostetter and Arden Smith, "A Mythology for England" and Anders Stenström, "A Mythology? For England?" in *Proceedings of the J.R.R. Tolkien Centenary Conference*, 1992, also Jane Chance, *Tolkien's Art: A Mythology for England*, University Press of Kentucky, 2001.

3. The outdated notion that *The Lord of the Rings* was an allegory of World War II can safely be dismissed, but the more general mood of the story is certainly directly connected to the war-torn twentieth century

4. Any doubt that the works belong together and project the same vision can be resolved by consulting the conversation on the Stairs of Cirith Ungol where Sam suddenly realizes by way of the Phial of Galadriel, that he and Frodo are in the Silmarillion and the story is still going on.

5. His first efforts at the mythology, a poem called "The Voyage of Earendel" and a school notebook titled in pencil "The Book of Lost Tales," were begun in 1914 and 1917 respectively. *The Lord of the Rings* was begun in 1938 and was roughly three-quarters finished by 1945.

A Post-modern Medievalist

1. See Shippey's discussion of cultural parallels in *J.R.R. Tolkien: Author of the Century* 91–92.

2. See Wilson, Edmund, "Oo Those Awful Orcs!" in *Nation* 182 (14 April 1956).

3. See Bonniejean Christensen's article, "Gollum's Character Transformation in *The Hobbit*" in *A Tolkien Compass*, ed. Jared Lobdell, re-issued 2003 by Open Court.

Taking the Part of Trees

1. In spite of its title, Patrick Curry's book does not so much defend Tolkien's Middle-earth as use Tolkien's Secondary World as the springboard for a defense of our more ecologically endangered Primary World.

2. *An Awfully Big Adventure*, produced by Julian Birkett. London: British Broadcasting Corporation, 1997.

3. It is not clear how much of the wresting was done by hobbits. Tolkien said in a letter that "it was a well-tended region when they took it over" (*Letters* 196), but stated in the Prologue to *The Lord of the Rings* that "the land . . . had long been deserted when they [the hobbits] entered it" (*FR* Prologue 14). The phrase "long deserted" carries with it the implication that nature (i. e., trees) must have begun to reclaim the land.

GILSON, SMITH, AND BAGGINS

1. Another real-life corollary to Frodo is Tolkien's second son Michael, described by Tolkien as "a much-damaged soldier" (*Letters* 86). As a result of 'severe shock to nervous system due to prolonged exposure to enemy action' (*Letters* 439 n74), Michael had been judged unfit for further military service. In a psychological sense, the same diagnosis could well be made for Frodo.

THE BODY IN QUESTION

1. A comparison may be made here to a work with which Tolkien was surely familiar, George MacDonald's *At the Back of the North Wind.* Though it is only tangentially and sporadically mentioned in the text, the child-hero of the story, little Diamond, is ill at the beginning of the book, and the entire story is an account of his physical illness and spiritual progress, a journey through life to death, which is not an end but an arrival at the back of the North Wind.

2. The word shadow has a psychological as well as a metaphoric meaning as one of Carl Jung's archetypal configurations of the human psyche. In Jungian psychology the Shadow is understood as the dark or un-admitted side of the personality; that part of ourselves we do not want to see, a part we reject and turn away from even as it follows us.

A DISTANT MIRROR

1. The episode from *The Hobbit* is not the only example of such use, it is just the most readily available. Tolkien also wrote some long narrative poems firmly seated in a medieval tradition. His alliterative "The Fall of Arthur" is a modern addition to the Arthurian canon (*Letters* 219). He described his "Völsungakvða en Nyja" as "an attempt to unify the lays about the Völsungs from the *Elder Edda*, written in the old eight-line fornyrðislag stanza" (*Letters* 379, 452n). That word "unify" is worth attention. Like the *Beowulf* manuscript, the *Edda* is corrupt. Not only that, one whole gathering, eight leaves, is missing, leaving a whopping gap in the story. The idea that writing fornyrðislag in modern English in the twentieth century he could "unify" a sequence of poems Old Icelandic written somewhere between the ninth and eleventh centuries is part of the same impulse that led him to "restore" in a modern children's book the corrupt passage in *Beowulf.*

Call it conceit or confidence. Whatever it was, it was an essential element of his art. He did it all the time. His early ambition to dedicate a mythology to England was intended to connect England's real history to the as yet unimagined mythology that should have preceded it. Something was missing and Tolkien was just the man to fill in the gap. From the time he began his mythology in 1917 he was looking for ways he could believably connect it to a real England. He called an early redactor of his tales Ælfwine, an English name that also translates as Elf-friend. He seriously considered having one of his demi-gods literally drag the Elvish island of Tol Eressëa loose from the seabed and re-position it as England.

These early efforts were clumsy and abortive, but by the time he got to *The Hobbit* and even later and better to *The Lord of the Rings* he was finding the range.

2. It is tempting to speculate that Tolkien might also have borrowed from this most Faërien of films. The gothic-arched, silver-embossed double doors of Oz before which Dorothy and her companions stand in awe as the soundtrack chorus sings "Open! Open!" are strikingly like the illustration of the gothic-arched, silver-engraved double doors of Moria at which Gandalf shouts "Open, open!" repeating the command "in every language that had ever been spoken in the West of Middle-earth" (*FR* II, vi, 319, 321). *The Wizard of Oz* was released in the United States in August of 1939 and in Britain in December of that year. According to Christopher Tolkien, the manuscript pages of what he terms the "Third Phase" of his father's narrative—going back to Bilbo's departure from Hobbiton (the second phase, like the first, had stopped at Rivendell)—was dated by his father "Aug. 1939." (*RS* 370) The earliest sketch of the subsequent Moria chapter was written as part of a continuous narrative from Rivendell through the journey South to the Mines of Moria. The sketch itself contains no reference to the Doors, nor to any difficulty in getting them to open. The draft chapter that follows it describes a scene very close to the one in *The Fellowship of the Ring* except that it shows Tolkien apparently hesitated between having a single Door or a pair (*RS* 449, 453). A new version, dated August 1940, and beginning again from the Rivendell chapter, makes a decisive change from "Door" to "Doors" and this was retained in the published version.

Works Cited

The American Heritage Dictionary of the English Language. Ed. William Morris. Boston: American Heritage, 1969.

Aneirin. *The Gododdin.* Trans. and ed. A.O.H. Jarman. Dyfed, UK: Gomer Press, 1990.

An Anglo-Saxon Dictionary. Based on the manuscript collection of Joseph Bosworth. Ed. J. Northcote Toller. Oxford: Oxford University Press, 1980.

An Awfully Big Adventure. Produced by Julian Birkett for BBC Television. London: British Broadcasting Corporation, 1997.

Barfield, Owen. *Poetic Diction.* London: Faber & Gwyer Ltd., 1928.

Belloc, Hilaire. *Cautionary Verses.* New York: Alfred A. Knopf, 1945.

Beowulf: A Dual-Language Edition. Trans. Howell Chickering. New York: Doubleday, 1977.

Bernheimer, Richard. *Wild Men in the Middle Ages.* Cambridge, Mass.: Harvard University Press, 1952.

Branch, M. A. Introduction to *Kalevala.* Vol. 1. Comp. Elias Lönnrot. Trans. W. F. Kirby. London: Athlone Press, 1985. xi–xxxiv.

Branston, Brian. *The Lost Gods of England.* New York: Oxford University Press, 1974.

Burns, E. Jane. Introduction to *Lancelot-Grail: The Old French Arthurian Vulgate and Post-Vulgate in Translation.* Vol. 1. Trans. Carol J. Chase. New York: Garland, 1993. xv–xxxii.

Carpenter, Humphrey. *Tolkien: A Biography.* London: George Allen & Unwin, 1977.

———. *The Inklings.* Boston: Houghton Mifflin, 1979.

Cassirer, Ernst. *Sprache und Mythos—Ein Beitrag zum Problem der Götternamen.* Studien der Bibliothek Warburg 6. Leipzig/Berlin: B.G. Teubner, 1925.

———. *Language and Myth.* Trans. Susanne Langer. New York: Dover, 1946.

Chance, Jane. *Tolkien's Art: A Mythology for England.* London: Macmillan, 1979.

Chaucer, Geoffrey. *The Canterbury Tales* in *The Riverside Chaucer.* Ed. Larry D. Benson. Boston: Houghton Mifflin, 1987.

Chrétien de Troyes. *Le Chevalier au Lion (Yvain).* Paris: Librairie Honoré Champion, 1968.

———. *Yvain, or, The Knight with the Lion.* Trans. Ruth Harwood Cline. Athens, GA: University of Georgia Press, 1984.

Christensen, Bonnijean. "Gollum's Character Transformation in *The Hobbit*." *A Tolkien Compass*. 2nd ed. Ed. Jared Lobdell. Chicago: Open Court, 2003. 7–26.

Cline, Leonard. *The Dark Chamber*. New York: Viking Press, 1927.

Comparetti, Domenico. *The Traditional Poetry of the Finns*. Trans. Isabella M. Anderton. London: Longmans, Green, 1898.

Corpus Poeticum Boreale. Vol. 1. Ed. and trans. Gudbrand Vigfusson and F. York Powell. Facs Brampton, Ontario: Ballantrae Reprints, 2007.

Curry, Patrick. *Defending Middle-earth: Tolkien, Myth and Modernity*. New York: St. Martin's Press, 1997.

Dasent, George. *Popular Tales from the Norse: With an Introductory Essay on the Origin and Diffusion of Popular Tales*. 2nd ed. Edinburgh: Edmonston and Douglas, 1859.

Davidson, Hilda Ellis. "Insults and Riddles in the *Edda* Poems." Edda*: A Collection of Essays*. Ed. R. J. Glendenning and Haraldur Bessason. Winnepeg: University of Manitoba Press, 1983. 25–46.

Dorson, Richard M. *The British Folklorists: A History*. 2 vols. Chicago: University of Chicago Press, 1968.

Doughan, David. "In Search of the Bounce: Tolkien Seen through Smith." *Leaves from the Tree: Tolkien's Shorter Fiction*. Ed. Alex Lewis. London: Tolkien Society. 17–22.

Dubs, Kathleen. "Fortune and Fate." *J.R.R. Tolkien Encyclopedia: Scholarship and Critical Assessment*. Ed. Michael D. C. Drout. New York: Routledge, 2007. 214–15.

——. "Providence, Fate, and Chance: Boethian Philosophy in *The Lord of the Rings*." *Tolkien and the Invention of Myth*. Ed. Jane Chance. Lexington: University Press of Kentucky, 2004. 133–42.

Dunne, J. W. *An Experiment with Time*. 3rd ed. London: Faber and Faber, 1935.

Eddison, E. R. *Zimviamvia: A Trilogy*. New York: Dell, 1992.

Fisher, Jason. "'Man does as he is when he may do as he wishes': The Perennial Modernity of Free Will." *Tolkien and Modernity*. Vol. 1. Ed. Frank Weinreich and Thomas Honegger. Zollikofen, Switzerland: Walking Tree, 2006. 145–75.

Flieger, Verlyn. *A Question of Time: J.R.R. Tolkien's Road to Faërie*. Kent, Ohio: Kent State University Press, 1997.

——. *Splintered Light: Logos and Language in Tolkien's World*. Rev. ed. Kent, Ohio: Kent State University Press, 2002.

——. "Taking the Part of Trees: Eco-conflict in Middle-earth." *J.R.R. Tolkien and His Literary Resonances: Views of Middle-earth*. Ed. George Clark and Daniel Timmons. Westport, Conn.: Greenwood, 2000. 147–58.

Fornet-Ponse, Thomas. "Freedom and Providence as Anti-Modern Elements." *Tolkien and Modernity*. Vol. 1. Ed. Frank Weinreich and Thomas Honegger. Zollikofen, Switzerland: Walking Tree, 2006. 177–206

Forster, E. M. *Howards End*. New York: Everyman's Library, 1991.

Fowles, John. *The French Lieutenant's Woman*. Boston: Little, Brown, 1969.

Gardner, John. *Grendel*. New York: Alfred A. Knopf, 1971.

Garth, John. *Tolkien and the Great War*. London: HarperCollins, 2003.

Gay, David Elton. "J.R.R. Tolkien and the *Kalevala*." *Tolkien and the Invention of Myth*. Ed. Jane Chance. Lexington: University Press of Kentucky, 2004. 290–304.

Geoffrey of Monmouth. *Life of Merlin*. Ed. and trans. Basil Clark. Cardiff: University of Wales Press, 1973.

Hammond, Wayne, and Christina Scull. *The Lord of the Rings: A Reader's Companion*. Boston: Houghton Mifflin, 2005.

Helms, Randel. *Tolkien and the Silmarils*. Boston: Houghton Mifflin, 1981.

Himes, J. B. "What J.R.R. Tolkien Really Did with the Sampo?" *Mythlore* 22.86 (2000): 69–85.

Hostetter, Carl. Personal communication, 2010.

Hostetter, Carl, and Arden Smith. "A Mythology for England." *Proceedings of the J.R.R. Tolkien Centenary Conference*. Ed. Patricia Reynolds and Glen H. GoodKnight. Milton Keynes and Altadena: Tolkien Society and Mythopoeic Press, 1995. 281–90.

Houghton, John. "Augustine of Hippo." *J.R.R. Tolkien Encyclopedia: Scholarship and Critical Assessment*. Ed. Michael D. C. Drout. New York: Routledge, 2007. 43.

Hughes, Daniel. "Pieties and Giant Forms in *The Lord of the Rings*." *Shadows of Imagination: The Fantasies of C. S. Lewis, J.R.R. Tolkien, and Charles Williams*. Ed. Mark Hillegas. Carbondale: University of Illinois Press, 1976. 81–96.

Hughes, Shaun. Review of *Tolkien and Modernity*. *Tolkien Studies* 5 (2008): 244–55.

An Icelandic-English Dictionary, 2nd ed. Initiated by Richard Cleasby. Rev. Gudbrand Vigfusson. 2nd ed. Oxford: Clarendon Press, 1937.

Isaacs, Neil, and Rose Zimbardo, eds. *Tolkien: New Critical Perspectives*. Lexington: University Press of Kentucky, 1981.

Jackson, Peter. *The Fellowship of the Ring*. New Line Cinema, 2001.

Joly, M.A. *De la Condition des Vilains au Moyen Age d'après les fabliaux en Mémoires de l'Académie nationale des sciences, arts et belles-lettres de Caen*. 1882.

Kalevala. Comp. Elias Lönnrot. Trans. W. F. Kirby. 2 vols. London: Dutton, Everyman's Library, 1907.

The Kalevala. Comp. Elias Lönnrot. Trans. Francis P. Magoun. Cambridge, Mass.: Harvard University Press, 1963.

Kocher, Paul. *Master of Middle-earth: The Fiction of J.R.R. Tolkien*. Boston: Houghton Mifflin, 1972.

Kristjansson, Jónas. *Eddas and Sagas: Iceland's Medieval Literature*. Trans. Peter Foote. Reykjavik: Hitíslenska bókmenntafélag, 1988.

Lang, Andrew. *Custom and Myth*. London: Longmans, Green, 1893.

———. Introduction to *Grimm's Household Tales*. Trans. Margaret Hunt. Vol. 1. London: G. Bell and Sons, 1884. xi–lxx.

Lewis, C. S. *The Collected Letters of C. S. Lewis*. Vol. 2. Ed. Walter Hooper. San Francisco: HarperSanFrancisco, 2004.

———. *Out of the Silent Planet*. New York: Macmillan, 1943.

———. *Perelandra*. New York: Macmillan, 1944.

———. *That Hideous Strength*. New York: Macmillan, 1946.

Lewis, W.H. *Brothers and Friends: The Diaries of Major Warren Hamilton Lewis.* Ed. Clyde S. Kilby and Marjorie Lamp Mead. San Francisco: Harper & Row, 1982.

Lindsay, David. *A Voyage to Arcturus.* London: Victor Gollancz, 1920.

Lobdell, Jared, ed. *A Tolkien Compass.* LaSalle, Ill.: Open Court, 1975.

Lucas, George. *Star Wars.* 20th Century and George Lucas Films, 1971.

MacCana, Proinsias. *Celtic Mythology.* London: Hamlyn, 1970.

MacDonald, George. *At the Back of the North Wind.* Philadelphia: J.B. Lippincott, 1909.

Malory, Sir Thomas. *The Winchester Malory: A Facsimile.* London: Oxford University Press for the Early English Text Society, 1976.

———. *The Works of Sir Thomas Malory.* Ed. Eugène Vinaver. 3rd ed. Rev. P.J.C. Field. 3 vols. Oxford: Clarendon Press, 1990.

Müller, Max. *Chips From a German Workshop.* 4 vols. New York: Scribner, Armstrong, 1871–76.

The New Arthurian Encyclopedia. Ed. Norris J. Lacey. New York: Garland, 1991.

Noad, Charles. "On the Construction of 'The Silmarillion.'" *Tolkien's Legendarium: Essays on* The History of Middle-earth. Ed. Verlyn Flieger and Carl Hostetter. Westport, Conn.: Greenwood Press, 2000. 31–68.

Oakeshott, Walter F. "The Finding of the Manuscript." *Essays on Malory.* Ed. J.A.W. Bennett, 1–6. Oxford: Clarendon Press, 1963. 1–6.

Oxford English Dictionary. 2nd ed. Ed. J. A. Simpson and E.S.C. Weiner. Oxford: Oxford University Press, 1989.

Parker, Douglass. "Hwaet We Holbytla. . . ." *Hudson Review* 9.4 (1956–57): 598–609.

Peasant Customs and Savage Myths: Selections from the British Folklorists. 2 vols. Ed. Richard M. Dorson. Chicago: University of Chicago Press, 1968.

Petty, Anne. "Identifying England's Lönnrot." *Tolkien Studies* 1 (2004): 69–84.

Plotz, Richard. "J.R.R. Tolkien Talks about Middle-earth." *Seventeen.* January 1967: 92+.

The Poetic Edda. Trans. Henry Adams Bellows. New York: Biblo and Tannen, 1969.

Ready, William. *The Tolkien Relation: A Personal Inquiry.* Chicago: Regnery Press, 1968.

Rosebury, Brian. *Tolkien: A Critical Assessment.* New York: St. Martin's Press, 1992.

Saunders, Corinne J. *The Forest of Medieval Romance.* Suffolk, UK: Boydell & Brewer, 1993.

Scull, Christina, and Wayne Hammond. *Chronology.* Vol. 1 of *The J.R.R. Tolkien Companion and Guide.* Boston: Houghton Mifflin, 2006.

———. *Reader's Guide.* Vol. 2 of *The J.R.R. Tolkien Companion and Guide.* Boston: Houghton Mifflin, 2006.

Shippey, Tom. "Allegory versus Bounce." *Journal of the Fantastic in the Arts* 12.2 (2001): 186–200.

———. *J.R.R. Tolkien: Author of the Century.* London: HarperCollins, 2000.

———. Review of *The Legend of Sigurd and Gudrún. Tolkien Studies* 7 (2010): 219–324.

———. "Long Evolution: The History of Middle-earth and Its Merits." *Arda.* Ed. Anders Stenström. Stockholm: Forodrim, 1987. 18–39.

———. *The Road to Middle-earth.* 2nd ed. London: HarperCollins Grafton, 1992.

———. "Tolkien and the Appeal of the Pagan: *Edda* and *Kalevala.*" *Tolkien and the Invention of Myth.* Ed. Jane Chance. Lawrence: University Press of Kentucky, 2004. 145–61.

"Tolkien as a Post-war Writer." Proceedings of the Tolkien Centenary Conference. Ed Reynolds and Goodknight, Milton Keynes and Altadena: Tolkien Society and Mythopoeic Press, 1995.

Shippey, Tom, and Andreas Haarder, eds. *Beowulf: The Critical Heritage.* London: Routledge, 1998.

Sir Gawain and the Green Knight. Ed. J.R.R. Tolkien and E. V. Gordon. Oxford: Clarendon Press, 1923.

Sir Gawain and the Green Knight, Pearl, and Sir Orfeo. Trans. J.R.R. Tolkien. Boston: Houghton Mifflin, 1975.

Snorri Sturluson. *Edda.* Trans. Anthony Faulkes. London: J.M. Dent, Everyman's Library, 1987.

———. *Edda: Prologue and Gylfaginning.* Ed. Anthony Faulkes. Oxford: Clarendon Press, 1982.

———. *The Prose Edda.* Trans. Jean Young. Berkeley: University of California Press, [n.d.].

Stenström, Anders. "A Mythology? For England." *Proceedings of the J.R.R. Tolkien Centenary Conference.* Ed. Patricia Reynolds and Glen H. GoodKnight. Milton Keynes and Altadena: Tolkien Society and Mythopoeic Press, 1995. 310–14.

Taylor, Archer. "The Varieties of Riddles." *Philologica: The Malone Anniversary Studies.* Ed. Thomas A. Kirby and Henry Bosley Woolf. Baltimore: Johns Hopkins University Press, 1949. 1–8.

Thomas, Paul. "Some of Tolkien's Narrators." *Tolkien's Legendarium: Essays on* The History of Middle-earth. Ed. Verlyn Flieger and Carl Hostetter. Westport, Conn.: Greenwood Press, 2000. 161–81.

Thomas, W. Jenkyn. *The Welsh Fairy Book.* Illus. Willy Pogány. London: T. Fisher Unwin, 1907.

Thomson, George H. "*The Lord of the Rings:* The Novel as Traditional Romance." *Wisconsin Studies in Contemporary Literature* 8.1 (1967): 43–59.

Timmons, Daniel. "Free Will." *J.R.R. Tolkien Encyclopedia: Scholarship and Critical Assessment.* Ed. Michael D.C. Drout. New York: Routledge, 2007. 221–22.

Tolkien, J.R.R. *The Adventures of Tom Bombadil.* London: George Allen & Unwin, 1962.

———. "*Ancrene Wisse* and *Hali Meiðhad.*" *Essays and Studies by Members of the English Association* 14 (1929): 104–26.

———. "*Beowulf:* The Monsters and the Critics." *The Monsters and the Critics and Other Essays.* Ed. Christopher Tolkien. London: George Allen & Unwin, 1983. 5–48.

———."*Beowulf:* The Monsters and the Critics." *Proceedings of the British Academy* 22 (1936): 245–95.

———. *The Book of Lost Tales* 1. Ed. Christopher Tolkien. Vol. 1 of *The History of Middle-earth.* Boston: Houghton Mifflin, 1984.

———. *The Book of Lost Tales* 2. Ed. Christopher Tolkien. Vol. 2 of *The History of Middle-earth.* Boston: Houghton Mifflin, 1984.

———. "Early Quenya and Valinoric." Ed. Patrick Wynne, Christopher Gilson, Carl F. Hostetter, and Bill Welden. *Parma Eldalamberon* 14 (2003).

———. "English and Welsh." *Angles and Britons: O'Donnell Lectures.* Cardiff: University of Wales Press, 1963. 1–41.

———. *Farmer Giles of Ham.* London: George Allen & Unwin, 1949.

———. *The Fellowship of the Ring.* London: George Allen & Unwin, 1954.

———. *The Fellowship of the Ring.* 2nd ed. Boston: Houghton Mifflin, 1965.

———. "The Grammar and Lexicon of the Gnomish Tongue." Ed. Christopher Gilson, Patrick Wynne, Arden R. Smith, and Carl F. Hostetter. *Parma Eldalamberon* 11 (1995).

———. *The Hobbit, or, There and Back Again.* Boston: Houghton Mifflin, 1966.

———. "The Lay of Aotrou and Itroun." *Welsh Review* 4 (1945): 204–66.

———. *The Lays of Beleriand.* Ed. Christopher Tolkien. Vol. 3 of *The History of Middle-earth.* Boston: Houghton Mifflin, 1985.

———. *The Legend of Sigurd and Gudrún.* Ed. Christopher Tolkien. London: HarperCollins, 2009.

———. *The Letters of J.R.R. Tolkien.* Ed. Humphrey Carpenter with the assistance of Christopher Tolkien. Boston: Houghton Mifflin, 1981.

———. *The Lord of the Rings.* London: HarperCollins, 1991 [i.e., 1994].

———. *The Lost Road.* Ed. Christopher Tolkien. Vol. 5 of *The History of Middle-earth.* Boston: Houghton Mifflin, 1987.

———. "Middle English 'Losenger': Sketch of an Etymological and Semantic Enquiry." *Essais de Philologie Moderne.* Bibliothèque de la Faculté de la Philosophie et Lettres de l'Université de Liège, Fascicule CXXIX. Paris: Société d'édition "Les Belles Lettres," 1953.

———. *Morgoth's Ring.* Ed. Christopher Tolkien. Vol. 10 of *The History of Middle-earth.* Boston: Houghton Mifflin, 1993.

———. "A neck-verse." Bodleian Library MS Tolkien A 13/1, c (folio 168 recto).

———. "On Fairy-stories." *The Monsters and the Critics and Other Essays.* Ed. Christopher Tolkien. London: George Allen & Unwin, 1983. 109–61.

———. "On Fairy-stories." *Essays Presented to Charles Williams.* Oxford: Oxford University Press, 1947. 38–89.

———. "On the *Kalevala.*" *Tolkien Studies* 7 (2010): 246–57.

———. "The Oxford English School." *Oxford Magazine.* May 29, 1930, 778–82.

———. *The Peoples of Middle-earth.* Ed. Christopher Tolkien. Vol. 12 of *The History of Middle-earth.* Boston: Houghton Mifflin, 1996.

———. "The Qenya Lexicon." Ed. Christopher Gilson, Carl F. Hostetter, Patrick Wynne, and Arden R. Smith. *Parma Eldalamberon* 12 (1998).

———. *The Return of the King.* 2nd ed. Boston: Houghton Mifflin, 1965.

———. *Sauron Defeated.* Ed. Christopher Tolkien. Vol. 9 of *The History of Middle-earth.* London: HarperCollins, 1992.

———. *The Shaping of Middle-earth.* Ed. Christopher Tolkien. Vol. 4 of *The History of Middle-earth.* Boston: Houghton Mifflin, 1986.

———. *The Silmarillion.* 2nd ed. Ed. Christopher Tolkien. London: HarperCollins, 1999.

———. *Smith of Wootton Major.* Ed. Verlyn Flieger. London: HarperCollins, 2005.

———. "The Story of Kullervo." Ed. Verlyn Flieger. *Tolkien Studies* 7 (2010): 211–78.

———. "The Story of Kullervo." Bodleian Library MS Tolkien B 64/6 (folios 1–25).

———. *Tolkien on Fairy-stories*. Ed. Verlyn Flieger and Douglas A. Anderson. London: HarperCollins, 2008.

———. *Tree and Leaf.* Boston: Houghton Mifflin, 1965.

———. *The Two Towers*. 2nd ed. Boston: Houghton Mifflin, 1965.

———. *Unfinished Tales of Númenor and Middle-earth*. Ed. Christopher Tolkien. Boston: Houghton Mifflin, 1980.

———. "Words, Phrases & Passages in Various Tongues: *The Lord of the Rings*." Ed. Christopher Gilson. *Parma Eldalamberon* 17 (2007).

Tuchman, Barbara. *A Distant Mirror.* New York: Alfred A. Knopf, 1978.

Villemarqué, Théodore Hersart de la. *Barzaz Breiz: Chants Populaires de la Bretagne*. Paris: Didier et Cie, 1867.

Walde, Alois. Vergleichendes Wörterbuch der indogermanischen Sprachen. Herousgegeben und bearbeitet von Julius Pokorny. Band II Berlin und Leipzig: de Gruyter, 1927.

Weinreich, Frank. "Brief Considerations on Determinism in Reality and Fiction." *Tolkien and Modernity*. Vol. 1. Zollikofen, Switzerland: Walking Tree, 2006. 135–44.

Weinreich, Frank, and Thomas Honegger, eds. *Tolkien and Modernity*. Vol. 1. Zollikofen, Switzerland: Walking Tree, 2006.

West, Richard C. "The Interlace Structure of *The Lord of the Rings*." *A Tolkien Compass*. Ed. Jared Lobdell. LaSalle, Ill.: Open Court, 1975. 77–94

———. "Setting the Rocket off in Story." *Tolkien and the Invention of Myth*. Ed. Jane Chance. Lexington: University Press of Kentucky, 2004. 285–94.

———. "Túrin's *Ofermod*." *Tolkien's Legendarium: Essays on* The History of Middle-earth. Ed. Verlyn Flieger and Carl Hostetter. Westport, Conn.: Greenwood Press, 2000. 233–45.

Weston, Jessie. *From Ritual to Romance*. Gloucester, Mass.: Peter Smith, 1958.

Williamson, Craig. *A Feast of Creatures: Anglo-Saxon Riddle-songs*. Philadelphia: University of Pennsylvania Press, 1982.

Wilson, A. N. *C. S. Lewis: A Biography*. New York: W. W. Norton, 1990.

The Wizard of Oz. MGM, 1938.

Woolf, Virginia. *Mrs. Dalloway*. New York: Classics House Books, 2009.

Yates, Jessica. "The Source of 'The Lay of Aotrou and Itroun.'" *Leaves from the Tree: J.R.R. Tolkien's Shorter Fiction*. Ed. Alex Lewis. London: Tolkien Society, 1991. 63–71.

Zimbardo, Rose. "Moral Vision in *The Lord of the Rings*." *Understanding* The Lord of the Rings*: The Best of Tolkien Criticism*. Ed. Rose A. Zimbardo and Neil D. Isaacs. Boston: Houghton Mifflin, 2004. 68–75.

Index